Creating Urban Agr

Creating Urban Agricultural Systems provides you with background, expertise, and inspiration for designing with urban agriculture. It shows you how to grow food in buildings and cities, operate growing systems, and integrate them with natural cycles and existing infrastructures. It teaches you the essential environmental inputs and operational strategies of urban farms, and inspires community and design tools for innovative operations and sustainable urban environments that produce fresh, local food.

Over 70 projects and 16 in-depth case studies of productive, integrated systems, located in North America, Europe, and Asia, are organized by their emphasis on nutrient, water and energy management, farm operation, community integration, and design approaches so that you can see innovative strategies in action. Interviews with leading architecture firms, including WORKac, Kiss + Cathcart, Weber Thompson, CJ Lim and Studio 8, and SOA Architectes, highlight the challenges and rewards you face when creating urban agriculture systems. Catalogs of growing and building systems, a glossary, bibliography, and abstracts will help you find information fast.

Gundula Proksch is a licensed architect and Associate Professor in the Department of Architecture at the University of Washington in Seattle, USA. With over 15 years of professional practice and teaching experience in London, New York City, and Seattle, her design, research, and scholarly work explore novel, sustainable design practices in architecture and landscape architecture.

"Never before has there been a more urgent need to rethink our urban systems. Gundula Proksch's comprehensive guidebook illustrates why, where, and how to grow food in our cities with the greatest attention to protecting and regenerating our environmental and human well-being."

Mia Lehrer, founding principal of the Los Angeles landscape architecture firm, Mia Lehrer + Associates

"Thoroughly researched and clearly illustrated, this insightful book combines themes, processes and cases to highlight the relation between urban agriculture and cycles, systems of operation, technologies and people. This is an essential research for architecture, planning and landscape professionals and students seeking to integrate urban agriculture in to their work."

Leila Marie Farah, PhD, Associate Professor, Department of Architectural Science, Ryerson University

Creating Urban Agricultural Systems
An Integrated Approach to Design

Gundula Proksch

NEW YORK AND LONDON

First published 2017
by Routledge
711 Third Avenue, New York, NY 10017

and by Routledge
2 Park Square, Milton Park, Abingdon, Oxon OX14 4RN

Routledge is an imprint of the Taylor & Francis Group, an informa business

© 2017 Taylor & Francis

The right of Gundula Proksch to be identified as author of this work has been asserted by her in accordance with sections 77 and 78 of the Copyright, Designs and Patents Act 1988.

All rights reserved. No part of this book may be reprinted or reproduced or utilised in any form or by any electronic, mechanical, or other means, now known or hereafter invented, including photocopying and recording, or in any information storage or retrieval system, without permission in writing from the publishers.

Trademark notice: Product or corporate names may be trademarks or registered trademarks, and are used only for identification and explanation without intent to infringe.

Library of Congress Cataloging in Publication Data

Names: Proksch, Gundula, author.
Title: Creating urban agriculture systems : an integrated approach to design / Gundula Proksch.
Description: New York, NY : Routledge, 2017. | Includes bibliographical references and index.
Identifiers: LCCN 2016002711| ISBN 9780415747912 (hardback : alk. paper) | ISBN 9780415747936 (pbk. : alk. paper) | ISBN 9781315796772 (ebook)
Subjects: LCSH: Urban agriculture.
Classification: LCC S494.5.U72 P76 2017 | DDC 630.173/2--dc23
LC record available at https://lccn.loc.gov/2016002711

ISBN: 978-0-415-74791-2 (hbk)
ISBN: 978-0-415-74793-6 (pbk)
ISBN: 978-1-315-79677-2 (ebk)

Acquisition Editor: Wendy Fuller
Editorial Assistant: Grace Harrison
Production Editor: Ed Gibbons

Typeset in Avenir and DIN
by Servis Filmsetting Ltd, Stockport, Cheshire
Printed and bound in Great Britain by
Ashford Colour Press Ltd, Gosport, Hampshire

To Dan, Robin, and Jordan

Contents

Foreword — ix

Preface — x

Acknowledgments — xii

Introduction: Urban Agriculture and the Built Environment — 1

Part I Environmental Resources — 5

1. Nutrients: Growing Systems and Zero Waste Future — 7
   - Catalog 1: Soil-Based Growing Systems in Urban Agriculture — 27
   - Catalog 2: Hydroponic Growing Systems in Urban Agriculture — 31

2. Water: Connecting the Cycle — 43
   - Catalog 3: Alternative Water Sources — 63

3. Energy: Solar-powered Photosynthesis and Greenhouses — 69
   - Catalog 4: Greenhouse Typologies — 87
   - Catalog 5: Greenhouse Cover Materials — 93
   - Catalog 6: Lighting Technologies — 96

   Innovative Greenhouses and Vertical Farms
   - Case Study 1: Aquaponic Solar Greenhouse — 100
   - Case Study 2: Granpa Domes — 108
   - Case Study 3: Sky Greens — 115
   - Case Study 4: Vertical Harvest — 123
   - Case Study 5: Plantagon — 130
   - Case Study 6: Vertical Indoor Farming: A Comparison — 137

Part II Human Expertise — 151

4. Operation: Farm Management, Business Planning, and Financing — 153

   Complex Urban Agricultural Operations
   - Case Study 7: Growing Power — 172
   - Case Study 8: Brooklyn Grange — 183
   - Case Study 9: The Plant — 193
   - Case Study 10: Lufa Farms — 203
   - Case Study 11: Commercial Hydroponic Rooftop Farms: A Comparison — 215

5. Community: Education and Social Integration	**231**
Community-Based Projects	
Case Study 12: Prinzessinnengarten	245
Case Study 13: Organopónicos	251
Case Study 14: R-Urban	257
Case Study 15: The Stop Community Food Centre	263
Case Study 16: School Gardens: Microcosms of Urban Agriculture	269
6. Design: From Urban Visions to Building Integration	**283**
Profiles of Architecture Firms	
Architect's Profile 1: CJ Lim/Studio 8 Architects	299
Architect's Profile 2: Kiss + Cathcart, Architects	308
Architect's Profile 3: Weber Thompson	315
Architect's Profile 4: SOA Architectes	323
Architect's Profile 5: WORKac	331
Glossary	**346**
Selected Bibliography	**350**
Image Credits	**353**
Index	**357**

Foreword

Will Allen, urban farmer, founder, and CEO of Growing Power; MacArthur Fellow; and author of the book *The Good Food Revolution: Growing Healthy Food, People, and Communities.*

Our work of over 20 years has focused on living systems that are economically feasible and produce sustainable food year round. Our urban farms help to provide equal access to healthy, high-quality, safe and affordable food for people in all communities through the development of Community Food Systems. These experiences have taught us that we must change our food system to be more local and sustainable. Environmental stewardship and human contributions are equally essential to the urban agricultural movement.

Improving our food system starts with education and expanded knowledge. The Good Food Revolution and urban agriculture grow by building skills within a community and sharing these skills with others. To be accessible and effective, an introduction to the field should include an overview of the environmental systems involved in growing food while also covering the practical techniques, community connections, social movements, and the economics required to create and operate urban farms.

Creating Urban Agricultural Systems: An Integrated Approach to Design will encourage communities to develop and share the skills required to implement urban agriculture in their neighborhoods. This sourcebook makes the science and technology associated with urban farming accessible to a wide audience of design professionals, students, farmers, entrepreneurs, local politicians, community leaders, and citizens. The book highlights what is required for a successful urban agricultural operation—from funding opportunities to leadership structure and from planting methods to harvest. Lastly, it offers inspiring ideas to help reconnect people and communities to their natural environments and their source of food.

By offering insights from the many professional disciplines involved in urban agriculture, *Creating Urban Agricultural Systems* provides interdisciplinary teams a shared knowledge base. It presents a spectrum of approaches to urban agriculture that helps develop a multitude of design ideas into viable projects. It offers a toolkit that can be referred to—almost like a menu—to advise teams on how best to implement an urban agricultural operation. Comprehensive and catalog-like, the book allows all of us—farmers, practitioners, students, community leaders, and community members—to discover opportunities to integrate urban agriculture into our cities.

Creating Urban Agricultural Systems is a must-have book and an inspirational reference. Keep it close by.

Preface

Urban agriculture is an interdisciplinary topic *par excellence*, and designing with urban agriculture offers the opportunity for interdisciplinary work between architecture, landscape architecture, and urban planning. It challenges architects and allied practitioners to develop new ways to approach sustainability, community integration, and visions for urban futures. Urban agriculture also affords the fascination of working with living, tactile elements, environmental systems, and the local climate. It reconnects us with nature and the sources of our food.

Luscious, green lettuce heads moving through a vertical greenhouse in front of a corporate, high-rise office turns the building skin into a productive system. Tasty heirloom tomatoes harvested on the rooftop of a local restaurant minimize the distance from field to fork. Productive vegetable gardens on warehouse roofs generate opulent green roofscapes and improve the urban microclimate of previously barren neighborhoods.

Evocative images and compelling ideas such as these drove my students' and my design work since Seattle's "The Year of Urban Agriculture" in 2010. While these ideas are compelling, they pose many questions about the construction and operation of urban agriculture. These questions remain largely unanswered; it is difficult to find sources that comprehensively record, investigate, and explain the systems at play. While many design professionals and students share a passionate interest in urban agriculture, many lack a fundamental understanding of the biological, environmental, and operational systems involved in urban farming. Recognizing this need, I conceived of the idea for a sourcebook for designers working to integrate urban agriculture.

Creating Urban Agricultural Systems: An Integrated Approach to Design documents the current state of urban agricultural design to inspire architects, landscape architects, urban planners, students, community groups, and interested residents in this growing movement. The book helps designers develop holistic, interdisciplinary approaches to urban agriculture through understanding its most important inputs: environmental resources and human expertise.

The book's distinctive approach collects first-hand data from this rapidly evolving field and connects technical instruction with design inspiration. It juxtaposes scientific information—for example, about biogeochemical cycles and plant physiology—with an analysis of existing building systems, new growing technologies, techniques for integrating into urban infrastructure, and different design approaches. *Creating Urban Agricultural Systems* illustrates and explains these connections. As a sourcebook, it introduces design professionals and students to designing with urban agriculture, helping to expand this dynamic, interdisciplinary field.

NOTE ON MEASUREMENTS

All quantitative data has been included in imperial units followed by metric units in parentheses, except weight in tons, which has been listed in short tons (US) only.

- To convert short tons (US) into metric tons, multiply the value by the factor 0.9.

    short ton (US) = 2000 lb = 907 kg
    metric ton = 1000 kg = 2,205 lb
    metric ton = short ton (US)/1.1023

Acknowledgments

Writing this book on the emerging field of urban agriculture required collecting case studies, first-hand accounts, and experiences. I am profoundly grateful to the contributing farmers, founders, urban entrepreneurs, nonprofits, and architects who shared their insights with me and allowed me to feature their operations and projects. In particular, I would like to thank Will Allen, Amale Andraos, James Biber, Jerry Caldari, Nicole Caprizzi, Colin Cathcart, John Edel, Ben Flanner, Zach Gould, Gregory Kiss, Tom Kubala, CJ Lim, Kurt Lynn, Penny McBride, Robin Elmslie Osler, Oscar Rodriguez, Franz Schreier, Joe Swain, Scott Thompson, Becky Warner, and Nona Yehia for their time and contributions. Also special thanks to those who generously provided permission to include their photographs and images in this book.

I am grateful to my colleagues, Branden Born, Myer Harrell, Susan Jones, Shannon Tyman, and Ken Yocom, for their collaboration and for fruitful discussions about engaging this new field through alternative research agendas, pedagogies, and design approaches.

Thank you to all students of my graduate seminar, "Designing with Living Systems," who directly or indirectly supported this project, and to my research assistants for helping me gather, weed, process, and represent the expanding amounts of information in the field of urban agriculture. I would like to especially acknowledge and thank Betsy Anderson for her outstanding research and editorial skills, Elissa Favero for her careful final edits, and Kristopher Chan and Bennett Sapin for their dedicated, creative support in helping me generate the visualizations.

The University of Washington, the College of Built Environments, and the Department of Architecture supported my research and development for this book through their interdisciplinary research framework and funding provided by the Royalty Research Fund and Johnston-Hasting Publication Endowment.

At Routledge, I would like to thank Alex Hollingsworth for encouraging me to tackle this subject, Wendy Fuller for shaping the book's format, and Grace Harrison and Ed Gibbons for their support of the final production.

Last but not least, I would like to thank my family and friends for their unwavering support and patience while I was completing this book. Special thanks to my parents for instilling their passion for architecture, landscape architecture, and gardening into me; my brother Stephan for his scientific input; Robin and Jordan for tolerantly sharing me with this book project; and Dan for his love, encouragement, and support.

Introduction

Urban Agriculture and the Built Environment

The urban agricultural movement is growing in popularity and has become an important part of the urban lifestyle in cities in North America, Europe, and Asia. It promises to help reestablish urbanites' lost connections to nature and to the source of their food while improving the environmental quality of cities and strengthening urban communities through social and economic benefits. Architects, landscape architects, planners, and students are increasingly interested in designing with urban agriculture to incorporate these benefits into their design work. Designing with living, productive systems and integrating them with urban infrastructure and building systems, however, require multidisciplinary skills. Many designers need to expand their knowledge about the underlying natural, technical, and operational systems to take full advantage of the design opportunity this movement affords. Integrating urban agriculture requires knowledge of ecological cycles, food systems, community networks, and other dynamic systems, as well as collaborating and coordinating with multidisciplinary design teams. Because it relies on these diverse considerations, urban agriculture may serve as a powerful catalyst for new approaches to sustainable design and urban futures.

Creating Urban Agricultural Systems: An Integrated Approach to Design is a sourcebook and design resource for an interdisciplinary audience, including architects, landscape architects, urban planners, design students, urban farmers, entrepreneurs, community leaders, and engaged citizens. It documents emerging strategies, current practices, and working case studies to show the environmental, systemic, technical, and operational considerations involved in urban agriculture. The research presented synthesizes information on inputs and outputs, resource efficiencies, environmental benefits, and operational achievements. It is based on numerous site visits, examinations of outstanding case studies, and interviews with the farmers, founders, consultants, architects, and landscape architects behind innovative farm operations.

Based on this first-hand information, the book develops a new focus for evaluating urban agriculture. It examines the potential for synergies across urban agriculture, infrastructure, and the built environment. It seeks to promote the broad integration of agricultural systems into building and urban projects in order to contribute on multiple levels to creating sustainable cities. Urban farming promotes the principle of intelligent use of urban resources—both environmental and human—by developing closed-loop, cyclical systems and careful integration with existing infrastructure, building systems, and networks.

This book investigates these systems in two parts, structured around the most important inputs necessary for successful urban agricultural operations:

Part I, environmental resources—or nutrients, water, and solar energy—and Part II, human expertise—or farm operation, community integration, and design. This examination is reinforced by more than 80 exemplary projects, case studies, and profiles of architecture firms, all of which demonstrate that interconnections across resource systems, human expertise, and the existing urban environment are the key to success. In this way, the book helps designers develop a better, more holistic understanding of environmental cycles and systems, human inputs, and their synergies with the built environment.

RESPONSE TO ENVIRONMENTAL CHALLENGES

Environmental inputs are not only critical for cultivating crops; they are also implicated in some of today's most pressing global challenges. Urban agriculture offers a more sustainable alternative to untenable anthropogenic activities and current industrial agricultural practices, including the use of synthetic fertilizers, overuse of fresh water resources, and combustion of fossil fuels, which harm the environment by accelerating the disturbance of global biogeochemical cycles. These industrial agricultural practices cause or exacerbate many global environmental problems, such as eutrophication, water scarcity, and global warming. Injecting large quantities of carbon, nitrogen, and phosphorus compounds and using massive amounts of fresh water in industrial agriculture have brought immense short-term gains in production and prosperity. However, they threaten long-term degradation of essential ecological systems.

Urban agriculture, on the contrary, relies on more sustainable processes, which help rebalance large biogeochemical flows, such as the carbon, nitrogen, phosphorus, and water cycles. Emerging methods of urban agriculture may, for example, demonstrate composting and alternative waste management, practice water conservation, or reduce the use of transportation and machinery. The urban agricultural movement has begun to develop strategies that exploit urban growing conditions. These approaches may be applied to large-scale agricultural operations as well. Researchers such as Sarah Taylor Lovell and Sam Wortman at the Department of Crop Sciences, University of Illinois at Urbana-Champaign, view urban agriculture as an important model for managing the escalating challenges of climate change in industrial agriculture.[1]

OPERATIONAL ALTERNATIVES

Designing urban agricultural operations demands a thorough understanding of operational requirements and the potential effects on the urban food system. In general, urban agriculture has increased awareness about flaws in the existing food system and has developed promising strategies to solve some of its greatest challenges. The centralized, industrial food system is in the hands of a few national and multinational distributors, which control crop selection, handling, distribution, and revenue flows. Consumers are increasingly disconnected from the sources of their food, and they lack physical, economic, and conceptual access to fresh, whole foods.

During the development process, design professionals need to understand how an urban agricultural project may be operated and integrated into the larger food system. Who grows what? Urban farms have the opportunity (and commitment) to produce for the local market, to address community needs, and to create successful niche markets. Urban farms develop distribution models that foster direct consumer relationships to keep the supply chain short and the economic benefits in the local community. They also build on diverse community integration strategies and create social benefits for their neighborhoods.

SYNERGIES BETWEEN URBAN AGRICULTURE AND CITIES

Urban farms make opportunistic use of space in the city. Integrating environmental and human systems works especially well when the urban farm is able to adapt to available resources while fulfilling urban needs. Paul de Graaf is a Rotterdam-based architect whose design and research focus on relationships between architecture, landscape, and ecology. In his recent work, he investigates reciprocal relationships between the supplies and demands of urban agriculture and cities to more successfully incorporate urban agriculture in industrialized cities.[2] The challenge and often underestimated opportunity for designers lie in identifying and leveraging synergies to solve urban problems by way of integrating urban agriculture.

Urban resources can fulfill a plant's basic needs for nutrients, water, and solar energy. For example, urban organic waste and wastewater contain essential nutrients. Recycling and composting these waste materials make use of them for plant cultivation while reducing the amount of biodegradable waste that goes into landfills, producing less methane, one of the most potent greenhouse gases. Similarly, cities offer potentially large amounts of rainwater as an alternative water source that can be collected on rooftops. Rainwater collection and retention will reduce the stormwater volume and load on wastewater treatment systems. In addition, urban rooftops typically offer unobstructed access to sunlight. The ambient temperatures in cities are higher due to the heat island effect, which extends the urban growing season. In return, urban farming offers extended evapotranspiration and cooling to reduce urban heat. Moreover, urban agriculture offers other benefits, such as education, jobs and job training, green space, and improved biodiversity. These opportunities align well with interested citizens, job seekers, and volunteers in cities and offer the potential to transform underutilized urban space.

Leveraging these synergies to create more sustainable urban environments is the greatest opportunity but also the greatest challenge for designers working with urban agriculture. Environmental synergies can be applied on multiple scales, from integrating with building systems to improving urban infrastructures. Similarly, the social benefits and services urban farms offer align well with the community needs of many neighborhoods. Urban farms support individuals with healthy food and opportunities for work and education while improving the livability of an entire community.

Creating Urban Agricultural Systems provides an understanding of the environmental and operational science, systems, and strategies at work in urban agricultural projects. The book's case studies of working operations, tested prototypes, and farms under development demonstrate how these systems are interconnected to respond to site-specific qualities. Finally, in the architects' profiles, practicing architects share their visionary ideas and provide inspiration for integrating urban agriculture in design work. Together, these examples vividly illustrate how urban agriculture can cultivate new spatial, architectural, and conservation practices using existing urban resources.

NOTES

1. Sam E. Wortman and Sarah Taylor Lovell, "Environmental Challenges Threatening the Growth of Urban Agriculture in the United States," *Journal of Environmental Quality* 42.5 (2013): 1291.
2. Paul A. de Graaf, "Room for Urban Agriculture in Rotterdam: Defining the Spatial Opportunities for Urban Agriculture within the Industrialized City," in *Sustainable Food Planning: Evolving Theory and Practice*, ed. André Viljoen and Johannes S.C. Wiskerke (Wageningen: Wageningen Academic Publishers, 2012), 533–545.

Part I | Environmental Resources

Chapter 1

Nutrients

Growing Systems and Zero Waste Future

ABSTRACT

Most cities maintain waste streams that do not sufficiently return nutrients to the natural cycle. Simultaneously, many ecosystems are threatened by pollution through agricultural runoff and over-fertilization. Urban agriculture offers a more holistic approach to nutrient resource management in cities, based on closed-loop systems that follow the principles of natural nutrient cycles, which are the basis for all life on Earth. This chapter provides the knowledge necessary to re-establish these recirculating systems by aligning the nutrient needs of plants with efficient growing systems and recycling strategies, such as composting, anaerobic digestion, and alternative waste management. It also illustrates their potential for integration in building systems and their beneficial impact on building performance. Chapter 1 concludes with two catalogs that provide an overview of soil-based and hydroponic growing systems and their application to urban farming.

CLOSING THE NUTRIENT CYCLE

The natural nutrient cycle provides a closed-loop system in which nutrients are recirculated and made available for each new growing cycle. Mineral nutrients move through the food chain from autotrophic plants—the primary producers, which transform inorganic substances under the presence of sunlight into their food—to herbivores and carnivores, then to decomposers, and back into a nutrient pool in the soil to be absorbed again by plants. This process is the basis for ecological recycling. Human interventions and industrialization, however, have disturbed this natural cycle.

Though the effects of human activity on the carbon cycle, such as global warming, are widely recognized and publicized, human impacts on the nutrient cycle remain less acknowledged. This lesser-known cycle is composed of the two great biogeochemical cycles of nitrogen and phosphorus.[1] As with the carbon cycle, the injection of vast quantities of nitrogen and phosphorus into the environment through chemical fertilizers has dramatically increased agricultural outputs and short-term prosperity without developing the closed-loop systems that support perpetual soil fertility. Furthermore, the extreme use of fertilizer threatens to cause long-term degradation of essential natural systems and aquatic ecosystems. Industrial agriculture and the modern economy depend on the circulation of nitrogen and phosphorous compounds primarily as fertilizer

◀ Figure 1.1

Red wigglers, an essential component for vermicomposting

and detergents and produce nitrogen dioxide through the combustion of fossil fuels. Unfortunately, the increased volume of these two elements is a serious source of pollution, and the potential to recycle and divert them from conventional waste streams remains underutilized.[2] As long as these opportunities are not realized, municipalities will expend enormous resources treating wastewater, while industrial agriculture will continue to rely on synthetic fertilizers.

Urban agriculture applies many strategies that help recycle nutrients and can mitigate related environmental challenges by mimicking the closed-loop character of the natural nutrient cycle. These practices enable synergies between urban food production and urban waste management by supporting the use of alternative nutrient sources and the recovery of energy created as a byproduct of natural decomposition processes.

NUTRIENT NEEDS OF PLANTS

While it is important to understand the larger environmental and global implications of the nutrient cycle, designers must also consider the resource and nutrient needs of plants when designing urban agricultural systems. Plants consist primarily of three non-mineral elements—carbon (C), hydrogen (H), and oxygen (O_2). These elements are acquired from water (H_2O) and from carbon dioxide (CO_2) in the air and account for 99.5% of fresh plant material. Water alone makes up 95% of a plant, and its presence is therefore the main factor for plant growth (Figure 1.2). In the remaining dry matter, C accounts for approximately 45% of the mass, O_2 for 40–45% and H for 5–7%. Plants absorb C in the form of CO_2 during photosynthesis; transform it into glucose, which they store in their tissue; and produce O_2 as a byproduct. Artificially elevating CO_2 levels, referred to as CO_2 fertilization, is a technique to increase plant growth and productivity. While plants create O_2 during photosynthesis, they also use O_2 for respiration during dark periods and to grow roots. Therefore plants require well-aerated soils or must receive aeration when grown in nutrient solutions.

While nutrients account for only 0.5% of a plant's volume, these inorganic salts and trace minerals found in the soil (or provided in a growing solution) are necessary for plant growth. Nitrogen (N), phosphorus (P), potassium (K), sulfur (S), calcium (Ca), and magnesium (Mg) are considered macronutrients since they are required in relatively large amounts by plants. Copper (Cu), zinc (Zn), cobalt (Co), manganese (Mn), molybdenum (Mo), boron (B), and chlorine (Cl) are micronutrients required in relatively small amounts.

Nitrogen (N), phosphorus (P), and potassium (K) are the primary nutrients needed by plants. The NPK rating system is used to specify the relative content of these chemical elements in a fertilizer. Each crop needs a slightly different composition of nutrients, which may change during different growth periods. Liebig's Law of the Minimum states that growth is limited not by the total amount of resources available but by the scarcest resource—the nutrient in the smallest quantity relative to the plant's need. Therefore it is important to provide all nutrients in sufficient proportions to prevent deficiencies and uncontrolled over-fertilization, which detrimentally affects plants and the environment.

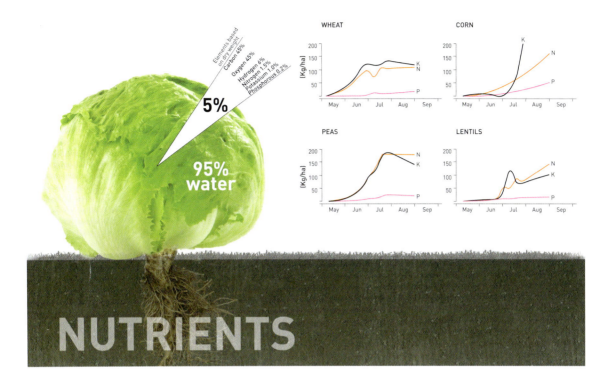

▲ Figure 1.2

Chemical composition of a typical plant and the nutrient needs of different crops during their growing period

Data adapted from Howard M. Resh, *Hydroponic Food Production: A Definitive Guidebook of Soilless Food-growing Methods* (Mahwah, NJ: CRC Press, 2004), 35; International Plant Nutrition Institute, 1998.

THE NITROGEN CYCLE

Nitrogen is vital for all living things. As a component of amino acids, it is necessary for the synthesis of proteins, enzymes, hormones, chlorophyll, and DNA. The atmosphere is the most important source of nitrogen, containing 78% of elemental nitrogen (N_2), an inert gas that cannot be used by most plants directly. Only leguminous plants such as beans, peas, lentils, alfalfa, and clover, in symbiosis with rhizobium bacteria, can synthesize nitrogen from the air through nitrogen fixation. All other plants absorb nitrate-ions (NO_3^-) in the soil through their roots as their main nitrogen source. Decomposition of humus—the organic matter in the soil—and its mineralization into usable inorganic forms replenish the nitrogen content in the soil. Since the beginning of the twentieth century, human activities such as synthetic nitrogen fixation by the fertilizer industry and the uncontrolled exhaust of pollutants have doubled the amount of biologically available nitrogen readily absorbable by plants.[3] This increased volume of nitrogen ends up in the wrong places with detrimental effects on the environment. Nitrogen compounds from agricultural runoff leach into groundwater and pollute aquatic ecosystems, leading to eutrophication (Figure 1.3). Too much nitrate in drinking water can lead to restricted oxygen transport in the bloodstream, which poses a health risk, especially to infants. Furthermore, the removal of excess nitrate in wastewater is very cost-intensive. Nitrous oxide (N_2O) is a very potent greenhouse gas and the third largest contributor to global warming after carbon dioxide and methane.

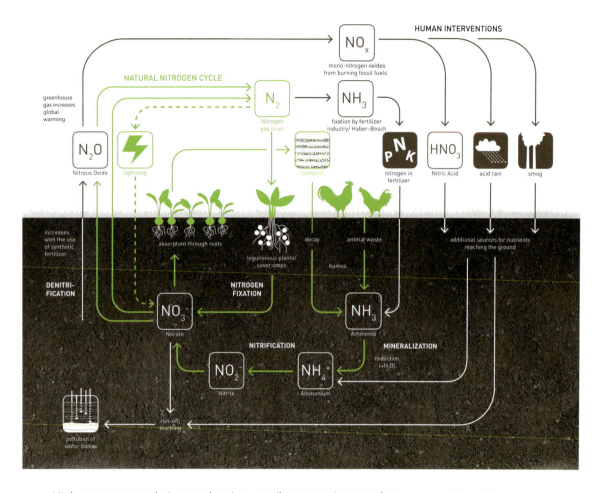

▲ Figure 1.3

The nitrogen cycle—natural cycle and human interventions

Data adapted from Hannah Hislop, ed., *The Nutrient Cycle: Closing the Loop* (London: Green Alliance, 2007), 10.

High temperatures during combustion contribute to an increased creation of mono-nitrogen oxides (NO) and nitrogen dioxide (NO_2). The higher the temperature during combustion, the more NO_x is produced. Ammonia and nitrogen oxides contribute to smog and acid rain, which damage plants and increase the nitrogen input into ecosystems. Over-fertilization can lead to nitrogen saturation, which reduces plant productivity and impairs the health of flora, fauna, and humans.

Energy Needs of Fertilizer Production

In 1909, Fritz Haber and Carl Bosch, two German scientists, developed an industrial process to synthesize ammonia, which became the basis for fertilizer production and other chemical processes. This process transforms inert nitrogen (N_2) from the air into ammonia (NH_3). It requires large amounts of energy and uses hydrogen from natural gas as a source material. The energy needs for ammonia production are 600 kWh per ton. The energy used to produce

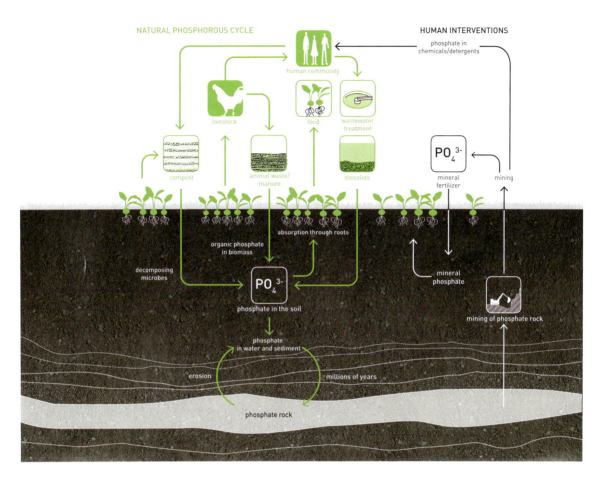

▲ Figure 1.4

The phosphorus cycle—natural cycle and human interventions

Data adapted from Vaclav Smil, "Phosphorus in the Environment: Natural Flows and Human Interferences," *Annual Review of Energy and the Environment* 25 (2000): 53–88.

nitrogen fertilizer from ammonia is a large part of the overall carbon footprint of agriculture, accounting for about 40% of the energy used to grow a corn crop. In the search for more sustainable fertilizer production, alternative energy sources and water as an alternate hydrogen source have been tested, though none of the experimental processes have proven industrially or commercially viable.[4]

THE PHOSPHORUS CYCLE

Phosphorus (P) is a nonmetallic chemical element important for plant growth. Plants absorb phosphorus through their roots as phosphate ions ($H_2PO_4^-$ and HPO_4^{2-}). In nature, decomposing organic matter and animal and human waste replenish phosphorus in the soil (Figure 1.4). In industrial agriculture, mineral fertilizers provide an additional source of phosphorus. The fertilizer industry comprises about 90% of the global phosphorus demand, for which the primary source is currently phosphate rock.[5] The amount of biologically available phosphate has tripled since phosphorus mining began at the end of the nineteenth century.[6] With growing demand for food, the global demand for phosphorus is predicted to increase by 50–100% by 2050. Phosphorous rock is a non-renewable resource, and commercial reserves will be depleted in 50–100 years.[7]

While many of the challenges around phosphate mining are similar to those associated with oil, there are two distinct differences. First, oil can be replaced with renewable energy sources, but there is no biochemical substitute for phosphorus. Second, energy stored in oil becomes unavailable after combustion, whereas phosphorus can be recovered from organic waste. Countries without direct access to phosphate rock invest in the production of renewable phosphorus fertilizer through composting and reclamation from sewage sludge to assure food security. They lead the way in utilizing the ecological recycling potential of this resource, while reducing their dependence on phosphorus imports.[8] Although phosphorus is a precious, essential, and finite resource, at elevated levels it also becomes a pollutant that causes eutrophication through agricultural runoff.

Industrial Agriculture

The large-scale application of fertilizer in industrial agriculture has dramatically increased agricultural yields. This upsurge, often celebrated as the Green Revolution, has also brought about immense global population growth. Feeding the growing global population with inadequate existing food systems remains one of the world's largest challenges. Rarely is industrial agriculture itself acknowledged as partly responsible for the exponential population growth at the root of the issue (Figure 1.5). Today, when the Earth's capacity to increase agricultural productivity with conventional methods is environmentally, economically, and socio-politically irresponsible, alternative methods that close the nutrient cycle have to be applied on a much larger scale; they must become the new normal.

Waste Management

In tandem with the widespread break in the nutrient cycle, most contemporary waste streams are still linear. Large amounts of biodegradable waste are dumped in landfills, where they create considerable amounts of methane, a potent greenhouse gas that contributes to global warming. Preventing waste and diverting biodegradable waste from landfills and the wastewater stream not only reduces greenhouse gas production but also helps to reconnect the nutrient cycle. Waste management has for a long time been a large-scale operation in need of large infrastructure. Today even alternative waste handling, like composting, often develops into industrialized operations. Urban agriculture demonstrates ways to decentralize these practices and transform them into nimble on-site solutions.

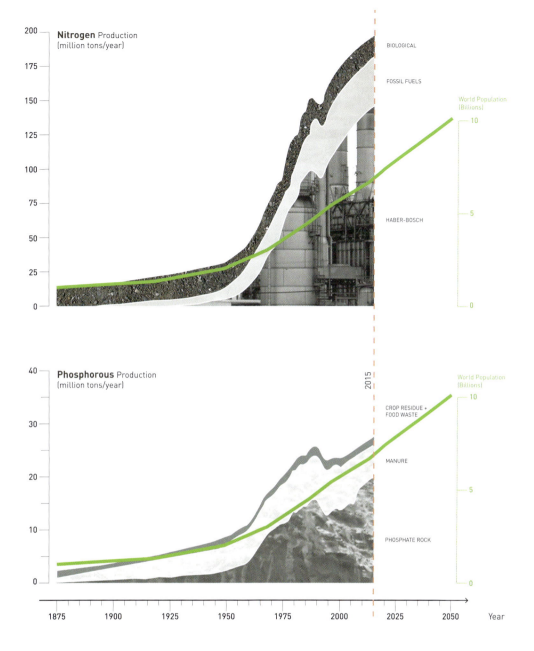

▲ Figure 1.5

Timeline of global nitrogen production, phosphorus production, and population growth

Data adapted from Peter M. Vitousek, et al., "Human Alteration of the Global Nitrogen Cycle: Sources and Consequences." *Ecological Applications* 7, no. 3 (1997): 737-50; Dana Cordell, et al., "Towards Global Phosphorus Security: Systemic Framework for Phosphorus Recovery and Reuse Options." *Chemosphere* 84, no. 6 (2011): 747-58; US Census Bureau, International Data Base, July 2015 Update.

URBAN AGRICULTURE'S POSITIVE IMPACT ON THE NUTRIENT CYCLE

Most urban agricultural projects take environmental approaches to their nutrient streams and replenishment. Urban farms are often committed to more sustainable growing methods and nutrient sources due to their environmental ethics, their goals to generate holistic cycles and organic operations, and their smaller scale. Commonly used practices fall into two larger categories: (1) the use of resource-efficient growing methods; and (2) the mining of alternative nutrient and energy sources.

Resource-efficient Growing Methods

Compared to conventional farming, growing methods used in urban agriculture are intensive, integrated, and use space effectively to achieve higher yields per area footprint. In addition, intercropping, multi-cropping, and vertical growing strategies utilize available space and growing seasons more efficiently. Sustainable approaches to resource management range from ecological methods that mimic natural systems to ensure long-term soil health to high-tech closed systems, such as hydroponics, that conserve water and nutrient resources. Other urban agriculture operations, like aquaponic systems, develop nutrient cycles that run through several stages of self-fertilization, irrigation, and purification. The environmental benefits that come with these methods are extensive. All of these methods environmentally outperform conventional agriculture.

Mining Alternative Nutrient and Energy Sources

In combination with resource-efficient growing methods, urban agriculture often utilizes alternative nutrient sources instead of the synthetic or mineral fertilizers typically used in industrial agriculture. Urban farms embrace either regenerative farming techniques, such as permaculture or biointensive farming, or urban nutrient resources—which have conventionally been considered waste—through composting and alternative waste treatment methods. While transforming waste into biologically available nutrients, some systems also extract energy as a valuable byproduct, such as heat recovery from composting and methane production from anaerobic digestion to support farm operations.

GROWING METHODS USED IN URBAN AGRICULTURE

Urban agriculture generates many approaches and growing systems while adapting to local conditions and taking advantage of urban resources. Different growing systems and typologies may be distinguished primarily by their growing medium and approach to nutrient management, their degree of building integration, and their level of environmental control. Additional criteria include expertise, labor, capital, energy, resources, and supplemental lighting required to construct and operate the growing system, as well as achievable outputs, yields, and environmental benefits.[9]

Growing systems fall into two main categories by growing medium: (1) soil-based systems, which cultivate plants in natural soil or a soil-like growing medium (see Catalog 1 below); and (2) hydroponic (soil-less) systems, which provide plants with nutrients through a nutrient solution (see Catalog 2 below). The range of growing methods generates a gradient from productive ecosystems to high-tech constructed systems (Figure 1.6). The degree of building integration ranges from constructed grounds that provide soil in barren places to controlled-environment agriculture (CEA), which engineers optimal indoor growing conditions.

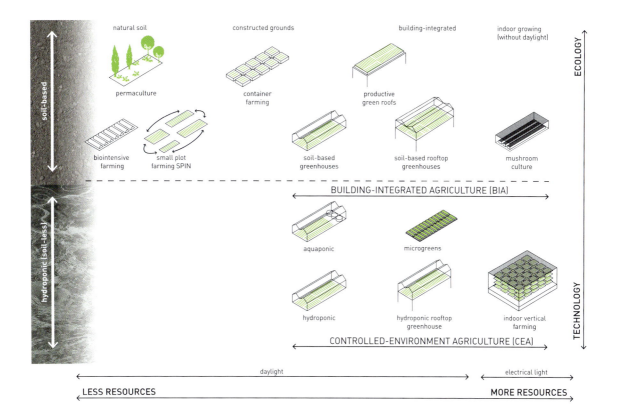

▲ Figure 1.6

Matrix of growing systems used in urban agriculture

Evaluation and Design Integration of Growing Systems

Soil-based natural growing systems, such as permaculture and organic farming methods, are perpetual in nature. Over time they actively build nutrient-rich soil and promote clean water storage, biological diversity, on-site resource maintenance, and high yields, while using natural fertilizer and reducing energy expenditures. These methods prioritize sustained harvests over immediate and short-lived returns and emphasize the farmer's role as a steward. Potential sites for this type of system need to offer an acceptable soil quality; at the very minimum, the site needs to have a connection to uncontaminated ground. The most important human input for this approach is expertise in how to establish an "agroecosystem." Natural soil-based systems offer the possibility of integrating conventional waste products as nutrient sources while aiming for a return to the environmental qualities lost with the development of industrial agriculture.

Soil-based constructed grounds are often the easiest way to grow crops in cities. Container gardens, raised beds, and productive green roofs import soil to underutilized urban sites, such as roofs, parking lots, vacant sites, and brownfields, bringing a variety of environmental benefits to previously barren sites. This approach uses a combination of simple constructed and natural systems that can take diverse forms at any scale. It often takes advantage of organic agriculture strategies, such as composting, to maintain soil quality.

Hydroponic soil-less growing systems recirculate nutrient solutions based on synthetic and mineral inputs. These systems use technology to reduce resource inputs, raise water and nutrient efficiency, and increase productivity. The use of controlled-environment agriculture (CEA) in greenhouses ensures the monitoring of the growing conditions, eliminates most sources of pollution, and extends the growing season. Indoor hydroponic systems require the highest up-front capital investment. They generate very high yields, however, and offer more opportunities for building integration than ground-based systems.

Aquaponic systems combine the benefits of highly controlled hydroponic systems with the qualities that natural, organic growing system offer. A closed-loop nutrient system replaces the negative aspects of hydroponics (mineral and synthetic fertilizer use) with self-fertilization, while potentially using the sophisticated distribution systems developed in hydroponic cultures (Figure 1.7). Aquaponic systems also require CEA conditions for their operation. For a detailed description of all growing systems, see Catalogs 1 and 2.

Potential Yields

The potential yields of different growing systems are another important criterion for their evaluation, though accurate numbers are difficult to establish. The productivity of growing systems depends on many components, including the type and variety of crop, environmental factors such as soil quality and nutrient access, water supply, sunlight exposure, natural climate, and the level of environmental control, as well as the planting density, system efficiency, and planting schedule.[10] Little comprehensive research has been conducted to date on the effect of urban growing conditions on yields. Traditionally, yields are established based on the productivity per growing area. With the increasing diversity of growing methods in urban agriculture, other factors become critical. Measuring "yields per unit of input" provides a valid alternative.[11] Additionally, Wortman and Lovell have observed that "water use efficiency (WUE) may become a critical metric for evaluating the performance of food production systems" with increasing water scarcity.[12] In connection with other environmental challenges, important units of input might include fertilizer, energy, carbon footprint, and volume of waste created. In terms of resource inputs, urban agricultural projects typically outperform conventional agriculture. However, if yields are measured against labor and operational costs, small urban farms have a hard time competing with industrial operations, let alone establishing economic viability.[13]

SYNERGIES BETWEEN URBAN AGRICULTURE, URBAN WASTE STREAMS, AND ENERGY RECOVERY

To maintain productivity, growing systems have to constantly replenish their nutrient pool. Most urban agricultural systems avoid synthetic and mineral fertilizers and attempt to mine alternative nutrient sources instead. Nutrients are mainly contained in what Western societies consider waste. Changing the

▶ Figure 1.7

Comparison: growing systems used in urban agriculture

Data adapted from catalog 1 and 2 sources and references.

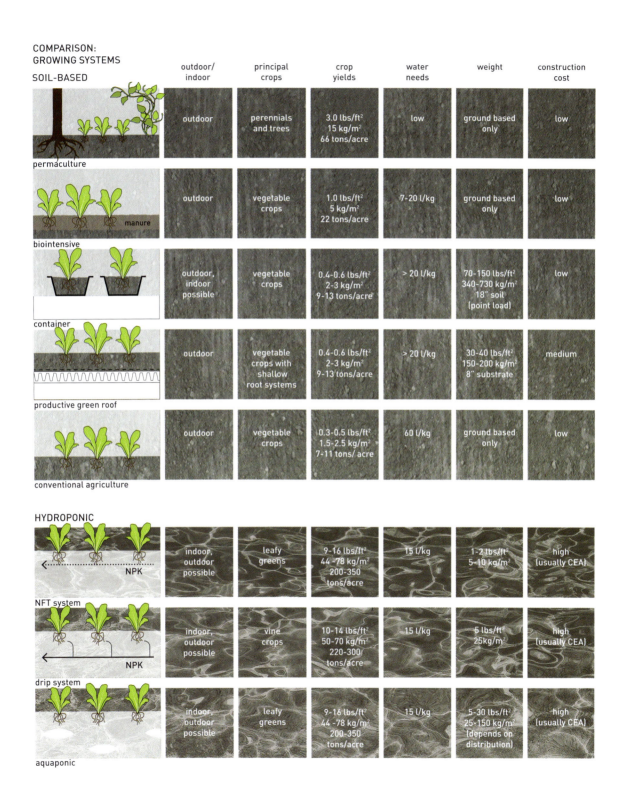

public perception of these valuable resources is the first step towards recovering them through alternative treatment options and capitalizing on synergies with urban waste management. Urban agriculture supports the movement away from the large infrastructure needed for conventional waste management towards smaller, decentralized operations for handling waste and returning nutrients on-site. In addition, cities' rich supplies of nutrients, biodegradable waste, and sewage also contain large amounts of carbon and energy. Organic matter is broken down during decomposition processes and transformed into heat and biogas. Several urban agricultural operations aim to retrieve some of this urban energy to cover their own operational energy needs.

COMPOSTING

Once biodegradable waste enters the landfill, it creates methane under anaerobic conditions. Methane is a greenhouse gas 24 times more potent than CO_2. Diverting organic waste from landfills into controlled composting, which generates CO_2 under aerobic conditions, reduces the greenhouse gas emissions of landfills and creates compost and soil amendments. Thus composting has an important place in urban agriculture and creates strong synergies with urban waste streams through improvements to soil quality, increased productivity, and additional environmental benefits.

The integration of compost into the soil generates long-term improvements to the physical structure of soils, their organic matter content, and their moisture retention capability. Compost releases nutrients slowly, offers the nutrient mix that plants need, and retains inorganic nutrients, reducing agricultural runoff.[14] The amended soil sequesters carbon through direct carbon storage and the addition of non-reactive humus compounds that decompose very slowly.[15] In addition, it has the ability to restore and repair soil and perform *in situ* lead stabilization of contaminated soils. Other research has shown that compost application suppresses plant pathogens.[16]

Microorganisms produce metabolic heat during aerobic composting. Based on the temperature generated during the decomposition process, composting methods are defined as either hot composting or cold composting. Cold composting is usually backyard or on-site composting conducted by residents or urban farmers who generate only small quantities of organic waste. Hot composting is a larger-scale operation in which the compost reaches temperatures between 130°F and 150°F (55–65°C) for an extended period of time. Hot composting generates compost faster, breaks matter down into finer humus, and destroys pathogens through exposure to high temperatures. To keep the temperature high and avoid anaerobic conditions that lead to methane production, compost piles or windrows need to be aerated regularly. Aerated turned windrow composting creates long compost piles that are manually or mechanically turned at regular intervals. Aerated static pile composting ventilates from below through specific piling techniques or by air blowers. Aerobic in-vessel composting uses special containers for environmental control, aeration, and agitation of the organic material. Vermicomposting is a special composting

▲ Figure 1.8

Large-scale windrow composting, Growing Power headquarters, Milwaukee

method that uses earthworms, especially red wigglers and red earthworms, to refine the compost, and their castings.[17]

Municipalities are increasingly installing large-scale composting systems to divert biodegradable waste from landfills, due to regulations controlling the amount of organic waste allowed in them. The EU Landfill Directive obliges member-state municipalities to reduce the amount of biodegradable waste in each landfill to 35% of 1995 levels by the year 2016.[18] Urban farms usually produce their own compost, but some also use industrially produced compost material for the initial establishment of planting beds and for soil amendments. Growing Power, a nonprofit urban farm and advocacy organization, is essentially built on a soil production system that combines composting and vermiculture (Figure 1.8). It is an outstanding example of a small-scale compost operation that has turned into an urban-scale endeavor (see Case Study 7).

Compost Heat Recovery Systems

To increase environmental benefits, large-scale aerobic composting operations have devoted more and more attention to heat recovery over the past few years. These recovery systems capture the metabolic heat produced by microorganisms through negatively aerated fan systems (Figure 1.9). They blow hot compost vapor against heat exchangers to pre-heat water in a large tank for heating and hot water preparation. The water in the tank can maintain a temperature between 90°F and 146°F (32–63°C), depending on the compost feedstock and other variables.[19]

Nutrients: Growing Systems

The most advanced heat recovery units (developed by Agrilab) capture both the thermal energy in the hot air and in the water molecules of the vapor stream itself. This increases the efficiency, since the hot water vapor contains 63% of the heat generated within a compost pile, while the hot air contains only 13%. The remaining heat is usually lost from the compost pile through natural convection and radiation.[20] These systems are not yet widely implemented but have been tested in research and pilot projects. Increased heat recovery will increase the overall energy balance, environmental benefits, and economic viability of composting operations.

Some urban agricultural projects implement effective, low-tech heat recovery strategies without the need for large infrastructure. Growing Power, for example, locates compost piles in and around its hoop houses during the winter to keep their interiors above freezing and operational during the cold season in Milwaukee. Other farms have developed compost heat recovery systems with coiled pipes integrated into their stationary compost piles. R-Urban, a Paris-based network of urban resilience, has developed a more compact heat recovery system that captures up to 140°F (60°C) in a mobile composting container (see Case Study 14). The heat transfer works much like a hot water heater: a coiled copper pipe in a copper sleeve is pushed into the compost pile. Water circulated through the system transfers the heat to a radiator to partially heat nearby buildings during the winter.[21]

▼ Figure 1.9

Industrial composting with heat recovery system

Data adapted from Matt Smith and John Aber, "Heat Recovery from Compost," *BioCycle. The Organics Recycling Authority* (February 2014), available at: www.biocycle.net/2014/02/21/heat-recovery-from-compost/.

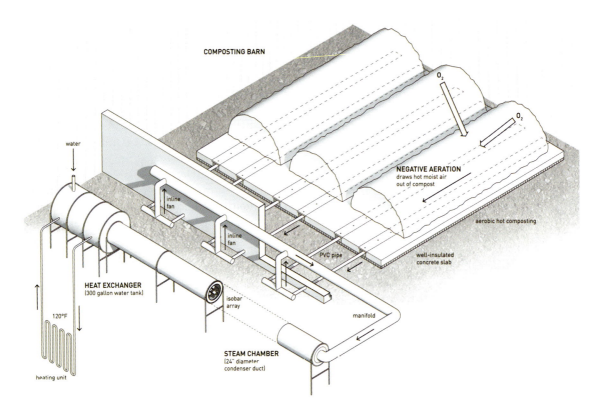

ANAEROBIC DIGESTION

Anaerobic digestion is a biological process that utilizes biodegradable waste to produce energy in an anaerobic digester, a vessel that works like a mechanical stomach. Anaerobic bacteria convert organic matter into biogas and digestate in the absence of oxygen. The biogas is a mixture of methane (55–80%), carbon dioxide (20–40%), and other gases (up to 10%). The digestate can be used as organic fertilizer and can be mechanically separated into liquid components and fiber with a solid, soil-like consistency. Based on the temperature to which the digester is heated, the process is considered mesophilic (70–105°F/20–40°C) and thermophilic (above 120°F/50°C). In comparison to mesophilic digestion, thermophilic digestion produces more biogas per unit time, requires smaller tanks for a given volume of feedstock, and kills more pathogens; however, it also requires more expensive infrastructure, more energy input, and a higher level of monitoring.[22]

Anaerobic digesters are large-scale infrastructure with a high up-front investment. Research for digester use in industrial agriculture suggests a payback period of 5–16 years depending on whether the digesters run under optimal or worst conditions and if access to free waste is available.[23] The interest in renewable energy and potential incentives or grant funding might reduce the amortization period. One example is The Plant in Chicago, which integrated an anaerobic digester into its energy system to cover its high energy demands (Figure 1.10). This installation was partly funded by a $1.5 million grant by the Illinois Department of Commerce and Economics. Once completed, the digester will consume approximately 30 tons of food waste per day, or around 10,000 tons annually, including all of the waste produced in the facility and by neighboring food manufacturers (see Case Study 9).

Comparison of Anaerobic Digestion and Aerobic Composting

It is difficult to compare the processes of aerobic composting and anaerobic digestion, since their effectiveness primarily depends on the type and scale of the operation. The criteria used to evaluate the two processes should be their emissions, environmental efficiency, energy balance, the quality of compost, and the operational cost. The emissions of both processes are similar: both produce compost, release biogas and evaporated water into the air, and generate wastewater and post-treatment waste. The percentages of the different outputs vary between the two processes. Both processes yield about 25–30% of compost as output. Anaerobic digestion produces methane as biogas, while aerobic composting produces CO_2 and heat. In terms of waste products, anaerobic digestion produces much more wastewater with higher water treatment costs and more post-treatment waste. Compost evaporates about 50% of the input as water, therefore the wastewater production is very small, as is the amount of post-treatment waste.

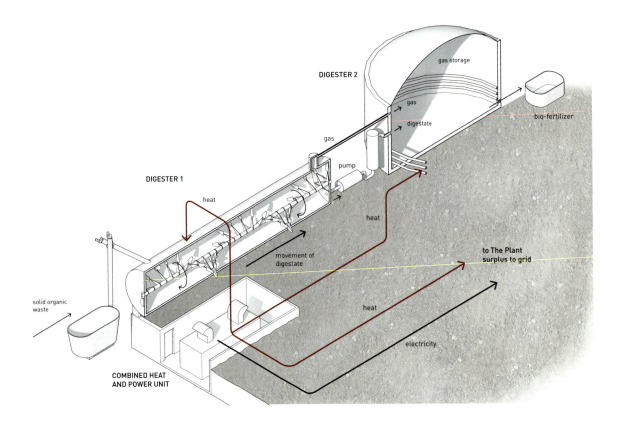

▲ Figure 1.10

Anaerobic digester (as installed by The Plant in Chicago)

Anaerobic digestion requires more energy input, primarily to heat the tank, but overall the energy balance is positive through the production of methane gas, a recognized alternative energy source. Composting requires less operational energy input, and energy in the form of heat can be recovered, though the technologies for heat recovery are still in the testing phase. Conclusive research on the comparative energy balance is missing. The quality of compost produced has to be monitored in both systems, since it is largely determined by the quality of waste input into the system and the ability of the facility to deal with post-treatment and maturing of the compost. Cost efficiency depends on the size of the operation and the source of the biodegradable waste. In general, the establishment of an anaerobic digester is more capital-intensive and the operational expenses are higher.

WASTEWATER AS NUTRIENT SOURCE

Nutrients contained in wastewater are a valuable but taboo nutrient source. Largely derived from human excrement, this source bears serious health risks that can be adequately addressed with safe technologies that kill pathogens. Public lack of confidence in these recycling methods is the main constraint against effective use of this resource and closure of the nutrient loop. Urban sewage is usually treated in large, municipal wastewater treatment plants. Urban agriculture can benefit from the two highly regulated outputs of these plants: reclaimed water for irrigation and sewage sludge or biosolids for fertilization.

Biosolids

Sewage sludge is the nutrient-rich organic byproduct created through the removal of solids during the wastewater treatment process. Instead of being dumped into landfills—once standard practice—sewage sludge can be recycled as a soil amendment for crop production, enriching soil by restoring valuable nutrients and carbon. An inexhaustible resource, all sludge is treated and regularly tested for quality and safety before use. Anaerobic digestion is the most common method of conventional sludge treatment. The process kills 90–95% of pathogens and reduces the volume of the solids. The methane gas thereby produced is used for combined heat and power generation to help run the treatment plant. Treated sludge may be applied to farmland as a liquid product but is increasingly dewatered mechanically to reduce transportation costs and produce a soil-like material. The dewatered, treated sludge is referred to as "biosolids" to distinguish it from untreated sludge.

Washington State's King County Loop biosolids are created following precise Environmental Protection Agency (EPA) standards for solids removed from treated wastewater before it is discharged into the adjacent Puget Sound or used as reclaimed water. Biosolids contain the full suite of nutrients needed by plants and are used as fertilizers and soil conditioners in agriculture and forestry. A portion of the biosolids is mixed with sawdust, composted by a private company, and sold as GroCo for use in landscaping and gardening. Both products offer the same improvements to soil quality as compost.[24]

The list of environmental benefits provided by biosolids is long. They offer high nutrient values, a slow release of nutrients, increased organic matter, reduced carbon footprint (based on carbon accounting), and protection for water bodies from agricultural runoff (due to their capacity to hold and store water and nutrients). Regardless of these benefits, the use of biosolids has been slow to take hold in agriculture due to the public's suspicion of any material made from human waste. Even usually pro-environmental companies such as Whole Foods prohibit the use of biosolids to grow produce sold in their stores.[25]

Energy Recovery

Biosolid production also offers the opportunity to recover energy produced during anaerobic digestion, improving the energy balance of the treatment process. Some publications suggest that the incineration of biosolids might be a potential energy source. Incineration disposes of biosolids by burning them, a less preferable option—in terms of sustainability—than using biosolids as soil amendment. During incineration, the high water content in biosolids must be reduced before combustion can start.[26] If the solids are dewatered to a relatively high degree and their heat value is sufficient, the combustion process might be self-sustaining but with little capacity to generate additional power from the incineration process. Supplemental energy, in fact, is always needed to start the process and to accommodate fluctuations in the feedstock.[27] Therefore incineration is only justified (and currently the only viable option) to dispose of contaminated sludge and should not be counted as a potential energy source.

Source Separation

Source separation goes a step further. It offers alternative approaches to handling and recycling human excrement before it enters the urban wastewater stream. The separation of human waste allows easier access to the nutrients within it. Separate treatment of urine and feces is also more energy- and cost-effective. The idea of sanitized reuse of nutrients (by returning them to the land) is simple but has been obscured by the success of the sewage system, though variations of this principle are already extensively used in China, Central America, and Sweden. Over the past two decades, trials have been conducted to divert urine and feces by using dry or wet source separating or urine diversion toilets.[28]

Given their chemical composition, both urine and feces are potential resources that can supplement the nutrient and energy cycles. Largely sterile urine contains nitrogen (15–19%), phosphorus, and potassium (both up to 5%) and can be used immediately as fertilizer. Feces, however, are high in pathogens and carbon (40–55%) and need to be either composted as fertilizer or treated with regular wastewater in a treatment plant or anaerobic digester. Urine's high nutrient content, instantaneous recycling options, and gentler public image suggest that it might become a nutrient resource for agricultural production in the future.[29]

Eco-Machines

Eco-Machines, first developed by John Todd in 1974 under the name Living Machine at the New Alchemy Institute, perform ecological sewage treatment by mimicking and accelerating the natural purification processes of wetlands (Figure 1.11). These contained systems are engineered by combining bacteria, microorganisms, algae, and aquatic flora and fauna. Following the same principles as aquaponic growing systems, bacteria turn ammonia into nitrates, which are consumed by algae and plants that feed zooplankton and fish. In addition, specific plants absorb and render toxins harmless. In northern climates, parts of (or even entire) treatment systems are protected from the local climate by a greenhouse to guarantee year-round operation and to raise the rate of biological activity. To date, Eco-Machines have been integrated into several small-scale projects. Their aesthetic as "productive" water features offers opportunities to integrate them indoors and outdoors.

Todd and his wife Nancy have also developed ideas for the Eco-Machine's urban integration. In their book, *From Eco-Cities to Living Machine*, they sketched out the idea of "city farming," including urban farming in several building-integrated project types. In the book, Eco-Machines serve as neighborhood sewage treatment facilities in the form of "solar sewage walls" that treat raw effluent, provide nutrient-rich water for other growing facilities, and transform the streetscape through the integration of greenhouses.[30]

DESIGN CONSIDERATIONS

The creation of an integrated nutrient system in an urban agriculture project depends on the selection of the growing system and the potential use of an alternative nutrient source for replenishment. Soil-based systems can incorporate any form of organic matter or humus as a nutrient source. The most commonly used source is compost, but digestate and biosolids are possible alternatives. Hydroponic systems cannot easily use organic or in-house nutrient sources. These highly controlled systems require a solution with either mineral nutrients or recycled, organic nutrients that have been processed for this purpose. The only alternative, or organic, version of the hydroponic system is the aquaponic system, which self-generates its nutrients. Aquaponics generate their own closed nutrient cycle with fish feed as the main input into the system.

The main challenge for designers is to identify potential alternative nutrient sources. Which sources are locally available and complement the other aspects of the project? For example, if the project benefits from biogas besides the alternative fertilizer, then the integration of an anaerobic digester is indicated, as demonstrated by The Plant in Chicago (see Case Study 9). Or can the project take advantage of the excess heat produced during composting to heat, for example, a greenhouse or grow space?

▼ Figure 1.11

Eco-Machine, diagrammatic flow of wastewater through processing steps

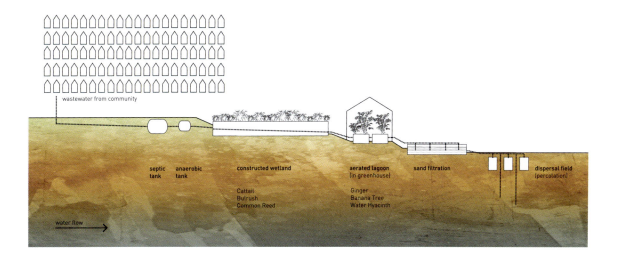

The next question is whether the recycling process is intended to happen on-site or whether the alternative fertilizer is produced off-site and delivered. If on-site treatment is intended, the designer is challenged to visualize the recycling process to demonstrate to the user of the building or site that the nutrient cycle is closed. Eco-Machines, for example, integrate well with the established aesthetics of water features in landscape and building design and make the different phases of water treatment easy to see and understand. Other recycling processes require more substantial infrastructure—for instance, anaerobic digesters and hot composting—and approaches for design integration for these processes have yet to be established.

Together with the design integration of nutrient recovery and waste management processes, cities, farmers, and designers have to take the scale of the operation and the capital investment needed for the infrastructure into consideration. How much compostable organic matter, organic waste, or wastewater needs to be processed?

Currently, the scale of alternative nutrient recovery infrastructure is also regulated by code. Many municipalities restrict the integration of alternative nutrient sources through rigid, unprogressive code requirements. For example, a Chicago ordinance limits on-site compost processing to 5–10 cubic yards (4–8 m^3) at any given time. For larger volumes, a city permit is required.[31] Even tougher restrictions apply for on-site wastewater treatment in many cities. Those interested in closing the nutrient cycle need to determine whether the loop should be closed on-site or in a network on the district scale. How many users need to collaborate to process waste effectively? Scale also affects feasibility. Large-scale infrastructure for hot composting, anaerobic digestion, and wastewater treatment is costly and requires a constant stream of feedstock, but it is also highly efficient. Smaller systems offer the opportunity for on-site treatment of organic waste and wastewater, which can develop into a decentralized network whose collective efficiency can rival that of a larger operation, if managed properly. This offers a real alternative to prevailing large-scale waste handling operations.

CATALOG 1: SOIL-BASED GROWING SYSTEMS IN URBAN AGRICULTURE

In nature, soil acts as the interface between the Earth's atmosphere and lithosphere, where energy, water, and gases are exchanged. Plant roots connect to soil processes, providing a pathway for water, nutrients, and oxygen, while physically anchoring plants to their growing medium. Plants absorb inorganic elements; both organic and inorganic components must be decomposed before they can be taken up by the plant.[32] As humus decomposes, it slowly releases nutrients as mineral elements and ions. Most soil-based growing systems strive to replenish their nutrient content through this process. Many of them build the nutrient levels and health of the soil slowly, increasing the soil's productivity over time.

Natural Soil-Based Systems

Permaculture Techniques
Permaculture—originally "permanent agriculture"—generates self-sustaining agriculture systems by mimicking natural ecosystems.[33] Developed by Bill Mollison and David Holmgren in Australia in the 1970s, permaculture is an integrated system of design that engenders diverse, high-yielding, "cultivated ecosystems." It vertically organizes four to seven layers of cultivation primarily composed of perennials, including trees, shrubs, herbaceous plants, and rhizomes. These polycultures simulate the ecosystem of a forest edge in both diversity and production.[34] The driving forces behind this design approach are mutually beneficial relationships. More than the sum of their parts, permaculture designs minimize waste and require minimal inputs and human labor once they are established. These unique characteristics allow permaculture to improve—both aesthetically and ecologically—underused and degraded public green spaces found in many parks, schoolyards, and public housing complexes. This design and growing practice reduces maintenance needs and offers educational opportunities to highlight cyclical systems in nature (Figure 1.12).[35]

Biointensive Farming Methods
Biointensive agriculture is an organic farming method focused primarily on improving and maintaining soil fertility to produce maximum yields on a minimum area of land. This technique combines two European growing methods: (1) the historic French intensive method; and (2) Rudolf Steiner's biodynamic technique developed in the early 1920s. Most recently promoted by John Jeavons, this farming method uses raised beds, close spacing, and deep soil preparation, which builds soil by loosening it to a depth of 24 inches (60 cm). It involves nutrient recycling through composting, closing the nutrient cycle on-site. When properly applied, biointensive farming can build soil up to sixty times faster than nature. The additional organic matter in the soil increases its water retention potential and reduces the water consumption per unit of production to well below that of commercial agriculture. The yields can be two to six times higher

◂ Figure 1.12

Food Forest, Martin Crawford, Dartington Estate in South Devon, UK

than that of average conventional US agriculture. The increased yields make this soil-based operation more feasible on small urban sites.³⁶

Constructed Soil-Based Grounds

Container Gardens
The cultivation of crops in containers can help surmount the common urban dilemmas of sealed surfaces, contaminated soil, and infeasible remediation. This growing method is usually applied whenever the ground is incompatible for cultivation or when flexibility and mobility are desired. Containers used in urban agriculture range from bags used as soft planters to industrially fabricated or recycled crates to designed and custom-built containers. With these different options, it is relatively easy to set up rooftop gardens (Uncommon Ground, Chicago), farms on vacant sites (Prinzessinnengarten, Berlin, see Case Study 12), and art/architecture installations (PF1, New York by WORKac, see Architect's Profile 5). These strategies may bring vegetation to previously inhospitable sites, improving the microclimate and offering many environmental benefits.

With the restricted soil volume of the container, crops are vulnerable to temperature fluctuation, soil loss (especially in exposed growing situations), and soil drying, which leads to higher water needs and irrigation loads. These challenges increase with a decreasing container volume; self-watering containers, for

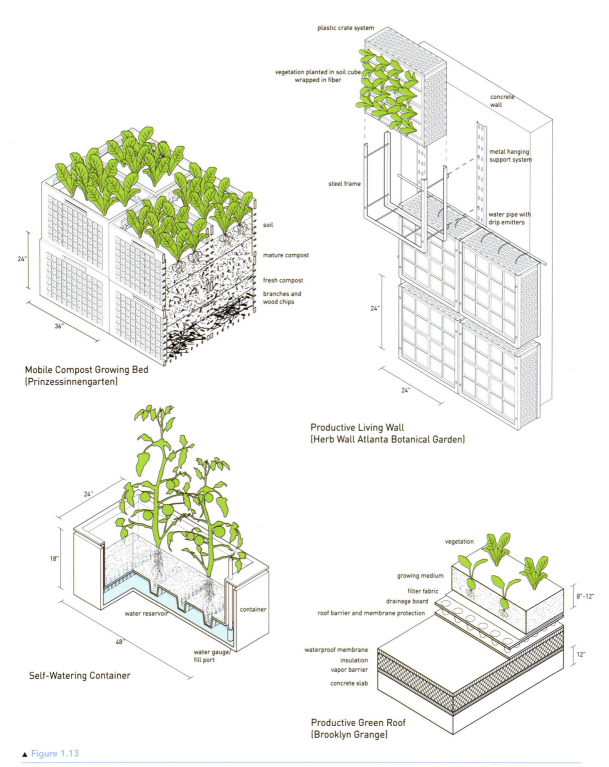

▲ Figure 1.13

Constructed soil-based growing systems

Nutrients: Growing Systems

example, by Earthbox, Growbox, and Biotop, counteract this problem. Raised beds are larger, more permanent, built-in-place or prefabricated containers. They offer a more continuous growing area with a larger soil volume that produces higher yields and mitigates temperature and humidity fluctuations.[37] The imported soil needs to be of high quality, such as a rich compost and soil mix, for intense cultivation. To maintain the nutrient supply, the containers have to be frequently fertilized with compost or additional organic matter. When installed on rooftops, weight restrictions and load capacities are similar to those for green roofs, though not all of the environmental and building performance improvements conferred by continuous green roofs can be realized.

Productive Green Roofs

Productive green roofs transform underused urban roofs into new vegetated areas. They especially benefit dense urban areas and warehouse districts that lack adequate space and infrastructure for ground-based urban agriculture and green spaces.[38] In addition to the benefits of food cultivation in the city, green roofs offer environmental benefits such as rainwater retention and detention as well as improvements in microclimates, urban habitats, and the performance of the host buildings.

Crops are grown in the substrate layer of the green roof, which covers the roof continuously. The substrate layer retains water and anchors the plants of the vegetation layer, while a drainage layer evacuates or stores excess water.[39] A waterproofing membrane and root barrier separate these water-carrying layers from the actual roof structure, which consists of an insulation layer and the roof slab or structural support.

Vertical Growing Structures

Space constraints have led to the exploration of vertical growth systems for urban agriculture, which make use of small spaces as long as they receive ample sunlight. There are currently two types of soil-based vertical systems: green façades and living (or green) walls. Green façades are made up of vines, climbers, or trained fruit trees rooted at the base of supporting trellis structures that are either anchored to a wall or freestanding. Plants suited for this growing technique include perennials, such as grapevines, that take three to five years to develop full coverage, and annuals, such as climbing beans. The soil volume and quality need to be sufficient to support the proportionally large plant volume.

Living walls, on the other hand, employ pre-vegetated wall panels, vertical modules, or planted blankets with irrigation and nutrient-delivery systems in addition to structural support. Living walls are intended for smaller plants that usually grow on horizontal surfaces. This growing system has not been extensively tested for edibles yet. Primary challenges associated with living walls include even water distribution and identifying crops suitable for vertical cultivation. Most of the realized productive living walls have been relatively small in scope and used to improve public spaces. Atlanta's Botanical Garden has built a vertical herb wall, which consists of 24-inch (60-cm) square metal frames hanging from tracks bolted to a masonry wall (see Figure 1.13). The frames hold rows of pre-planted panels with 16 herb plants apiece. Each row is irrigated from the top by a drip line.

CATALOG 2: HYDROPONIC GROWING SYSTEMS IN URBAN AGRICULTURE

Hydroponic or soil-less growing systems employ nutrients dissolved in water to cultivate plants without using soil as a nutrient source. The nutrient solution provides water, nutrients, and oxygen to the plants. Urban agriculture projects usually apply closed hydroponic systems that recirculate the nutrient solution. Only recirculating systems grant hydroponics the environmental benefits of resource efficiency, elimination of agricultural runoff, and potential integration with building systems. The recirculation process requires nutrient solution filtration, sterilization, aeration, and the restoration of the original volume, pH level, and nutrient content.[40]

The formula of the nutrient mix depends on the nutrient requirement of the crop, distribution method, and application frequency. Dissolving inorganic salts in water is the typical method used to create the nutrient solution. More recently, organic fertilizers generated from recycled organic matter have been available for hydroponic cultures. This important development may address the daunting sustainability issues affecting synthetic and mineral fertilizers. Crops grown hydroponically produce higher yields and growth rates than those associated with soil-grown plants.[41] The higher levels of control—both in terms of nutrient injection and controlled growing environment—are the main reason for the increased productivity. The delivery of nutrients and oxygen directly to the root ball accelerates the growth and allows additional growing cycles in one year. The greenhouse environment, furthermore, extends the growing season. In combination, these factors allow hydroponic systems to generate more than ten times higher yields than conventional, soil-based agriculture.[42]

The method used for distributing the nutrient solution distinguishes hydroponic systems from one another. The most commonly used systems fall into two large categories: (1) aggregate cultures, which use inert rooting materials; and (2) truly hydroponic water cultures (Figure 1.14). Most urban farms install hydroponic systems in greenhouses or other controlled environments to achieve year-round production, but versions of these systems could also operate outside.

Aggregate Cultures

The Flood-and-Drain System
The flood-and-drain system, also known as the ebb-and-flow system, is primarily used commercially for deep-rooted vegetables, such as tomatoes, that are grown in aggregate-filled containers placed in large-scale beds covering the entire greenhouse floor. The substantial weight of the watering beds and their potential for leakage pose challenges for building and rooftop integration. Because of this, urban agriculture projects usually use a secondary application of the flood-and-drain system, which consists of small-scale bench systems for raising seedling transplants.[43]

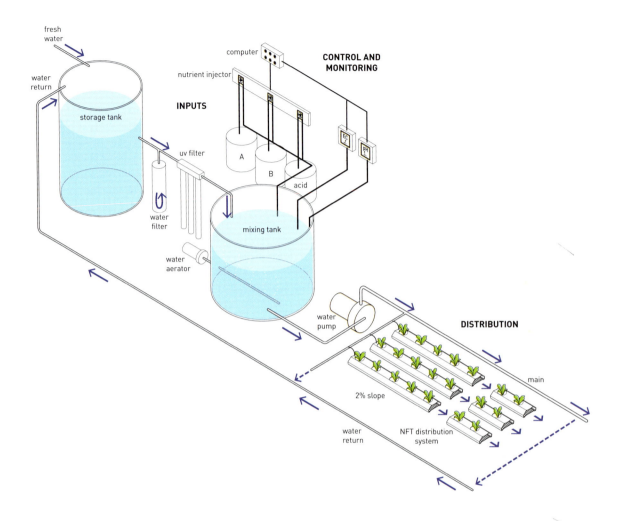

▲ Figure 1.14

Prototypical hydroponic growing system shown with nutrient film technique (NFT) distribution system

Data adapted from Howard M. Resh, *Hydroponic Food Production: A Definitive Guidebook for the Advanced Home Gardener and the Commercial Hydroponic Grower* (Boca Raton, FL: Newconcept Press, 2013).

The flood-and-drain system is a sub-irrigation method. This method involves the cultivation of plants in an inert rooting medium set in a water-tight rooting bed. The bed is periodically flooded with nutrient solution by a mechanical pump, ensuring absorption by the growing medium and plant roots. The bed is then drained via gravity to a nutrient tank, where the solution is replenished, while the roots receive access to oxygen. The cycle period of the flood-and-drain system depends on the crop, atmospheric conditions, and the growth medium absorption rate.

The Drip System
Drip-irrigation hydroponic systems, or Dutch bucket systems, are the preferred method for growing vine crops, such as tomatoes, cucumbers, peppers, and other plants with deeper root structures.[44] For these crops, a high-wire production system is usually integrated to train the plant into a single stem. Due to their relatively light weight, flexibility, and low infrastructure needs, drip systems are

Flood-and-Drain System (also Ebb-and-Flow System)

Drip Hydroponic System (also Dutch Bucket System), Lufa Farms, Montréal

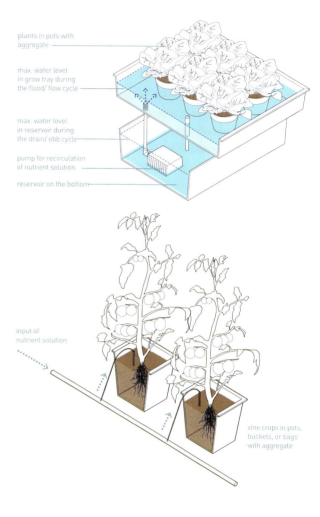

▲ Figure 1.15

Hydroponic aggregate cultures—flood-and-drain system and drip system

also suitable for rooftop applications as demonstrated by Lufa Farms (see Case Study 10) (Figure 1.15).

In the drip system, plants sit in growth-medium-filled slabs or containers, and nutrient solution drips onto the plant's root ball. Irrigation lines carry nutrient solution to each row of containers and feed each plant with an individual emitter. The drip rate is determined by crop type, atmospheric conditions, and growth stage. Most drip systems assume no overflow; the plant is intended to absorb nearly all the solution. Advantages to this system include well-aerated roots, as the solution is constantly mixing with air, and high yields owing to the high level of control. Water efficiency is also fairly high if measures are taken to prevent evaporation. The greatest disadvantage of the drip system is its lack of robustness and redundancy due to its dependence on the pump. Plants will very quickly die in the case of pump failure. Pumps may fail if the lines—which easily clog with minerals—are not cleaned regularly.

Water Cultures

Raft Culture

The most direct water culture in hydroponics is the raft culture, or deep-water technique. This growing technique involves the submersion of plant roots in a relatively deep bed of nutrient solution. The raft culture technique efficiently uses floor space in greenhouses, using around 85% of the floor area for growing beds, but it requires an extensive horizontal plane.[45] The weight of the water-filled pools makes it less applicable for building integration and rooftop farming. It can, however, be an extremely efficient technique for ground-level or basement urban farming sites. For example, The Plant in Chicago effectively integrates this system on the basement level, avoiding load problems (see Case Study 9).

The raft culture method is used commercially for lettuce and herb production by floating the plants on perforated Styrofoam rafts. For lettuce production, the nutrient solution beds are usually 8 inches (20 cm) deep, relatively narrow, and often span the entire length of a greenhouse. In commercial systems, two-week-old seedlings are transplanted into rafts on one side of the growing bed. Adding seedlings every day guarantees continuous production, while the rafts are slowly pushed to the other side of the pool, where they are harvested after a growing period of about 30 days. The nutrient solution constantly recirculates to a tank where it is sterilized, aerated, and replenished before being pumped back to the other end of the bed.[46]

Nutrient Film Technique

The nutrient film technique (NFT), introduced in the 1970s and publicized as the growing method of the future, has become one of the most productive and frequently employed hydroponic growing methods for leafy greens worldwide. NFT setup and construction costs are relatively low. Its lightweight infrastructure makes the system very flexible, space-efficient, and ideal for building integration and rooftop installation. Used by commercial hydroponic rooftop farms such as Lufa Farms, Gotham Greens, and BrightFarms, it is their preferred growing system for lettuces and leafy greens (see Case Studies 10 and 11).

The process suspends plant roots in a long narrow trough through which the nutrient solution trickles. This technique constantly recirculates the nutrient solution, sterilizing, aerating, replenishing, and pumping it back to the high points of the troughs. The recirculating stream is shallow, providing water, nutrients, and oxygen to the plants. Despite its advantages, NFT comes with limitations. Plants at the top of the tray tend to extract inputs from the solution, depleting the concentration by the time it gets to the bottom of the tray. Growing root masses sometimes divert the water, further depriving plants lower in the trough of resources. Though NFT is the highest-yielding hydroponic growing method, it requires close monitoring and careful calibration, making it labor-intensive.[47]

Aeroponics

Arguably the most novel of the hydroponic growing systems, aeroponics systems spray plant roots with a mist of nutrient solution. Plant roots are suspended in an enclosed rooting chamber consisting of a box, an A-frame, a teepee, or a

Raft Culture, Educational Hydroponic Farm, Windy City Harvest, Chicago

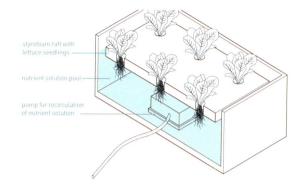

Nutrient Film Technique (NFT), Lufa Farms, Montréal

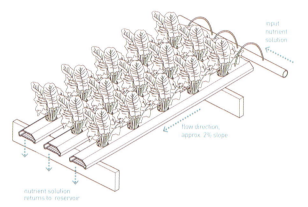

Aeroponics with Open Rooting Chamber Consisting of a Box

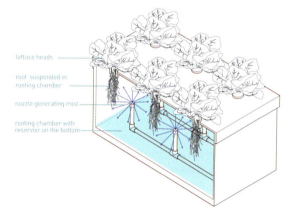

▲ Figure 1.16

Hydroponic water cultures—raft culture, Nutrient Film Technique (NFT), and aeroponics

lean-to structure. Vertical systems are often leveraged to create the enclosure for the misting chambers. While the aeroponics technique is rarely applied on a large commercial scale, this system offers many opportunities for building integration (Figure 1.16).

    This technique works for the cultivation of small plants, such as lettuce and herbs, particularly herbs and medical plants whose roots will be harvested

Nutrients: Growing Systems   35

for consumption or for use in drugs or vitamins. Tower Garden is a popular system applied by many small urban farms or kitchen gardens; these 5–7-ft-high (1.50–2.00 m) vertical tubes feature slots for growing spaces and a water reservoir as a base.

High pressure misting generates finer nutrient solution droplets with greater potential for root adherence. Uninterrupted exposure of the roots to a fine mist has been proven to yield improved results when compared with recurrent spraying or misting. In contrast to other hydroponic techniques, aeration is integral to this system, given that the plant roots are effectively cultivated in air. This method also requires a refined infrastructure. Nutrient solution filtration is essential to prevent clogged nozzles, and adequate dispersal of the nutrient solution through small nozzle openings requires high-pressure pumps.[48]

Vertical Hydroponic Growing Structures
The lightweight nature of the NFT system easily allows the vertical arrangement of growing troughs to maximize the growing area. Advances in vertical systems also specifically target building integration. One of the simplest vertical versions of the NFT system, the "cascade" system, uses standard troughs arranged in a stepping zigzag pattern.[49] The Vertically Integrated Greenhouse (VIG) by Kiss + Cathcart, New York Sun Works, and Arup develops this system into a vertical façade application (see Architect's Profile 2 in Chapter 6).

Water distribution in vertical hydroponic systems proves less challenging than in vertical soil-based systems. Gravity provides a relatively constant flow of the nutrient solution through vertically connected trays, resulting in consistent water availability for the individual plants. In general, vertical hydroponic systems use a similar amount of water as horizontal hydroponic systems when measured by the number of plants. The planting density and the efficient use of vertical space, however, lead to higher overall water needs per area footprint.

The Aquaponic System
A hybrid of aquaculture and hydroponics, aquaponics generate self-fertilizing, recirculating ecosystems that concurrently produce both fish and plants in a symbiotic environment.[50] In simple terms, an aquaponic system is a hydroponic system consisting of three living components that create a closed-loop system—fish, plants, and microbial communities. The microbes transform toxic waste from the fish excrement into plant fertilizer, fortifying the nutrient solution. Beneficiary plants extract the nutrients and clean the water to sustain the fish population (Figure 1.17). Fish feed is thus the primary input into this system. For the well-being of the fish, the water temperature and oxygen level must be monitored. For successful plant cultivation, the nutrient mix and concentration in the water should be monitored and missing nutrient components added. Each of these three critical components needs to be kept in balance as the crops and fish population grow.[51]

As an organic, natural ecosystem, aquaponic systems will ideally move towards a position of equilibrium between the amount of nutrients the plants

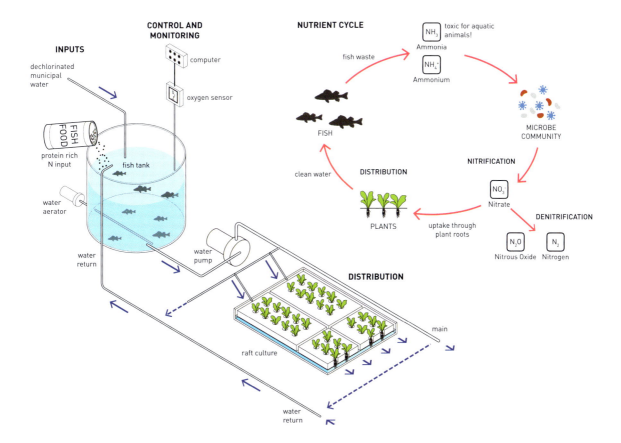

▲ Figure 1.17

Prototypical aquaponic growing system shown with raft culture distribution system

Data adapted from Sylvia Bernstein, *Aquaponic Gardening: A Step-by-Step Guide to Raising Vegetables and Fish Together* (Gabriola, BC: New Society, 2011).

need and the excrement the fish produce. To achieve this balance, a careful study of optimal tank size, fish species, number of fish versus the growing area, crop species, and number of plants has to be conducted. Once properly established, an aquaponic system produces higher yields than a traditional hydroponic system while using a sustainable nutrient source for the crops.[52] Several urban agriculture projects demonstrate the use of aquaponic systems, such as the Aquaponic Solar Greenhouse, Growing Power, and The Plant (see Case Studies 1, 7, and 9).

Mulberry Dike-Pond System
Aquaponic cultures have a long tradition in China's Zhujiang Delta. Motivated by the need to support a large population and protect against flooding, farmers have been perfecting a method of integrated agriculture aquaculture for over one thousand years (Figure 1.18).[53] The dike-pond system combines fish farming with crop cultivation in a large, closed-loop system of materials and energy that involves smaller-scale, layered subsystems. Shallow ponds are deepened, providing a habitat for fish cultivation while the excavated soil serves as dikes for crop production above the flood level.[54]

The excrement of pigs, humans, and silkworms serves as the primary fertilizer for this system of ponds. Within each pond, different species of fish with distinct feeding and habitat requirements are raised. While a portion of fish

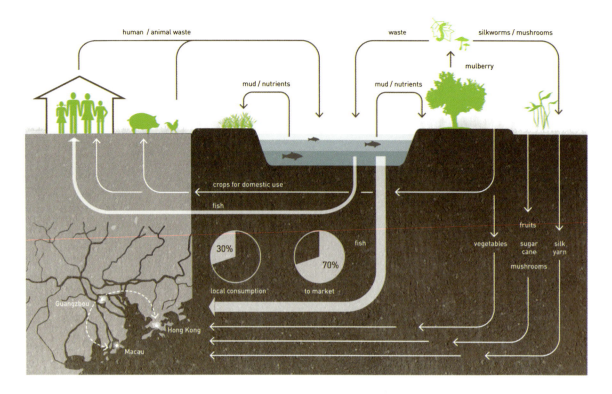

▲ Figure 1.18

Mulberry dike-pond system of the Zhujiang Delta, China

yields are consumed locally, most enter the market, providing the largest source of income for the region's agricultural sector. On the dikes surrounding each pond, a range of linked subsystems functions in a program of year-round planting and harvesting. Mulberries, sugar cane, and fruit—the chief commercial crops—are interplanted with a wide range of crops produced for domestic use, livestock fodder, and fish feed. The organically enriched mud, dredged from the pond two or three times each year, is used to fertilize and stabilize the upper surface of the dike. Silkworms reared in nearby sheds are sent to a filature for the production of yarn, yielding wastewater, cocoon waste, and dead larvae, which are returned to enrich the pond and feed the fish. Pond mud is also used to make mud-beds for mushroom cultivation on the floor of the silkworm sheds in winter, when silkworms cannot be raised.

NOTES

1. Hannah Hislop, ed., *The Nutrient Cycle: Closing the Loop* (London: Green Alliance, 2007), 3.
2. Ibid., 3.
3. Ibid., 3.
4. Steve Savage, "Moving Towards Fossil-Energy-Independent Nitrogen Fertilizer," *Science* 2.0 (April 2, 2013), www.science20.com/agricultural_realism/moving_towards_fossilenergyindependent_nitrogen_fertilizer-108036.

5. Vaclav Smil, "Phosphorus in the Environment: Natural Flows and Human Interferences," *Annual Review of Energy and the Environment* 25 (2000): 53–88.
6. Hislop, *The Nutrient Cycle*, 4.
7. Ingrid Steen, "Phosphorus Availability in the 21st Century: Management of a Nonrenewable Resource," *Phosphorus and Potassium* 217 (1998): 25–31.
8. D. Cordell, J.O. Drangert, and S. White, "The Story of Phosphorus: Global Food Security and Food for Thought," *Global Environmental Change* 19.2 (2009): 292–305.
9. Paul A. de Graaf, "Room for Urban Agriculture in Rotterdam: Defining the Spatial Opportunities for Urban Agriculture within the Industrialized City," in *Sustainable Food Planning: Evolving Theory and Practice*, ed. André Viljoen and Johannes S.C. Wiskerke (Wageningen: Wageningen Academic Publishers, 2012), 533–545.
10. Kubi Ackerman, "Urban Agriculture: Opportunities and Constraints," in *Metropolitan Sustainability: Understanding and Improving the Urban Environment*, ed. Frank Zeman (Sawston, Cambridge, UK: Woodhead Publishing, 2012), 127.
11. Ibid., 128.
12. Sam E. Wortman and Sarah Taylor Lovell, "Environmental Challenges Threatening the Growth of Urban Agriculture in the United States," *Journal of Environmental Quality* 42.5 (2013): 1291.
13. Ackerman, "Urban Agriculture," 127.
14. Hislop, *The Nutrient Cycle*, 31–34.
15. EPA, "Composting," www.epa.gov/climatechange/wycd/waste/downloads/composting-chapter10-28-10.pdf.
16. Wortman and Lovell, "Environmental Challenges Threatening the Growth of Urban Agriculture in the United States," 1286.
17. EPA, "Types of Composting," available at: www.epa.gov/compost/types.htm.
18. European Commission Environment, "Biodegradable Waste," http://ec.europa.eu/environment/waste/compost/.
19. Matt Smith and John Aber, "Heat Recovery from Compost," *BioCycle. The Organics Recycling Authority* (February 2014), www.biocycle.net/2014/02/21/heat-recovery-from-compost/.
20. Nickolas J. Themelis, "Control of Heat Generation during Composting," *BioCycle: The Organics Recycling Authority* (January 2005), www.biocycle.net/2005/01/21/control-of-heat-generation-during-composting/.
21. R-Urban, "Un chauffage alternative," http://r-urban.net/wp-content/uploads/2012/03/RURBAN_Chauffage-compost.pdf.
22. EPA, "Biosolid Technology Fact Sheet: Multi-stage Anaerobic Digestion," http://water.epa.gov/scitech/wastetech/upload/2006_10_16_mtb_multi-stage.pdf.
23. Agri-Facts, "Economic Feasibility of Anaerobic Digesters," *Alberta Agriculture and Rural Development*, www1.agric.gov.ab.ca/$department/deptdocs.nsf/all/agdex12280/$file/768-6.pdf?OpenElement.
24. Loop, "What Is Loop?" King County Wastewater Treatment Division, www.loopforyoursoil.com/what-is-loop/.
25. Eliza Barclay, "Whole Foods Bans Produce Grown with Sludge. But Who Wins?," Food for Thought, NPR, www.npr.org/blogs/thesalt/2014/01/17/263370333/whole-foods-bans-produce-grown-with-sludge-but-who-wins.

26. EPA, "Biosolids Technology Fact Sheet: Use of Incineration for Biosolids Management," http://water.epa.gov/scitech/wastetech/upload/2005_07_28_mtb_incineration_biosolids.pdf.
27. Hislop, *The Nutrient Cycle*, 20.
28. J.O. Drangert, "Fighting the Urine Blindness to Provide More Sanitation Options," *Water SA* 24.2 (1998): 158.
29. Ibid., 163.
30. Nancy Jack Todd and John Todd, *From Eco-cities to Living Machines: Principles of Ecological Design* (Berkeley, CA: North Atlantic Books, 1994).
31. City of Chicago, "Composting Ordinance," www.cityofchicago.org/city/en/depts/streets/supp_info/composting/composting_ordinance.html

Catalog 1

32. Howard M. Resh, *Hydroponic Food Production: A Definitive Guidebook for the Advanced Home Gardener and the Commercial Hydroponic Grower* (Boca Raton, FL: CRC Press, 2013), 15.
33. T. Hemenway, *Gaia's Garden: A Guide to Home-scale Permaculture* (White River Junction, VT: Chelsea Green Publishing, 2009).
34. Ross Mars, *The Basics of Permaculture Design* (White River Junction, VT: Chelsea Green Publishing, 2005), 1–3.
35. De Graaf, "Room for Urban Agriculture in Rotterdam," 540.
36. John Jeavons, "A Perspective for the Future," *How to Grow More Vegetables: (and Fruits, Nuts, Berries, Grains, and Other Crops) than You Ever Thought Possible on Less Land than You Can Imagine* (Berkeley, CA: Ten Speed, 2002), 2.
37. Lauren Mandel, *Eat Up: The Inside Scoop on Rooftop Agriculture* (Gabriola, BC: New Society Publishers, 2013), 26.
38. Gundula Proksch, "Urban Rooftops as Productive Resources: Rooftop Farming versus Conventional Green Roofs," in *Considering Research: Proceedings of the Architectural Research Center Consortium Spring Research Conference, Detroit, MI, April 2011* (Southfield, MI: Lawrence Tech University, 2011), 497–509.
39. J. Mentens, D. Raes, and M. Hermy, "Green Roofs as a Tool for Solving the Rainwater Runoff Problem in the Urbanized 21st Century?," *Landscape and Urban Planning* 77.3 (2006): 217–226.

Catalog 2

40. Resh, *Hydroponic Food Production*, 254.
41. S. Bernstein, *Aquaponic Gardening: A Step-by-Step Guide to Raising Vegetables and Fish Together* (Gabriola, BC: New Society, 2011), 3.
42. Resh, *Hydroponic Food Production*, 89.
43. Ibid., 155.
44. Ibid., 245.
45. Ibid., 106.
46. Ibid., 98.
47. J.B. Jones Jr., *Hydroponics: A Practical Guide for the Soilless Grower* (Boca Raton, FL: St. Lucie, 1997), 127–141.
48. Ibid., 142–143.

49. Resh, *Hydroponic Food Production*, 148.
50. Bernstein, *Aquaponic Gardening*, 1–6.
51. Growing Power Workshop on Aquaponic Fish Farming, June 2012.
52. Bernstein, *Aquaponic Gardening*, 4–5.
53. Kenneth Ruddle and Gongfu Zhong, *Integrated Agriculture-Aquaculture in South China: The Dike-Pond System of the Zhujiang Delta* (New York: Cambridge University Press, 1988).
54. C.J. Lim and Ed Liu, *Smartcities + Eco-warriors* (London: Routledge, 2010).

Chapter 2

Water
Connecting the Cycle

ABSTRACT

Availability of fresh water will be the most critical environmental challenge facing the planet in future years. With its wasteful consumption of 70% of all accessible supplies, industrial agriculture is the single largest user of water in the world. Cities, meanwhile, struggle to secure water resources and fail to take advantage of on-site sources such as rainfall, which instead may damage the environment through urban stormwater runoff. As this chapter illustrates, urban agriculture is well poised to mitigate these water challenges by embracing water-efficient strategies integrated with existing urban infrastructure, building systems, and management approaches. These best practices—described in Catalog 3—take full advantage of urban resources, which are currently underutilized and discharged into the wastewater treatment stream.

WATER CHALLENGES

Water has long been seen as an inexhaustible resource. In reality, clean, safe, available fresh water is a limited resource that totals a mere 0.008% of all water on earth.[1] While the consumption rates of non-renewable resources such as petroleum, coal, natural gas, and minerals are carefully monitored, fresh water reserves are not, even though they are increasingly threatened by pollution, climate change, and excessive, highly unsustainable water-use patterns. The rapid pace of human development in recent decades has dramatically disrupted the very water cycle that is needed to support growing populations, urbanization, and intensive agriculture. Problems arise when fresh water is used beyond the rate at which it can be naturally replenished by the hydrologic cycle.[2] Water management demands in cities receive more scrutiny even though industrial agriculture is the largest contributor to increased global water consumption. Especially in regions of extreme water scarcity, cities and industrial agriculture compete for the same limited resource.

By readily adapting to local climate conditions, urban agriculture embraces emerging water management strategies that are a valuable component of green infrastructure. The term "green infrastructure" describes the strategic use of natural processes to improve urban environmental conditions through actions such as habitat enhancement, improvement of air and water quality, and stormwater management. The positive effects of urban agriculture projects on the

◀ Figure 2.1

Fresh water, a vital resource for plant cultivation.

hydrologic cycle are two-fold: (1) they demonstrate water-efficient agricultural methods, which can be adopted by industrial agriculture; and (2) they support low-impact urban water management through numerous synergies between water systems and the built environment.

Urban Water Challenges

Urban areas, with their high concentration of inhabitants and industrial processes, place a severe strain on existing water resources. Municipal authorities are responsible for providing urban residents with an adequate water supply and acceptable water quality.[3] To support their water needs, most cities import water by either pumping it from underground sources (aquifers and wells) or transporting it a long distance from surface sources (reservoirs, lakes, or rivers). During transport and handling, dilapidated infrastructure causes a loss of up to 50% of potable water. These losses occur not only in newly industrialized countries but also in the metropolitan areas of the Western world.[4] Additional threats to water resources and water security of cities include pollution as well as the over-pumping of groundwater and aquifers. Most groundwater near major cities, industrial developments, or leaking landfills already contains contaminants.[5]

Buildings and transportation infrastructure are composed of sealed surfaces that prohibit water infiltration and evaporation and thus increase runoff volumes.[6] Runoff captures and transports pollutants to receiving water bodies such as rivers, lakes, and oceans. In cities with combined sewer systems, overflow events add sewage to this harmful discharge. To combat this disruption of the hydrologic cycle, most cities have developed complex urban water management systems involving hard infrastructure for urban drainage, flood control, and wastewater treatment. This infrastructure requires expensive maintenance and is increasingly undersized for more severe storm events. Its treatment processes are also often energy- and cost-intensive. Only recently have communities started to move toward more sustainable, low-impact water management by implementing green infrastructure.

Water Use in Industrial Agriculture

Global water consumption has grown exponentially since the 1950s (Figure 2.2). Industrial agriculture accounts for 70% of water use worldwide and is the largest contributor to global water consumption today. Overall, 40% of all food is produced using irrigation, and almost 20% of all arable land is irrigated. While there are large regions that require almost no irrigation, other regions irrigate more than 75% of agricultural land.[7] Intensive irrigation in arid regions is one of the most destructive aspects of industrial agriculture.[8] Up to 60% of all irrigation water could be reduced with the use of up-to-date, appropriate, and properly managed equipment.[9]

Even more problematic is the fact that 15–35% of irrigation withdrawals are unsustainable and cannot continue without causing irreversible damage.[10]

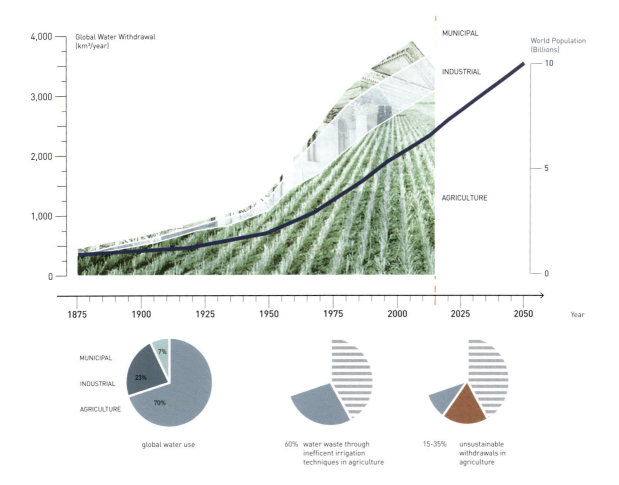

▲ Figure 2.2

Timeline of global water use and population growth

Data adapted from Igor A. Shiklomanov, "Appraisal and Assessment of World Water Resources." *Water International* 25, no. 1 (2000): 11-32; US Census Bureau, International Data Base, July 2015 Update.

Groundwater over-pumping and aquifer depletion are now occurring in many of the world's most important crop-producing regions. In the western United States, water tables are dropping 3 feet a year, signaling that groundwater use has exceeded its limit. A large portion of the world's food supply is now produced through unsustainable water use. One estimate suggests that up to 10% of the world's grain is being produced by water that will not be renewed.[11]

Recognizing the True Cost of Water

Many of the fastest-growing cities in the United States, including Austin, Houston, San Antonio, Phoenix, Salt Lake City, and San Diego, are located in arid regions. These cities must compete with surrounding farms for the same limited water supply, further amplifying pressures on the resource.[12] Arid states are only able to support the water needs of both their cities and intensive agricultural operations through enormous infrastructure projects to transport water over long distances and with unrealistically low or subsidized water prices. The substantial energy and environmental costs of supplying these cities with fresh water demand a rigorous reexamination of water conservation efforts.[13]

The situation in industrial agriculture is even worse. Farmers in California, for instance, pay about 1.4% of what the state's urban residents pay for water.[14] Large subsidies for agricultural water keep water prices artificially low, generate little incentive to use water efficiently, and continue to discourage investments in more efficient irrigation methods.[15] This subsidization conveys the false message that water is abundant and can be wasted, even as rivers dry up and aquifers are depleted. Water pricing reflecting the resource's true cost would create incentives to promote both water efficiency and reuse. It would encourage growers and manufacturers to implement water conservation measures and to allocate water more productively.[16] Water efficiency, not water's extensive overuse, needs to be subsidized.

Most urban agricultural projects do not benefit from these agricultural subsidies. Urban agriculture projects should therefore be a model illustrating how crop cultivation and food prices are affected by realistically priced water. Based on their production ethics and economic constraints, urban farms develop far more water-efficient growing methods. Their enormous popularity shows that many consumers are willing to pay the true water costs of their food.

Water Footprint

Besides water subsidization, the amount of water needed to produce different crops and food products is a challenging aspect of the current food system. The virtual water footprint of a food product is defined as the volume of fresh water used in the food production process and thereby "invisibly" contained in the product. In developed countries, food production accounts for 925 gallons (3,500 liters) of water per person per day. That represents 92% of the average daily water per capita consumption. In contrast, water used for the production of industrial products accounts for 4.5% and domestic uses for only 3.5%.[17]

Different food products have different water footprints, so consumers' daily food choices affect global water consumption (Figure 2.3). The production of meat and dairy products, for example, consumes the largest amount of water, accounting for 27% of humans' water footprints. In industrialized countries, carnivores consume 36% more water than vegetarians, or 345 gallons (1300 liters) of additional virtual water per person per day.[18] Food products imported from water-scarce regions are also a challenge. Higher product transparency would allow consumers to make choices about which products they buy, based on the water footprint, production method, and water availability at the location of origin. Urban agriculture offers this transparency while providing local, more sustainable food alternatives. Through the development of water-efficient growing methods, it also reduces the amount of water needed to cultivate the same produce in comparison to industrial agriculture.

▶ Figure 2.3

Water footprint of food products, Iimm Kekeritz (original size 33 x 47 inches/0.85 x 1.20m).

WATER FOOTPRINT
virtual water embedded in products

2500 Coconut

50 Orange

70 Apple

560 Mango

100 Banana

650 Barley

650 Wheat

2500 Millet

1700 Rice

450 Corn

2500 Cheese

2400 Chocolate

750 Cane Sugar

650 Toast

125 Potato

1000 Milk

90 Tea

840 Coffee

150 Beer

720 Wine

4650 Beef

1830 Sheep Meat

1440 Pork

1200 Goat Meat

1170 Chicken

2500 Burger

4250 Leather

2700 Cotton

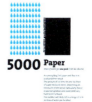
5000 Paper

200 Egg

WATER NEEDS OF PLANTS

Integrating agriculture into cities and building systems requires an understanding of the threats that urban water management, industrial agriculture, and unsustainable developments impose on the global water cycle. Understanding the specific water needs of plants is equally important. Familiarity with the basics of plant physiology allows designers to not only estimate the water needs of urban agricultural operations, but also to successfully integrate plants and living systems into buildings.

Plant Physiology

Water is the primary resource required by plants. Not only does it typically constitute up to 95% of the mass of growing plant tissues, it is also the principal factor affecting plant growth. With no other limiting factors, plant growth and total crop production are proportional to the amount of water a plant transpires.[19] Water is fundamental to all physiological processes; however, a plant uses only 5% of the water taken up by its roots to maintain primary metabolic functions, including photosynthesis and respiration. The remaining 95% of water intake is transpired directly into the atmosphere. Transpiration refers to the water lost to the atmosphere in the form of vapor, emitted through small pores (stomata) on the surface of a plant's leaves. This process creates a cooling effect so that plants avoid heat stress. Continual water movement—from root to stomata—is fueled by the upward driving force of evaporation, cohesion of the water molecules, and the capillary dimensions of a plant's vascular tissue.[20] Transpiration rates are dependent on the availability of water and sufficient energy from solar radiation to vaporize that water. Accordingly, sunny weather increases the transpiration rate and the amount of water a plant needs.

Evapotranspiration

"Crop water requirement," or evapotranspiration, is a value that helps quantify how much water plants need. Because the processes of evaporation and plant transpiration take place concurrently, evapotranspiration, or "ET," refers to the sum of the two processes. The quantity of water required to offset evapotranspiration loss (plus 5% for metabolic functions) is defined as the "crop water requirement." The crop water requirement can be based on a daily, weekly, or growing-season timetable. It is determined by crop type and can be influenced by numerous variables, including soil water availability, precipitation, stage of growth, root depth, amount of solar radiation, humidity, temperature, and wind.

The net irrigation water requirement represents the amount of irrigation water needed to fulfill crop water needs not provided by soil water or precipitation. The frequency and timing of irrigation, as well as its timely application during dry and hot periods, are as important as the total amount of water

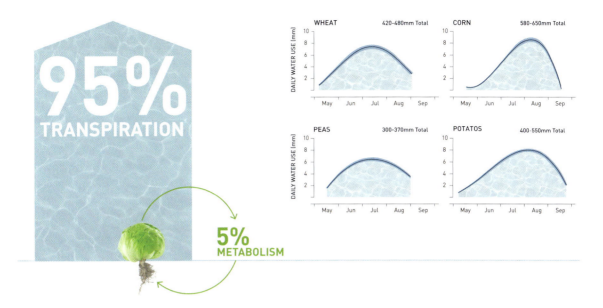

▲ Figure 2.4

Water needs of plants and crop water requirements

Data adapted from Ross H. McKenzie and Shelley A. Woods, "Crop Water Use and Requirements," *Agri-Facts, Alberta Agriculture and Rural Development*, November 2011, 1-4.

provided. A prolonged water deficit or water stress, especially at critical growth phases such as germination, flowering, or fruit expansion, will detrimentally affect a crop.

Most vegetables require between 0.75 and 1.5 inches (2–4 cm) of water per week during the growing season. Cauliflower, for example, only develops flowers (the desirable portion of the plant) in the presence of adequate moisture. Beans and peas require moisture, especially during flowering, to develop filled pods and large fruits. Plants require a specific amount of water to flower and produce. This is especially important for the cultivation of vegetables and edible crops (Figure 2.4).

URBAN GROWING CONDITIONS

Plants growing in urban conditions are exposed to unique water demands not encountered by those growing in rural areas. These factors include elevated temperatures caused by the urban heat island effect, increased sun and wind exposures of rooftop growing locations, limited soil volume, and higher soil temperatures in container-growing conditions. Evapotranspiration rates and resulting crop water requirements are unquestionably higher in urban climates, though the causes and consequences of the increase are varied and complex.[21] The results of a study investigating temperature effects on evapotranspiration and irrigated agriculture indicate that a 5.4°F (3°C) increase in temperature prompts a 14% increase in potential evapotranspiration, or PET, rates.[22] Despite producing increased water needs, elevated temperatures from urban heat islands also yield positive outcomes, such as a lengthened growing season, resulting in higher growth rates and productivity in the presence of no other limiting factors. Conversely, the microclimate surrounding an urban growing area will benefit from the cooling effect of evapotranspiration, which mitigates the heat island effect and reduces the cooling load and energy required for air-conditioning in adjacent buildings.

URBAN AGRICULTURE'S POSITIVE IMPACT ON WATER CHALLENGES

Urban agriculture has a positive effect on both halves of the urban water cycle: the supply of fresh water and the disposal of stormwater and wastewater. On the supply side, urban agriculture employs powerful strategies to increase the water efficiency of food production and resource conservation through intensive growing methods, selection of crops based on their low water requirements, targeted irrigation systems, and the use of alternative water sources. This is especially important because the integration of agricultural operations in cities will otherwise increase the urban demand for fresh water.[23] To avoid straining municipal water supplies, urban agricultural operations must minimize their water needs and, if possible, should become water self-sufficient by harvesting alternative water sources such as collected rainwater, greywater, building wastewater, and reclaimed water (see Catalog 3).

On the water management side, this potential use of alternative water sources creates symbiotic relationships between urban agriculture and urban water infrastructures. It reduces the volume of rainwater, greywater, and building wastewater that enters the wastewater stream. This is a relatively clean water resource, and consequently it reduces the required capacity of wastewater treatment plants. The use of reclaimed water better utilizes the resources involved in cost-intensive conventional treatment processes. In addition, urban agriculture works as green stormwater infrastructure (GSI), reducing stormwater management problems. Generally, GSI is defined as a set of best management practices for reducing stormwater runoff by simulating the natural ecosystem processes of retention, evapotranspiration, and infiltration. Urban agriculture provides these benefits through rainwater harvesting and increased plant cultivation in otherwise barren locations. GSI recharges the groundwater table, increases soil water availability, and improves the microclimate of the site. Additional vegetation increases evapotranspiration rates, which in turn lowers the ambient temperature and reduces the heat island effect. Stormwater treatment at its source reduces the energy expended on water treatment and reduces harmful combined sewer overflow (CSO) events in cities with aging combined sewer systems.[24] In addition, stormwater detention prevents pollutants from being washed directly into urban water bodies.

These advances of efficient water consumption, use of alternative water sources, and increased synergies with low-impact stormwater management

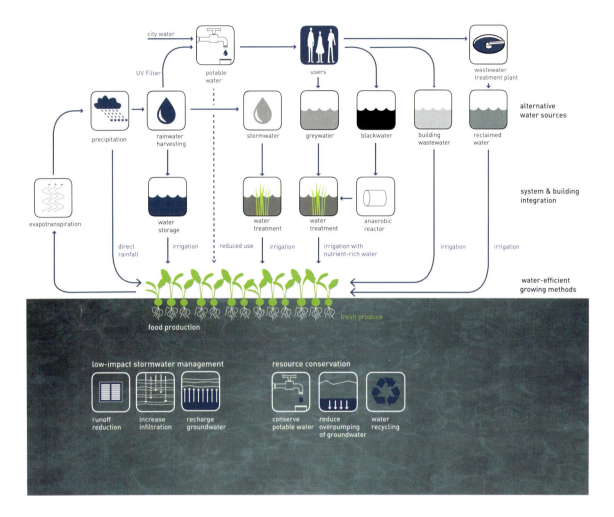

▲ Figure 2.5

Symbiosis between urban agriculture and the urban water cycle

foster the development of closed-loop water systems and their integration with buildings and infrastructures, greatly improving the overall urban water cycle (Figure 2.5).

WATER EFFICENCY AND RESOURCE CONSERVATION

The starting point for more effective water use is local adaptation. Outdoor and soil-based growing situations require adaptation to climatic and environmental factors, including temperature, solar exposure, humidity, wind speed, natural water availability, and soil conditions. In outdoor growing situations, ambient conditions must determine appropriate growing systems, irrigation systems, and crop species. In regions where water is a scarce commodity, selecting crop species based on their water efficiency becomes imperative in terms of environmental and economic sustainability. A comparison of a crop's water needs with a location's total water availability throughout the growing season and its average monthly precipitation allows an agricultural operation to take advantage of direct rainfall, reducing the need for irrigation and the chance of crop failure. The cultivation of crop varieties with abbreviated growing seasons (and thus reduced water intake from germination to harvest) can also help reduce overall water use.[25]

In the case of urban agriculture, additional urban-specific site conditions must be considered for the success of any farming operation. These constructed conditions present many opportunities, including the potential for rainwater harvesting on-site, utilization of alternative water resources, and integration with existing building systems and infrastructure, as discussed at the end of this chapter.

Irrigation Strategies

The intensive growing methods used in urban agriculture are inherently water-efficient. In addition, selecting an appropriately designed, accurately installed, and properly managed irrigation or watering system will achieve the largest reduction of water use. Its selection must be specific to the crop, climate, site, and soil conditions to optimize the amount and timing of moisture in the root zone, which will allow the crop to use the water productively.[26] Therefore, localized irrigation systems, such as drip irrigation, micro-irrigation, sub-irrigation, and manual irrigation deliver water directly as a small discharge to the root zone of each plant. These systems are well suited to urban agricultural situations, as they are water-efficient, require relatively minimal infrastructure, and are applicable to small-scale operations.

Complete coverage systems, such as sprinkler and basin surface irrigation, are inefficient in terms of water use and are associated with industrial agricultural practices. As a reference, conventional sprinkler irrigation systems may distribute 60–180 GPH (gallons per hour, 240–720 liters per hour), while the most efficient drip irrigation systems operate at low flow rates of 0.5–4 GPH (2–16 liters per hour). Due to the inefficiency of complete coverage systems and better applicability to large-scale operations, these systems are not typically used in urban agricultural situations (Figure 2.6).

Most importantly, irrigation systems can only reduce water consumption when they deliver the right amount for the proper length of time, at the correct time of day, and at the right frequency. The efficiency of a system thus depends more on proper management than on equipment. Moreover, the scheduling and quantity of water distribution require constant—ideally daily—monitoring and adjustment. These decisions have typically been the responsibility of the farmer. Recently, however, weather-based irrigation controllers, which manage irrigation based on real-time weather data, have started to supplement human expertise. If properly programmed, these controllers save 20–40% more irrigation water than conventional controllers.[27]

Hydroponic systems combine irrigation and nutrient supply by growing plants in nutrient solution. Hydroponic systems are popular for their high water efficiency, primarily achieved through recirculation of the nutrient solution.

▶ Figure 2.6

Comparison: irrigation systems used in urban agriculture

Data adapted from The USGS Water Science School, "Some irrigation methods," USGS, http://water.usgs.gov/edu/irmethods.html.

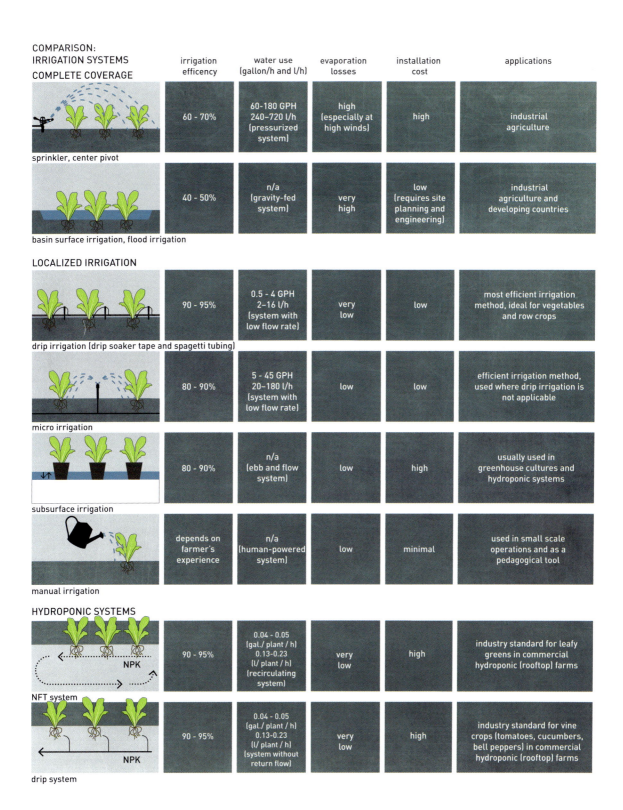

Hydroponic growing operations use various localized irrigation techniques to distribute the nutrient solution. The average daily water use of a hydroponic system ranges from 5–30% of the system volume depending on the size of the operation, tank size, growing area, plant number, type, and growth stage. The solution volume circulating in the system has to be kept relatively constant in order to ensure adequate plant growth. Plants take up the water much more rapidly and at a higher rate than they do added nutrients and essential elements. As water is removed from the solution, the volume of the solution decreases and the concentration of nutrients increases. Best practices allow the nutrient solution volume to fluctuate equally on both sides of the original level.

SYMBIOSIS BETWEEN URBAN AGRICULTURE AND WATER INFRASTRUCTURE

Urban agriculture has the potential to develop symbiotic relationships with water infrastructure at the building and urban scales. These synergies generate multiple benefits while supporting closed-loop systems to ultimately improve the urban water cycle.

Alternative Water Sources

Alternative water sources allow urban agriculture operations to become independent of the municipal water supply, offering opportunities to conserve fresh water resources. Alternative, underused water resources need to be identified for individual projects. Their use is primarily constrained by regulations that aim to protect human and environmental health. Many municipalities, for example, define any water that is not potable as wastewater. They thereby fail to consider many viable sources for irrigation, including precipitation, domestic wastewater, and building wastewater (see Catalog 3).

Some of these "degraded" water sources have very few contaminants. Regardless, they are all discarded into one sewer system, rendered blackwater, and made unrecyclable without costly water treatment. More sophisticated classification and source separation of different water streams is the first step toward more sustainable water management and use in urban agriculture.

Urban Agriculture As Stormwater Management Tool

Capturing water for crop cultivation slows down, mitigates, and reduces the volume of stormwater runoff that would otherwise be discarded into the sewage system or discharged untreated into urban water bodies.

Rainwater Harvesting

Rainwater harvesting is an obvious but often underused GSI strategy for improving urban water management. Rainwater is collected at its source for plant irrigation, decreasing the consumption of potable water for this purpose. The local climate, water availability, and annual distribution of precipitation determine the rainwater endowment. The potential collection volume is further determined by the size of the catchment area and its surface condition. The catchment area's materiality, slope, and absorption and evaporation capacities affect harvest efficiency, which ranges from 90% for impervious, smooth surfaces to 80% for gravel and paved surfaces and 30% for natural soil.[28] To provide high-quality water, rainwater harvesting systems include a first-flush diverter (Figure 2.7), which routes the initial, most contaminated runoff from a rainstorm away from the main cistern.

▼ Figure 2.7

Elements of a basic rainwater harvesting system

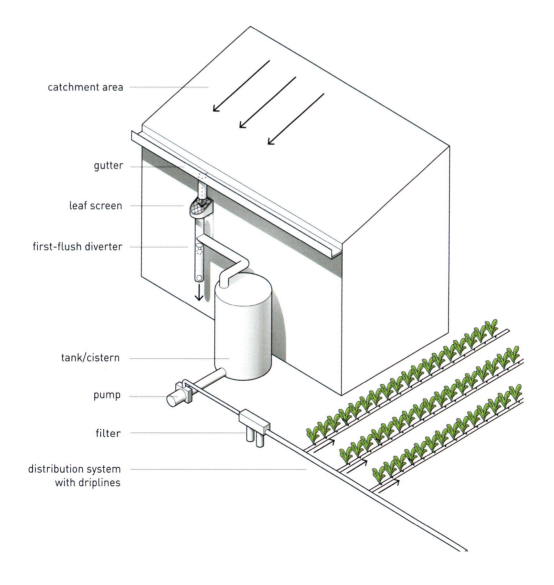

Water: Connecting the Cycle

While there is no consensus on acceptable levels of contamination, levels after first-flush diversion are generally considered safe for crop irrigation.[29]

The size, weight, and cost of water storage devices often become limiting factors for rainwater harvesting. The cost of tanks varies by type, material, and installation. They can be located above ground, buried below ground, or integrated into a building. The immense weight of these water storage tanks is an important consideration. A full 5,000-gallon (19-cubic meter) tank weighs approximately 21 tons (19,000 kilograms). The first step for a tank's integration into a building should be a load estimate and analysis of the structural system. Careful sectional studies of the site or building are necessary to develop gravity-fed systems, which reduce the energy needed for pumping.

Community gardens were among the first urban sites to integrate rainwater harvesting systems. These systems are adapted to local precipitation patterns. For example, Seattle and New York receive similar annual rainfalls of 38 and 50 inches (965 and 1,270 millimeters), respectively. Seattle receives most of its precipitation during the winter months, while New York's rainfall is evenly spread throughout the year. Seattle's gardeners need to install large tanks (up to 10,000 gallons/38,000 liters) to cover their irrigation needs for extended dry periods during the growing season, while New York's gardeners can cover dry spells between rainfalls with smaller tanks (1,000 gallons/3,800 liters).[30]

Rain Gardens

Rain gardens are GSI tools that slow stormwater runoff and collect it in low-lying gardens before infiltrating it into the ground, where the filtered water replenishes the groundwater table. These strategies can also be used to direct the water flow in soil-based gardens. In conjunction with the existing topography, the formation of swales, basins, and berms will slow water during heavy rain events and retain it on the site to allow slow infiltration. Plants and trees along these swales and basins benefit from the additional moisture and recharged groundwater. Planting Justice in Oakland, CA, frequently integrates these elements into their garden installations.[31]

Productive Green Roofs

Productive green roofs transform underused urban rooftops into new cultivation areas and green spaces. In addition to stormwater and urban heat island mitigation, the combination of green roofs and urban agriculture offers community and economic benefits (see Case Study 16). Moreover, in this symbiosis with the built environment, the additional layer of rooftop insulation improves the performance of the host building.

A green roof's substrate does much to determine its success. Effective installations delay and reduce stormwater runoff by 75–85%.[32] These "intensive" green roofs operate with a substrate depth of 6–24 inches (15–60 cm), in comparison to "extensive" green roofs, which are only 3–5 inches (7–12 cm) deep. In general, the deeper the substrate layer, the more water can be retained, though with added depth comes added weight and increased demands for the load capacity of the roof structure. Green roofs with a 6- to 8-inch substrate layer—such as those farmed by Brooklyn Grange (see Case Study 8)—have proven optimal in terms of balancing stormwater management potential, weight, and productivity.[33] With the ability to retain rainwater, green roofs provide additional environmental benefits, such as summer cooling, increased evapotranspiration, improved air quality, and noise reduction (Figure 2.8).

BUILDING-INTEGRATED, CYCLICAL SYSTEMS

Several urban agricultural projects have developed closed-loop systems that circulate water through different stages of plant irrigation, purification, and

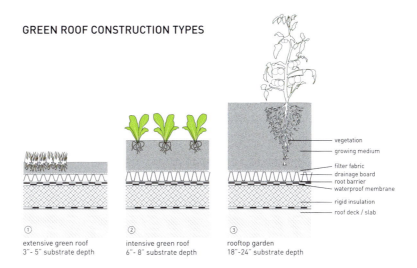

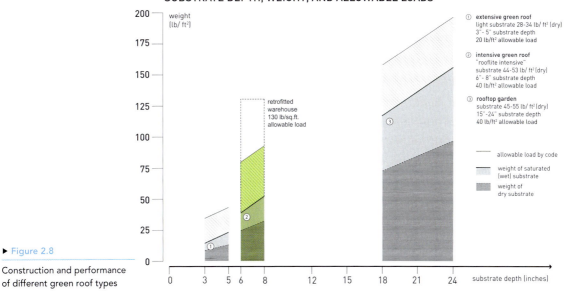

▶ Figure 2.8

Construction and performance of different green roof types

fertilization. These self-sustaining, water-efficient growing systems can be integrated into building systems to maximize resource efficiency, further expanding their benefits and synergies with the built environment.

Figure 2.9

East façade of the Bullitt Center, the Miller Hull Partnership, Seattle, Washington, 2013.

Integrated, Recirculating Growing Systems

Combining closed growing systems with alternative water sources yields the most water-efficient urban agricultural operations with the highest resource conservation. Hydroponic rooftop farms that collect rainwater are an example of this approach. Gotham Greens began operation in 2011 as the first commercial-scale hydroponic rooftop farm in the United States (see Case Study 11). Its first greenhouse in Greenpoint, Brooklyn, has a water demand of only 5 gallons (19 liters) to produce 1 kilogram of leafy greens. In this greenhouse, Gotham Greens produces an annual yield of 30 tons of fresh vegetables, primarily lettuce, basil, and leafy greens grown in recirculating NFT growing systems. The original farm provides irrigation water through rainwater collection on its 15,000-ft^2 (1,400-m^2) greenhouse roof. In comparison to a conventional greenhouse, this practice saves up to 1,056,700 gallons (4 million liters) of fresh water per year.[34] It also means that the farm uses 20 times less water than conventional farms. It additionally eliminates harmful agricultural runoff, a leading source of water pollution, and retains stormwater to prevent combined sewer overflows.

Building-Integrated, Net-Zero Water System

In order to increase the efficiency and sustainability of integrated systems, harvested water is ideally led through multiple systems to perform several tasks before it is treated on-site and returned to the cycle. The Bullitt Center in Seattle, completed in 2013, integrates multiple water reuse systems. Designed by Miller Hull to meet the Living Building Challenge, the building covers all its water needs independent of municipal water (Figures 2.9 and 2.10). It collects rainwater on its 13,400-ft^2 (1,250-m^2) PV roof and stores it in a 56,000-gallon (210,000-liter) cistern in the basement. The rainwater is filtered and treated with UV light to meet potable water quality standards and then used in drinking fountains, sinks, and showers in the building. Used water collected as greywater irrigates the green roof (a constructed wetland) and infiltrates rain gardens on-site. Currently, vegetation on the roof and in the rain garden are only intended to evaporate and infiltrate greywater, but a similar system could be developed to grow edible crops. The Bullitt Center avoids the creation of blackwater altogether through the use of micro-flush composting toilets.

Closed-Loop, Building-Integrated Agricultural Systems

Over the past few years, a number of building-integrated agricultural (BIA) projects have proposed circulating water systems. The Eco-Laboratory, an

Figure 2.10

Net Zero water system for the Bullitt Center, 2020 Engineers

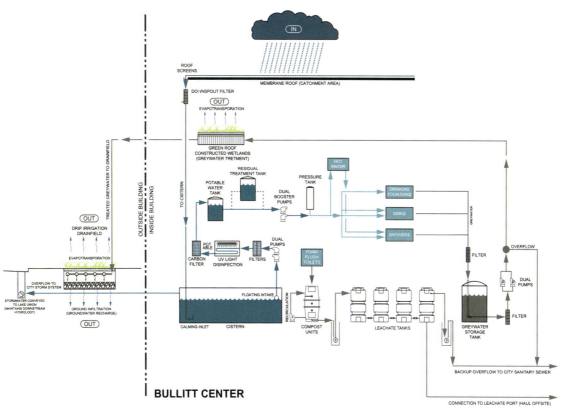

BULLITT CENTER

Water: Connecting the Cycle

award-winning building proposal by Weber Thompson (Figure 2.11), integrates rainwater collection, greywater use, and wastewater treatment in a closed-loop system involving outdoor and indoor growing components (see Architect's Profile 3).[35] Ecologically interconnected systems recycle water and promote its repeated reuse. Rainwater is collected, purified though wetlands and a UV filter, used as potable water in the building, and recaptured for use in greywater fixtures. A series of wastewater treatment systems treat blackwater for agricultural use. The nutrient-rich reclaimed water is used for growing crops outdoors and within interior hydroponic growing systems. Byproducts of the wastewater treatment process, such as methane gas, are given careful design consideration: methane is captured and used in hydrogen fuel cells to generate heat and electricity for the building. Thus, the by-product of one process becomes the resource for the next through these interlocking resource cycles.

▶ Figure 2.11

Site section and integrated water cycle of the Eco-Laboratory, competition project, Weber Thompson, Seattle, Washington, 2008

DESIGN CONSIDERATIONS

The interconnections between the selected growing system and the local climate are the starting point for the design of an integrated water system in urban agriculture. While all urban agricultural projects strive for water efficiency, soil-based and hydroponic growing systems take very different approaches. Soil-based systems conserve water with natural means, such as soil amendments, efficient irrigation, and crop selection; hydroponic systems reduce water consumption through recirculation, environmental controls, and distribution strategies.

The local climate does not determine the irrigation system per se, but the growing and irrigation systems have to be adjusted accordingly. Soil-based outdoor systems work best in temperate climates; they can work in warmer climates as long as enough water and shading are provided during summer droughts and intense solar radiation. Hydroponic growing as part of controlled-environment agriculture (CEA) is the most regulated approach. It is used to extend plant cultivation beyond natural restrictions, regionally and temporally. CEA is used to extend the growing period in hot and dry climates as well as in locations that have cold and wet winter seasons. More complex system integration often starts with the identification of alternative water sources to connect the growing systems with other water systems in the built environment. Their availability depends on climatic factors, but the ability to develop an integrated water system is restricted by anthropogenic factors such as codes and regulations, the current approach to water infrastructure in cities, as well as the cost implications of these systems.

Water Infrastructure's Effect on Multiple Scales

Urban water management is often associated with major infrastructure, such as sewer systems, underground reservoirs, holding tanks, and wastewater

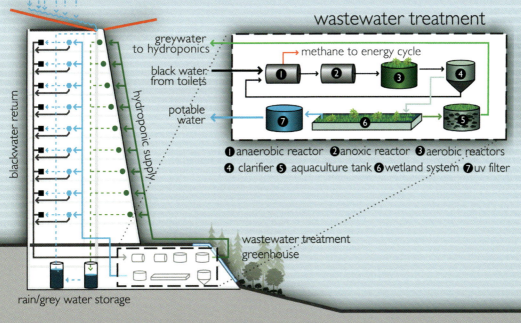

Water: Connecting the Cycle

treatment plants. Urban agriculture introduces small-scale, on-site strategies in the form of GSI and alternative water treatment options. While closed-loop water systems for urban agriculture are mainly conceived on the project scale, designers need to apply them in the larger context of the watershed. Although the scale of most urban agricultural projects is relatively small, the collective repercussions of cost-effective, decentralized infrastructure can be significant. Furthermore, urban farming operations serve as pioneers and case studies for subsequent projects. The integration of environmental water management strategies with urban agriculture creates more incentives through additional social and economic benefits.

Water infrastructure for urban crop cultivation is much less capital-intensive than conventional water-management infrastructure. A broader recognition of urban agriculture as green infrastructure results in additional funding opportunities through programs that incentivize low-impact stormwater management—documented by Brooklyn Grange's grant from the Department of Environmental Protection's (DEP's) Green Infrastructure Stormwater Management Initiative (see Case Study 8)—which creates a win-win situation for cities and urban farms.

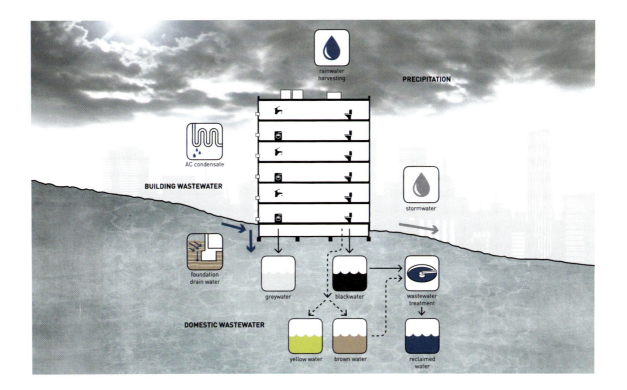

▲ Figure 2.12

Alternative water sources available in the city

CATALOG 3: ALTERNATIVE WATER SOURCES

Precipitation

Rainwater
Harvesting is the collection and storage of precipitation from elevated structures before it comes into contact with the ground and turns into surface runoff. For millennia, rainwater collection and storage in cisterns have been an important source of water, especially in arid climates. The main advantage of this technique over other alternative sources is its high water quality. Many urban farmers favor rainwater over municipal water because it is not treated with chlorine and other chemicals, which kill microorganisms. Microbes are critical to many farming techniques, including the cultivation of organic soil and vermiculture composting.

Cistern size is calculated based on local precipitation rates and water needs during the growing season. These rates may vary widely. For example, annual precipitation levels in major cities range from 7 inches (177 millimeters) in Phoenix to 29 inches (737 millimeters) in London to 50 inches (1,260 millimeters) in New York to 90 inches (2,286 millimeters) in Singapore. In addition to regional variations, seasonal variations will mean fluctuating rainwater abundance and demand throughout the year. Most water can be collected during wet periods, while the need is greatest during the warm, dry season.

Stormwater
Runoff is generated when precipitation comes into contact with ground-level impervious surfaces. In the United States, 60–95% of developed areas are covered by sealed surfaces, contributing to heavy runoff. About 75% of city rainfall turns into stormwater runoff.[36] This surface runoff often accrues large amounts of contaminants, such as debris, oil, chemicals, and sediment, most dramatically during the first rain following an extended dry period when pollutants have accumulated on impervious surfaces. Due to high and unmanageable pollutant levels, stormwater is not suitable for urban agriculture. Ground-level catchment areas can only be used to collect irrigation water if contaminants do not come into contact with them.

Domestic Wastewater

Greywater
Greywater is defined as wastewater that originates from washing machines, bathtubs, showers, or sinks—but not from toilets, urinals, kitchen sinks, or dishwashers. Greywater can be collected separately from sewage and accounts for typically 60–80% of domestic wastewater.[37] A person produces about 40 gallons (150 liters) of greywater per day. In conventional homes, this large volume of relatively clean water finds its way into the blackwater system. A dual plumbing system would lead to responsible source separation of these two water streams, enabling the alternative use of greywater as a seasonally consistent water supply for urban agricultural irrigation. For irrigation with greywater, basic guidelines apply. Plumbing systems must prevent human contact with greywater, as it could potentially contain pathogens. And greywater should not be stored more than 24 hours, as it might begin to emit unpleasant odors. Drip irrigation is the preferred distribution method, as it allows water to infiltrate directly into the ground. The use of sprayers and sprinkler with greywater is prohibited, since it could release airborne pathogens and put the edible parts of the plants in contact with the greywater.

Blackwater
Blackwater is generated from facilities containing fecal matter or urine. Due to its biological contamination, treatment is required before blackwater can be used for irrigation purposes. Conventionally, it is sent to municipal sewage treatment plants for a fairly costly, energy- and water-intense treatment process, which generates "reclaimed water." In rural areas, blackwater is infiltrated into the ground through private septic systems.[38] More localized and environmentally sound methods of treating blackwater with biodigesters and Eco-Machines make nutrients available on-site.

Yellow water and Brown Water
Yellow water and brown water systems promote the source separation of blackwater. These systems split human waste into urine (yellow water) and feces (brown water); they also reduce blackwater's dilution before entering the sewer (blackwater contains 98.3% water and only 1.7% human waste). The separation

of human waste allows urine and feces to be treated separately, which is more energy- and cost-effective. Given their chemical composition, both substances are resources that can supplement the nutrient and energy cycles, but they require different treatments: urine can be used immediately as fertilizer, while feces need to be composted or treated like blackwater.

Reclaimed Water
Reclaimed water is former municipal wastewater that has been treated to meet specific water quality criteria for reuse. The term "recycled water" is synonymous with "reclaimed water."[39] In the context of urban agriculture, it might be used for irrigation and the recharge of groundwater aquifers. Despite the high cost of treatment, reclaimed water conserves water resources in contrast to discharging treated water into rivers and oceans. While reclaimed water is objectively clean and safe to use for irrigation, it is not always perceived as such. Since consumers may reject crops grown with reclaimed water, many municipalities undertake efforts to change negative perceptions and promote reclaimed water as irrigation water.[40] Reclaimed water offers another asset to urban agricultural use, as its high nutrient content offsets needs for additional fertilization.

Building Wastewater

Foundation Drain Water
Foundation drain water is groundwater that has the potential to harm the foundations of a building (Figure 2.12). Foundation drain systems convey groundwater away from a building foundation to an appropriate discharge point using gravity. Most foundation drain systems discharge this relatively clean surplus water into the sewer. Though easily diverted for irrigation, unfortunately this and other alternative outputs have not yet been incorporated into most foundation drain water systems. The quality and volume of the available groundwater are largely dependent on water table depth, climate and seasonal variations, the permeability and chemical composition of sediments, and the proximity of nearby watercourses. A single office building, for example, can discharge up to 900,000 gallons (3,400 m^2) per day.[41]

Air-conditioner Condensate
Air-conditioner condensate is formed through the condensation of moist air on the refrigeration coils of an AC unit. Although it is high-quality water, it is conventionally drained into the sewer system. This condensate is potentially simple to source and ideal for irrigation applications, due to its low mineral content as well as its abundance during hot summer seasons that see high supplemental water demand. Because it does not need to be stored, this supply is also inexpensive. Commercial buildings, which produce sizeable amounts of condensate due to their higher cooling load, are ideal candidates for condensate collection. With yields as high as 10 gallons per day per 1,000 square feet (38 liters per day per 93 square meters) of air-conditioned space, a 50,000-ft^2 (4,650-m^2) office building can produce up to 500 gallons (1,900 liters) of water per day.[42]

NOTES

1. Sandra Postel, "Dividing the Waters," *Technology Review* 100.3 (1997): 57.
2. Godrej Dinyar, "Precious Fluid," *New Internationalist* 354 (2003): 12.
3. Raquel Pinderhughes, *Alternative Urban Futures: Planning for Sustainable Development in Cities Throughout the World* (Lanham, MD: Rowman & Littlefield, 2004), 19.
4. Udo Rettberg, "Wasser wird zum Spekulationsobjekt," www.zeit.de/wirtschaft/2010-08/wasser-rohstoff-investition.
5. Dinyar, "Precious Fluid," 14.
6. Pinderhughes, *Alternative Urban Futures*, 22.
7. "Agricultural Irrigated Land," http://data.worldbank.org/indicator/AG.LND.IRIG.AG.ZS.
8. Dinyar, "Precious Fluid," 15.
9. Postel, "Dividing the Waters," 61.
10. J. Griffiths and Eva Zabey. "Water Facts and Trends, Version 2," *World Business Council for Sustainable Development* (2009), http://wbcsdpublications.org/.
11. Sandra Postel, *Pillar of Sand: Can the Irrigation Miracle Last?* (New York: W.W. Norton & Co., 1999).
12. Postel, "Dividing the Waters," 56.
13. Kubi Ackerman, "Urban Agriculture: Opportunities and Constraints," in *Metropolitan Sustainability: Understanding and Improving the Urban Environment*, ed. Frank Zeman (Sawston, Cambridge, UK: Woodhead Publishing, 2012), 133.
14. The cost of water for agricultural use is $.0719 per 1000 gallons compared to municipal use in San Francisco of $5.105 per 1000 gallons.
15. Pinderhughes, *Alternative Urban Futures*, 24.
16. Postel, "Dividing the Waters," 62.
17. Angela Morelli, "The Water We Eat," www.angelamorelli.com/water/.
18. Arjen Y. Hoekstra, "The Hidden Water Resource Use Behind Meat and Dairy," *Animal Frontiers* 2.2 (April 2012).
19. Vandana Shiva, *Water Wars: Privatization, Pollution and Profit* (Cambridge, MA: South End Press, 2002), 114.
20. Howard M. Resh, *Hydroponic Food Production: A Definitive Guidebook for the Advanced Home Gardener and the Commercial Hydroponic Grower* (Boca Raton, FL: CRC Press, 2013), 18.
21. H. Taha, "Urban Climates and Heat Islands: Albedo, Evapotranspiration, and Anthropogenic Heat," *Energy and Buildings* 25.2 (1997): 99–103.
22. Bryce Finnerty and Jorge Ramirez, "CO_2 and Temperature Effects on Evapotranspiration and Irrigated Agriculture," *Journal of Irrigation and Drainage Engineering* (1996): 155–163.
23. Ackerman, "Urban Agriculture," 133.
24. Ibid., 134.
25. Postel, "Dividing the Waters," 61.
26. Ibid., 61.
27. *Integrated Water Management Seminar for Buildings and Sites*, ed. 1.0. Participant's Manual, Green Roofs for Healthy Cities, 80.
28. Heather Kinkade-Levario, *Design for Water: Rainwater Harvesting, Stormwater Catchment, and Alternate Water Reuse* (Gabriola, B.C.: New Society Publishers, 2007).

29. Kubi Ackerman, "The Potential for Urban Agriculture in New York City: Growing Capacity, Food Security, and Green Infrastructure." *Urban Design Lab at the Earth Institute* (New York: Columbia University, 2011), 65, www.urbandesignlab.columbia.edu/sitefiles/file/urban_agriculture_nyc.pdf.
30. Ellen Kirby and Elizabeth Peters, *Community Gardening: Brooklyn Botanic Garden All-region Guides; Handbook #190*. (Brooklyn, NY: Brooklyn Botanic Garden, 2008), 88.
31. Janett Nolasco,"Sustainable Water Management for Urban Agriculture: Planting Justice, Oakland," *Pacific Institute* (December 9, 2011), 7.
32. J. Mentens, D. Raes, and M. Hermy, "Green Roofs as a Tool for Solving the Rainwater Runoff Problem in the Urbanized 21st Century," *Landscape and Urban Planning* 77.3 (2006): 217–226.
33. Gundula Proksch, "Urban Rooftops as Productive Resources: Rooftop Farming versus Conventional Green Roofs," in *Considering Research: Proceedings of the Architectural Research Center Consortium Spring Research Conference, Detroit, MI, April 2011* (Southfield, MI: Lawrence Tech University, 2011), 497–509.
34. D. Gould and T. Caplow, "Building Integrated Agriculture: A New Approach to Food Production," in *Metropolitan Sustainability: Understanding and Improving the Urban Environment*, ed. Frank Zeman (Sawston, Cambridge, UK: Woodhead Publishing, 2012), 162.
35. "Eco-Laboratory," *Weber Thompson*, www.weberthompson.com/eco-laboratory.html.

CATALOG 3

36. L. Frazer, "Paving Paradise," *Environmental Health Perspectives* 113 (2005): 457–462.
37. *Integrated Water Management Seminar for Buildings and Sites*, 29.
38. Ibid., 30.
39. EPA, "Guidelines for Water Reuse," (2004), www.epa.gov/NRMRL/pubs/625r04108/625r04108.htm.
40. Dana D. Clarke, Kristen McIvor, and Sally Brown, "Safety of Reclaimed Water for Edible Food Crops" (King County, Washington State).
41. *Integrated Water Management Seminar for Buildings and Sites*, 24.
42. Ibid., 31.

Chapter 3

ENERGY

Solar-powered Photosynthesis and Greenhouses

ABSTRACT

Photosynthesis converts solar energy into chemical energy and establishes the carbon cycle, which powers all life on Earth. This biogeochemical cycle is currently out of balance: the rapidly increasing carbon dioxide (CO_2) concentration in the atmosphere is driving accelerated climate change. Urban agriculture has the potential to exert a positive influence on this crisis, however, through more sustainable energy use and a reduction of fossil fuel consumption, achieved through the elimination of synthetic fertilizer, reduced use of machinery, increased local food production, and alternative distribution systems. This chapter will investigate the factors that need to be considered in implementing a sustainable, energy-efficient urban agricultural operation. These factors include the solar needs of plants, the potential extension of growing seasons indoors, and associated passive solar gains for buildings. An overview of greenhouse typologies, cover materials, and lighting systems identifies methods to optimize energy use and production in a variety of environmental situations. Chapter 3 additionally examines the potential for photosynthesis and the carbon cycle to make use of the exhaust systems of buildings so that used, CO_2-rich air and excess heat can support crop cultivation. Intersections among the nutrient, water, and energy cycles are further explored in a series of case studies that demonstrate the breadth and diversity of current urban agricultural practice.

THE CARBON CYCLE

Together with the water cycle and nutrient cycles, the carbon cycle provides fuel for the biotic processes that sustain all life on Earth. This cycle traces the movement of carbon as it is recycled and reused throughout the biosphere. Sunlight-driven photosynthetic uptake of carbon from the atmosphere and oceans is the basis of the carbon cycle. Photosynthesis is the Earth's principal biochemical process driven by solar energy. It converts carbon dioxide (CO_2), a common waste product of respiration and combustion, together with water and sunlight into two vital substances: carbohydrates—a biological energy source—and oxygen (O_2). Respiration, the reverse process of photosynthesis, occurs when cells break down carbohydrates in the presence of oxygen to release the stored energy. All living organisms respire oxygen and exhale carbon dioxide and water. However, only plants that contain chlorophyll are able to perform

◀ Figure 3.1

Sunlight, the energy source for photosynthesis

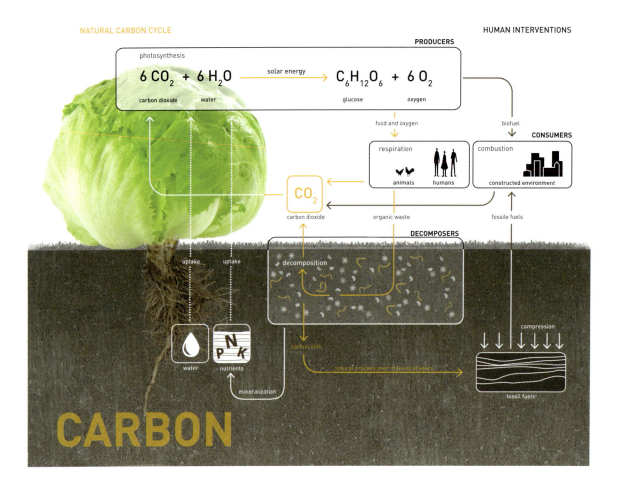

▲ Figure 3.2

The carbon cycle driven by photosynthesis

photosynthesis. Together, these two metabolic processes—with their associated CO_2 capture and expiration—drive the carbon cycle (Figure 3.2).

Natural Carbon Pools and Sinks

On a global scale, carbon is found in four major sources, or pools: (1) the terrestrial biosphere; (2) the atmosphere; (3) the ocean; and (4) the lithosphere. Carbon moves between these pools with a time scale ranging from seconds (in the case of photosynthesis) to millions of years (for geological processes that transfer carbon from the lithosphere to the other carbon pools).[1]

The terrestrial biosphere, encompassing vegetation and soil, holds the largest biological reservoir of carbon. Reduced carbon, which is integrated into organic compounds, makes up about half of the mass of all organic matter on Earth. Terrestrial vegetation contains nearly as much carbon as the atmosphere, and soil contains at least twice as much carbon as vegetation.

The atmosphere is the smallest and most dynamic carbon pool. Carbon in the atmosphere exists primarily as CO_2 and in much smaller quantities as methane (CH_4). Both gases are responsible for the "greenhouse effect" in the atmosphere, which allows life on Earth, though the increased concentrations of CO_2 and CH_4 cause the negative effects of global warming.

The carbon pool in the oceans is divided into two strata: the thin layer of surface waters and the intermediate to deep ocean waters, which hold 97% of the ocean carbon pool. The surface water interacts with the atmosphere and contains similar quantities of carbon as the atmosphere and terrestrial vegetation. Only a fraction of this carbon exists in organic forms, contained in marine organisms and biomass. While marine organisms account for a very small carbon pool, they cycle as much carbon annually as terrestrial vegetation.[2]

Finally, the geological carbon pool contains more than 99% of all carbon on Earth and is stored inertly in the lithosphere. Most of this carbon was stored in the Earth's crust when the planet formed; only a small percentage in the form of fossil fuels was created through sedimentation of organic carbon from the biosphere. Naturally, this pool cycles very slowly (at the rate of millions of years), depending on the geological processes associated with the rock cycle, the movement of continental plates, volcanism, uplift, and weathering.[3]

Anthropogenic activities have a significant influence on the global carbon cycle by adding extra carbon dioxide emissions. Combustion of fossil fuels, which releases CO_2 stored in the geological pool, is the largest and most direct human influence on the carbon cycle. Cement production, meanwhile, releases CO_2 from carbonate rocks, adding it to the active CO_2 cycle. Land use changes, including deforestation and the transformation of grassland into agricultural land, release carbon through biomass burning and enhanced decomposition of the soil. These human interventions have been changing carbon pool sizes in greater dimensions since the beginning of industrialization. Annually, these anthropogenic fluxes are equivalent to 10–15% of the carbon cycled by the terrestrial or the marine pool. Combined human activities therefore constitute the third largest flux of carbon to the atmosphere (Figure 3.3).[4]

Global Warming

In April of 2014, the National Oceanic and Atmospheric Administration (NOAA) stated that the measured CO_2 concentration in the atmosphere had reached 400 parts per million (ppm) for the first time in millions of years.[5] This is a significant increase from the beginning of the Industrial Revolution in the late eighteenth century, a period which had one of the lowest CO_2 concentrations in the Earth's history (below 300 ppm).[6] Anthropogenic emissions of CO_2 and other greenhouse gases (GHGs) have contributed most to this GHG-induced warming. The majority of GHGs come from the combustion of fossil fuels, the production of petroleum products, and industrial processes, but industrial agricultural practices, deforestation, and land use changes have also increased the concentration of greenhouse gases in the atmosphere. All emissions can be directly or indirectly traced back to a release of carbon from natural carbon pools.

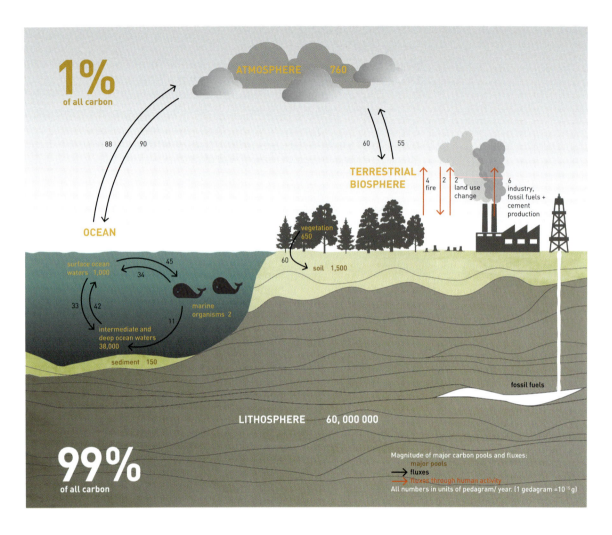

▲ Figure 3.3

Natural carbon pools and sinks and human interventions

Data adapted from F. Stuart Chapin, P.A. Matson, and Harold A. Mooney, *Principles of Terrestrial Ecosystem Ecology* (New York: Springer, 2002), 336.

The warming of the Earth's atmosphere is driven by the "greenhouse effect," so called to evoke the warming of a closed greenhouse by the sun, although atmospheric warming is actually propelled by a different mechanism. Atmospheric temperature increases because GHGs absorb thermal radiation from the planetary surface and then reradiate it in all directions. Some of it is reradiated towards the Earth, which results in a rise of the average temperature. The "greenhouse effect" is a natural process that is necessary to support life on Earth by keeping the atmospheric temperature in a moderate range. However, greater GHG concentration reinforces the effect and leads to a steady increase in the atmospheric temperature. This climate change is manifested by heat waves and altered precipitation patterns, resulting in floods and droughts that trigger dangerous effects on ecosystems. The higher temperatures cause the oceans to warm, the glaciers and ice caps to melt, and the sea levels to rise. Agriculture, food production, and food security are threatened by extreme and unpredictable weather events and the potential destruction of low-lying

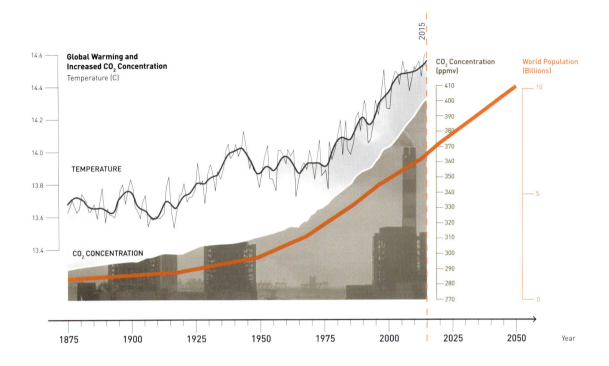

▲ Figure 3.4

Timeline of global warming, increased CO2 concentration and population growth

Data adapted from GISS Surface Temperature Analysis, "Global Mean Land-Ocean Temperature Index," NASA, http://data.giss.nasa.gov/gistemp/graphs_v3/; Global Monitoring Division, "Atmospheric CO₂ at Mauna Loa Observatory," NOAA, http://www.esrl.noaa.gov/gmd/ccgg/trends/full.html, US Census Bureau, International Data Base, July 2015 Update.

farmland in coastal regions. The increased agricultural production that occurred through industrialization allowed a rapid growth of the global population; now industrialization's side effects threaten the world's food supply (Figure 3.4).

Industrial Agriculture's Effects on the Carbon Cycle

Industrial agriculture affects climate change directly through GHG emissions and a reduction of carbon storage in the terrestrial carbon pool. All told, it accounts for 10% of all GHG emissions in the United States.[7] Conventional soil management activities account for 40% of these agricultural emissions, primarily through the application of nitrogen fertilizer and the consequent release of nitrous oxide (N_2O), an extremely potent GHG. The second source of GHG emissions is enteric fermentation, a natural digestive process in animals (predominantly beef and dairy cattle), which produces 30% of the emissions in the form of methane. Livestock manure management accounts for an additional 14%, and other industrial agriculture practices, including rice cultivation and the burning of crop residues, make up 6%. Energy use, finally, is the fourth largest source of emissions (10%). Industrial agriculture, like other industries, has a negative effect on the carbon cycle through the direct use of fossil fuels to power big machinery, mechanized operations, food processing, and transport over long distances. Indirect energy use includes emissions for the production of commercial fertilizer and other energy-intensive farm inputs.

Statistics gathered by the Environmental Protection Agency (EPA) and other research institutions show that current soil management practices—over-fertilization, denitrification, and carbon loss from the soil—are the primary sources of agriculturally produced GHGs. Improving agricultural practices by organically managing soils and reducing the application of synthetic fertilizer can turn the soil back into a carbon sink. Land use practices and land use changes further precipitate carbon loss. Land use conversions, for example, the tilling of grassland into cropland and deforestation for agriculture and livestock, reduce the capacity of the land to store carbon. While pasture and grassland have higher carbon retention than cropland, the current standard practice of overgrazing diminishes the performance of grassland as a carbon sink.

Agricultural practices and performance are closely tied to consumer choices. Production of meat and dairy products, for example, has grown to meet demand. In turn, large-scale livestock farming has increased methane gas production, fertilizer use (to produce feed), and the tendency for overgrazing. All three are unsustainable practices and increase GHG production in different ways. Therefore, consumer education, lifestyle choices, and conscious consumer decisions will significantly influence agricultural practices.

SOLAR ENERGY AND CARBON DIOXIDE NEEDS OF PLANTS

Urban and building-integrated agricultural systems offer an alternative to industrial agriculture and may mitigate the global threat of climate change. In order to implement a successful system, it is fundamental for designers to understand the solar needs of plants growing both outside and indoors. For example, light that passes through structures and glazing materials to reach interior plants may be significantly diminished when compared to unobstructed light outside.

Photosynthesis is the starting point for understanding the solar energy needs of plants. Occurring inside the chloroplasts of plant cells, photosynthesis is driven by solar radiation and transforms carbon dioxide and water into carbohydrates (glucose) and oxygen. It can be represented by the following equation:

$$6\ CO_2 + 6\ H_2O \rightarrow C_6H_{12}O_6 + 6\ O_2$$

Based on the critical inputs of this reaction, the following sections investigate how light levels, CO_2 levels, and ambient temperatures affect photosynthesis rates. Up to a certain level, the increase of these three factors will increase photosynthetic productivity, as long as there are no other limiting factors, such as water and nutrient availability.

Light Quality and Intensity

The characteristics of light that affect plant growth in urban agriculture are quality and intensity. Light quality denotes the color or wavelength spectrum of radiation reaching a plant's leaves. Photosynthetically active radiation

(PAR), consisting of wavelengths between 400 and 700 nanometers (nm), falls just inside the visible spectrum of humans—between 380 and 770 nm. While humans perceive the entire visible spectrum as white light, there is actually a continuous spectrum of colors. From the smallest to the largest wavelengths, the spectrum is made up of violet, indigo, blue, green, yellow, orange, and red light (Figure 3.5). Wavelength and quantum energy are inversely associated. This means the smaller the wavelength, the greater its energy content.[8]

The light spectrum absorbed by plants is an important consideration when selecting greenhouse cover materials (see Catalog 5). The absorbed light spectrum should also be matched by electric light sources selected

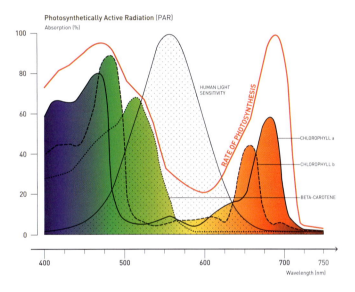

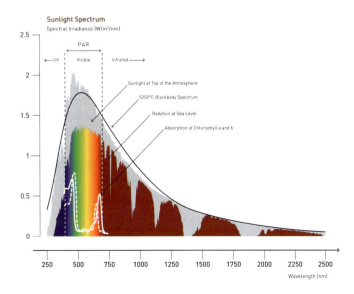

▶ Figure 3.5

Photosynthetically Active Radiation (PAR) and the sunlight spectrum

Data adapted from Lincoln Taiz and Eduardo Zeiger. *Plant Physiology*. 3rd ed. (Sunderland, Mass.: Sinauer Associates, 2002), 113-115.

for supplemental lighting and sole-source lighting for indoor growing (see Catalog 6).

As first shown by Thomas Engelmann in 1882, the blue and red wavelengths have the greatest effects on plant growth. Blue light contributes primarily to vegetative or leaf growth, while red light (in the presence of blue light) promotes flowering and fruiting. Green light has generally been deemed least effective since a large portion of it is reflected, giving plants their green color. More recent studies have shown, however, that green light, together with the total light spectrum, is utilized as an energy source for photosynthesis. Blue and red light are more efficient at powering photosynthesis on the upper sides of leaves, where these light colors are absorbed through the plant pigments chlorophyll a and b. Green light, on the other hand, has been found to penetrate further into the leaf, thus powering carbon fixation more efficiently in the deeper leaf layers. Green light primarily affects the plant pigment (carotenoid) beta-carotene, which serves as an accessory pigment in the photosynthesis process. The photosynthesis rate is thus an accumulation of the absorption processes of the three pigments chlorophyll a and b and beta-carotene, as shown in the PAR graph in Figure 3.5.

Increased sunlight intensity will increase a plant's photosynthetic rate proportionally, but only to a certain extent. At the maximum light intensity, which is different for each plant, the curve flattens out. Some plants even experience photoinhibition, or a reduction of photosynthesis rates at very high light levels. Light intensities during the summer are routinely higher than the photosynthetic capacity of most plants, which require shading for optimal growth. However, during winter days, the light intensity in northern latitudes is so low that plants cannot perform photosynthesis effectively. Therefore, year-round greenhouse operations in these regions require supplemental lighting during winter months.

Carbon Dioxide Levels

Plants grow well at ambient CO_2 levels that are between 350 and 400 ppm. Commercial greenhouse operators consider CO_2 a nutrient and increase CO_2 concentrations to enhance productivity, plant growth, and vigor. An increase in CO_2 results in a proportionate increase of photosynthetic activity. Doubling the CO_2 concentration to 800 ppm will increase yields by 30% if all the other growing factors, including ample PAR, are available. A drop in the CO_2 levels by 50% in closed greenhouses, resulting from active photosynthesis, will proportionally reduce the plants' ability to perform photosynthesis. Therefore, sufficient ventilation or CO_2 fertilization in greenhouses is important. Higher CO_2 concentrations will shorten the growing period by 5–10%, increase plant mass and volume, and improve quality and yield (Figure 3.6).[9]

Ambient Temperature

Plant growth and productivity are also influenced by average temperature, the thermo period (the period a plant is exposed to a particular temperature), and

▶ Figure 3.6

Effects of light intensity and CO_2 concentration on photosynthesis rate

Data adapted from Lincoln Taiz and Eduardo Zeiger. *Plant Physiology*. 3rd ed. (Sunderland, Mass.: Sinauer Associates, 2002), 178; Ontario Ministry of Agriculture, Food and Rural Affairs, "Carbon Dioxide in Greenhouses," www.omafra.gov.on.ca/english/crops/facts/00-077.htm.

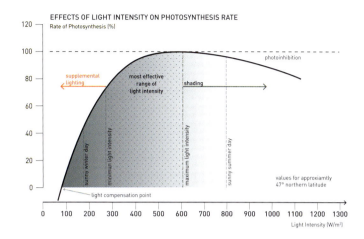

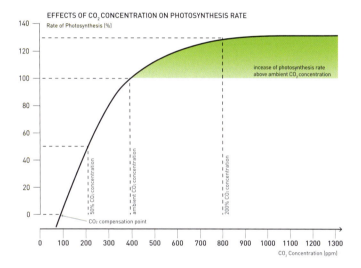

daily temperature changes. Just as a plant's photosynthetic rate will increase with increased sunlight, respiration rates rise with increasing temperatures. Plant growth is dependent on photosynthesis rates being greater than respiration, and as temperatures reach the upper growing limits for the crop, respiration rates can exceed the rate of photosynthesis so that the products of photosynthesis are expended faster than they can be supplied. Similarly, reduced rates of photosynthesis are associated with low temperatures, resulting in poor growth and diminished yields.

Not all crops experience optimal growth in identical temperature ranges. As guidance for farmers and gardeners, hardiness zone maps specify the average annual minimum temperature projected for geographic areas. Together with the plant specifications, the hardiness zone helps identify which crop species will grow in a specific region. The zones are defined by temperature variation, each separated by a 10°F (5.5°C) difference in average annual minimum temperature. In 2012, the US Department of Agriculture issued a revised USDA Hardiness

Zone Map that documents the northward shift of zones in recent years due to global warming. This revision highlights extended growing seasons in previously colder areas, which often come with destabilized local ecosystems that now mismatch the blooming schedules of plants and availability of insects for pollination.

URBAN GROWING CONDITIONS

In an urban environment, microclimates determine the actual growing conditions and can be more telling of crop prospects than a hardiness zone map. Factors including solar exposure, thermal heat mass, wind exposure, and elevation can cause urban farms to exhibit temperatures considerably warmer (or colder) than their surrounding locales. A south-facing exposure typically indicates a hot and dry situation, while a north-facing exposure will exhibit cool and moist conditions.

In general, the temperatures in cities are higher than the surrounding areas due to the heat island effect. The large building masses, paved surfaces, and minimal vegetation of urban settings mean that the heat received through solar radiation is stored. Mechanical heat released by cooling and heating equipment, traffic, and industry further increases temperatures. On hot summer days, the temperature in large cities can exceed the surrounding rural areas by as much as 22°F (12°C). The average temperature of most large cities has been found to increase by 0.56°F (0.31°C) per decade. These temperature increases occur almost twice as fast as those in rural areas, the rates for which average 0.29°F (0.16°C) per decade.[10]

Higher emissions from increased combustion of fossil fuels in cities create higher rates of CO_2 concentration in urban areas, resulting in urban CO_2 domes. These "domes" exist only in the lower levels of the atmosphere over cities and cause health-damaging air pollution and ozone concentrations. This identifies high CO_2 as a primarily urban problem, which needs to be addressed at its source.[11] Measurements in Phoenix, for example, found a 40–75% increase in CO_2 levels near the ground in comparison to surrounding rural areas. The effect of these higher levels of GHG on the urban ambient temperature, however, is low in comparison to the temperature increase of 9–18°F (5–10°C) caused by the urban heat island effect.[12]

URBAN AGRICULTURE'S POSITIVE IMPACT ON THE CARBON CYCLE

Urban agriculture often increases plant cultivation (outdoor and indoor) in previously desolate urban areas with little or no vegetation. The photosynthesis performed by these urban crops exerts a direct local impact on the carbon cycle. In addition to the output of energy in the form of local produce, photosynthesis also increases CO_2 sequestration and O_2 production. Additional vegetation will also help improve microclimates through evapotranspiration, provide a cooling influence on the heat island effect, and improve air quality through air filtration by trapping particulates on the surface of the plants' leaves. As corollary, crops often benefit from the higher temperatures and extended growing seasons in cities, and the additional vegetation has a cooling influence on the heat island effect.

Through soil-based systems, urban farms either bring more soil to barren places or increase soil quality and its ability to sequester carbon through organic practices, such as the use of cover crops, composting, mulching, no-till farming, and permaculture. These urban agricultural practices also lead to greater plant density through more intense growing systems and operations, which lead to higher photosynthesis rates overall. Controlled-environment agriculture (CEA), such as hydroponic greenhouse growing, also increases CO_2 sequestration through the production of large quantities of crops or biomass in a protected environment.

Local food production reduces additional CO_2 emissions through the reduction of food miles: less fossil fuel is used for long-distance transportation, heavy machinery, and processing than is typically used in industrial agriculture. Moreover, urban agriculture practices often abstain from using synthetic fertilizer, herbicides, and pesticides, which require energy for production. Instead, many farms rely on composting and other organic soil improvements that divert organic waste from landfills and boost soil quality and carbon-storing ability.

SYMBIOSIS BETWEEN URBAN AGRICULTURE AND SOLAR ENERGY IN URBAN ENVIRONMENTS

Favorable Urban Climate

Urban growing conditions have long exerted a beneficial effect on agriculture. Walled urban gardens were the basis of successful crop cultivation in cities such as Paris from medieval times through the nineteenth century.[13] High, protective walls absorbed heat during the day and reradiated it at night and during the winter months. These sheltered microclimates allowed for almost year-round food production in comparison to the more exposed climates of rural areas.

Today, extended growing seasons in temperate cities through the northward shift of hardiness zones and an increase in average regional temperature could be considered one of the very few positive effects of the urban heat island effect. Cities with limited growing seasons especially profit from these higher average temperatures. Soil-based outdoor gardens in urban spaces benefit most directly, due to the lack of other means to control the growing environment. CEA, and more specifically high-tech greenhouses, benefit through better environmental performance, as they need less energy for heating during the winter months.

Urban agricultural systems can greatly benefit from higher temperatures, as long as they are able to provide sufficient quantities of all other inputs. These other inputs, however, could easily turn into the limiting factors (Liebig's Law)—for example, if higher temperatures create a shortage of water. Similarly, the same climate changes can cause negative effects in arid climates. Droughts and heat waves will make agricultural production in these regions even more challenging.

BUILDING INTEGRATION

To take better advantage of urban growing conditions and to further exploit synergies with the built environment, architects have begun to integrate agriculture with buildings and building systems. The spectrum ranges from "passive systems," such as green roofs and container growing, to actively integrated greenhouses, vertical façade systems, and stacked indoor growing facilities.

Productive green roofs, the most effective passive system, improve the performance of their host buildings greatly without being directly integrated with the building systems. The added layer of substrate and vegetation offers environmental benefits, including stormwater retention, carbon sequestration, and additional insulation value, while taking full advantage of the often underutilized solar radiation on urban roofs.

Greenhouses

Greenhouses—on rooftops and along south-facing façades—are the most prominent form of active building integration, commonly referred to as building-integrated agriculture (BIA). These greenhouses operate with resource efficient methods, such as recirculating hydroponic systems and rainwater harvesting, to reduce their water needs. For heating, the greenhouses utilize the energy provided by solar radiation and by host building by-products, such as exhaust heat and air. The energy captured in the built environment lowers the energy demand from other sources. The greenhouses also improve the environmental performance of their host buildings. They provide additional insulation, summer cooling, and potential pre-tempered and oxygen-enriched air to the host building (see Case Studies 10 and 11). Some farm systems have integrated crop cultivation in vertical spaces—such as double façades—as well as mechanized transportation systems that equalize access to natural light, increase the possible height of the growing structure, and simplify the maintenance and harvest of the upright cultivation system (Figure 3.7 and Case Studies 4 and 5). This approach exploits solar radiation on south-facing vertical building façades. At 40° northern latitude, these surfaces receive about 70–80% of the solar radiation that a horizontal roof surface collects.[14]

Stacked Indoor Growing Facilities

Indoor growing in warehouse-like settings is another form of BIA, one that explicitly does not take advantage of the PAR in sunlight. This growing method has seen increased interest in urban agriculture, and it works by replacing natural daylight with electrical lighting, which is arguably not very sustainable. The environmental performance of these farms depends largely on the source of the electrical power used and its associated carbon footprint. With the development of technically sophisticated, highly productive, energy-efficient, and reasonably priced LED grow lights (see Catalog 6), however, indoor growing facilities seem to have reached economic viability in recent years (see Case Study 6).

▲ Figure 3.7

Vertical farm, Wigan University Technical College (UTC), Greater Manchester area, UK, 2013

ENVIRONMENTAL SYSTEMS SUPPORTING INDOOR GROWING

Both greenhouses and indoor growing facilities need to control their indoor climates and improve environmental performance to facilitate effective and economical plant cultivation. The main concerns are keeping excess heat (from solar radiation or electrical lighting) out, preventing heat loss during the night, and controlling the availability of resources. While greenhouse operations largely take advantage of passive systems, indoor growing in warehouse-like environments relies primarily on mechanical systems.

Providing irrigation, ventilation, and a tolerable temperature range in a greenhouse is necessary. Supplementing naturally available energy and resources—such as sunlight, heat, and CO_2 content—is, however, optional. Supplementation will boost yield, especially during darker, cooler winter months, and allow for year-round production in regions where it would otherwise not be possible. Indoor growing requires the provision of all growing inputs, including PAR, because grow spaces are sealed off from natural resources. The economics and environmental effects of these supplements and essential resources need to be identified for each case. The energy sources (fossil versus alternative), energy cost, and associated carbon footprint also need to be carefully considered.

Ventilation

Ventilation systems help regulate air temperature by preventing overheating and replacing moist air with drier outside air to reduce the risk of disease. Ventilation also supplies CO_2, which plants quickly consume in an indoor air volume. Outside air, or air with a high CO_2 concentration, needs to be consistently provided, and air movement is needed to generate an equal concentration of this gas in the entire greenhouse or grow space.

Greenhouses can be designed to encourage natural ventilation by inserting ridge vents along the full length and side vents along the base of one sidewall (Figure 3.8). Propelled by the thermal gradient between inside and outside air, warm air will rise to the top of the greenhouse and exit through the ridge vents, while cooler air will enter through the side vents. To utilize wind in this process, the ridge of the greenhouse needs to be perpendicular to the direction of prevailing summer winds. The wind flows over the roof and generates a vacuum on the leeward side of the ridge, which pulls hot air out of the

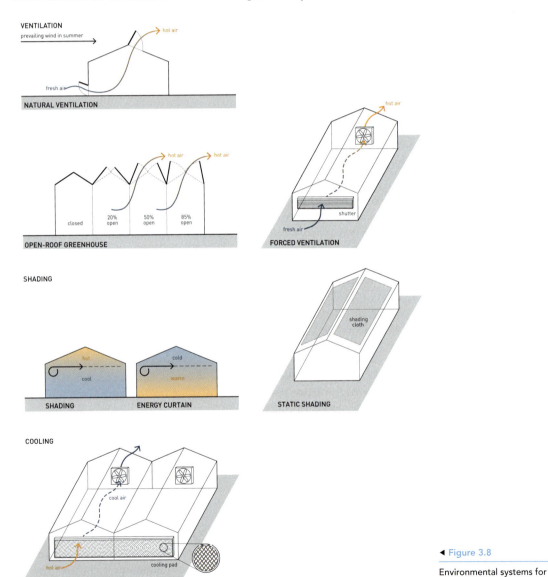

◀ Figure 3.8

Environmental systems for climate control in greenhouses

ridge vents. Alternative methods of natural ventilation have been developed in the high-tech greenhouse industry. Open-roof greenhouses offer retractable, infinitely variable roofs that can extend to be up to 85% open to the sky. This technology offers plants exposure to the outside climate and reduces energy needs for ventilation and cooling.

In forced or mechanical ventilation systems, fans pull air through the greenhouse. Air enters through a shutter on one end wall and leaves through exhaust fans on the other end wall. This method is often used in hoop houses or polyethylene tunnels in which ridge vents are difficult to install. The ventilation of indoor growing spaces is similar, with extractor fans that pull exhaust air out of the grow space. In either application, the energy consumption for fan ventilation is high.

Shading Systems and Energy Curtains

Most greenhouses integrate shading systems to screen excess solar radiation, prevent overheating, and reduce the overexposure of the plants to light. Depending on the geographic region, this task may be more challenging than heating the interior. There are two general approaches to greenhouse shading: static or directly applied shading elements and movable screens.

Simple approaches to shading include directly applied compounds such as "whitewash" painted or sprayed onto the greenhouse, or the application of woven shading cloth on the exterior, which can be designed to block out 10–90% of the sunlight. A more advanced static and still experimental approach is the use of building-integrated technologies. European greenhouse operators and producers have started to install arrays of transparent PV panels in greenhouse glassing. The PV cells work as shading devices and produce electricity at the same time (Figure 3.9). The Aquaponic Solar Greenhouse (Case Study 1) takes this idea to the next level by developing an operable louver system that integrates PV cells.

Mechanized shading screens, pulled horizontally through the interior of the greenhouse, are technically more sophisticated but also ten times more expensive than shading cloths. Movable screens, however, can respond to the actual daylight conditions and can be opened on overcast days during the summer to let more daylight in.

Adjustable shading systems like these often function simultaneously as integrated, horizontal energy curtains that prevent heat loss during the night. These screens are also known as thermal screens, movable curtains, or heat blankets. The insulation works most effectively if the crop zone below the curtain is completely sealed off from the unheated gable zone above. In addition, the material properties of the curtain are critical. Semi-porous material offers the best performance due to its ability to roll or fold up well to minimize shading during the day and drain water that collects on top of the fabric, as well as its heat retention rate of 50–75%.[15] Neither strategy applies to indoor growing operations since they use opaque warehouses and basement spaces that block out sunlight entirely.

◀ Figure 3.9

Greenhouse with integrated photovoltaic cells, municipal greenhouse called "Palmenhaus," Munich, Germany, renovation, 2004

Cooling Systems

If ventilation and shading in greenhouses do not provide enough cooling, evaporative cooling through fan or pad systems is the most effective alternative. These systems lower temperature, increase humidity, and therefore reduce the water needs of plants. To generate these effects, air moves through a porous wet screen. The energy needed to evaporate this water (enthalpy or heat of vaporization) is extracted from the air and cools the air. This method works most effectively when the humidity levels of the outside air are low. Indoor growing facilities use electrical air conditioning (AC) systems, which cool the air using a refrigeration cycle, generating a higher energy demand.

Electrical Lighting

Efficient supplemental lighting is critical for the economic viability of year-round greenhouse operations in northern latitudes. While most crops will benefit from additional lighting during limited light conditions, electrical lighting is only profitable if increased photosynthesis and crop quality lead to higher revenue. The monetary cost and environmental impact (or carbon footprint) associated with the use of electricity in urban farming are worthy of serious consideration, given the growing number of indoor urban farms that rely exclusively on electrical lighting. A range of technologies for supplemental lighting is available (see Catalog 6) depending on the type of farm operation as well as the crop and growing cycle. Light-emitting diodes (LED) are currently the preferred technology for both supplemental and sole-source lighting for urban agriculture.

Heating

Conventional greenhouses are heated primarily to counteract heat loss during winter nights. Passive strategies such as energy curtains help reduce supplemental heating requirements. To determine the feasibility of supplemental heating, it is critical to consider the investment required for implementation, the operating cost, and the carbon footprint of the energy source. Energy sources range from fossil fuels to alternative heating with biomass to the recovery of waste heat from buildings and industry. Alternative sources have often been dismissed in conventional greenhouse operations but are more widely available for greenhouses operated in cities. The heat island effect in cities lowers the heating demand in general. The use of passive solar greenhouses (see Catalog 4) will eliminate the need for heating almost entirely and should therefore receive primary consideration.

Carbon Dioxide Fertilization

CO_2 fertilization is a standard practice used in commercial greenhouse operations to increase crop yields. Conventionally, growers increase the CO_2 concentration in greenhouses by releasing compressed food-grade CO_2 from tanks or by burning natural or propane gas. It is counterproductive to burn fossil fuel for CO_2 fertilization while sustainability goals require increased CO_2 sequestration. Very rarely, controlled flue gases are discharged into greenhouses. This is an excellent practice to increase synergies between building exhausts and CO_2 supplementation and should be more widely implemented. The main concern for food production is that flue gas may contain potentially hazardous chemicals. Methods for purification, which guarantee food safety, require further study.

Symbiosis through Cogeneration Technology

Supplemental lighting, heat, and CO_2 fertilization are co-dependent. Increased light intensity in greenhouses leads to higher rates of photosynthesis, which can only be maintained through CO_2 fertilization. This biochemical process also requires constant minimum temperatures. If well coordinated, supplementation increases crop yields significantly. Cogeneration technology connects all three supplemental systems and leads to more sustainable and efficient energy production. The principle is simple: a cogeneration engine powered by natural gas produces heat and electricity. The heat warms the greenhouse while the electricity is used for supplemental lighting or fed into the grid. The exhaust of the gas engine is purified and used for CO_2 fertilization in the greenhouse. The Plant in Chicago uses this technology in the most integrated way demonstrated to date (see Case Study 9). Instead of burning natural gas, The Plant produces its own biogas in an anaerobic digester, thus reducing its carbon footprint even further.

DESIGN CONSIDERATIONS

Growing crops in urban environments has several energetic advantages, including the use of passive solar and excess energy from buildings. The urban heat island effect extends the length of the growing season for outdoor growing and reduces the need for heating when greenhouses are operated in cities instead of rural areas. Passive strategies that increase the gain of solar radiation and prevent heat loss at night reduce the energy consumption even further. Urban density encourages the reuse of "waste" energy emitted by buildings. BIA projects are poised to take advantage of excess heat and exhaust air to supplement CO_2 and exploit synergies with building systems and the urban environment.

While urban agriculture requires energy to construct viable growing systems in cities—for example, healthy soil, constructed grounds, containers, and recirculating hydroponic systems—it also exerts a positive effect on the carbon cycle. The additional CO_2 sequestration generated through large soil volumes and amendments, as well as the biomass produced, is beneficial in cities where CO_2 concentrations are high. It is therefore important for designers to consider the energy balance and carbon cycle effects of each urban agriculture project. The analysis of energy inputs and outputs follows the concept of life-cycle assessments, including the energy expended for construction, operation, and distribution as well as biomass or calories generated through the plant material.

Energy Balance of Growing Systems

Healthy soil-based outdoor operations are passive systems that retain and generate resources such as nutrients, carbon, water, and heat with little additional input. The output largely depends on the farmer's ability to manage these natural systems. Green roofs can also fall under this category.

Rooftop greenhouses allow urban farmers to use water-efficient growing methods in controlled indoor environments and to produce large amounts of vegetables all year round. While primarily powered by solar energy, rooftop farms also require supplemental lighting and heating for year-round operation. Indoor growing depends on systems that artificially provide and control all growing resources. Lights, pumps, fans, and cooling aggregates are all powered with electricity. Such a farm can thus be costly to operate and have a large carbon footprint.

Despite their high productivity, CEA operations in northern latitudes typically result in a carbon footprint that needs to be carefully weighed against other options. Growing tomatoes in northern latitudes in conventional greenhouses takes about twelve times as much energy as producing field-grown tomatoes. Shipping field-grown tomatoes from warmer regions, meanwhile, takes only about three to six times more energy.[16] The increased energy efficiency of BIA and the necessary infrastructures and a growing demand for fresh, local vegetables in cities have, however, started to shift the balance in favor of local CEAs.[17] While a few hydroponic farms have reached economic feasibility (see Case Studies 6, 10, and 11), most farms do not disclose their energy needs and sources. Therefore their carbon footprint might still be in contradiction with the generally shared environmental ethics of the urban agricultural movement.

CATALOG 4: GREENHOUSE TYPOLOGIES

The primary purpose of a greenhouse is to protect crops from adverse weather, including extreme temperatures, severe winds, and excessive precipitation. The underlying principle is simple: a translucent cover transmits sunlight and the greenhouse absorbs this energy and reradiates it as longer-wave infrared energy to warm the air in the greenhouse interior. The translucent cover prevents the heat from leaving the interior.

In addition to ensuring the transmission of sunlight to heat the growing space, the design of a greenhouse needs to safeguard the transmission of PAR, which lies within the visible spectrum of sunlight. The higher the transmission rate of the cover material and the smaller the shading caused by the greenhouse structure, the better. The thermal mass in a greenhouse increases the warming effect: thermal mass can be provided by the ground, concrete floors, masonry walls, water tanks, and potentially the host building. The more solar energy that is captured and absorbed, the more heat can be reradiated during cloudy intervals and colder nights.

Three fundamental greenhouse typologies are discussed below: low-tech, high-tech, and passive solar (Figure 3.10). For each typology, the two most critical performance factors are the structure's orientation relative to the sun and the type of glazing material installed. Any greenhouse needs to be oriented to maximize its solar gain. To support winter farming and year-round production in northern latitudes, the orientation of the greenhouse needs to maximize light interception during the winter months. Urban site constraints often make it impossible to orient a greenhouse due south. If site obstructions or the orientation of the host building require a different alignment, derivation from true south by 15–20 degrees will still provide 90% of the maximal solar capture.

Greenhouse Typologies in Urban Agriculture

The wide variety of greenhouse construction types parallels the spectrum of urban agricultural operations, ranging from low-tech to high-tech growing and from soil-based to hydroponic. Consequently, the construction methods used to amend these growing environments vary from simple, low-tech structures that solely capture solar radiation to high-tech, controlled growing environments that regulate most growing factors via computerized controls. In addition to these two commonly used approaches, a growing number of alternative greenhouse construction methods have been implemented or are under development for urban agricultural operations.

Passive solar greenhouses are an interesting alternative typology intended to foster more sustainable energy performance. Their energy use is much more efficient than that of a low-tech greenhouse, and their requirements for energy and fossil fuel inputs are greatly diminished when compared to high-tech greenhouses. Other greenhouses experiment with alternative lightweight construction methods: air-supported or pneumatic greenhouses are examples. These

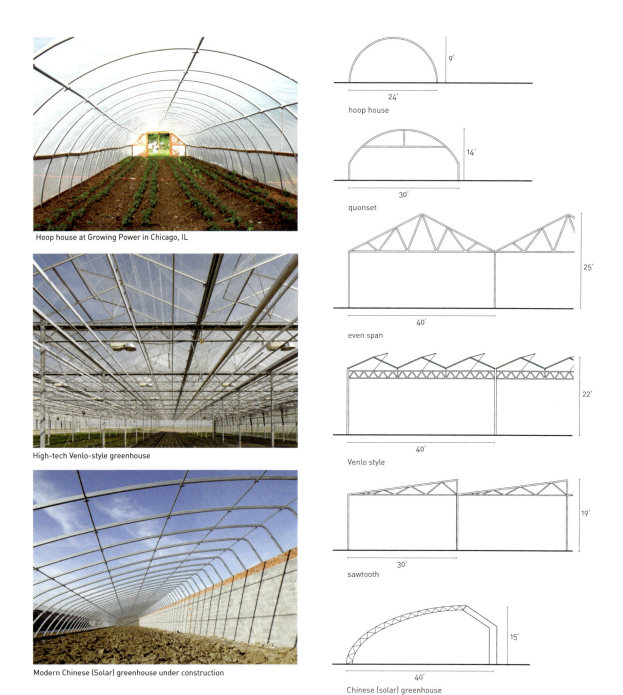

▲ Figure 3.10

Greenhouse typologies: low-tech, high-tech and Chinese (solar) greenhouse

approaches allow for mobility and large, column-free spaces. Other proposals further integrate growing technologies with buildings, such as vertical greenhouses included in façade systems. Outstanding examples of greenhouse technology will be discussed in the case studies at the end of this chapter.

Low-Tech Greenhouses
Any construction with a transparent enclosure that captures solar energy to create favorable growing conditions can be considered a low-tech greenhouse. The most common type is the hoop house, also known as a polytunnel, polyhouse, or high tunnel. Hoop houses are simple, inexpensive, easily installed, and fully accessible greenhouses. Cold frames are smaller in scale and even easier to install: these low, simple structures cover only one growing bed at a time. Farmers access the crops and service the growing beds by lifting the transparent enclosure.

Many ground-based urban agriculture farms include one or more hoop houses as an energy-efficient way to extend their growing operation into the shoulder season or year-round. Hoop houses are used to germinate seedlings, produce starts in early spring, or expand produce variety to include sensitive specialty crops that otherwise would not grow in that location. A prolonged growing season is especially beneficial in regions with long winters and a short growing season, as it lengthens the timeframe for the production and marketing of local produce.

The construction of hoop houses is simple and inexpensive; the structure that supports the hoop or tunnel is composed of a series of bow frames made of metal or plastic (PVC) pipes, covered with one or two layers of polyethylene (PE) film. In an array, hoop houses remain detached with enough distance between them (usually equivalent to twice the height) to prevent shadows and snow build-up, which would compromise their stability. Hoop houses use only solar energy to modify the growing climate. They use no additional heating, except in rare cases where alternative heat sources such as livestock or compost piles keep the temperature in the hoop house well above freezing, as demonstrated by Growing Power's operations in the Upper Midwest (see Case Study 7).

The cover material is the weak point of this typology; typical PE film has to be replaced after one or two years. High-quality PE film, improved through UV inhibitors, anti-condensate coating, and IR barriers, offers increased performance and doubles the longevity but also increases the cost. Still, the relatively inexpensive construction costs of hoop houses make them widely accessible (Figure 3.11). The USDA High Tunnel Initiative, a pilot project that tests the environmental benefits of hoop houses in real-world situations, established a cost of four dollars per square foot for the construction of hoop houses, including material and labor.

High-Tech Greenhouses
High-tech greenhouses, at the other end of the technology spectrum, are engineered to create fully regulated growing environments for controlled-environment agriculture (CEA) operations. "High-tech" here refers to the level of

COMPARISON: GREENHOUSE TYPOLOGIES

	support structure	cover materials	growing method	energy input	expected yields/year (kg/m²)	investment costs ($/m²)
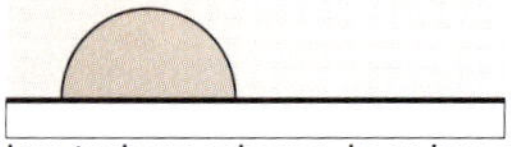 low-tech greenhouse, hoop house (Growing Power)	metal pipe or PV pipe, wood	single layer of PE film	soil-based with drip irrigation (manual)	solar radiation, compost, passive cooling	10-20 kg/m² 45-90 tons/acre tomatoes	25-30
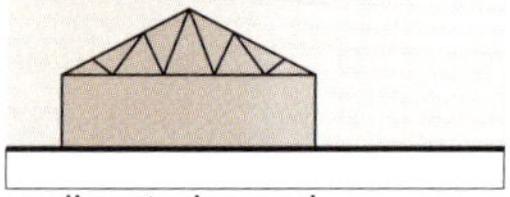 medium-tech greenhouse	steel frame	double PE film or rigid plastic	soil-based or hydroponic with drip irrigation	solar radiation, passive + active controls (fans + vents) with or without heating	20-50 kg/m² 90-225 tons/acre tomatoes	30-100
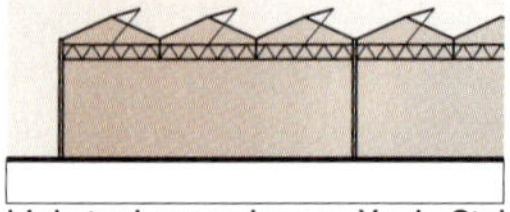 high-tech greenhouse, Venlo Style	steel frame or aluminum frame	glass, polyethylene, polycarbonate	recirculating hydroponics, high wire aggregate drip culture and NFT	solar radiation, forced ventilation, evaporative cooling, heating, CO_2 fertilization, energy curtains	50-70 kg/m² tomatoes, up to 80 kg/m² lettuce (225-360 tons/acre)	150-300 and more
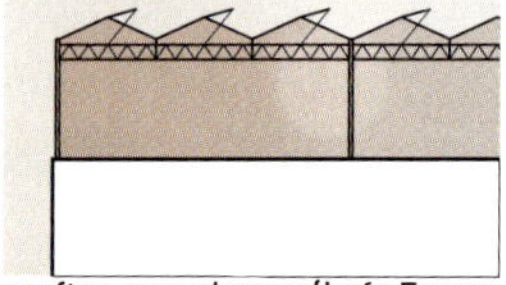 rooftop greenhouse (Lufa Farms, Gotham Greens)	steel frame or aluminum frame	glass	recirculating hydroponics, high wire aggregate drip culture and NFT	solar radiation, forced ventilation, evaporative cooling, heating, CO_2 fertilization, energy curtains	50-70 kg/m² tomatoes, up to 80 kg/m² lettuce (225-360 tons/acre)	300-500
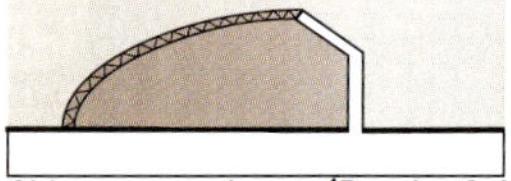 Chinese greenhouse (Passive Solar Greenhouse)	steel trussed (low tech: bamboo)	single layer of PE film	soil based	solar radiation, thermal blanket	30 kg/m² 135 tons/acre all vegetables	25-30 (steel) 6-10 (bamboo)
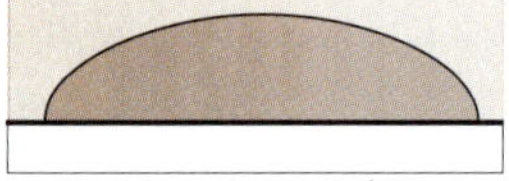 pneumatic greenhouse (Granpa Domes)	fan to create positive pressure	ETFE film	recirculating hydropnic raft culture	solar radiation, forced ventilation, heating + cooling through fans, vents + misters	30 kg/m² 135 tons/acre lettuce	600

technology required for the control systems used in the greenhouse to optimize plant growth and maximize productivity and crop quality. Almost exclusively, these greenhouses rely on recirculating hydroponic systems. Automated control systems regulate temperature, irrigation, nutrient concentration, shading, lighting, and CO_2 supplementation.

Typical high-tech greenhouses are steel or aluminum structures, often erected as large horizontal arrays. In these multi-bay, gutter-connected (or ridge and furor) constructions, the greenhouses share common rows of support structures on their interior, which creates large floor areas with a proportionally small exterior envelope. The improved ratio between floor area and exterior walls improves the environmental performance of the greenhouses.

▲ Figure 3.11

Comparison: greenhouse typologies

Data adapted from Gene Giacomelli, "Designing the Greenhouse to Meet Your Expectations: What's Your Technology Level?," Controlled Environment Agriculture Center CEAC, University of Arizona, Tucson, http://ceac.arizona.edu/.

In urban agriculture, high-tech greenhouses are primarily used for hydroponic rooftop farms. These farms utilize underused urban rooftop space that receives consistently ample sunlight. The first hydroponic rooftop farms were built in large cities with temperate climates and cold winters. For more details, see Lufa Farms in Montréal (Case Study 10) and Gotham Greens in New York (Case Study 11).

The gutter-connected greenhouse types are differentiated by their roof forms. These include even-span roofs with two slopes of equal pitch and equal length; Venlo-style greenhouses, whose low-profile roofs have small pitch angles and ridge ventilation; and uneven span or mono-pitch roofs connected into a multi-span, sawtooth design. The last are good for high-latitude locations, allowing low light angles to enter the growing space. In general, the smaller the pitch angle, the smaller the roof area and greenhouse volume, which reduces heating costs. Most of these greenhouses use flat, tubular, or angle steel to form their trusses. The material determines the width of the greenhouse bay—for example, steel pipe frames can span up to 40 feet (12m). High-tech greenhouses are preferably covered with glass or rigid plastic sheets. Depending on the control systems included, construction costs of high-tech greenhouses range from \$15–25/ft^2 (\$160–270/m^2).[18] When constructed on rooftops, they are much more expensive, with costs increasing to \$35–45/ft^2 (\$375–485/m^2).[19]

Passive Solar Greenhouses
All greenhouses collect solar energy. Solar greenhouses, however, are conceived to be heated solely by solar energy. Substantial thermal mass in solar greenhouses stores solar energy in the form of heat that is reradiated during cloudy periods, at night, and even during the winter months. The first widespread interest in alternative energy—and hence solar greenhouses—was during the first oil crisis in the 1970s. Despite a few publications, individual initiatives, and prototypes, however, this form of greenhouse did not establish itself in the United States and Europe. In China, however, the development of solar greenhouses began in the late 1970s and has been very successful ever since. Single-slope, energy-efficient solar greenhouses cover 1.83 million acres (0.74 million hectares) in China, almost 75 times the area of high-tech greenhouses in the Netherlands (Figure 3.12). They are primarily located north of the Huai River and in the larger region around Beijing, between 32 and 43 degrees northern latitude.[20]

Solar greenhouses are characterized by a transparent, south-facing arched wall and roof as well as a massive, insulated wall and partial roof on the north side. The northern wall acts as a thermal mass to absorb solar energy during the day and reradiate it into the greenhouse at night. Arched trusses span from the peak of the roof to the ground and are clad with a single layer of transparent film. To retain more heat in the interior at night, the southern face can be covered with an insulation blanket.[21]

Solar energy is the only source of light and heat for crop production in these greenhouses. The exposure to the sun determines the light conditions inside the greenhouse, which vary according to the season, latitude, greenhouse structure, quality and aging of the plastic film, and duration of daylight

◀ Figure 3.12

Chinese greenhouse

hours. In northern latitudes, low light intensities and temperatures during the winter months are usually the limiting factors. Regardless, the interior temperature of solar greenhouses can usually be maintained at above 61°F (16°C), while low outside air temperatures typically vary between -3 and -4°F (-16 to -20°C) in some regions of China during the winter months.

Given their relatively low construction cost, passive solar energy utilization, and low CO_2 emissions, solar greenhouses would be a good alternative for urban agriculture in northern latitudes. The urban agricultural movement would provide a second chance to establish passive solar greenhouses in Western countries. Their success in China, together with the interest in sustainable operation, creates a strong argument for this typology. To date, though, only a few solar greenhouses have been built in Europe or the United States. The Aquaponic Solar Greenhouse of Energy Biosphere Food (EBF) in Germany (Case Study 1) is a remarkable example of the development potential of this typology.

CATALOG 5: GREENHOUSE COVER MATERIALS

The selection process for the cover material for an urban greenhouse is complex. Architects have to consider the code requirements for the intended application, the goals and budget of the project, and the performance of the cover material. To evaluate the material performance and its suitability for an urban agricultural project, several factors need to be considered, including the transmission of solar radiation, heat transfer resistance or insulation value, structural characteristics, weight, and longevity.

The transmission of photosynthetic active radiation (PAR) is of primary interest. Ultraviolet radiation (UV), with shorter wavelength (smaller than 400 nanometers) and higher energy content, might be undesirable in areas with high infestation pressure of certain virus-vectoring insects. Reducing the UV transmission supports the pest management.[22] Infrared radiation (IR), with a longer wavelength (greater than 700 nanometers) and reduced energy content, is desirable because it regulates the growth and flowering of plants. Too much IR, however, can be harmful because it creates heat stress.

The heat transfer resistance or insulation value (R-value) of a cover material determines the ability of a greenhouse to retain heat. The higher the R-value of a construction material, the better the material resists energy transfer.

Structural characteristics of the glazing materials determine the support member spacing (trusses and purlins), which also has an effect on the PAR transmission. Less structure means less obstruction and shading, resulting in a higher light transmission. The weight of the cover material affects the design of the support member and is an important aspect to consider in building integration (Figure 3.13). Material costs and expected lifespans are also critical criteria for the realization of greenhouses. Materials with long lifespans are more sustainable, while materials with less longevity require more frequent replacement. In this case, the material and labor costs need to be multiplied by the number of replacements required.

Glass

Until the 1950s, glass was the only option for greenhouse glazing and is still the traditional greenhouse cover material. It offers very high PAR transmission rates and one of the longest life spans, at more than 30 years. Its disadvantages are shorter spans and more substantial support members required because of its weight. These reduce potential light transmission by casting shadows. Tempered or laminated glass is stronger and requires fewer support structures. Low-iron glass has a higher light transmission, up to 92%. Higher-quality glass improves the performance even further, but it is also more expensive. Insulated glazing units are heavier and require more structure, but their thermal performance is more than three times better than single glazing, which has a small insulation value. The material itself as well as the necessary structure and installation are relatively expensive. Glass is currently seen as the material best suited for building integration and is often required by code to comply with fire-safety regulations.

COMPARISON: COVER MATERIALS

		radiation transmission			insulation value R-value	support member spacing	weight	expected lifespan
		UV (280-400nm)	PAR (400-700nm)	infrared (700-1000nm)	(ft²°Fh/Btu)/(m² K/W)	(ft/m)	(lbs/ft² and kg/m²)	(years)
GLASS								
glass, single layer	float glass, 6mm	70%	89%	<3%	1.0 / 0.17	2' - 3'3" / 0.60 - 1.00 m	3.0 lbs / 15 kg	30+ years
glass, double layer	2 layers float glass, 6mm	48%	78%	<3%	2.0 / 0.33	2' - 3'3" / 0.60 - 1.00 m	6.0 lbs / 30 kg	30+ years
RIGID PLASTIC								
acrylic panel (PMMA)	16mm twin wall	44%	82%	<3%	2.3 / 0.4	4' / 1.20 m	0.9 lbs / 4.4 kg	15-30 years
polycarbonate panel (PC)	16mm triple wall	<3%	70%	<3%	2.4 / 0.44	4' - 6' / 1.20 - 1.80 m	0.55 lbs / 2.7 kg	10-15 years
glass fiber reinforced plastic (GRP)	0.05"/ 1.3mm	0-10%	86%	12%	0.8 / 0.15	2' - 4' / 0.60 - 1.20 m	0.4 lbs / 2.0 kg	10 years
FILMS								
polyethylene film (PE), single layer	PE film, 6 mil / 150 μm	3-60%	85-88%	50%	0.8 / 0.14	4' / 1.20 m	0.1 lbs / 0.5 kg	1 - 2 years (without coating) 3 - 5 years (with coating)
ETFE film, single layer	ETFE, 100 μm	70%	95%	95%	1.0 / 0.17	up to 8' / 2.50 m	0.07 lbs / 0.34 kg	30+ years
ETFE film, triple layer	ETFE, 3 x 100 μm installed in pillows, ca. 2.5 m	34%	83%	85%	3.0 / 0.5	up to 8' / 2.50 m	0.21 lbs / 1.0 kg	30+ years

◄ Figure 3.13

Comparison: greenhouse cover materials

Data adapted from Johannes F. J. Max, Ulrich Schurr, Hans-Jürgen Tantau, Urbanus N. Mutwiwa, Thomas Hofmann, and Andreas Ulbrich. "Greenhouse Cover Technology" in Horticultural Reviews, Vol. 40, (2012): 259-397.

Rigid Plastic

Rigid plastic panels such as acrylic, polycarbonate, and fiberglass-reinforced plastic offer an alternative to glass. The PAR transmission rates for these materials are almost as good as those for glass, though they decrease over time due to aging and yellowing caused by UV radiation. Plastic panels are much lighter than glass and require fewer structural support members, which increases their relative performance. Since they are often manufactured as twin- or triple-wall sheets, their heat transfer resistance is also higher, with enclosed air space acting as an insulator. But rigid plastic panels, though less expensive than glass, often cannot be integrated into buildings due to code regulations that restrict their use because of high flammability.

Films

Polyethylene plastic film is usually considered to be the cheap alternative to more durable covering materials. The PAR transmission, however, deteriorates rapidly through exposure to UV radiation so that regular film lasts only one to two years. Treatment with UV inhibitors increases longevity to three to four years, and other special coatings further improve performance. Additionally, anti-condensate coating prevents condensation droplets and improves light transmission. It also prevents the dripping of condensate on crops by channeling the condensate water off to the side. An IR barrier prevents the reradiation of IR out of the greenhouse (at night) to prevent heat loss. The application of two layers of PE film with an inflated air space of approximately 4 inches (10 cm) as insulator improves the heat retention significantly. PE film is extremely light and requires a minimal structural system, and the material cost is very low. Due to the need for frequent replacement, however, the cost over a 30-year period increases, primarily because of labor costs.

There is one film with exceptional performance. Ethylene tetrafluoroethylene (ETFE) film offers high-performance characteristics equivalent to or higher than those of glass. The PAR transmission of ETFE film is 93–95%, which means it transmits the full solar spectrum through its UV transparency. This guarantees better growing results and higher productivity. ETFE film is lightweight and has a high tensile strength, which helps minimize the structure of the greenhouse, resulting in more light exposure and greater crop productivity. Lightly tensioned ETFE film spans up to 8 feet (2.5 meters) between light lattice girders. Additional material properties of ETFE include UV stability, longevity, mechanical strength, robustness, anti-adhesion, self-cleaning properties, and non-flammability, all contributing to a material lifespan of over 30 years (equal to that of glass). These properties make ETFE an ideal greenhouse cover material, with a cost similar to that of glass.

CATALOG 6: LIGHTING TECHNOLOGIES

Controlled-environment agriculture (CEA) uses electrical lighting for two distinct applications—supplemental lighting in greenhouses, which amends the naturally available sunlight, and sole-source lighting in enclosed controlled indoor environments, which entirely substitutes sunlight. Supplemental lighting in greenhouses is most beneficial in northern latitudes with overcast skies that receive less than 4.5 hours of sunshine per day during the winter months. Technically, the accumulated amount of PAR a plant receives is measured as the daily light integral (DLI)—the amount of light (expressed in number of photons) received in a particular area. The naturally occurring outdoor DLI in the United States ranges from 5–60 moles per square meter per day (mol/m^2/day) in summer to 1–30 mol/m^2/day in winter. For plants in greenhouses, only 35–75% of this light is available due to transmission losses and structural obstructions.[23]

Vegetable crops require more light than other kinds of plants to thrive: lettuces need a minimum of 12 mol/m2/day, while vine crops need at least 15 and preferably more than 20 mol/m2/day.[24] The amount and quality of supplemental lighting needed depends primarily on the geographic location and the naturally available daylight. Attaining sufficiently high DLIs for crop production in northern latitudes requires high-intensity lighting at least from October until February. Supplemental lighting in southern latitudes is less critical, though it will increase crop production during the winter months. The long-term feasibility of supplemental and sole-source lighting depends primarily on the local cost for electricity and its energy source, which defines its environmental footprint. In 2014, the cost of electricity for the commercial sector in the United States ranged from 7.85 cents/kWh in Washington State (primarily hydroelectric) to 18.22 cents/kWh in California (primarily natural gas) and 34.74 cents/kWh in Hawaii (primarily petroleum).[25]

For both supplemental and sole-source lighting, a range of technologies are available (Figure 3.14). In general, the following criteria need to be taken into consideration to select the appropriate light source: spectral light quality, light intensity, PAR efficiency, energy consumption, heat production, placement options and distance from plants, life span, and life cycle cost.

Fluorescent

The recent development of T5 linear fluorescents and compact fluorescent lights (CFL) provides a worthy alternative to other types of greenhouse lights. The new fluorescents offer three times the light intensity of traditional fluorescent fixtures with relatively low energy consumption. An electrical current in mercury vapor generates ultraviolet light, which causes the fluorescent coating inside the tube to glow. Their low heat emission allows these lamps to be placed very close to plants, which helps to compensate for their still comparatively low intensity. The tubes and bulbs are available in a cool spectrum (6500 K) supporting vegetative growth and a warm spectrum (3000 K) for flowering and fruiting. They can be combined to generate a more complete color spectrum or used at different times in the growing cycle.

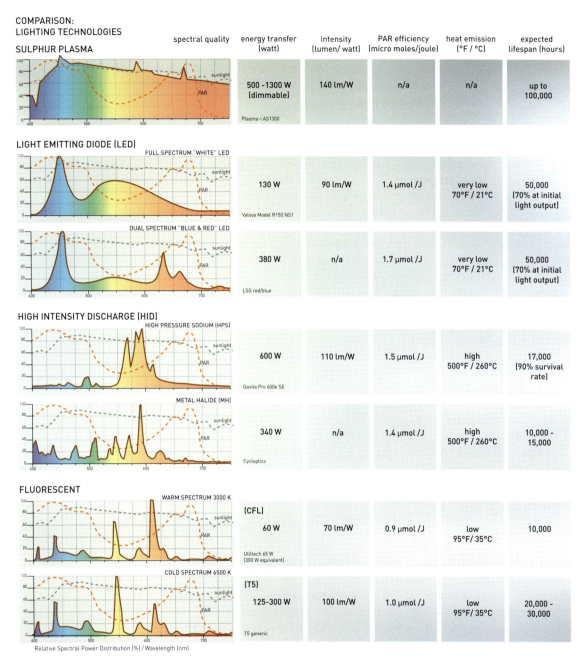

▲ Figure 3.14

Comparison: greenhouse lighting technologies

Data adapted from C. Wallace and A.J. Both, "Evaluating operating characteristics of light sources for horticultural applications." *Acta Horticulturae*. 1134 (2016): 435-444; Jacob A. Nelson and Bruce Bugbee. "Economic Analysis of Greenhouse Lighting: Light Emitting Diodes vs. High Intensity Discharge Fixtures." *PLoS One 9*, no. 6 (2014); Plasma International Lighting Systems, www.plasma-i.com/index.html.

High-Intensity Discharge (HID)

Overhead high-intensity discharge (HID) lamps are still the current standard in greenhouse supplemental lighting because of their high-intensity broad-spectrum light emission. They operate similarly to fluorescent lights by introducing an electrical arc into an elemental gas mixture contained in a clear quartz tube. Different combinations of gases and metal salts are available depending on the type of HID.

High-pressure sodium (HPS) is the most commonly used technology for high-intensity lighting for commercial vegetable production in greenhouses. HPS lamps produce light in the orange-red spectrum, which supports flowering and fruiting in plants. The lamps are available in 300-, 400-, 600-, and 1000-watt (W) sizes. The 600-W size is the most frequently used, with an efficiency of 110 lumens per watt (lm/W) and a high PAR efficiency. The lamps and fixtures are relatively inexpensive. However, they have an inefficient conversion rate (30%) of electricity into useful light. The remaining energy is emitted as heat, which can provide 25–40% of the greenhouse heating requirements during the winter months, but is impractical for indoor growing.

Metal-halide (MH) lamps produce light in the blue spectrum (6500–7200 K), which is most beneficial for vegetative plant growth. Most fixtures allow MH and HPS lamps to be used interchangeably. MH lamps are less efficient in the conversion of electricity into useful light (20%) and are less durable than HPS lamps.

Light-Emitting Diodes (LED)

LED grow lights have become increasingly popular with the rapid development and growing affordability of this technology. They are the current standard in sole-source lighting for indoor growing operations and will be increasingly utilized for customized supplemental lighting in greenhouses. LED lamps produce light by passing an electric current through a semiconductor material. The electrons moving through the material release photons, particles carrying energy in the form of light. This technology is very energy-efficient, using up to 80% less energy than HID and 30% less energy than fluorescent technology, thus reducing energy and operation costs. LED lamps produce 90–130 lm/W and convert 80–90% of the electricity used into PAR while releasing little energy as heat in the light beam. Additional heat produced by the LED is directly conducted into a thermal pad and heat sink within the device. In turn the cool, photon emitting surfaces of LEDs allow novel placements of light fixtures—such as close-canopy overhead lighting and within-canopy lighting, which reduce the electrical energy required and the need for cooling and ventilation of the greenhouse or grow space.[26]

Leading manufacturers of LED technology—for both sole-source and supplemental lighting—offer fixtures for production with custom (but fixed) light spectra for different crops and applications, as well as fixtures with dynamic, programmable spectra based on four-channel LEDs. The latter are primarily used as "research tools" in grow labs to generate a precise spectrum of light by adjusting the balance of wavelengths. LEDs have a long lifespan of 50,000 hours (to 70% of the initial light output).[27]

Plasma

Some predict that plasma lights will be the next revolution (after LEDs) in the field of greenhouse lights. Plasma lamps generate light by activating plasma (an ionized gas) through radio frequency emissions. Currently this technology is still prohibitively expensive.

The sulfur plasma lamp is one version of this electrode-less lamp typology. Argon gas and sulfur are contained in a quartz bulb and are activated by microwaves generated by a magnetron.[28] The plasma lamp's most significant benefit is that it generates the full spectrum of sunlight and therefore effectively simulates growing with daylight. It produces intense light (140 lm/W) and demonstrates a 93% conversion rate of electricity into useful light (at full power). While not implemented in large numbers yet due to its high price, the lamp has potential, especially because of its light spectrum and its extremely long life span of 100,000 hours.

◀ Figure 3.15

Greenhouse interior with custom-made photovoltaic panels, Franz Schreier, Aquaponic Solar Greenhouse, Neuenburg am Rhein, Germany, 2015

CASE STUDY 1: AQUAPONIC SOLAR GREENHOUSE

Organization: Energy Biosphere Food GmbH
Founder/Engineer: Franz Schreier
Location: Heppenheim and Neuenburg am Rhein, Germany
Operation: prototypes in operation since early 2011
Growing System: aquaponic system in passive solar greenhouse
Growing Area: 1100 ft² (100 m²)
Growing Season: year-round growing season (with energy efficiency prioritized over productivity in the winter months, 48°–49° N latitude)
Annual Yield/Main Distribution: not yet specified

The Aquaponic Solar Greenhouse was inspired by the UN mandate for Integrated Food and Energy Systems (IFES) to counteract the fossil fuel dependence of the current food system.[29] Franz Schreier, a German physicist with substantial experience in energy management, developed this energy-integrated growing system. The greenhouse runs exclusively on passive solar energy, uses custom-made photovoltaic panels for energy transformation and shading, employs high-performance materials such as ethylene tetrafluoroethylene (ETFE) greenhouse film, and integrates other technologies to supplement available daylight. This passive solar greenhouse yields carbon-neutral produce (measured over an annual cycle) and transforms excess radiation into usable electrical and thermal energy.

Growing System and Background

The solar greenhouse operates a water- and resource-efficient recirculating aquaponics growing system. It integrates fish, plant, and microbe cultivation into an "agroecosystem." This greenhouse technology has been in development since 2006, and several prototypes have been consistently operated and monitored since 2011. The first fully functional prototype greenhouse is equipped with a fish tank and a 15-m^3 circulation system that houses 20 Russian sturgeons. A raft culture system offers growing space for lettuce and leafy greens, and a customized drip system accommodates tomatoes and other vine crops. The system loses about 1% (40 gallons or 150 liters) of the water in circulation per day to plants and evaporation. A much larger prototype (1040 ft^2/100 m^2) has recently been completed (Figure 3.18).

Solar Energy

Schreier studied plant physiology and plant science, including the light spectrum and light intensity needed by plants, and has invested in pioneering greenhouse technologies to develop his innovative integrated food and energy system. All innovations revolve around different cutting-edge uses of solar energy: (1) the greenhouse runs exclusively on solar energy; (2) it maximizes light transmission through its ETFE film enclosure; (3) it transforms excess solar radiation into electrical energy through custom-made PV panels; (4) it makes the most effective light spectrum for photosynthesis available through wavelength conversion; and (5) it uses sulfur plasma lamps, a very energy-efficient and energy-effective supplemental light source.

Passive Solar Energy

The greenhouse design is adapted from the Chinese passive solar greenhouse typology—heated solely by the sun—in order to create a controlled environment with the minimum heating and cooling loads necessary to extend the

◂ Figure 3.16

Construction of second prototype, Franz Schreier, Aquaponic Solar Greenhouse, Heppenheim, Germany, 2014

growing season. The ETFE film-covered, south-facing wall and roof of the greenhouse capture daylight and solar energy (Figure 3.17). The northern wall and two short sidewalls act as thermal mass. Schreier's system functions to -4°F (-20°C) and maintains an internal temperature of 43°F (6°C).

The aquaponic system also lowers the greenhouse's heating and cooling loads and energy demands. The fish tanks provide additional thermal mass, which buffers temperature swings in the greenhouse (Figure 3.18). The joint fish and plant cultivation recycles nutrients and creates a closed carbon cycle: CO_2

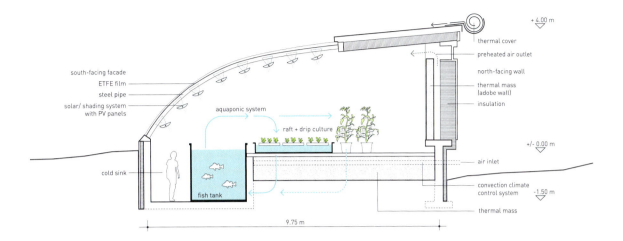

▲ Figure 3.17

Diagrammatic building section, the Aquaponic Solar Greenhouse

exhaust from the fish and O_2 production from the plants balance each other and reduce the need for ventilation, which would bring cold air into the greenhouse during the winter.

Maximum Light Transmission

The Aquaponic Solar Greenhouse uses ETFE film to maximize the transmission of the full spectrum of sunlight, as indicated by its PAR transmission rate of 93–95%. This guarantees good growing results and high productivity. ETFE film also has a high tensile strength; in the prototype greenhouse it spans 8 feet (2.5 meters) between girders. ETFE's capacity to span long distances minimizes the

▼ Figure 3.18

Greenhouse interior with growing beds and covered fish tanks, Franz Schreier, the Aquaponic Solar Greenhouse, Neuenburg am Rhein, Germany, 2015

amount of supporting structure needed and maximizes the light-transmitting surface area of the greenhouse. Less structure means less shading and more light reaching the plants. Additionally, ETFE's light weight, UV transparency, UV stability, longevity, mechanical strength, robustness, anti-adhesive quality, self-cleaning nature, and non-flammability make it an ideal greenhouse cover material.

Transforming Excess Solar Energy into Electrical Energy

The solar greenhouse operates on the rule of thumb that plants require a minimum of 250–300 W/m^2 of solar energy. On clear days, the sun provides up to 1000 W/m^2. Studies have shown that too much light inhibits plant growth; therefore greenhouses have shading systems, operated when light levels exceed 600W/m^2. The integrated PV system of the solar greenhouse transforms solar insolation into electrical energy to power operation while also providing shade and optimal light and temperature conditions for plant growth. In total, the PV panel integrates six functions in one element:

1. The PV cells are mounted on top of the aluminum frame of a rotating panel (Figure 3.20). Each 8-ft- (2.5-meter-) long panel produces up to 100 W of electrical energy. The PV panels are wrapped in ETFE, which improves their performance in comparison to glass as cover material.

▼ Figure 3.19

Multi-functional custom-made photovoltaic panels, the Aquaponic Solar Greenhouse, Neuenburg am Rhein, Germany

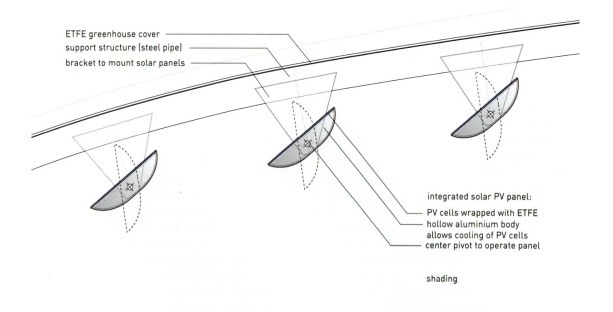

▶ Figure 3.20

Custom-made photovoltaic panel for the Aquaponic Solar Greenhouse

2. The panel cogenerates electricity and heat. The cavity in the aluminum body of the panel can extract heat, which in turn increases the productivity of the PV panels. While high-temperature PV modules (developed for use in the desert) are integrated in the panels, their output is higher when the ambient temperature is lower.
3. The extraction of heat helps cool the greenhouse, which increases plant productivity and growth on hot summer days. To increase cooling, cool air can be blown through the cavity.
4. In reverse, warm air can be blown through the hollow lamella for heating purposes. In its closed position, the panel works as an energy shield, simulating an energy curtain to retain heat within the greenhouse.
5. The operable panels serve as shading devices to block out intensive sunlight in adjustable positions relative to the sun angle. The panels have only one thin, sharp edge that reflects light. Therefore most of the light enters the greenhouse when the panels are in the open position relative to the sun angle (Figure 3.20).
6. The greenhouse produces more electrical energy than needed for its operation. The surplus is fed into the grid.

The PV panels replace several conventional systems usually included in a high-tech greenhouse, such as energy curtains, heating systems, and shading devices. This increases the value of the panels and reduces the initial cost for the greenhouse since only one system has to be installed.

Wavelength Conversion

To amplify photosynthetic activity during poor light conditions, green light is transformed into red light with wavelength conversion film. A red, transparent ETFE film hangs as curtains in the north–south direction inside the greenhouse and converts the wavelength of light that passes through it. Filled with water, the filter turns into a PAR light enhancing water wall and buffers the heating and cooling loads of the greenhouse.

Efficient Supplemental Lighting

To expand the photoperiod in northern latitudes, the solar greenhouse integrates supplemental lighting. It uses sulfur plasma lamps, which are the most powerful electrical growing lights currently available. Microwaves activate sulfur plasma until it glows and creates a spectrum approximating that of sunlight (see Catalog 6).

Strengths and Innovations

The strength of this greenhouse and growing system is its combination of low-tech passive solar strategies with high-tech technologies and materials to optimize the energy performance and increase the output of the growing system. The primary innovation of the greenhouse is the multifunctional PV panel system developed by Franz Schreier. It generates enough electricity to operate the entire greenhouse—even in Germany, where solar access is limited—while also operating as a shading device and providing supplemental heating and cooling. Besides this advanced use of PV panels, the greenhouse integrates several

▼ Figure 3.21

South façade of passive solar greenhouse, Franz Schreier, Aquaponic Solar Greenhouse, Neuenburg am Rhein, Germany, 2015

cutting-edge technologies, such as the application of ETFE film as a greenhouse cover, PAR light film, and sulfur plasma lamps (Figure 3.21). These technologies enhance the performance of the growing system and energy balance, but they are not essential for the operation of the outstanding passive solar and photovoltaic systems of the greenhouse.

Currently being tested in several prototypes, the strategies used in the Aquaponic Solar Greenhouse could be implemented at much larger scales. Franz Schreier continues to refine and expand this greenhouse technology. As the energy consultant for the Gemüsering, a network of German vegetable producers, he is presently working on the application of his photovoltaic integrated system for a 10-acre (4-hectare) commercial greenhouse.

The first Aquaponic Solar Greenhouse in the United States is under development in collaboration with City Farm Fish and Brooklyn Grange in the Brooklyn Navy Yard. The 1,500 ft^2 (140 m^2) facility will be constructed adjacent to Brooklyn Grange's rooftop farm on the northwest corner of the same roof. This project aims to connect carbon-neutral food production with sustainable urban fish farming in a local, financially viable business ownership that has the potential to transform urban futures.

◄ Figure 3.22

Interior of pneumatic greenhouse with circular hydroponic raft growing system, Granpa Domes, Japan

CASE STUDY 2: GRANPA DOMES

Organization: Granpa Co., Ltd.
Founder: Abe Takaaki
Location: Yokohama, Kanagawa, Japan (headquarters)
Operation: company established 2004, expanding
Growing System: hydroponic system in greenhouses, raft culture
Growing Area: 6,200 ft² (580 m²) per dome
Growing Season: year-round (35°–39° N latitude)
Annual Yield: 18 tons per dome
Main Distribution: direct-from-farm marketing

The Japanese company Granpa Co., Ltd. has developed a unique approach to hydroponic farming organized around "plant factories" in pneumatic (air-supported) circular domes, which house mechanized, rotating growing systems.[30] These facilities use space more efficiently and require less labor and fewer resources than conventional greenhouses. This inventive concept, which could be widely implemented across the globe, aims to spark the interest of Japanese youth in agriculture while tackling issues associated with climate change.

Background and Milestones

In 2004, after a 28-year career in finance, Abe Takaaki founded Granpa Co., Ltd. Operations began with hydroponic raft cultures in conventional greenhouses, which continue to be in operation. Takaaki was unhappy, however, with the labor-intensive operation of conventional greenhouses in which plants must repeatedly be manually moved to new rafts with larger spacing to give them adequate growing area. This system proved difficult to operate profitably, which led Takaaki to search for a better way to use greenhouse space and human labor. Takaaki got the idea for his innovation from the Tokyo Dome, a pneumatic baseball stadium. Its circular form effectively accommodates large crowds of people and supports a lightweight roof with minimal structure, and it inspired the domed form of the Granpa system.

Currently, Granpa operates 19 domes with more than 117,000 ft^2 (10,800 m^2) of growing area in four locations in Japan. After patenting its greenhouse system, Granpa built 56 additional domes for affiliated farms, totalling 345,500 ft^2 (32,100 m^2), and is looking to sell its technology to other farms nationally and overseas. To further disseminate this growing model, Granpa provides farmers with training programs, helps farmers secure bank loans, and aids with land leasing and crop distribution. The company's aim is to remove hurdles for young urban farmers to further develop this new approach to agriculture, and it has received support from the Japanese Ministry of Economy, Trade, and Industry to further these goals. Following the Tōhoku earthquake and tsunami in 2011, the government subsidized construction of a Granpa facility in Rikuzen Takata, which provided jobs and fresh produce to local communities recovering from the disaster.

Growing System

Each pneumatic greenhouse dome contains a circular hydroponic pool that is 66 feet (20 meters) in diameter, about 8 inches (20 cm) deep, and elevated 3 feet (1 meter) off the ground. Granpa uses a unique raft culture in which the raft is composed of a series of 250 wedge-shaped, plastic plates that are radially aligned. The large plates are supported floating above the shallow tub, which is filled with nutrient solution by a series of circular rails. Between each triangular plate segment, small, tub-like pots are suspended. These hold individual lettuce plants so that the plant's root system can access the nutrient solution

◀ Figure 3.23

Transplanting of seedlings into raft structure, Granpa Domes, Japan

(Figure 3.23). A mechanical system circulates the plates for about one hour per day, slowly rotating newly planted seedlings in a spiralling motion towards the outer edges of the pool (Figure 3.24). The circular geometry of the pool ensures more space between the plants the closer they travel towards the edge of the pool. This prevents any overcrowding of plants as they grow. Fully-grown plants arrive at the perimeter of the pool ready to be harvested. At that point, the plants are about 1 ft (30 cm) apart from each other.

The nutrient solution is carefully monitored and constantly pumped through a process of filtration, aeration, and sterilization. Computers control the solution volume, nutrient level, pH level, and temperature. A series of sensors attached to the center of the domed roof monitors the interior and exterior climate conditions and triggers computer-controlled fans, vents, and misters.

Greenhouse Structure

Currently more than 80 pneumatic greenhouse domes have been built, all clad with ETFE, a common greenhouse cover material in Japan. Like all pneumatic structures, they use the pressure of slightly compressed air for their structural integrity. Fans maintain the higher pressure, and air locks at the entrance mitigate pressure loss. Each dome is anchored to a 5-ft- (1.5-m-) high circular steel truss, which stabilizes the low sidewalls and provides ballast to hold

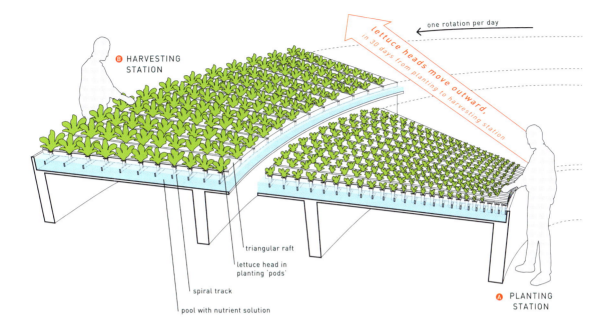

▲ Figure 3.24

Diagrammatic section through Granpa hydroponic raft growing system, Granpa Domes, Japan

the pressurized structure to the ground, effectively replacing more permanent foundations. The dome's pneumatic structure provides a 6,200-ft² (580-m²) column-free, uninterrupted space for the hydroponic pond. Additionally, the structure-free, pneumatic design of the domes reduces the interior shading to only 2%, in comparison to an average shading of at least 17% in conventional greenhouses (Figure 3.25). The ETFE cover has a very high light transmission efficiency, and its translucent finish reflects incoming light within the interior. The domes are twice as productive as conventional greenhouses while using 40% less energy.

Operation

The domes produce lettuce and leafy greens all year round. Each growing cycle from seed to harvest takes about six weeks. Seeds germinate in sterilized rooms in a separate structure. After two days, they are moved to benches along the sidewalls of the domes, where they remain for two weeks in their germination trays. Workers then transport the seedlings across a catwalk to the center of the growing pool, a 9-ft- (3-m-) wide circular cutout (Figure 3.26).

Once transferred to cylindrical pots partly suspended in the nutrient solution, the plants are automatically moved from the center of the pool outwards. This circular system requires no labor to transplant plants as they increase in size—the further they travel from the center, the more space plants have to grow. Conventional raft-based hydroponic systems, in contrast, require the rearrangement of plants several times from seed to harvest to maximize space in the greenhouse. After about 30 days, the fully grown lettuce heads arrive at the

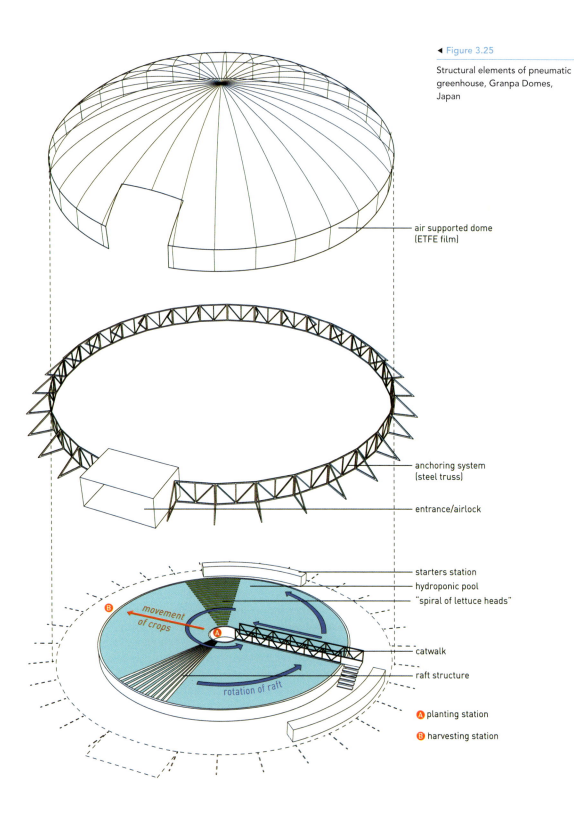

◀ Figure 3.25

Structural elements of pneumatic greenhouse, Granpa Domes, Japan

▲ Figure 3.26

Interior of pneumatic greenhouse with catwalk across raft structure, Granpa Domes, Yokohama, Japan

perimeter of the pool, where they are harvested. Lettuce heads are individually packaged in clear plastic bags for retail and distributed by Granpa. Each dome produces 400–450 heads of lettuce per day, or 18.1 tons per year. Up to 15,000 heads of lettuce at various stages of growth can occupy a single dome.

Strengths and Innovations

The strength of the Granpa domes is the powerful design synergy between their pneumatic greenhouse structure and their circular, partly automated hydroponic system. The operation makes excellent use of the column-free space provided by the air-supported greenhouse structure (Figure 3.27). The growing system, in turn, brilliantly utilizes the circular geometry of the nutrient solution pool to accommodate the expanding size of the maturing lettuce heads. The circular and automated design of the hydroponic system and the centrifugal movement of the plants are the true innovations of the system.

Currently, the pneumatic greenhouse and automated system come at a higher cost than the construction of a conventional greenhouse. In comparison to typical raft culture greenhouse systems, however, the Granpa domes outperform the standard by being twice as productive and economically viable

▲ Figure 3.27

Exterior of pneumatic greenhouse, Granpa Domes, Yokohama, Japan

through their efficient use of energy, space, and labor. This last consideration is particularly important since labor costs are a primary expense for most urban agricultural operations located in high-wage areas.

The higher weight and large footprint of the nutrient solution pool (in comparison to an NFT hydroponic system) reduce the versatility of this growing system for building integration and make installation on rooftops more difficult. But the ease of construction and the mobility of the pneumatic greenhouses are advantages, as their nimble steel structures do not require permanent foundations. This makes the Granpa domes useful for fast deployment in disaster relief, as tested in Rikuzen Takata after the Tōhoku earthquake and tsunami.

▶ Figure 3.28

Greenhouse with "A-Go-Gro" vertical growing structures, Sky Greens, Singapore

CASE STUDY 3: SKY GREENS

Organization:	Sky Greens
Founder and engineer:	Jack Ng
Location:	Singapore
Operation:	prototypes since 2009, commercial since October 2012, expanding
Growing System:	soil-based vertical farming in greenhouse; can be adapted for hydroponics
Growing Area:	over 760 growing towers (November 2015), equivalent to about 2.5 acres of horizontal growing area
Growing Season:	year-round (1° N latitude)
Yield:	up to 1 ton per day; 360 tons per year
Main Distribution:	direct-from-farm marketing to local supermarket chain

Limited landmass and high density prevent Singapore from growing most of its crops through traditional means and make it dependant on food imports. Sky Greens, Singapore's first commercial vertical farm, addresses this challenge by using an innovative A-frame structure to hold large stacks of slowly rotating growing troughs. By growing vertically and using largely renewable energies and abundant local resources, Sky Greens reduces inputs and increases production to five to seven times that of horizontal farming operations.[31] The Sky Greens model is a useful precedent for designers working in increasingly crowded, compact urban settings.

Background and Milestones

A highly urbanized city-state with a population of around 5 million and little land for crops, Singapore currently imports over 90% of its produce. However, the city-state intends to continue to increase its current domestic production to 10% of the domestic consumption. The city also has no native fresh water supplies and relies on a combination of import, recycling, desalination, and rainwater harvesting to satisfy its demand. Sky Greens is a first step towards Singapore's goal to expand domestic food production by actively supporting urban agricultural operations.

In 2009, Jack Ng, creator of Sky Greens, began testing vertical farming prototypes. The following year, he began collaborative research with the Singapore government's Agri-Food and Veterinary Authority (AVA). This partnership led to the development of the "A-Go-Gro" vertical farming system, consisting of an A-frame structure with rotating growing troughs. Honored with a Minister of National Development merit award for its unique and efficient solution to crop growth challenges, the project began commercial operation in 2012.

Growing System

"A-Go-Gro" growing towers installed in greenhouses are the key to Sky Greens' highly efficient operations. The A-frame structures carry growing troughs, which are rotated by a patented water-driven pulley system to ensure that the plants obtain uniform sunlight even though the A-frames are closely spaced. The conveyor belt that moves the troughs is fastened to the aluminum tower frame, and the A-frames are anchored to the steel structure of the greenhouse (Figure 3.29). The modular growing system is customizable in scale: Sky Greens' first towers are 20 ft (6 m) tall, while later versions measure 30 ft (9 m) (Figure 3.30). The growing towers are powered almost entirely by rainwater, an abundant but often underutilized resource in Singapore, which receives at least 6.7 inches (170 mm) of precipitation every month, or a total of 92 inches (2,340 mm) per year. The rainwater is collected from the greenhouse roofs and stored in tanks to irrigate plants and hydraulically power the pulley modules.

Sky Greens uses a soil-based system, with growing trays filled with growing medium and irrigated with rainwater. The company currently uses conventional

▶ Figure 3.29

"A-Go-Gro" vertical growing structure, axonometric diagram, Sky Greens, Singapore

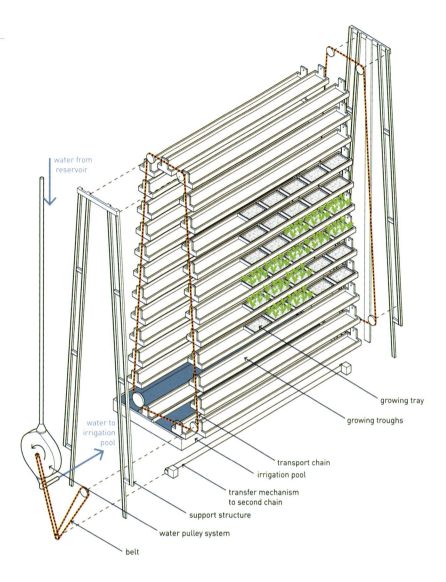

fertilizer but is experimenting with aquaponics systems as a more sustainable nutrient source. The growing troughs slowly rotate, completing between three full rotations (for the 30-foot [9-meter] towers) and four full rotations (for the 20-ft [6-m] towers) each day. When the troughs return to the base, they are dipped in a pool of water (Figure 3.31). This recirculating sub-irrigation system requires much less water than other irrigation systems.

Yield and Efficiency

The growing system is water-, energy-, and labor-efficient and easy to maintain. The amount of energy used to operate the growing towers is small in

◀ Figure 3.30

"A-Go-Gro" vertical growing tower, Sky Greens, Singapore

comparison to the energy needs of conventional farming. Due to its use of stored waterpower, the system is largely emission-free and almost independent of outside energy sources. These efficiencies ensure low production costs.

Each tower occupies an area footprint of only 58 ft² (5.4 m²) but offers a much larger growing area. The 20-ft (6-m) towers consists of 22–26 planting tiers each, equivalent to a horizontal growing area of 240 ft² (22 m²); the 30-feet (9-meter) tower consists of up to 38 tiers each, equivalent to a horizontal growing area of 370 ft² (34 m²). The towers increase the growing area by 5–7 times, achieving correspondingly higher yields than a horizontal growing system with the same footprint. Currently, Sky Greens operates 760 growing towers with a daily output of up to 1 ton of vegetables, or 360 tons per year. The company is in the process of building additional growing towers to increase production to 2 tons per day, or 720 tons per year.

Greenhouse Design

Singapore's equatorial location results in a tropical climate with an average temperature of 82°F (28°C) and high, consistent solar exposure throughout the year. Unmitigated, this tropical solar exposure is too strong for some of the vegetables

▶ Figure 3.31

"A-Go-Gro" vertical growing structure, diagrammatic section of transport and growing system, Sky Greens, Singapore

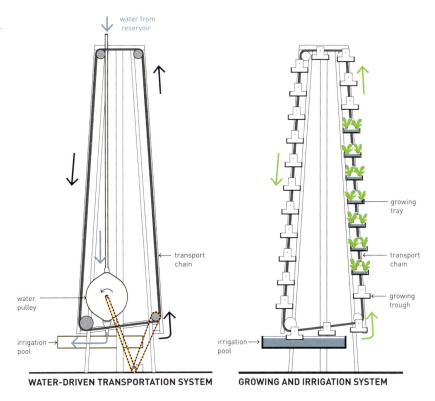

WATER-DRIVEN TRANSPORTATION SYSTEM   **GROWING AND IRRIGATION SYSTEM**

grown by Sky Greens. Translucent PVC roofing and netting on the exterior of the greenhouse structure protect the plants from sun overexposure and extreme weather during the monsoon season (Figure 3.32). Twelve-hour days throughout the year make supplemental light unnecessary. If adapted to non-equatorial climates, the reduced solar intensity and seasonal shifts of solar exposure need to be considered. Sky Green's greenhouse structures are very tall to accommodate their growing towers, and they are composed of a three-dimensional, closely spaced structural grid with each member spanning 10–13 ft (3-4 m). This steel structure not only supports the greenhouse enclosure but also provides lateral support for the A-frame growing systems (Figure 3.33).

Operation

The automated maintenance of the "A-Go-Gro" structures reduces manual labor to the transplantation of seedlings and harvesting. Seedlings are kept in a germination station for two weeks until they reach their primary growth stage. They are then transplanted into the medium-filled growing trays. Six to eight plants fit in each tray. After approximately four weeks on the "A-Go-Gro" structure, the plants are ready to be harvested. Similar to the planting process, harvesting, weighing, and packaging must be done manually to ensure a quality

▲ Figure 3.32

Greenhouse exterior, Sky Greens, Singapore

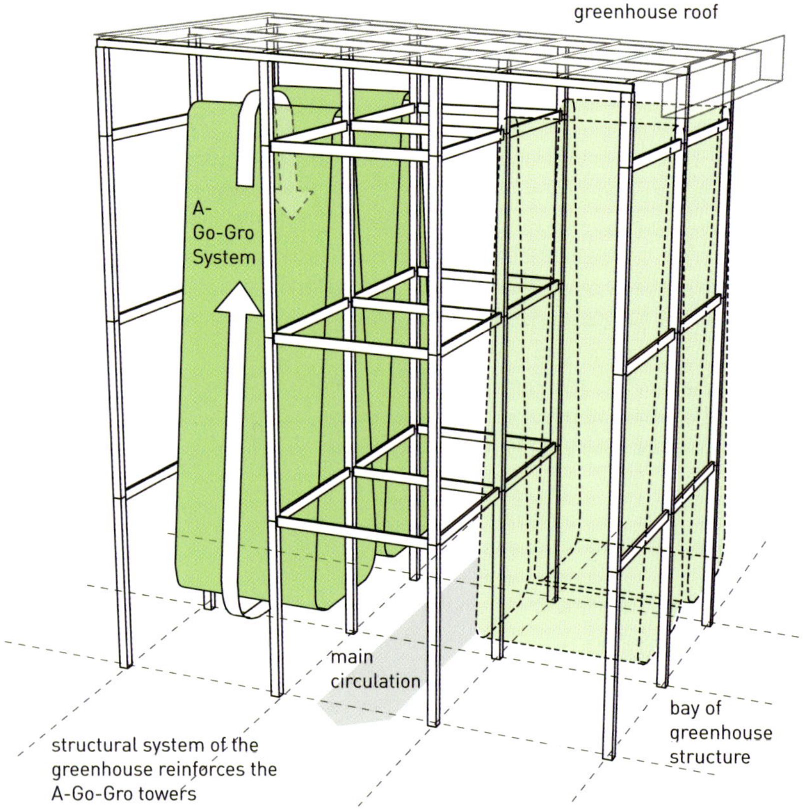

◀ Figure 3.33

Integrated structural support for greenhouse and vertical growing structure, Sky Greens, Singapore

Environmental Resources

▲ Figure 3.34

Harvesting, weighing, and packaging between "A-Go-Gro" vertical growing structures, Sky Greens, Singapore

crop reaches consumers (Figure 3.34). New trays with transplanted seedlings replace the harvested trays on the rotating troughs to start a new growing cycle. This continuous planting allows for an increased number of crop cycles and higher productivity.

Sky Greens' vegetable production focuses on leafy greens for the local market. The farm currently produces lettuce, bok choy, and Chinese cabbage. It markets this produce directly to local supermarkets chains. Imported produce remains 10% cheaper than Sky Greens' produce, but the fresh, local, and chemical-free product attracts consumers nonetheless.

Strengths and Innovations

Sky Greens tackles two major food-production challenges in Singapore. It addresses local land scarcity and food security through its vertical growing system that multiplies the available cultivation area. In response to the city-state's water scarcity issues, the vertical farm also collects rainwater as an alternative water source.

Sky Green's strong public-private partnership with the AVA illustrates how wide-reaching partnerships can lead to unique, sustainable, and profitable

Energy: Solar-Powered Photosynthesis

solutions in urban agriculture. For the government and AVA, it is a valuable demonstration project to encourage other vertical farm projects to improve Singapore's food security. Singapore's government and citizens have become more concerned with the country's sustainability and resilience. One of their priorities is to support projects that make their country less reliant on food and water imports. Additional sustainable side effects of local food production are a reduction of food miles and thus a smaller carbon footprint associated with the food supply.

Sky Greens combines an efficient growing system with a successful approach to urban agriculture. While it clearly capitalizes on local climatic and political conditions, the system would also be viable in other locations with adaptation to climate, solar exposure, and rainwater availability. The sustainable and economic uses of space, alternative energy, and water resources are essential benefits of successful urban agricultural operations.

▶ Figure 3.35

Living wall atrium and vertical rotating growing system, Vertical Harvest, Jackson, Wyoming

CASE STUDY 4: VERTICAL HARVEST

Organization:	Vertical Harvest
Cofounders:	Penny McBride and Nona Yehia
Architects:	E/Ye Design
Greenhouse Engineers:	Thomas Larssen Ltd, Denmark
Location:	Jackson, Wyoming, United States
Operation:	under development since 2009, groundbreaking December 2014, start of operation early 2016
Growing System:	vertical hydroponic and high-wire farming in greenhouse
Growing Area:	approximately 9,000 ft² (840 m²) in a three-story greenhouse
Growing Season:	year-round (43° N latitude, high altitude)
Annual Yield:	100,000 lbs (50 tons) at 250 tons/acre (expected)
Main Distribution:	local restaurants, grocery stores, and directly to customers

Energy: Solar-Powered Photosynthesis

The agribusiness Vertical Harvest incorporates the principles of vertically integrated greenhouse design with other sustainable growing methods in a three-story greenhouse. The project has both commercial and social missions: while producing vegetables year-round in the extreme, high-altitude climate of Jackson, Wyoming, the farm offers training and employment to individuals with disabilities.[32] To support its dual mission, Vertical Harvest operates according to a unique financial model that offers opportunities for a socially and environmentally progressive public-private partnership.

Background and Milestones

Vertical Harvest was co-founded by sustainability consultant Penny McBride and architect Nona Yehia in 2010. E/Ye Design, Yehia's architecture firm, led the greenhouse design team for this low-profit, limited liability company (L3C). To design a productive year-round operation for Jackson's short growing season (only four months), the team worked with the expert Danish greenhouse engineering firm Larssen Ltd, which has extensive experience working in extreme climates. The greenhouse itself was manufactured by KUBO, a Dutch company selected for their track record in building complex greenhouse systems.

The project was developed and financed as a public-private partnership between the Town of Jackson and Vertical Harvest. The greenhouse is located on an empty, south-facing lot owned by the town (Figure 3.36). Measuring 30 feet by 150 feet (9 meters by 46 meters), the parcel is located next to a public parking garage. Groundbreaking took place in December of 2014, and the three-story greenhouse started successful crop cultivation and farm operations in early 2016.

Growing Systems

The vertical farm utilizes different hydroponic systems in various locations and both natural and supplemental lighting to produce a variety of crops, including tomatoes, lettuce, herbs, and microgreens. The most innovative feature is the vertical rotating growing system that stretches from the ground to the second floor of an unobstructed south-facing façade. Hydroponic gutters are connected to a vertical chain system that moves them up and down. This vertical track turns 90 degrees and creates a horizontal plane of crops on the second floor (Figure 3.37). In addition, the second floor holds the germination room and propagation tables as well as a growing area specifically for microgreens. A similar growing area is planned on the ground floor for other specialty crops. The third floor under the glassed greenhouse roof contains high-wire growing structures for tomatoes and other vine crops, which have the highest demand for daylight. The center of the three-story greenhouse is occupied by a "living wall atrium" that features the rotating growing system in a three-story-tall vertical configuration and viewing platforms on all levels, allowing visitors views into the different growing areas.

▶ Figure 3.36

(a) Site before construction; and (b) rendering of vertical greenhouse, Vertical Harvest, Jackson, Wyoming

Energy Requirements

Jackson experiences a humid continental climate with long, cold winters and short, warm summers. The high altitude of 6,237 feet (1,901 meters) exaggerates the difference between day and night temperatures—an average disparity of 35°F (20°C), with variations that can reach close to 100°F (55°C) on extreme days. These daily fluctuations, especially the cold nights, are the main energetic challenge for the greenhouses. Thomas Larssen, Vertical Harvest's greenhouse engineer, has consulted on commercial projects in similarly extreme climates in Maine, Greenland, Iceland, and Siberia. In Jackson, the team applied

Energy: Solar-Powered Photosynthesis

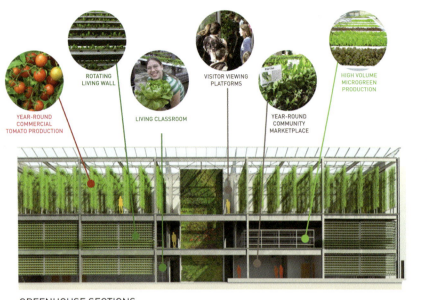

GREENHOUSE SECTIONS

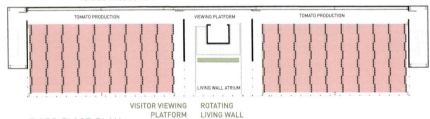

THIRD FLOOR PLAN

SECOND FLOOR PLAN

FIRST FLOOR PLAN

Environmental Resources

◀ Figure 3.37

Vertical greenhouse section and floor plans, Vertical Harvest, Jackson, Wyoming

state-of-the-art active and passive environmental control systems used in these previous projects.

Yield and Efficiency

With their diversified growing systems, Vertical Harvest anticipates producing 22 tons of tomatoes annually on approximately 4,000 ft^2 (370 m^2) of floor area, 12 tons of lettuce and herbs on vertical growing carousels, and 9 tons of microgreens and baby greens in two 1000 ft^2 (95 m^2) special grow spaces. This equals about 43 tons of production in about 9,000 ft^2 (840 m^2) of growing area (208 tons/acre). Vertical Harvest claims that this is equivalent to what can be grown on 5 acres of traditional agricultural land.

Operation

In this public-private partnership, the Town of Jackson owns the land and greenhouse. Vertical Harvest will rent the greenhouse, own the growing equipment, and operate the vertical farm. Vertical Harvest has been incorporated as a

▼ Figure 3.38

Building systems, Vertical Harvest, Jackson, Wyoming

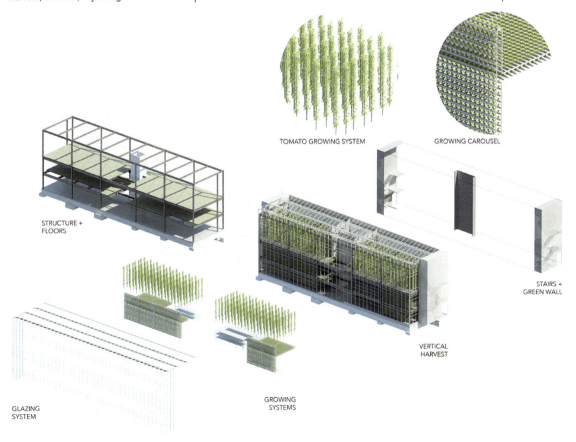

Energy: Solar-Powered Photosynthesis

low-profit, limited liability company (L3C) to address its social ambitions as well as the financial challenges of the project. This hybrid model allows a for-profit organization to pursue a charitable goal by uniting the legal and tax flexibility of a traditional LLC with the social and tax benefits of a nonprofit organization.

Collaboration with Arthur and Friends

Like many urban farms, Vertical Harvest is challenged with integrating their social mission into their operation. To achieve their goal to provide work for individuals with disabilities, Vertical Harvest has partnered with the New Jersey-based nonprofit organization, Arthur and Friends. This organization has developed training and employment opportunities in hydroponic greenhouse operations for individuals with disabilities since 2008 and shares its approach by selling the operational strategies to interested partners. Arthur and Friends helped Vertical Harvest develop its operation by making its business plan available, assisting with the hiring of management-level personnel, overseeing the installation of the growing system, and facilitating the implementation of a vocational training program. The New Jersey organization supports Vertical Harvest's efforts to build a sustainable business that offers individuals with disabilities a place to work year-round.

Distribution

Vertical Harvest sells its hydroponically grown vegetables to local restaurants, grocery stores, and at a retail store on the ground floor of the greenhouse. Due to their fundraising success, 95% of their production is already under pre-purchase agreement with local businesses and consumers.

Financing

The project's first and most important step towards realization was a $1.5 million grant from the state of Wyoming in 2012. This was followed by Vertical Harvest's successful kickstarter.com campaign, which raised $36,000 and a $300,000 loan without interest from the Town of Jackson to further integrate energy-efficient technologies. This loan was later converted into a grant. These early fundraising successes covered the entire estimated cost of the project. Since then, the anticipated construction cost has more than doubled. Public funds still covered $1.8 million; Vertical Harvest invested $500,000 for the growing equipment; and their business partners and private contributors paid the remaining amount. The primary reason for this cost increase was that the vertical greenhouse had to be constructed to meet office building standards instead of the code for agricultural structures. The building codes, safety regulations, and structural requirements are far more extensive for a three-story office building than for a one-story agricultural building.

▶ Figure 3.39

Vertical rotating growing system under construction, Vertical Harvest, Jackson, Wyoming, 2015

▶ Figure 3.40

Vertical greenhouse exterior under construction, Vertical Harvest, Jackson, Wyoming, 2015

Strengths and Innovations

Vertical Harvest is the first three-story greenhouse that operates a mechanized vertical growing system primarily based on the adaptation of existing commercial growing systems. As such, it illustrates the feasibility of vertical growing systems in BIA.

Vertical Harvest's business model combines for-profit and nonprofit organizational structures, a strategy observed in many successful urban agricultural projects. The operation realizes this through the use of the low-profit limited liability company (L3C) model, which encourages the company to have a strong social impact on the larger community. Environmentally and energetically, the vertical greenhouse is a stand-alone operation. Relying on energy-efficient and sustainable systems, it is independent of larger urban energy or waste streams.

◀ Figure 3.41

Office building with double-skin façade greenhouse, rendering, Plantagon, Linköping, Sweden

CASE STUDY 5: PLANTAGON

Organization:	Plantagon International AB
Cofounders:	SWECORP Citizenship Stockholm AB and Onondaga Nation
Architects/Engineers:	SWECO, architecture and environmental engineering
Inventor, Greenhouse System:	Åke Olsson (Sustainovation AS)
Location:	Linköping, Sweden
Operation:	organization formally founded 2008
Growing System:	hydroponic vertical greenhouse with special tray conveyer belt
Vertical Greenhouse:	4,300 ft² (400 m²) footprint
Growing Area:	approximately 48,440 ft² (4500 m²)
Growing Season:	indoor year-round (58° N latitude)
Annual Yield:	330–550 tons per 1/10 of an acre footprint
Main Distribution:	directly to customers and farmers markets

Plantagon, a Swedish organization that promotes innovation in the field of urban agriculture, has proposed an ambitious approach to vertical farming in partnership with a Swedish government initiative. Their freestanding, building-integrated vertical greenhouse proposals are designed around a patented transportation helix, which allows automated vertical movement of crops through multi-story growing spaces. The greenhouses support space-efficient, high-volume agricultural production in cities, engaging urban energy and waste streams to foster holistic and sustainable forms of urban development.[33]

Milestones

In 1985, organic farmer Åke Olsson imagined a helix-based greenhouse system. In collaboration with Plantagon, he eventually developed and patented the design. In February 2012, their first building project came to fruition with the ambitious design for an integrated double-skin façade greenhouse in Linköping, Sweden. The 17-story high-rise structure combines food production and office space.

Growing System

The core element of Plantagon's vertical hydroponic growing system is a spiraling transportation structure that slowly moves trays with leafy greens downwards in a vertical, 20-foot- (6-meter-) wide, south-facing greenhouse to provide homogeneous daylight distribution. The overall sloped façade maximizes daylight exposure.

The operations in the greenhouse are highly automated in a closely controlled environment. Germination and planting occur on the basement-level service floor, and from here trays with young plant starts are taken to the top of the helix in a freight elevator. The trays of young leafy greens travel horizontally on U-shaped tracks on each floor before a transport belt takes them down to the next floor (Figure 3.42). Three horizontal levels of plant trays correspond to one office floor; therefore the greenhouse includes three interlocking (corkscrew) transport spirals.

The growing system makes efficient use of resources. The planting trays are watered three times a day with an ebb-and-flow hydroponic system, and naturally available daylight is supplemented with electrical lighting only when necessary. Plantagon anticipates that the plants will receive 50% natural and 50% electrical lighting over the course of a year. After a growing period of approximately 30 days, the trays will return to the service floor in the basement, where the mature plants will be harvested. The trays will then be disinfected and replanted to start a new growing cycle and vertical journey through the greenhouse. Plantagon anticipates 10–11 consecutive growing cycles of leafy greens per year, producing 330–550 tons of produce annually.

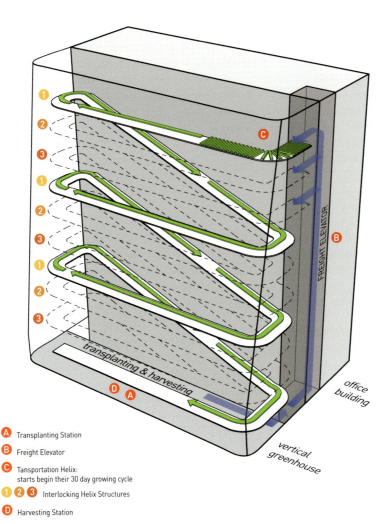

◀ Figure 3.42

Operation of the vertical greenhouse with transportation helix, Plantagon, Linköping, Sweden

Ⓐ Transplanting Station
Ⓑ Freight Elevator
Ⓒ Tansportation Helix: starts begin their 30 day growing cycle
① ② ③ Interlocking Helix Structures
Ⓓ Harvesting Station

Energy Systems

Plantagon's project in Linköping is part of a larger Swedish initiative, "SymbioCity," that promotes sustainable urban development. The greenhouse project will be connected to several large urban energy systems to improve its operational efficiency and environmental mission. It will join a network of public and private industries to promote the holistic advancement of urban development.

Plantagon calls this strategy "PlantaSymbioSystem" (Figure 3.43). The organization works directly with the local power plant, sewage treatment plant, and biogas company to create symbiotic relationships that keep energy costs and the project's carbon footprint low. Conventional commercial greenhouse projects use significant amounts of fossil fuels for heating and CO_2 fertilization. Plantagon's greenhouse will use peak waste heat from the power plant and biogas facility as a heat source, while the byproducts of these facilities—CO_2

▶ Figure 3.43

PlantaSymbioSystem, energy flows between Plantagon's vertical greenhouse and the SymbioCity, Linköping, Sweden

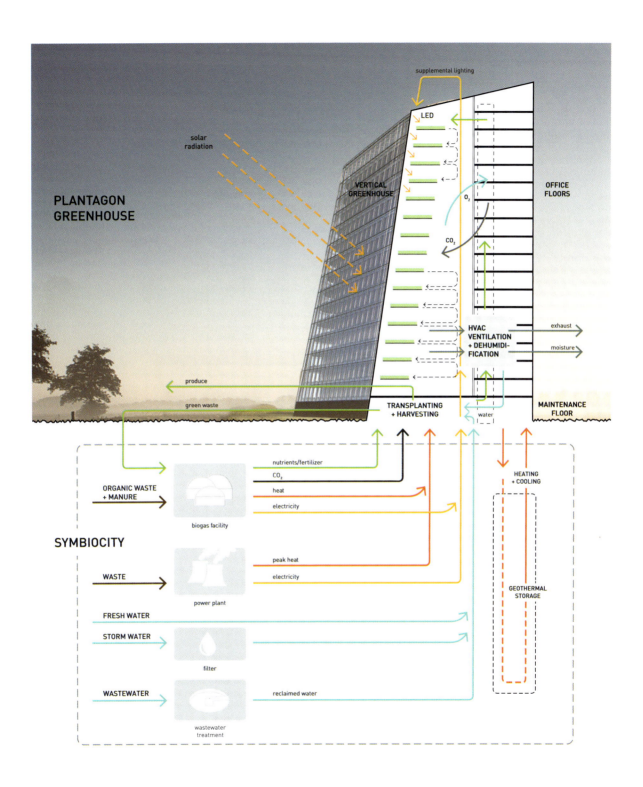

Energy: Solar-Powered Photosynthesis

and digestate from the biogas plant—will be used for fertilizer. Green waste from the greenhouse will, in turn, become biomass for the biogas facility.

Building Integration

The vertical greenhouse will be integrated with the host building in several ways. It will be structurally connected to the high-rise, which makes multi-story food production possible and is a unique feature of Plantagon's approach and invention. The façade greenhouse will receive CO_2 and excess heat not only from the biogas and power plants, but also from the tenant office spaces (Figure 3.44). In return, oxygen produced in the greenhouse will be conveyed into the offices of the high-rise building. The greenhouse façade will also contribute to the

▼ Figure 3.44

Façade section, double-skin façade greenhouse, Plantagon

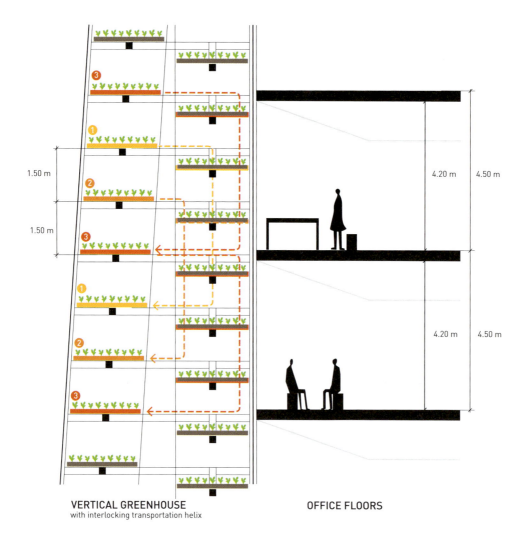

▲ Figure 3.45

View into the vertical greenhouse towards office spaces, rendering, Plantagon, Linköping, Sweden

energy performance of the host building by shading and insulating its interior. The direct visual connection to vegetation will increase human well-being and therefore raise the value of the tenant spaces (Figure 3.45).

Operation

A combined for-profit company and nonprofit organization, Plantagon describes itself as a "companization." The two primary business partners are the Swedish entrepreneur Hans Hassle and the Native American Onodaga Nation in New York State. Their "companization" has expanded beyond its headquarters in Stockholm to offices in New York, New Delhi, and Singapore, and has established a research center in collaboration with the Tongji University in China. Plantagon's design, technology, marketing, and political strategies are global, yet their greenhouse and infrastructural proposals are customized to the local conditions. Design proposals have been developed for several different types of vertical greenhouse—building-integrated, attached, and stand-alone—however, the design for the greenhouse in Linköping is the closest to realization.

Business Model and Financing

Plantagon's projects integrate both long- and short-term sources of revenue to ensure more resilient business models. The estimated construction cost for the greenhouse in Linköping is $30.5 million, projecting that the rent of the office spaces will create a profit after only five or six years. The company sees the sale of greenhouse produce as an additional, long-term revenue source that is not part of the short-term financing model. Using an established financing model based on the construction of commercial office real estate takes pressure off the urban farm to turn a profit immediately.

Strengths and Innovations

Once constructed, Plantagon's vertical greenhouse in Linköping will not only provide important proof of the feasibility of BIA, it will also represent the tallest vertical growing system ever realized. Its impressive height of over 170 ft (52 m) can only be achieved through structural integration with the host building. The innovations of this system are primarily reflected in its transportation system, based on the principles of a conveyer belt, as well as its adaptation of existing hydroponic systems.

As part of the Swedish governmental initiative, Symbiocity, Plantagon combines organizational structures of for-profit and nonprofit operations, a strategy observed in other successful urban agricultural projects, such as the low-profit limited liability company (L3C) model used by Vertical Harvest. Instead of applying an existing legal business model, Plantagon developed and operates under its own hybrid system of "companization."

Plantagon's greenhouse in Linköping strives for integration with the larger urban contexts and connects to larger urban energy and waste streams. When realized, the project will be an excellent example of BIA integration with large-scale urban systems.

▲ Figure 3.46

Stacked indoor growing system with LED lights, Caliber Biotherapeutics, Bryan, TX

CASE STUDY 6: VERTICAL INDOOR FARMING: A COMPARISON

Cultivating vegetable crops in entirely controlled environments or "plant factories" has been an important practice in Japan for over 30 years now. After the Tōhoku earthquake and tsunami in 2011, interest in indoor growing operations—especially those relying entirely on electrical lighting—grew exponentially due to concerns about food security and safety. Between 2011 and 2013, the number of these enterprises in Japan tripled to over 200.

As light-emitting diode (LED) grow lights have become more technically sophisticated, energy-efficient, and price-effective, interest in indoor growing facilities has also grown in North America and Europe. In the last three years, in fact, urban farms with stacked growing shelves seem to have reached economic viability. With LED lights placed in close proximity above plants at each shelf or level, these units are easily stacked, usually between 4 and 15 levels high. Commercial production farms including FarmedHere, AeroFarms, Growing Underground, and Mirai—as well as research facilities like PlantLab and Caliber Biotherapeutics—are successfully employing this growing method with highly controllable LED lights.

FARMEDHERE

Organization: FarmedHere
Cofounders: Jolanta Hardej, Paul Hardej, and Steve Denenberg
Location: Bedford Park, IL, United States
Operation: founded in 2008, Bedford Park facility started operation in 2013
Growing System: vertical aquaponics system stacked up to six layers high
Growing Area: 90,000-ft^2 (8,300-m^2) warehouse
Growing Season: year-round (fully contained environment; 41° N latitude)
Annual Yield: 500 tons (approximately 500 tons/acre footprint growing area)
Main Distribution: direct through Whole Foods and other supermarkets

FarmedHere's third farm—located in Bedford Park, Illinois, on the outskirts of Chicago—is a 90,000-ft^2 (8,300-m^2) CEA indoor vertical farm using an aquaponics growing system. The plants are grown in beds stacked up to six levels high (Figure 3.47). Whole Foods, which sells the company greens in their Chicago stores, helped finance this large facility. In addition, FarmedHere will offer underserved local youth agricultural training and jobs in partnership with Windy City Harvest apprenticeship program.[34]

▼ Figure 3.47

Stacked indoor growing system with LED lights, FarmedHere, Bedford Park, IL

AEROFARMS

Organization: AeroFarms
Cofounders: David Rosenberg, CEO; Ed Harwood, CTO; and Marc Oshima, CMO
Location: Newark, NJ, United States
Operation: founded in 2004, Newark facilities started in 2016
Growing System: vertical aeroponics system stacked up to 12 layers high
Growing Area: 70,000-ft^2 (6,500-m^2) and 30,000-ft^2 (2,800-m^2) warehouses
Growing Season: year-round (fully contained environment, 40° N latitude)
Annual Yield: 1000 tons (approximately 1000 tons/acre footprint growing area)
Main Distribution: supermarkets, restaurants

AeroFarms is an agricultural operation with over 10 years of growing expertise. Its mission is to "grow locally flavorful, safe, healthy food in a sustainable and socially responsible way." The company developed its own patented clean-tech growing technology using aeroponics and LEDs. In 2016, AeroFarms installed this system in two repurposed warehouses in Newark, NJ (Figure 3.48), making it the largest indoor farm by production volume today.[35]

▼ Figure 3.48

Rendering of indoor grow space, AeroFarms, Newark, NJ

Energy: Solar-Powered Photosynthesis

GROWING UNDERGROUND

Organization:	Growing Underground
Cofounders:	Richard Ballard and Steven Dring, backed by two-star Michelin chef Michel Roux Jr.
Location:	London, United Kingdom
Operation:	founded in 2012, in operation since 2014
Growing System:	vertical hydroponic system stacked four layers high
Growing Area:	65,000-ft^2 (6000-m^2) deep-level bomb-shelter tunnel
Growing Season:	year-round (fully contained environment, 51° N latitude)
Annual Yield:	not specified
Main Distribution:	restaurants, direct to customer via hyper-local online supplier

Growing Underground operates a hydroponic farm in a tunnel of a deep-level air-raid shelter 100 ft (33 m) below the ground near Clapham North in South London. The farm started operation in 2014 and primarily supplies high-end restaurants with microgreens. It will be, according to its founders, carbon-neutral by partnering with a renewable energy company.

MIRAI

Organization:	Mirai, Co., Ltd
Cofounders:	Shigeharu Shimamura, CEO, and Tomohiro Shimamura
Location:	Tagajo, Miyagi Prefecture and 25 additional farm locations in Japan
Operation:	founded in 2004, Miyagi Prefecture farm in operation since 2014
Growing System:	vertical hydroponic system stacked 15 layers high
Growing Area:	25,000-ft^2 (2,300-m^2) abandoned semiconductor factory warehouse
Growing Season:	year-round (fully contained environment, 38° N latitude)
Annual Yield:	400 tons
Main Distribution:	supermarkets

Mirai, which translates as "the future," currently operates 25 farms of all sizes, from demonstration projects in schools and shopping malls to large-scale, high-production warehouse facilities, both as retrofits and new construction. The company installed a small facility in the Japanese Syowa Research Station in Antarctica, has exported its technology to Mongolia, and has plans to expand to Hong Kong, Russia, and China.[36]

CALIBER BIOTHERAPEUTICS

Organization:	Caliber Biotherapeutics
Executive Team:	Tony Goosmann, CEO; Barry Holtz, CTO
Location:	Bryan, TX, United States
Operation:	research lab and product facility of a biotechnology company since 2011
Growing System:	vertical hydroponic system stacked up to 50 ft (15 m) high
Growing Area:	150,000-ft² (14,000-m²) facility
Growing Season:	year-round (fully contained environment, 30° N latitude)
Annual Yield/Distribution:	undisclosed, research facility

Caliber Biotherapeutics is a biotechnology company based in Bryan, Texas, with a focus on protein-based therapeutics to treat cancer and other diseases. The company's "pinkhouse" (so called because the glow of the blue and red LEDs is tuned to specific wavelengths) houses 2.2 million plants stacked up to 50 ft (15 m) high and employs a hydroponic system (Figure 3.49). The facility gives Caliber Biotherapeutics' scientists tight control over the growing environment for their expensive crops.[37]

▼ Figure 3.49

"Pinkhouse," indoor grow space, Caliber Biotherapeutics, Bryan, TX

PLANTLAB

Organization:	PlantLab
Cofounders:	John van Gemert, Leon van Duijn, Marcel Kers, Gertjan Meeuws
Location:	's-Hertogenbosch, the Netherlands
Operation:	research lab since 1994, development of plant production units since 2013, and new research facility since 2014
Growing System:	hydroponic system
Growing Area:	66,000-ft² (14,000-m²) research facility
Growing Season:	year-round (fully contained environment, 51° N latitude)
Annual Yield/Distribution:	undisclosed, research facility

PlantLab is a research branch of the HAS University of Applied Sciences in 's-Hertogenbosch, the Netherlands. In September 2014, it opened its new 66,000-ft² (14,000-m²) research and development center. The organization performs research to improve efficiencies of controlled environment agriculture (CEA). The goal is to develop Plant Production Units (PPUs) that function on a variety of scales from household use to warehouse production.[38]

Growing Systems

Indoor farms use contained, stacked, hydroponic growing systems to grow primarily lettuce, leafy greens, and microgreens. Sealed environments allow for controlled lighting (spectrum, intensity, and duration), CO_2 enrichment, and temperature. Hydroponic systems, in turn, supply water, oxygen, and a mix of nutrients to plants. Nutrient levels are carefully monitored and adjusted to meet individual crop specifications. Mirai and PlantLab, in particular, work on "recipes" to micromanage the mineral contents, tastes, textures, and appearances of plants, and then market this research with their growing systems. As distribution systems, most farms use a variation of the nutrient film technique (NFT) with mineral solution. AeroFarms uses a patented aeroponic system (Figure 3.50), and FarmedHere utilizes an aquaponic system to generate nutrients while also producing tilapia. The sealed clean-room environments of these indoor farms create a barrier between the growing operation and any pests or infections that may damage the crop, allowing the plants to remain free of pesticides and genetic modification.

These indoor growing systems are also very efficient with water, so much so that the different farms report that they use only 1–10% of the water used by traditional farming methods. Unlike regular hydroponic farms, indoor farms can be operated as fully enclosed systems. All water used within the nutrient feed is recycled, and even plant transpiration can be recycled through the use of the dehumidifiers, though this equipment requires large amounts of electricity.

▲ Figure 3.50

Stackable aeroponic growing system, AeroFarms

Electrical Lighting

Until three years ago, fluorescents and other lights were considered feasible for indoor growing. Now, a new generation of LEDs has become the lighting technology of choice. Energy-efficient LEDs can be programmed to precisely regulate the light spectrum, and they emit very little heat, which allows growing shelves to be packed tightly. Mirai also reports an effect on plant quality: Lettuces and leafy greens grown under LEDs are perceived as crispier than those grown with fluorescent light.

Electrical light also has unlimited availability, making it much more productive than daylight. The naturally available growing hours in northern latitudes (around 50°), for example, are about 1,000–1,500 hours per year, but LED lighting can provide growing hours year-round. In the Netherlands, PlantLab, for instance, uses up to 7,300 hours of growing hours per year (20 hours per day), which is up to five times more than natural conditions would allow.

The energy needed for LEDs, however, presents the significant drawback of indoor growing systems. Although the new generation of LEDs requires only a fraction of the energy that other grow-lamp technologies need, the energy costs associated with year-round farming with electrical light can be very high, depending on the cost of electricity in a given location. Mirai, for example, reports that energy costs make up approximately 25% of their operation costs.

Energy: Solar-Powered Photosynthesis

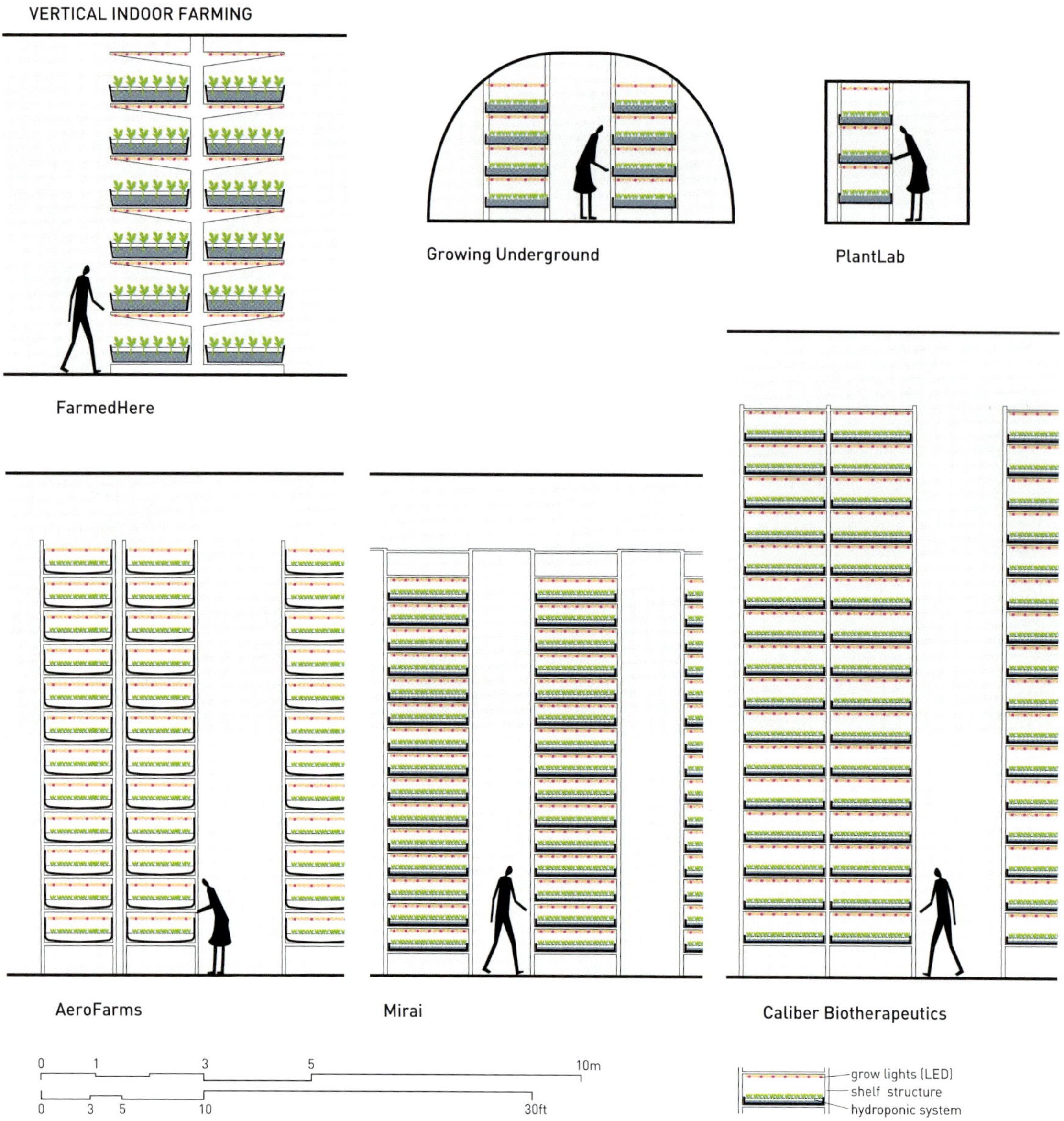

VERTICAL INDOOR FARMING

FarmedHere

Growing Underground

PlantLab

AeroFarms

Mirai

Caliber Biotherapeutics

grow lights (LED)
shelf structure
hydroponic system

In addition to cost, environmental considerations, such as the carbon footprint of the electricity available, need to be considered.

Operations, Designs, and Building Integrations

Farms growing lettuce and leafy greens, which have short growing cycles, need their produce to be delivered extremely fresh. Microgreens, which have even

▲ Figure 3.51

Stacked indoor growing system: FarmedHere, Growing Underground, PlantLab, AeroFarms, Mirai, and Caliber Biotherapeutics, diagrammatic sections

Environmental Resources

COMPARISON: VERTICAL INDOOR FARMING	footprint growing area	stacked growing	growing method	grow lights	projected production/ year	estimated size of operation
FarmedHere Chicago, IL (Bedford Park) formerly abandoned warehouse 90,000 ft² since 2013	47,000 ft² / 1.08 acre	15 ft high, 6 levels	Aquaponics, baby leafy greens and herbs	LED (Illumtex) and fluorescent lamps	500 tons	40 employees
AeroFarms Newark, NJ reuse of steel plant 69,000 ft² expected 2016	46,000 ft² / 1.06 acre	30 ft high, 12 levels	Aeropopnics, baby leafy greens and herbs	LED	1000 tons, 22 cycles / year	75 employees
Growing Underground London, UK reuse of bomb shelter 65,000 ft² since 2014	ca. 25,000 ft² / 0.57 acre (once built out)	4 levels	Hydroponics, microgreens	LED	still in development	still in development
Mirai Tagajo, Miyagi Prefecture abandoned Sony factory 90,000 ft² since 2014	25,000 ft² / 0.57 acre	15 levels	Hydroponic (NFT), 15 varieties of lettuce	17,500 LED lights, (GE Japan) and fluorescent lamps	400 tons	30 employees
RESEARCH FACILITIES						
Caliber Biotherapeutics Bryan, TX new warehouse facility 150,000 ft² since 2011	150,000 ft² / 3.45 acre	50 ft high, 15 levels	Hydroponics, Healing plants	LED	research facility, not reported	125 employees
PlantLab 's-Hertogenbosch, Netherlands new building 66,000 ft² since 2014	66,000 ft² / 1.5 acre	PPUs of varying sizes	Hydroponic, leafy greens and other cultivars	LED (Illumtex)	research facility, not reported	not reported

▲ Figure 3.52

Comparison: vertical indoor farms

Data adapted from Case Study 6 sources and references.

shorter growing cycles and higher retail values, are a similar case. Digital controls can support the growing process, though the success of an indoor farm depends largely on the expertise of at least one highly qualified expert. Labor is primarily needed for transplanting and harvesting crops, which accounts, for example, for a quarter of Mirai's production costs. While a large budget item, these desirable green jobs secure political support for urban (indoor) farms.

Many commercial operations strive to be the next "world's largest" indoor farm. Mirai and PlantLab, meanwhile, both have goals to demonstrate that their growing systems or PPUs can work on multiple scales from small in-counter systems to full-floor systems in multistory warehouses. Currently, most of the commercial-scale operations use abandoned warehouses as a cost-effective solution for grow space but also as a political statement about reconstruction and reuse. Mirai, for example, repurposed a semiconductor plant in Tagajo, Miyagi Prefecture, which the Tohoku tsunami hit severely. Aerofarms supports the redevelopment of an industrial neighborhood in Newark, NJ, and receives funding from both developers and the city, since green businesses help increase the value of the neighborhood. Growing Underground, meanwhile, stands out by utilizing a very unusual space—a bomb shelter, which offers stable growing conditions and affordable rent compared to London's above-ground warehouse spaces.

Strengths, Innovations, and Challenges

Indoor growing facilities control all growing factors. Their sealed-off growing environments make them resource- (water-, nutrient-, labor-, and space-) efficient, protect them from infestation, and generate uniform, consistent crop quality. The ability to function without sunlight offers interesting scenarios for building and urban integration. It allows crop growth in any geographical location, even during winter months. What's more, crops can be stacked to create high-density growing environments (Figure 3.51), and daylit areas are left for human occupation. "Just-in-time" crop production for close-by consumers reduces food miles and waste during transport.

Despite these benefits, high up-front capital investment and energy expenditures remain major drawbacks. "Clean" power sources are a must for these operations to keep their carbon footprints small; otherwise, reducing food miles is useless. While the interest in and economic feasibility of this farm type are growing, more research around developing sustainable environmental footprints is needed before indoor farming should be implemented broadly.

NOTES

1. F. Stuart Chapin, P.A. Matson, and Harold A. Mooney, *Principles of Terrestrial Ecosystem Ecology* (New York: Springer, 2002), 337.
2. Ibid., 335–336.
3. Ibid., 337.
4. Ibid., 337.
5. NOAA's Earth System Research Laboratory, "Recent Global CO_2," www.esrl.noaa.gov/gmd/ccgg/trends/global.html.
6. Chapin, Matson, and Mooney, *Principles of Terrestrial Ecosystem Ecology*, 337.
7. United States Environmental Protection Agency, "Sources of Greenhouse Gas Emission," http://epa.gov/climatechange/ghgemissions/sources/agriculture.html.
8. A.J. Both, "Some Thoughts on Supplemental Lighting for Greenhouse Crop Production," *Bioresource Engineering*, Rutgers, New Brunswick, NJ (2000): 1–10.

9. Ontario Ministry of Agriculture, Food and Rural Affairs, "Carbon Dioxide in Greenhouses," www.omafra.gov.on.ca/english/crops/facts/00-077.htm#sourc.
10. Brian Stone, Jason Vargo, and Dana Habeeb, "Managing Climate Change in Cities: Will Climate Action Plans Work?," *Landscape and Urban Planning* 107.3 (15 September 2012), 263–271.
11. Louis Bergeron, "Urban CO_2 Domes Increase Deaths, Poke Hole in 'Cap-and-Trade' Proposal, Stanford Researcher Says," *Stanford News* (16 March 2010), http://news.stanford.edu/news/2010/march/urban-carbon-domes-031610.html.
12. R.C. Balling Jr., R.S. Cerveny, and C.D. Idso, "Does the Urban CO_2 Dome of Phoenix, Arizona, Contribute to Its Heat Island?," *Geophysical Research Letter* 28.24 (2001), 4599–4601.
13. J. Cockrall-King, *Food and the City: Urban Agriculture and the New Food Revolution* (Amherst, NY: Prometheus Books, 2012), 81–105.
14. Gregory Kiss, "Solar Energy in the Built Environment: Powering the Sustainable City," in *Metropolitan Sustainability: Understanding and Improving the Urban Environment*, ed. Frank Zeman (Sawston, Cambridge, UK: Woodhead Publishing, 2012), 431–456.
15. Scott Sanford, "Thermal/Shade Curtains," *Rural Energy Program*, www.uwex.edu/energy/pubs/ThermalCurtains.pdf.
16. Michael Bomford, "Getting Fossil Fuels off the Plate," in *The Post Carbon Reader: Managing the 21st Century's Sustainability Crises,* ed. Richard Heinberg and Daniel Lerch (Healdsburg, CA: Watershed Media, 2010), 119–127.
17. Kubi Ackerman, "Urban Agriculture: Opportunities and Constraints," in *Metropolitan Sustainability: Understanding and Improving the Urban Environment*, ed. Frank Zeman (Sawston, Cambridge, UK: Woodhead Publishing, 2012), 118–146.

Catalog 4

18. Gene Giacomelli, "Designing the Greenhouse to Meet Your Expectations: What's Your Technology Level?," *Controlled Environment Agriculture Center CEAC, University of Arizona, Tucson*, http://ceac.arizona.edu/.
19. Ackerman, "Urban Agriculture," 127.
20. Li-Hong Gao, M. Qu, H.-Z. Ren, X.-L. Sui, Q.-Y. Chen, and Z.-X. Zhang. "Structure, function, application, and ecological benefit of a single-slope, energy- efficient solar greenhouse in China." *HortTechnology* 20, no. 3 (2010): 626.
21. Ibid., 627.

Catalog 5

22. Johannes F. J. Max, Ulrich Schurr, Hans-Jürgen Tantau, Urbanus N. Mutwiwa, Thomas Hofmann, and Andreas Ulbrich. "Greenhouse Cover Technology". *Horticultural Reviews*, Vol. 40, (2012): 286.

Catalog 6

23. Paul Fisher and Caroline Donnelly, "Evaluating Supplemental Light for Your Greenhouse," factsheet, Cornell University, NY, www.greenhouse.cornell.edu/crops/factsheets/SuppLight.pdf.

24. Erik Runkle, "Lighting Greenhouse Vegetables," http://flor.hrt.msu.edu/assets/Uploads/Lightingvegetables.pdf.
25. United States Energy Information Administration, "Electric Power Monthly," www.eia.gov/electricity/monthly/epm_table_grapher.cfm?t=epmt_5_6_a.
26. Cary A. Mitchell, M.P. Dzakovich, C. Gomez, R. Lopez, J.F. Burr, R. Hernández, C. Kubota, C.J. Currey, Q. Meng, E.S. Runkle, et al. "Light-emitting diodes". *Horticultural Reviews*, Vol. 43, (2015): 1–87.
27. Jacob A. Nelson and Bruce Bugbee. "Economic Analysis of Greenhouse Lighting: Light Emitting Diodes vs. High Intensity Discharge Fixtures." *PLoS One* 9, no. 6 (2014).
28. Plasma International Lighting Systems, www.plasma-i.com/index.html.

Case Study 1: Aquaponic Solar Greenhouse

29. This case study is based on presentations by and an interview with Franz Schreier and completed with his permission. Additional sources: Franz Schreier, "Aquaponic Solar Greenhouse: An Integrated Food and Energy System (IFES) for Sustainable Food and Energy Production," www.ebf-gmbh.de/pdf/Food_and_Energy.pdf. Argus, "Light and Lighting Control in Greenhouses," www.arguscontrols.com/resources/Light-and-Lighting-Control-in-Greenhouses.pdf. City Farm Fish, "We Teach Cities How to Fish," http://cityfarmfish.com/#projects.

Case Study 2: Granpa Domes

30. This case study profile is partly based on preliminary research conducted by Matthew McDonald in the author's graduate seminar. Sources: Granpa, http://granpa.co.jp/Granpa, https://ssl.entrys.jp/granpa_inq/images/common/granpa_english.pdf. Sawaji Osamu, "Growing the Business of Agriculture," *The Japan Journal* 9.8 (2012): 10–13, www.japanjournal.jp/tjjpdf/1211e_light.pdf. AJW by The Asahi Shimbun, "Harvesting Nears for Lettuce Grown in Disaster-stricken City," http://ajw.asahi.com/article/0311disaster/recovery/AJ201207110019.

Case Study 3: Sky Greens

31. This case study profile is partly based on preliminary research conducted by Thanakorn Wongphadungtham in the author's graduate seminar. Sources: Sky Greens, www.skygreens.com/. Ravindra Krishnamurthy, "Vertical Farming: Singapore's Solution to Feed the Local Urban Population," The Permaculture Research Institute, http://permaculturenews.org/2014/07/25/vertical-farming-singapores-solution-feed-local-urban-population/. Jessica Lim, "Design Acclaim for 9m-tall System which beats more than 1,000 Entries from 72 Countries," *The Straits Times*, www.straitstimes.com/singapore/vertical-farming-invention-wins-global-award. Esther Ng, "Veggies from a Vertical Farm," *Today* (January 29, 2011), http://wildsingaporenews.blogspot.com/2011/01/vertical-farming-boosts-production-of.html#.VSMI4l3F9rJ. Kalinga Seneviratne, "Farming in the Sky in Singapore," *Our World*, http://ourworld.unu.edu/en/farming-in-the-sky-in-singapore.

Case Study 4: Vertical Harvest

32. This case study is based on an interview with Penny McBride and architect Nona Yehia and completed with their permission. Additional sources: Vertical Harvest, www.verticalharvestjackson.com/. Suzanne Zimmer Lowery, "Where Dreams (and Greens) Sprout," http://njmonthly.com/articles/restaurants/where-dreams-and-greens-sprout.html. Ben Graham, "High-rise greenhouse sees price grow again," www.jhnewsandguide.com/news/town_county/high-rise-greenhouse-sees-price-grow-again/article_5ec8d007-6a20-5892-8cbc-21a22ba019cd.html.

Case Study 5: Plantagon

33. This case study profile is partly based on preliminary research conducted by Heli Ojamaa in the author's graduate seminar and an interview with Joakim Ernback of Plantagon. Sources: Plantagon, http://plantagon.com. Hans Hassle, "Building for Cultivating Crops in Trays, with Conveying System for Moving the Trays," World Intellectual Property Organization: Patent WO 2013/066253 A1 (May 10, 2013). Magnus Hjelmare, "Greenhouse Development, Plantagon," Urban Agriculture Summit, Linköping, 2013. Romain Vuattoux, "Intensive Vertical Urban Agriculture: Rethinking Our Cities' Food Supply. Moving towards Sustainable Urban Development" master's thesis, Malmö University's Sustainable Urban Management: Built Environment, 2012.

Case Study 6: Vertical Indoor Farming: A Comparison

34. FarmedHere, http://farmedhere.com/. "FarmedHere, Nation's Largest Indoor Vertical Farm, Opens in Chicago Area," *Huff Post Chicago*, www.huffingtonpost.com/2013/03/22/farmedhere-nations-largest-vertical-farm_n_2933739.html.
35. AeroFarms, http://aerofarms.com/. C. J. Hughes, "In Newark, A Vertical Indoor Farm Helps Anchor an Area's Revival," *The New York Times*, www.nytimes.com/2015/04/08/realestate/commercial/in-newark-a-vertical-indoor-farm-helps-anchor-an-areas-revival.html?_r=2.
36. Gloria Dickie, "Q&A: Inside the World's Largest Indoor Farm," *National Geographic*, http://news.nationalgeographic.com/news/2014/07/140717-japan-largest-indoor-plant-factory-food/. Kazuaki Nagata, "Future Appears Bright for Indoor Veggie Farms," *The Japan Times*, www.japantimes.co.jp/news/2014/08/11/business/tech/future-appears-bright-indoor-veggie-farms/#.VeSuurxVhBe.
37. Caliber Biotherapeutics, www.caliberbio.com/. Jeff Reinke, "Caliber Recognized for Excellence in Technology," *Pharmaceutical Processing*, www.pharmpro.com/articles/2014/03/caliber-recognized-excellence-technology.
38. PlantLab, http://plantlab.nl/. Hal Hodson, "Shoots in the Dark: Farming without Sunlight," *The Independent* (September 26, 2011), www.independent.co.uk/news/science/shoots-in-the-dark-farming-without-sunlight-2360833.html. TEDxTalks, "TEDxBrainport 2012 – Gertjan Meeuws – Indoor Farming, Plant Paradise," YouTube video (June 8, 2012), www.youtube.com/watch?v=ILzWmw53Wwo. 100.

Part II | Human Expertise

Chapter 4

Operation

Farm Management, Business Planning, and Financing

ABSTRACT

This book describes the multiple scales and diverse methods associated with urban agriculture, from ground-based to building-integrated approaches, ranging from site-specific to city-wide networks. These multiple scales and diverse methods are also reflected in the management approach for each farm, which may operate on a personal, community, or commercial level, or some combination thereof. An effective operational system is vital to the success of any urban agricultural initiative, and new approaches to the production and marketing of food that increase the transparency of food origin and inputs are establishing alternatives to the existing, unsustainable food system. This chapter examines urban farm operations on multiple levels, from farm management to production and processing methods. Essential to an operation's success are considerations including start-up funding, financing, business models, and profitability, and we demonstrate a variety of effective approaches in a series of case studies. While nonprofit, community, educational, and personal urban agricultural practices are significant branches of the movement, this chapter focuses on commercial endeavors and identifies what designers need to know when planning a viable farm operation.

OPERATIONAL CHALLENGES

Urban agriculture offers promising solutions to some of the largest operational challenges facing the industrial food system. One prime concern is the growing distance—an average of 1500–2500 miles (2400–4000 kilometers)—that food travels before reaching its consumers.[1] This extended transport results in increasingly untenable energy use related to transportation, storage, and processing as well as a high volume of food waste due to spoilage.[2] A highly centralized food distribution model with long, complicated supply chains has negative implications for food quality, food security, and environmental and human health.[3]

Such a centralized model also has a negative economic effect on most communities. The conventional food system concentrates economic value in the processing and distribution phases. As a result, farmers see few of the economic benefits of their work because small, local food businesses cannot compete with large agribusinesses. Money spent by consumers therefore leaves the local economy and is instead diverted to national or multinational distributors. Variety

◀ Figure 4.1

CSA Boxes at Lufa Farms' pick-and-pack

and quality of produce suffer, as crops are selected for their durability and capacity to withstand industrial harvest, transport, and storage.[4]

In addition, the industrial food system presents a troubling imbalance of power in the production, processing, and distribution cycles: large retail chains are increasingly influencing the type of food that is grown and who grows it. As large distributors control ever-larger portions of the food market, they are able to demand high volumes of durable, homogeneous produce, meeting standards of quality and quantity that are impossible for smaller farmers to attain.

While urban agriculture is uniquely poised to address these problems, it presents its own suite of operational complexities that are crucial to understand in order to design for a successful program. In particular, those planning an urban agricultural operation must be aware of the full breadth of the system from production to consumption, including all inputs, outputs, and constraints. Knowledge of the complexity of the "urban foodshed" allows designers to properly embed an operation into existing urban systems, leveraging spatial, social, ecological, and economic synergies to the greatest degree possible.[5]

URBAN AGRICULTURE'S POSITIVE EFFECT ON THE FOOD SYSTEM

Local Adaptation and Value

In contrast to conventional agriculture, urban-produced food is more likely to be locally consumed and responsibly grown. Most urban agricultural operations are adapted to the local climate and culture and grow produce sustainably, with minimum resource input. Additionally, many urban farms recycle the rich supply of waste materials produced in urban environments (such as organic waste, waste heat, and rainwater and greywater), incorporating them into the food production system to fulfill energy, water, and nutrient requirements.

In addition, practitioners of urban agriculture are more likely to see the economic benefit of their work remain in their community instead of being siphoned off by a remote distribution network. Urban agriculture also spurs associated small- or larger-scale local agribusiness opportunities. These can range from local restaurants, to processing of added-value products, and jobs that provide supplies, irrigation equipment, and recycled organic matter.[6]

Urban agriculture is characterized by short supply chains, and its production and distribution relationships tend to be more local and more equitable. Due to the proximity of growers, distributors, and consumers, urban agricultural operations are more responsive to shifts in the market, adapting to local needs and wants, and developing an identity associated with a particular place. Local valuation is a promising component of urban agriculture since value is determined not only by price but also by quality, establishing a trusting relationship between producer and consumer with positive environmental and community benefits.[7]

Niche Products and Markets

Unlike the conventional food system, which favors staple crops that can travel long distances, urban agriculture allows for specialty varieties that are often highly perishable, difficult to find commercially, and culturally important to the community. Indeed, the ability to trade in niche products is critical to the success of many urban agricultural ventures. Identifying a target market, including potential niches, is an essential first step in designing an operation. Everything in the urban agricultural cycle—from growing methods and spatial requirements to packaging, distribution, and business models—will hinge on the target crop and how best to grow it in an urban setting.

Distribution Methods

While conventional agriculture is focused on exports and wholesale, urban agriculture is invested in direct buyer relationships and local networks. Urban farmers often invest time in personally selling their produce at farmers' markets in order to develop direct relationships with their customers. In addition, they often strive to establish a loyal customer base of local restaurants that are willing to pay premium prices for reliably high-quality produce. Other farms establish advanced payment plans or long-term business contracts with customers to help finance farm operations. The latter are especially advantageous for farms with high infrastructure investment.

Practices and Farm Models

Perhaps the most significant operational difference between commercial and urban agriculture is the complexity and heterogeneity of urban food production practices. Urban agriculture encompasses an enormous breadth of scale, ranging across all levels of cost and technological expertise. In fact, multiple approaches reaching from ground-based community gardens to high-tech, building-integrated systems are available. Market and operational priorities should determine which approach is selected or if several approaches can be combined. The designer's role is to have a full understanding of the urban food cycle and the choices available to successfully integrate production goals with the built environment.

DESIGNING AN OPERATION

Assembling a Team

Many individuals are involved in establishing and operating a farm. First and foremost are the farmers themselves, who offer direction about crop selection, planting, maintenance, and business models. Members of the distribution network—whether restaurant or grocery store owners—should also be consulted early on to help define the target market for the farm's produce. A team will also include architects, landscape architects, and engineers who will address the system design, structural requirements, and infrastructural needs (Figure 4.2). Product manufacturers and suppliers may also be involved for their expertise on soil, green roof components, greenhouse structures, and specialized growing systems such as those for hydroponics, aquaponics, or supplemental lighting. At this early stage, urban agricultural initiatives may also consult with nonprofit community organizations to learn about how to integrate social programs into farm management, approach research institutions for funding or other resources, or confer with local or national governments about financial assistance and regulatory compliance. Lastly, it is vital to involve the farm's future consumers in early planning decisions and to design the farm with their specific needs and wants in mind.

▼ Figure 4.2

Interdisciplinary team necessary to establish and operate an urban farm

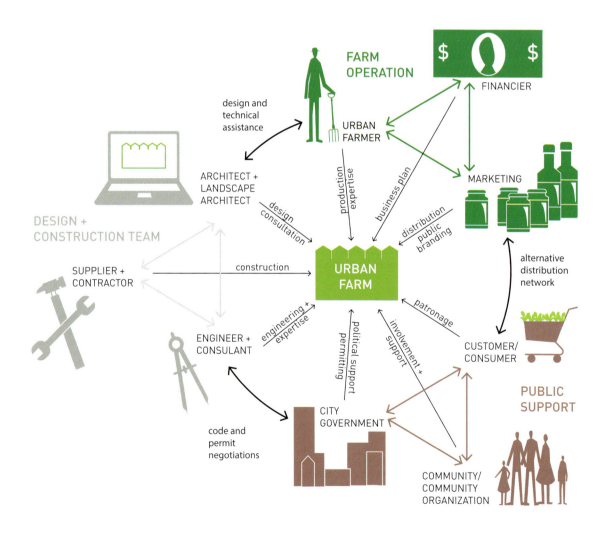

The Economics of Different Farm Models

The types of farm operation and commercial models available to urban agriculturalists vary widely and determine which crops may be successfully grown (see Figure 4.3). In identifying a method of farming, it is necessary to understand the opportunities and constraints of the available spatial resources. For example, if only outdoor space is available for the operation, hardy varieties must be selected, whereas if greenhouse or interior space is accessible, a farmer may undertake the year-round cultivation of species, such as tomatoes or lettuces, that may be too tender to survive outside in the cold season. The different farm types range from soil-based to controlled-environment agriculture (CEA) and vary in size, ownership model, recommended crops, growing season, harvest cycles per season or year, and operation costs.

Soil-Based Urban Farms

Soil-based urban farms often operate with biointensive growing methods to achieve higher yields on small urban sites. Some may operate as small plot intensive (SPIN) or distributed urban farms, which cultivate several small plots to aggregate larger growing areas in urban neighborhoods. These small urban farms are characterized by low up-front investment but also relatively low production and income. Their exact productivity depends largely on local conditions, such as the length of the growing season and the quality of the soil at the different sites. The small number of consecutive crop cycles per growing season—usually two to three, ideally four with very good farm management—limits the possible yields substantially. Due to these constraints, farmers often cultivate heirloom varieties and gourmet produce to generate more revenue. In general, it is very difficult to make a living from these small farms; therefore, most of them are operated as a part-time job for additional earnings. A viable soil-based urban farm managed by two full-time farmers and support staff needs a site of at least 2 acres. A start-up investment of $0.50/ft^2 ($5/m^2) can usually cover soil amendments and basic infrastructure.

Hoop-House Farms

Soil-based farms can increase their productivity by adding hoop houses. These low-tech greenhouses help extend the growing season, cultivate starts in early spring, and grow specialty crops that would otherwise not tolerate the local climate. With the protective cover of the greenhouse, the farm can support up to seven harvesting cycles per growing bed each year. The necessary investment is still moderate, at $4/ft^2 ($43/m^2), but the potential yields multiply with the additional harvest cycles.

The farm Growing Power is an advocate of hoop houses (Figure 4.4). It uses them at its headquarters, employs them in neighborhood gardens,

COMPARISON: TYPES OF FARM OPERATION

	ownership model	preferred crops and yields	growing season	crop cycles per season	investment for infrastructure	operation cost and labor input
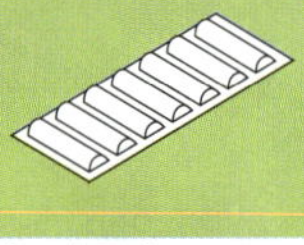 geoponic urban farm	land leased or owned	all vegetables, ideally high value crops for niche market, 20 tons/ acre	outdoors, natural growing season, 6-9 months	2-3 crops per growing bed per season	low, $0.50-1/ ft^2	low, after system has been set up well
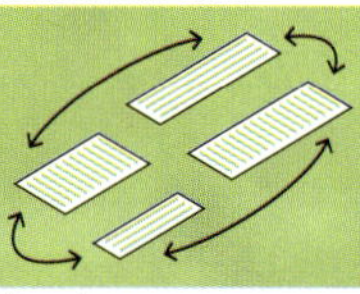 spin farming	farming plots owned by others, rent often in kind	all vegetables, ideally high value crops for niche market, 20 tons/ acre	outdoors, natural growing season, 6-9 months	3-4 crops per growing bed per season	low, $0.50-1/ ft^2	low, 4 hours per 1000 ft^2 / week
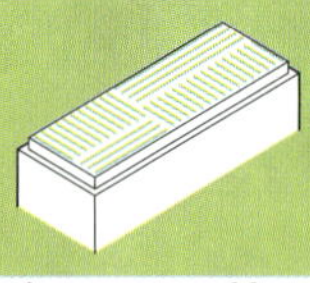 productive green roof farm	long-term lease of rooftop, (at least 10 years)	all vegetables, ideally high value crops for niche market, 10-12 tons/ acre	outdoors, natural growing season, 6-9 months	3-4 crops per growing bed per season	medium high, installation cost for green roof $5 - $14 per ft^2	medium, one farm manager, and 2-3 support staff
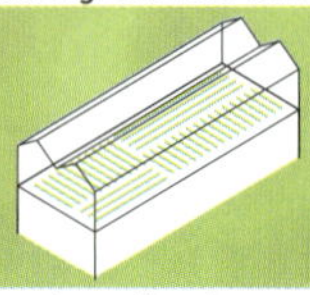 hydroponic rooftop farm	long-term lease of rooftop, (at least 10 years), ownership of greenhouse	lettuce, leafy greens, and tomatoes, 200-300 tons/ acre	indoors, 12 months year round	12 harvests of lettuce, continuous harvesting of vine crops	very high, installation cost for greenhouse $40 - $50 per ft^2	high energy and labor costs, greenhouse experts and daily harvest team
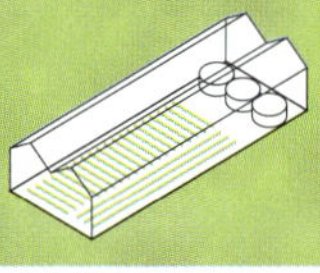 aquaponic farm	long-term lease of grow space, ownership of equipment	lettuce, leafy greens, and tomatoes, 200-300 tons/ acre	indoors, 12 months year round	12 harvests of lettuce, harvest of fish every 9-12 months	high, depends on the level of technology integrated	depending on size, aquaponic expert and harvest team
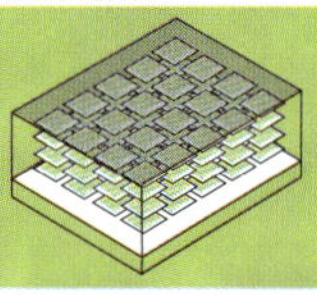 vertical indoor farming	abandoned warehouse, long-term lease, ownership of equipment	lettuce, leafy greens, and microgreens, 200-300 tons/ acre	indoors, 12 months year round	12-15 harvests of lettuce, continuous harvesting of microgreens	very high, depends on host building and density, $20 - $50 per ft^2	high energy and labor costs, indoor farm experts and daily harvest team
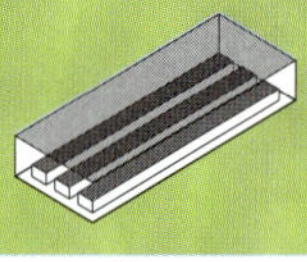 mushroom culture	abandoned warehouse or basement, low rent or left-over spaces	specialty mushrooms	indoors, 12 months year round	continuous harvesting	low, requires low-tech infrastructure	expert knowledge and low maintanance
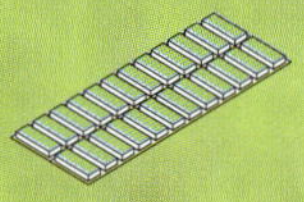 microgreens	very space efficient, often in existing greenhouse or indoor space	microgreens and baby leafy greens	indoors, 12 months year round	harvests every 7-10 days, 36-50 harvests per year	medium, depends on existing infrastructure	high enrgy, material, and labor costs

▲ Figure 4.3

Comparison: types of farm operation in urban agriculture

Data adapted from Case Study 6–11 sources and references.

▶ Figure 4.4

Hoop house farm, Growing Power, Milwaukee

and teaches workshops on their construction. Even in the extreme climate of Milwaukee, the farm generates almost year-round production in these hoop houses by using passive solar gain and compost piles as heat sources in the winter months to keep the interior above freezing (see Case Study 7).

Productive Green Roofs

Productive green roofs offer soil-based production plus the environmental advantages of green-roof technology. The green-roof infrastructure requires a high up-front investment of $12/ft² ($130/m²). Its stormwater management benefits, though, may make it eligible for funding from environmental protection grants, which can help offset the cost. Since green-roof production is equivalent to other soil-based farms, it is difficult to cover the investment with produce sales alone, but New York's Brooklyn Grange, which has operated two 1-acre green roofs since 2012, is one successful model. This farm helped finance its infrastructure through tax incentives and grant support based on stormwater management improvements. Brooklyn Grange has also leveraged several additional sources of revenue (see Case Study 8), as proceeds generated by the sale of produce alone cannot return the high up-front investment quickly.

Hydroponic Rooftop Farms

Controlled-environment agriculture (CEA) operations with hydroponic or aquaponics growing systems are the most expensive to install. This method is well suited for building integration and in situations where ground space is a limiting factor. To date, these farms have been successfully established in a few metropolitan areas with high-end produce markets. Lettuce, leafy greens, herbs, and vine crops are the most economically and logistically feasible produce for these operations (Figure 4.5).

This CEA farm model allows year-round harvesting, producing very high yields of 100–200 tons per acre each year. To achieve this rate of productivity in most northern climates, supplemental lighting and heating are required. Hydroponic rooftop farms are currently, however, the most profitable type of urban farm operation once the initial start-up funding and growing infrastructure are secured. The up-front investment is much higher than for other systems, reaching $50/ft^2 ($540/m^2). Funding for this type of farm is often provided by business development grants or by loans backed by long-term purchasing agreements with supermarket chains. In this arrangement, the supermarket commits to buying a certain amount of produce over the next 10 years (see Case Study 11).

Vertical Indoor Farms

The increasing affordability and efficiency of light-emitting diode (LED) grow lights have recently resulted in the development of several indoor farms that leverage vertical space for crop production (see Case Study 6). Stacked growing units maximize the growing area in crowded urban space, but require lighting, cooling, and ventilation powered by electricity, which results in a high operation cost and a potentially very high carbon footprint, depending on the energy source of the electrical power.

The up-front investment for the growing infrastructure—growing shelves, hydroponic delivery system, and light fixtures—can be equally high if not higher than for a hydroponic rooftop greenhouse. The investment per square foot depends on how densely the growing units are stacked and if an existing warehouse can be reused. The operation cost depends primarily on the local cost of electrical power and how much equipment needs to be operated.

Complementary Farming Operations

Once an urban farm has set up a controlled growing environment, microgreen production can be a profitable addition. Microgreens are seedlings of lettuce, vegetable, and herb plants that are harvested after the first set of leaves have emerged. They are grown in 7- to 10-day cycles, with each cycle requiring an intensive replenishment of nutrients to the soil. These high-value crops are typically grown for specialty markets or local restaurants, and they can offer a quick turnaround and constant income for a farm, although their intense production requirements result in high labor costs (Figure 4.6). To supplement income, farms may also experiment with mushroom cultures, which can be grown indoors with no light or very low light levels. Depending on the species, mushroom cultures grow on a variety of media, from compost to straw to pieces of tree trunks, creating interesting opportunities for design integration (Figure 4.7).

Beekeeping is also a popular complementary operation. Apiaries (collections of beehives) require little space and support fruit production through pollination while also generating a high-value product—honey. One beehive can produce between 50–100 lbs (23–45 kg) of honey per year. Some soil-based farms also complement their operation with animal husbandry—for example, raising chickens and goats. Animals add to the complexity, sustainability, and ambience of the farm, though the small-scale nature of these additions typically has no positive economic effect on the farm operation.

Start-up Funding

Necessary start-up funding varies greatly for different farm models and ranges from $0.50/ft^2 to $50/ft^2 ($5/m^2 to $540/m^2). Therefore, different farm models face different challenges in raising capital. One difficulty common to all projects is that urban agriculture is not broadly recognized as an established type of business. Many credit institutions are still reluctant to grant private loans for urban agricultural projects because of perceived risks and lack of collateral.

Long-term purchasing agreements, however, have increased the likelihood that projects can secure large loans. These agreements are established between a grower and a corporation—usually a recognized supermarket chain—that commits to buy large quantities of produce. With the help of a 10-year contract, a farm can secure loans to finance its growing infrastructure, typically an expensive hydroponic system.

Such contracts are modeled on the solar energy industry, specifically Power Purchase Agreements (PPAs), which allow solar power developers to establish photovoltaic (PV) systems on rooftops that they do not own. In addition to providing the necessary space for the PV system, rooftop owners agree to purchase the energy it generates for an agreed-upon period of time. This assurance of long-term revenue allows the operator to secure financing for the infrastructure. Gotham Greens appropriated this model for its first hydroponic rooftop greenhouse in 2009, establishing a high-profile partnership with Whole Foods Market. Based on this collaboration, Gotham

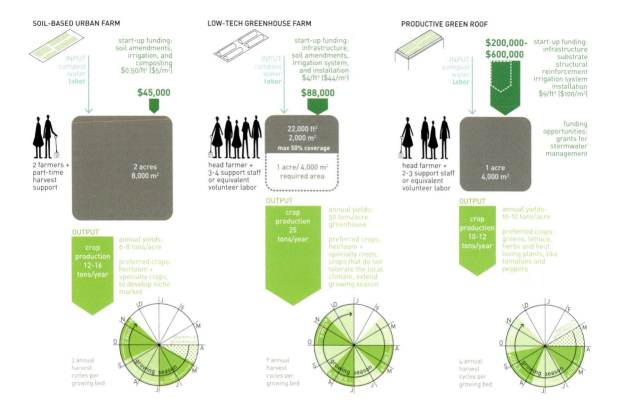

▲ Figure 4.5

Farm types and business models in urban agriculture

Data adapted from Case Study 6–11 sources and references.

Greens has been able to build three greenhouses in New York City and one in Chicago to date. In 2011, Paul Lightfoot, the CEO of another urban agriculture venture, BrightFarms, went as far as to rebrand the approach as a "Produce Purchase Agreement." While hydroponic greenhouses need far more capital than other farm models, an implementation model based on PPAs is seen as a promising investment strategy. Hydroponic urban farms are typically most successful if they can demonstrate that the operation has a credible management team and if they find an investor that gains marketing value from the collaboration.

New forms of building integration are very promising when it comes to start-up funding. In conjunction with large building projects, more complex funding models are possible as long as the investor is willing to take the risk of working with the new urban agricultural industry. Plantagon developed such a funding model for their office building with vertical greenhouse, in which the rent of the office spaces will create a profit after only five or six years (see Case Study 5). The company sees the sale of greenhouse produce as an additional, long-term revenue source that is not part of the short-term financing model, thus taking pressure off the urban farm to turn a profit immediately.[8]

Many commercial urban agricultural operations have also been fortunate to receive start-up funding in the form of grants. Even a small amount of grant support can give a farm the competitive advantage needed to raise more money

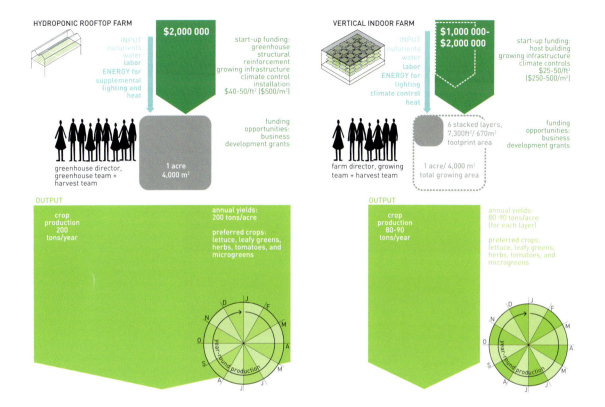

and begin operation. Grants prevalent in commercial urban agriculture fall into two categories: (1) grants for environmental improvement, such as stormwater management, or (2) business development grants from city or state governments to support innovative projects. Tax incentives work similarly to grants, fostering investment in environmental improvement from which urban farms can benefit. For example, New York City's tax abatement pays $4.50/ft^2 ($50/m^2) for the installation of green roofs. Brooklyn Grange made use of this incentive and qualified under special considerations for the maximum tax abatement of $100,000 with their first productive green roof (see Case Study 8).

With the growing presence of urban farms on social media, online fundraising has also become a successful tool to raise start-up funding and support for smaller projects. Using this platform, Vertical Harvest raised over $36,000 in their initial campaign. From a similar base of supporters, urban farms can also receive donations in the form of volunteer hours spent setting up the farms and in support of their operation.

Operation Cost

In general, labor is the most expensive part of urban agricultural operations due to scale and the fact that mechanized equipment is not used for planting,

◂ **Figure 4.6**

High value products in urban agriculture: Microgreens at The Plant, Chicago

◂ **Figure 4.7**

High value products in urban agriculture: Oyster mushrooms at The Plant, Chicago

irrigation, harvesting, or maintenance. It is therefore critical that farms balance their wage payments and income. Different growing methods have different labor needs, so it is also important to take these requirements into account when designing an operation.

Commercial hydroponic farms, with a large production volume, rely on a small number of experts in greenhouse management and a large team of harvesting and greenhouse aids. Soil-based farms, with lower production rates, build seasonal teams with one experienced farm manager plus support that is often provided by interns and volunteers. Successful commercial urban farms also have an increasing number of staff who work in public relations, management, and technical development. These specialists build the farm's brand and work on expanding the farm operation to additional sites. Some hydroponic rooftop farms have grown to operations with 30–100 employees and staff to address an increasing and varied workload.

The rent for the growing space—site, rooftop, or warehouse—in a city is also important to consider. To keep overhead expenses down, it is important to procure long-term leases, keep the rent low, or even find a site that requires no rent payment (for example, free use of publicly-owned land). High-tech farms in particular, which require expensive infrastructure, should secure long-term leases of at least 10 years. To negotiate rooftop rents, farmers and landlords have looked at prevailing rental rates for PV arrays as a model. Renting out urban rooftops is often a new surplus income for landlords, though many still hesitate to recruit urban farms as tenants. Rental costs to support facilities used for processing, sale, and education also need to be considered.

Energy can be another large operational expense, particularly the energy used for the supplemental lighting, heating, and ventilation required by high-tech greenhouses and indoor growing operations. Supplementing greenhouse operation in northern latitudes is necessary for year-round production. It is also usually critical to economic viability as long as the supplementation generates more revenue than operational costs.

DISTRIBUTION MODELS

Distribution models for urban agriculture are as diverse as its farming methods and are likewise closely linked to the crop and its intended consumers (Figure 4.8). Unlike the convoluted supply chains of industrial agriculture, distribution networks in urban agriculture are typically local and direct but vary according to product and business plan.

Direct to Buyer

The simplest distribution model is the farmer selling directly to the consumer, either from on-site produce stands or at farmers' markets. This approach involves minimal overhead, and with the growing popularity of farmers' markets in the United States, it is quickly becoming a profitable option. Farmers' market sales bring twice the return of selling to a conventional wholesaler.[9] On-site vegetable stalls and farmers' market sales can also be pursued alongside other distribution models. For example, at its flagship urban farm in Milwaukee, Growing Power offers an in-house market selling produce, meat, worm castings, and compost.[10]

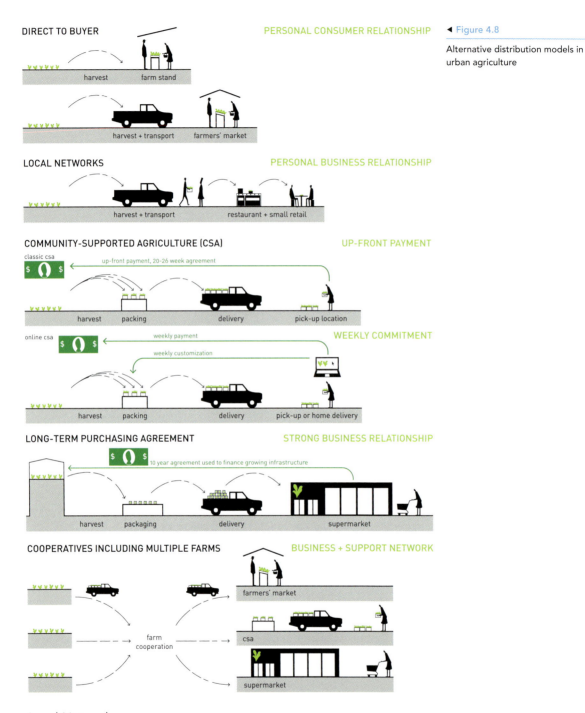

▲ Figure 4.8

Alternative distribution models in urban agriculture

Local Networks

A variety of local networks facilitate the distribution of urban agricultural products. The most straightforward is an exclusive relationship between a productive farm and a single distribution operation, such as a restaurant or market. Often referred to as kitchen gardens, growing operations may take place on the rooftop of a restaurant, serving the kitchen below. Uncommon Ground in Chicago, Bastille in Seattle, and Rosemary in New York are examples of restaurants that have established rooftop gardens as marketing tools. Such gardens also give the chef the opportunity to coordinate the crops that are grown.

An urban farming operation may also produce for several local restaurants and markets. Vegetables can be sold daily at a premium price and delivered by bicycle or truck, a highly visible advertisement for "locavorism," with food entering through the front door and not via a loading dock in the back alley. Restaurants and neighborhood specialty markets like these are at the forefront of developments in local food culture and economics, and these small-scale distribution networks stimulate pride and economic development in the community.[11] The Brooklyn Grange rooftop farm has leveraged these local networks with particular success, notably through their "Grown in NYC" branding campaign and their extensive and varied list of nearby clients, including restaurants, markets, and catering companies.[12]

Community-Supported Agriculture (CSA)

In recent years, community-supported agricultural programs have become increasingly popular in the United States. Traditionally, a CSA distribution model allowed a limited number of people to pay in advance for a weekly or bi-weekly share of fresh vegetables. These annual shares provided the farm with necessary capital at the beginning of the growing season in exchange for a regular supply of produce during the summer. The selection depended largely on what the farm was able to harvest each week. Vegetables were either delivered directly to the buyer or picked up at a central distribution point, reducing the number of miles that food had to travel. More recently, a growing CSA network and increasing online resources have improved communication to allow for greater customization (Figure 4.9). Farms with advanced websites now offer buyers the option to choose what they would like in their basket each week and pay upon delivery.

The CSA model has been applied to a variety of rural, peri-urban, and urban agricultural operations, ranging in scale from several hundred acres to a city rooftop. One example is Eagle Street Farm in Brooklyn, New York, which became the first rooftop CSA in the United States in 2010. On a 6,000-sq-ft green roof, the farm produces a diverse variety of crops, the most successful of which have been heat-loving species such as hot peppers, cherry tomatoes, and sage. In 2011, Eagle Street Farm initiated an "upstate/downstate" CSA share with upstate New York's Lineage Farm to expand the selection of produce they offer and to connect city consumers with their larger regional foodshed.[13]

◀ Figure 4.9
Lufa Farms' CSA box augmented with marketplace products

Long-Term Purchasing Agreement

Long-term purchasing agreements are established between a grower and a franchised or corporate entity. The distributor commits up-front to buy large quantities of produce for (usually) the next 10 years. The food is then marketed by the retailer as locally grown and is branded with the name of the farm. The farm usually leverages this pre-arrangement to finance its growing infrastructure.

Cooperatives

Cooperative associations are another prevalent distribution model that takes advantage of local networks and market proximity. Programs such as the Rainbow Farmers' Cooperative, run by Growing Power, allow small-scale Midwestern farmers to pool their resources in order to better compete in markets in Chicago, Madison, and Milwaukee. Growing Power assists in collectively marketing these farms' produce to restaurants, retailers, and small wholesalers while providing centralized cool storage to ensure quality.[14] Britain's East Anglia Food Link recently made the case for developing a similar cooperative depot in London, where small farmers, including urban agriculturalists, could collectively market and distribute their produce.[15]

PROCESSING, PACKAGING, AND BRANDING

How much urban farming products are processed and packaged depends on the type of crop and the target distribution method. For example, while locally grown vegetables sold at a farmers' market require little packaging or processing, a year-round hydroponic farm with larger-scale distribution through supermarkets may have substantial packaging needs to brand its products.

Processing can also confer added value on a farm's products. Many operations, for example, supplement income from fresh produce by selling processed items such as sauces, jams, pickles, soup, and honey. This is an important tactic given that the bulk of the economic value in the conventional food system comes from processing and distribution,[16] and many urban farms have discovered that economic self-sufficiency can be difficult to achieve through the sale of produce alone. Additionally, such processing provides farms with branding opportunities. Initiatives like Food From the 'Hood (FFTH) illustrate the economic success that can be achieved through larger-scale processing and marketing. Established in 1992 with a student-run garden in south central Los Angeles, FFTH has expanded into a student-run natural foods company that distributes its salad dressings to stores nationwide, reinvesting profits in the community.[17]

Stringent regulations for commercial kitchens are an important concern for many entrepreneurial processing operations. In most US states, for example, food products need to be produced in a licensed commercial kitchen under the supervision of a permitted food handler, and commercial kitchens and their licenses are expensive to attain. This is one reason why The Plant's food business incubator will offer a rentable commercial kitchen to new businesses in the food industry (see Case Study 9 below). There are similar expenses for aquaponics operations that need to process their raised fish in a licensed kitchen; otherwise the fish need to be sold alive.

On-site cafés or nearby food carts offer another method of value-added processing. Operations such as Berlin's Prinzessinnengarten have taken full advantage of the retail opportunities presented by an in-garden café, creating a widely appealing experience that attracts customers from all over the city, regardless of their interest in the urban agricultural movement. This is reflective of a shift in branding and marketing that emphasizes place—i.e., the farm itself—over its individual products. Whereas the industrial food system is built around the branding of highly processed end products, in urban agriculture, value is increasingly associated with sites of food production—whether ground-based, rooftop, or CEA. Farms frequently rent their facilities to generate additional income. Brooklyn Grange, for instance, will rent its rooftop for weddings or other special events. In this way, urban farms can recoup economic value for some of the non-monetary benefits they provide, including ecological and aesthetic improvements to the built environment.

For commercial urban farms, this type of branding—together with a strong social media presence—is important to reinforce local food as a lifestyle choice. Successful urban farms have sophisticated websites that inform potential customers not only about where and how to purchase their products, but also about the farm's backstory and current events. A farm can further extend its reach through appearances in the local press, on radio stations, and on television.

COMMUNITY SUPPORT AND INTEGRATION

While branding and public relations are important to increase produce sales, they also generate community interest in local farms. Many farms offer tours, educational programs for youth, and workshops for interested farmers. To organize these programs, most commercial farms have established a nonprofit sub-organization. Dividing a business into two arms—one for-profit and the other nonprofit—has proved successful for operations trying to reconcile the need to make money with social and educational objectives. The nonprofit branch operates and is funded like a traditional nonprofit organization while the for-profit section focuses on maximum productivity and sales. The Plant in Chicago is organized in this fashion, and Brooklyn Grange is similarly arranged partnering with City Growers, a nonprofit entity that manages their educational programs.

Community outreach provides urban farms with an important mechanism to give back to their neighborhoods. This is especially true in communities with low-income residents who may not be able to access locally grown food at its premium market price. The high price point that farms require to profitably grow quality produce poses an ethical conflict for many urban farmers interested in making their crops more accessible to low-income consumers. In response, farms such as Growing Power have devised various methods to support their nearby communities, including donating surplus produce to food banks and other food security programs that support disadvantaged residents. Growing Power's Farm-to-City Market Basket Program is one of the oldest food security programs of this kind.

Engaged communities also provide an important source of volunteer labor for urban farms, and farms have started to organize volunteer participation events to provide effective instruction for special projects. Farmers also offer internship programs in which interns commit to a specific number of hours per day or week for an entire growing season. These programs help farms generate an additional labor force that they can train over time. In return, the interns receive a practical introduction to urban farming over the course of one summer. Indirectly, the internship programs support job training and help interns get jobs in urban agriculture or start their own operations. As a consequence, urban farms are also job creators. They usually offer jobs for a wide range of skill levels, from highly trained management opportunities to various support roles. Hydroponic farms in particular create a lot of jobs due to their need for a sizable staff to support the daily greenhouse harvest.

DESIGN CONSIDERATIONS

With the variety of operational strategies available, it is essential for designers to understand all aspects of the urban farm operation. Only with this expertise will they be able to fully integrate their urban farm project into a more sustainable food system and the local foodshed. Too often, designers focus on incorporating the physical (growing) systems into the building or urban context without considering the operational system. Who operates the farm? What are the most lucrative, viable crops to grow? And how will they be distributed? If these simple questions are not integrated into the design process from the beginning, urban agricultural projects are often doomed to failure.

Urban agriculture demands that design professionals expand their systems thinking from physical to operational systems. Working in this interdisciplinary field increases the designer's ability to think holistically about a project, a requirement for any successful project in the built environment. Designers must consider the entire cycle, from conception, programming, and financing to economic and sustainability planning and community integration.

▲ Figure 4.10

Hoop house, one of Growing Power's important growing strategies, Growing Power, Milwaukee

CASE STUDY 7: GROWING POWER

Organization: Growing Power
Founder: Will Allen, CEO
Architects: The Kubala Washatko Architects, Inc. (Vertical Farm)
Engineers: Michael Utzinger, University of Wisconsin-Milwaukee
Location: Milwaukee, WI (headquarters); Chicago, IL; United States
Operation: Milwaukee headquarters since 1993, Chicago branch since 2002
Growing Systems: field cultivation, hoop houses, and aquaponics
Growing Area: ca. 200 acres total, with 2 acres at headquarters in Milwaukee and 12 acres in Chicago
Growing Season: outdoor beds from May to October; hoop houses and aquaponics year-round (43° N latitude)
Annual Yield: 40 tons Milwaukee headquarters, 500 tons in total
Main Distribution: farm stand/store, market baskets, Rainbow Farmers' Cooperative, farmers' markets, restaurants, and supplier of public schools

A nonprofit organization located in Milwaukee, Growing Power seeks to better its local community by growing healthy, sustainable, and inexpensive food. Their focus on "growing" soil and developing sustainable growing methods, together with outreach opportunities, community empowerment, and education, is central to Growing Power's success. Growing Power seeks to change the relationship people have with the food they consume by teaching volunteers, employees, and underserved youth about various crops and growing systems.[18]

The actions of the organization embody their goal of "growing food, growing minds, and growing community."[19] Over the past 20 years, Growing Power has evolved into a multisite organization; its network includes their headquarters in Milwaukee, branches in Chicago and Madison, numerous farm sites, and 15 Regional Outreach Training Centers throughout the United States.

Background and Development

Growing Power has developed from one man's urban farm to an organization with several locations and a multilayered approach to intensive cultivation, education, and outreach. In 1993, Will Allen, son of sharecroppers and a former professional basketball player, purchased a 2-acre greenhouse nursery, the last remaining agriculturally zoned parcel within the city limits of Milwaukee. Initially, he intended to use the site as a farm stand to sell produce grown on his Oak Creek farm, which he started while working as a corporate executive at Procter and Gamble.[20] The existing greenhouses and nursery, however, quickly turned into a community food center and the organization's headquarters.

The development of Growing Power relied on several key tactics helpful in establishing community food systems. The organization's projects and approaches fall into four distinct categories, which all work together to create what Allen describes as the "Good Food Revolution" (Figure 4.11):

1. *Growing methods, composting operation, and expansion of farm sites.* Growing Power developed a variety of integrated farming methods suitable for the urban environment—including raised beds, hoop houses, and aquaponic cultures. In addition, the organization established a sophisticated composting operation to produce nutrient-rich soil, the foundation of their farming success. For the last 15 years, the farm has expanded its operation to underserved communities, large farm sites, and other cities. In 2002, Allen's daughter Erika spearheaded the expansion of the organization to Chicago.
2. *Food production and diversification of distribution methods.* The farm cultivates high-quality, healthy, affordable food and develops alternative distribution methods to make it available to all members of the community. Besides selling produce at farm stands and farmers' markets, Growing Power supports small farms through a cooperative network, reaches out to large-scale distributors to open up other markets, and use a food security program to reach economically disadvantaged residents.

▲ Figure 4.11

Growing Power's "Good Food Revolution," photomontage by Douglas Gayeton, Lexicon of Sustainability

3. *Youth engagement, education, and outreach.* Youth engagement has been a driving focus of the organization from the beginning. In 1995, Allen partnered with the YWCA to create opportunities for youth to learn urban farming skills. Today, the Youth Corps program is still an essential part of Growing Power's mission and trains several hundred underserved youth each year. In addition, the organization hosts several different educational programs, such as two- to three-day weekend workshops, as well as an in-depth Commercial Urban Agriculture Program that was established in 2008. Growing Power began expanding its educational network with the creation of six ROTCs in 2008; today the network includes 15 centers.

4. *Financing, grants, and awards.* As a nonprofit entity, the organization improves its operation through collaboration with other nonprofits, its increasing ability to secure large grants, and recognition through numerous awards. In 2008, Allen was named a MacArthur Fellow and received a $500,000 award. This prestigious award made his work broadly known outside the urban agricultural movement. It led to participation in First Lady Michelle Obama's "Let's Move!" campaign and being named one of the "World's Most Influential Foodies" by Michael Pollan and Forbes Magazine.

Growing Systems and the Nutrient Cycle

Growing Power has developed a variety of indoor and outdoor growing techniques mainly supported by their self-generated, nutrient-rich compost soil, including traditional field cultivation, soil-based growing beds and containers in greenhouses and hoop houses, microgreens cultivation, and aquaponics. In 1997, Growing Power started to embrace the practice of aquaponics from Toronto's Food Share program; since 2004, the organization has operated its own aquaponic model developed in collaboration with the University of Wisconsin-Milwaukee (Figure 4.12).

An extensive composting and vermicomposting operation largely contributes to Growing Power's success. The cultivation of nutrient-rich, healthy soil allows the organization to create new growing areas (even on non-arable sites using raised beds) and intensify cultivation through soil amendments (in soil-based cultures). In 1996, a partnership with Alison Cohen of Heifer Project International and a grant from the Kellogg Foundation intensified the compost operation. To supply the rapid expansion of its composting operation, Growing Power began to collect organic waste from a network of local businesses in 1999. The organization partnered with WasteCap Wisconsin to divert organic waste from landfills and created partnerships with businesses and institutions like Sendik's, a local grocery store; the Lakefront Brewery; Kohl's; Wal-Mart; and the University of Wisconsin-Milwaukee to receive their compostable waste.[21] Today, the program diverts over 400 tons of waste from landfills each week.

To optimize the composting process and output, Growing Power mixes 25% "green," nitrogen-rich organic waste and 75% "brown," carbon-rich organic matter in compost bins and windrows. This mixture needs to remain moist: water

▼ Figure 4.12

Greenhouse with aquaponics growing system and stacked growing beds, Growing Power, Milwaukee Headquarters

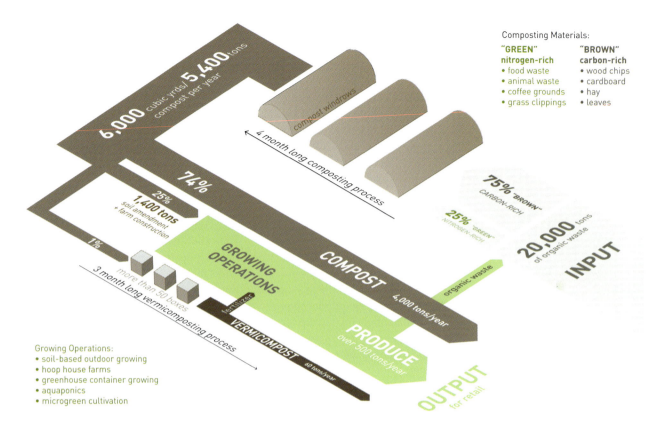

▲ Figure 4.13

Composting operation and nutrient flows, Growing Power, Milwaukee

is added if needed, and the mix is turned frequently. With the finished compost, Growing Power creates new growing beds—even on parking lots and brownfield areas—by layering 12 inches (30 cm) of soil on a bed of wood chips installed for drainage. Each year the company produces 6,000 cubic yards (4,600 m³) of soil from organic waste (Figure 4.13). One quarter of that compost is used in existing growing beds and new farm sites. The remaining three-quarters are sold.[22]

Some of the compost is further refined through vermicomposting, which produces a very effective fertilizer. The organization operates over 50 vermicomposting bins and several composting rows (Figure 4.14). Worms, primarily red wigglers and red earthworms, continue to digest the organic material in the compost and enrich it with worm castings. To start the 12-week composting process, alternating layers of worms and compost are stacked in a 36-ft³ (1-m³) wooden box. At the end of the processing cycle the top of the compost is covered with wire mesh, and a layer of fresh compost—ideally fruit—is added to attract the worms. About 80% of the worms will migrate through the mesh to the top layer and can be pulled out of the compost and used to start the next vermicomposting cycle (Figure 4.15). The worms reproduce quickly, often quadrupling their numbers in four months. Vermicompost boasts higher nutrient density than normal compost, and worm castings and worm mucus additionally improve soil moisture retention, preventing nutrients from washing away during first watering. As the worms process the organic material, they also remove contaminants and increase beneficial bacteria, which break soil nutrients down into more bioavailable forms.[23] Growing Power's refined vermicomposting cultures allow the organization to successfully pursue intensive growing practices in

▲ Figure 4.14

Vermicompost boxes, Growing Power, Milwaukee Headquarters

▶ Figure 4.15

Removal of earth worms from vermicompost box after composting process, Growing Power, Milwaukee Headquarters

containers, raised beds, and microgreen cultivation in their greenhouses. Since 2003, the operation has sold worm castings directly to the public as organic fertilizer and for the "Milwaukee Black Gold Tea" bag, a dried version that can be "steeped" to create liquid fertilizer.

Water and Energy Cycles

While Growing Power focuses on closing the nutrient cycle, it also experiments at its Milwaukee headquarters with strategies to reconnect the water and carbon cycles. The operation was awarded a $35,000 grant from the Milwaukee Metropolitan Sewerage District to construct a rainwater harvesting system. Rainwater from the greenhouse roofs feeds the aquaponic systems and is used to make "worm casting tea" as fertilizer. Each greatly benefits from the use of rainwater, as chlorinated municipal water would kill the valuable microorganisms essential to both systems.

On the roof of its south-facing market stand and between its greenhouse roofs, Growing Power has also installed photovoltaic panels to harvest solar energy. The electricity these create offsets about 25% of the farm's energy use,[24] thereby reducing its carbon footprint. The farm is also experimenting with an anaerobic digester; the methane this produces is intended to be an additional energy source.

Operation and Yields

Growing Power produces 40 tons of produce on its 2-acre headquarters site and an estimated 500 tons across all farm sites.[25] Between 150 and 200 different vegetable crops are planted annually. In addition, the farm produces honey, raises chickens and goats, and grows tilapia and yellow perch in its aquaponic systems.[26]

Distribution Models

Growing Power sells produce to local buyers from its headquarters' farm stand and through its market basket program, as well as selling wholesale to restaurants. This market basket program, which closely resembles a community-supported agriculture (CSA) model, provides lower-income neighbors with an affordable system of buying healthy, local foods.

In addition, Will Allen applies his sales talent and skills to developing new distribution methods. In 1993, Growing Power established the Rainbow Farmers' Cooperative (RFC) to support small farming operations by creating a network to increase marketing opportunities. Growing Power also distributes its produce at a dozen farm stands hosted by various corporate sponsors. In 2009, Growing Power partnered with Milwaukee Public Schools and their food distributor Sysco to provide local produce to public schools. The farm has since expanded the program to serve other Wisconsin and Chicago school districts. Under these partnerships, Growing Power sold 40,000 lbs (18,000 kg) of carrots, the largest farm-to-school fresh food procurement ever carried out in the United States, in January 2014.[27]

Financing and Business Planning

Allen states that to be able to survive as a nonprofit organization today, "We have to grow some of our own money, instead of just applying for grants."[28] This is especially important since Growing Power has grown to become a large farm operation on 200 acres of growing space, with around 150 full-time employees and 1700 volunteers annually, and supports an extensive outreach and educational network. Its revenue from produce ($750,000 worth of crops in 2014) and other products, sales of compost and soil, fees for workshops and educational programs, speaker honoraria, and consultancy on constructing growing systems[29] generate more than half of the organization's annual multimillion dollar operating budget ($2,850,000 in 2010) (Figure 4.16). The other portion is funded by grants.

To successfully secure these increasingly large grants, the organization works with professional grant writers. Most of the grant money supports Growing Power's expanding outreach and the dissemination of its educational mission nationwide. In 2011, Walmart awarded Growing Power a $1 million grant to strengthen existing ROTCs and create new ones. While Allen received heavy criticism for accepting the grant from a large corporation that supports the conventional food system, he thinks that companies such as Walmart have

▼ Figure 4.16

Resource flows at Growing Power's headquarters in Milwaukee

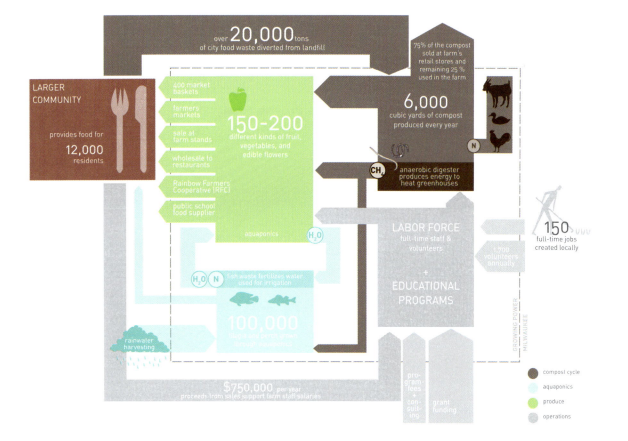

Operation: Farm Management, Business Planning

to be integrated into the Good Food Revolution to make change on larger scale possible.[30] One year later, Growing Power received a five-year, $5 million grant from the Kellogg Foundation to develop five community food centers in five different states. The centers will be modeled after Growing Power's headquarters in Milwaukee but tailored to local conditions and needs.[31]

Education

Growing Power spreads its vision and expertise through youth programs, weekend workshops, and intensive training programs in commercial farm operation. Weekend workshops cover the basics of aquaponics, composting and vermicomposting, stormwater management, animal husbandry, beekeeping, mycoscaping (mushroom growing), and year-round production, as well as business planning and marketing for urban farms. In-depth training covers the logistics of creating and sustaining community food systems and commercial urban agricultural projects.

Social Effects

Growing Power works to create sustainable food systems and increase food security primarily through community and social outreach, encouraging people to eat healthier, more nutritious food. It provides affordable access to local food in food deserts and offers nutrition education for children. From its first days, Growing

▼ Figure 4.17

Composting workshop with Will Allen, Growing Power, Milwaukee Headquarters

Power has engaged local youth in the cultivating, processing, and selling of produce. The Milwaukee headquarters alone had almost 400 youth corps graduates in 2014.[32] The organization also gives back to the community by sponsoring community gardens, including donating compost to 50 Milwaukee daycare mini-gardens. Growing Power's *Growing Food and Justice for All Initiative* (GFJI) aims to increase the role and input of minority communities in the sustainable food systems movement. The ROTCs are also integral to Growing Power's sustainable food system network because they host training sessions and community development programs in collaboration with local urban agriculture organizations. Finally, Growing Power seeks to influence policy through land trust work[33] and has succeeded in changing urban composting regulations.[34]

Design and Building Integration

Growing Power's agricultural systems are integrated insofar as its diverse operations—from soil production to crop cultivation to aquaponics—benefit and rely on each other for nutrients and growing media. These low-tech systems are in most cases, however, not integrated with greenhouse building systems. Exceptions include the rainwater harvesting system and the use of excess heat from composting piles to heat hoop houses. Growing Power's proposed vertical farm on the Milwaukee headquarters site, developed in collaboration with Kubala Washatko Architects, will provide possibilities to experiment with sophisticated, extensive building and systems integration.

Growing Power's Vertical Farm

Growing Power first approached Kubala Washatko Architects in 2006 to determine the feasibility of locating a training and office building at their Milwaukee headquarters. The building also needed to serve as a production and distribution facility. In 2010, the firm was asked to integrate a vertical greenhouse into the design. This culminated in a project that was fully vetted through the Wisconsin Building Code and approved by the city in 2010 (Figure 4.18).

Kubala Washatko Architects embraces a wide range of project types and has designed aquaponic systems at various scales. For Growing Power, the firm was able to leverage this experience to develop what they describe as a "site-specific resolution of highly complex needs on a very small parcel of land." The proposed vertical farm features four stories of cascading, south-facing aquaponic greenhouses with fish tanks below for year-round production. The greenhouses will capture solar energy and their roofs will collect rainwater to feed the aquaponic systems. Heat pumps will transport excess heat into underground storage to heat the greenhouse during the winter months. PV panels and thermal solar panels will generate electricity and hot water. To achieve energy and operational efficiency, the firm has consulted with engineer Michael Utzinger at the University of Wisconsin-Milwaukee as well as with the Madison-based energy modeling firm TESS (Thermal Energy Systems Specialists).

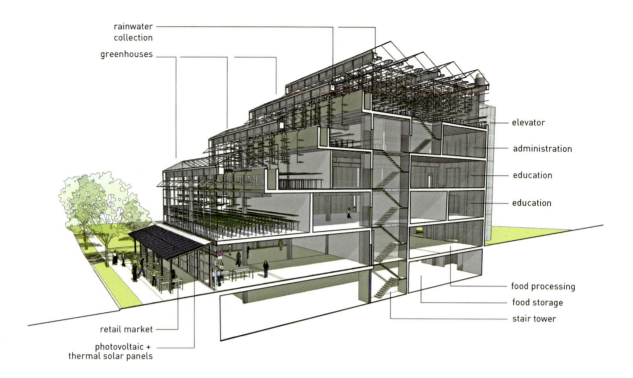

▲ Figure 4.18

Growing Power vertical farm, proposal by the Kubala Washatko Architects, Growing Power, Milwaukee headquarters

The greenhouses and classrooms in the vertical farm will receive primarily natural light. Below the cascading greenhouses will be classrooms, conference spaces, kitchens, and facilities for food processing, storage, and freezing.[35] Administrative offices, volunteer spaces, and staff support areas will be closely connected to the greenhouses and classrooms to increase interaction among students, workshop attendees, and staff. A retail space on the ground floor will support not only year-round sales but also Growing Power's commitment to be a community food center.[36] Although the vertical farm has yet to be built, its programmatic and operational integration of high-tech growing systems with production, education, and outreach space is a compelling precedent for other community-based urban farming initiatives.

Strength and Innovations

Growing Power stands apart for its capacity to engage the full cycle of the food system from the ground up. The program's holistic approach, which starts with the soil, promotes the growing and eating of wholesome food through educational, economic, political, and environmental strategies. Its strength lies in its ability to capitalize on a diverse array of food system networks, ranging from connections with small farmers to ties with conventional large-scale distributors such as Walmart and Sysco. Similarly, Growing Power embraces a versatile suite of methods and technologies to support a mission that has been both highly successful and highly visible.

▶ Figure 4.19

Open house, Brooklyn Grange rooftop farm, Northern Boulevard, Long Island City, Queens, New York

CASE STUDY 8: BROOKLYN GRANGE

Organization:	Brooklyn Grange
Cofounders:	Ben Flanner, Gwen Schantz, Anastasia Cole Plakias
Architects:	Bromley Caldari Architects PC and Allied Engineering (at Northern Boulevard site)
	Elizabeth Kennedy Landscape Architects (at Brooklyn Navy Yard site)
Location:	the Brooklyn and Queens boroughs of New York City, United States
Operation:	since 2010, expanding
Growing System:	productive green roof
Growing Area:	Northern Boulevard: 40,000 ft^2 (3,700 m^2)
	Brooklyn Navy Yard: 43,000 ft^2 (4,000 m^2) (on a 65,000 ft^2 or 6,000 m^2 roof)
Growing Season:	Nine months, March through November (40° N latitude)
Annual Yield:	10 tons per acre
Main Distribution:	Farm stand, farmers' market, restaurants and CSA model

Brooklyn Grange is a privately owned for-profit venture started in 2010 by a team of five young urban farmers and entrepreneurs in New York City.[37] Today, the company operates the world's largest (green roof based) rooftop farm, located on two roofs with close to one acre (4,000 m²) of growing area each. It began with a vision to create a commercially profitable urban farm to increase access to local, healthy, and fresh food in the city. In addition to growing and distributing local vegetables and herbs, Brooklyn Grange quickly expanded their services to include consulting about productive green roofs and installation services for clients worldwide. With this diversified approach, the farm has become a noteworthy urban agricultural operation and sought-after brand.

Milestones

Brooklyn Grange's success is based partly on lessons learned in green-roof vegetable cultivation during the development of the Eagle Street Farm. Ben Flanner, one of the managing partners of Brooklyn Grange, was also a cofounder of Eagle Street Farm's 6,000-ft² (560-m²) productive green roof, installed in spring 2009 on top of a music studio in Greenpoint, Brooklyn. The Greenpoint farm was implemented in collaboration with the landscape architects Goode Green.[38] The following winter, Flanner left the Eagle Street Farm leadership team and started Brooklyn Grange with four partners, including Gwen Schantz and Anastasia Cole Plakias. The team secured funding for a new rooftop farm and a 10-year lease for the roof of the Standard Motor Products Building on Northern Boulevard in Long Island City, Queens. Operations began in spring 2010 with the installation of the green roof. After two successful growing seasons, Brooklyn Grange expanded with an even larger green roof in the Brooklyn Navy Yard (Figure 4.20). The increased growing area allowed them to diversify their operation, expand their services, and install an apiary of 30 beehives in the Brooklyn Navy Yard. Meanwhile, Brooklyn Grange has consulted on and constructed numerous projects for clients and is seeking to expand their operation onto additional rooftops.

Nutrient Cycle and Growing Systems

Brooklyn Grange employs well-established green-roof technology by using the substrate layer for growing vegetables. Together with Skyland USA, a green-roof media supplier, Brooklyn Grange developed a special substrate for agricultural applications on rooftops. The blend is composed of compost mixed with lightweight, porous stones. These stones reduce the weight of the material (about 20% lighter than typical topsoil), and as the stones slowly break down, they add trace minerals needed by the vegetables. The thickness of the substrate is based on the structural capacity of the host building and determines the range of crops that can be grown. Brooklyn Grange's substrate layer averages 6 inches (15 cm), with growing beds that are 8–12 inches (20–30cm) deep and walkways with a 1-inch (2.5 cm) cover. Using this shallow substrate, the farm successfully cultivates a wide range of vegetables.

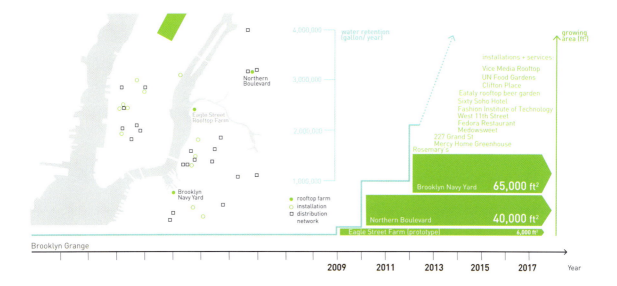

▲ Figure 4.20

Timeline and distribution network in New York City, Brooklyn Grange

Soil fertility is very important for productive green roofs. The agricultural substrate mix at Brooklyn Grange originally included a fertilizer, but after only two years of operation, the farmers found that soil fertility was declining. To mitigate the drop, the farm replenishes its growing substrate with 30 square yards (23 m³) of compost at the beginning of each growing season, all of which has to be brought up in a freight elevator. To further bolster soil fertility, Brooklyn Grange grows nitrogen-fixing cover crops such as rye, buckwheat, vetch, and clover during the winter months. These keep soil from blowing off the roof and are plowed back into the soil in the spring. Thanks to these steps, the farm preserves a high percentage of organic matter in its substrate.

Water Cycle and Water Retention

Brooklyn Grange improves the urban water cycle by retaining stormwater on its green roofs. By slowing and absorbing runoff by 70–85%, the operation is able to retain over one million gallons (3,800 m³) of rainwater each year, thus reducing nonpoint source pollution in adjacent water bodies and helping to eliminate harmful combined sewer overflows (CSOs). While Brooklyn Grange's environmental contribution is still very small relative to the size of New York City, it is an important demonstration of stormwater management. In recognition of its positive environmental performance, Brooklyn Grange has received a large Department of Environmental Protection (DEP) grant from the city.

Irrigation

Although the precipitation in New York City is relatively consistent throughout the year and the substrate layer retains rainwater, the city's rooftop farms need irrigation to grow produce successfully during the summer, much like ground-based farms in the region. What's more, the evapotranspiration rate in the city is higher due to the heat island effect and even higher on roofs due to unobstructed sun and wind exposure.

Brooklyn Grange uses efficient drip irrigation as its primary irrigation system along with some sprinkler irrigation for special applications. To minimize water use and evaporation, the paths between the growing beds are covered with mulch. The farm currently relies on municipal water for irrigation because potable water in New York City is relatively inexpensive. For environmental reasons and to avoid chlorinated water in their organic growing operation, the farm has investigated rainwater storage at strategic collection areas, such as skylights, bulkheads, and rooftop water towers. Storing water in barrels and tanks can be challenging, however, because it creates heavy loads that the host building's structure needs to accommodate. To date, Brooklyn Grange is still examining options for incorporating rainwater harvesting into their operation.

Diversified Operation and Business Strategies

Brooklyn Grange deliberately diversifies its production, distribution, and business strategies to meet the financial challenges. The main objectives are to run the farm profitably and to grow produce sustainably. The farm tracks its cultivation practices in spreadsheets to improve crop selection, timing, fertilization, and marketing from year to year. Brooklyn Grange diversifies its distribution model by selling to restaurants, at farmers' markets, and through a CSA. The two 1-acre (4,000 m²) rooftop farms allow for economies of scale to produce sufficient volume and diversity of crops (Figures 4.21 and 4.22), and the company plans to expand their operation to a third roof in order to increase efficiencies even further.

A second strategy to generate income involves sharing the farm's spectacular sites with others, and these gardens in dense industrial areas with stunning views of the Manhattan skyline have become popular venues. Brooklyn Grange rents out its rooftops as event spaces for farm dinners, movie nights, weddings, corporate events, and yoga classes and charges fees for guided tours and educational programs (Figure 4.23).

The farm's third income-generating approach is to market its expertise in building productive green roofs and rooftop farms. To that end, the company offers consulting and design-build services to help others realize rooftop farms (Figures 4.24 and 4.25). The partners also present at conferences and workshops.

Brooklyn Grange has likewise been successful at cultivating its public image. In addition to a professionally-run website and blog, the farm has a short weekly radio show on Heritage Radio, and the partners are additionally featured in numerous interviews in the press and on television.[39] This publicity and brand awareness extend far beyond New York City and widely increase recognition of the company's expertise and the farm's desirable setting.

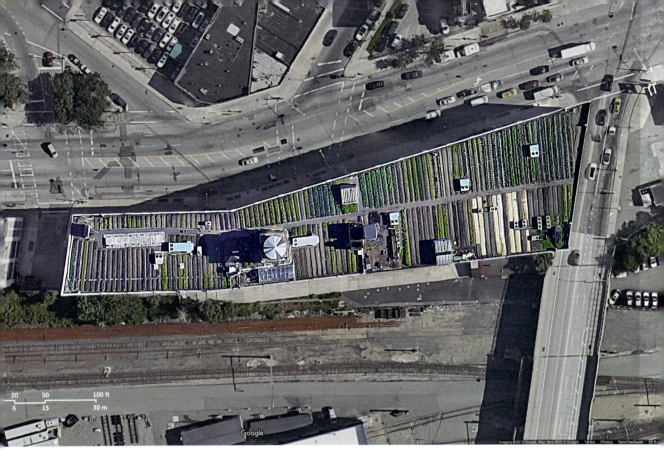

▲ Figure 4.21

Brooklyn Grange rooftop farm, Northern Boulevard, Long Island City, Queens, New York

▶ Figure 4.22

Brooklyn Grange rooftop farm, Brooklyn Navy Yard, Brooklyn, New York

Growing and Harvesting

Brooklyn Grange operates like any other soil-based farm and achieves high yields through rigorous farm management. The farm's goal is to grow four different crops in each growing bed per season. Thanks to the team's growing experience over the past five years, yields have increased to 10 tons per acre annually. In a relatively short nine-month outdoor growing season (March to November), Brooklyn Grange produces a wide variety of crops, which vary slightly from year to year. Crops include leafy greens, heirloom tomatoes (up to 20 varieties), peppers, kale, root vegetables, herbs, and other seasonal produce—totaling over 100 different types of vegetables.

Beginning in early spring, Brooklyn Grange grows most of its vegetable starts in its greenhouse at the Navy Yard and in a hoop house at the Northern Boulevard site. These starts are planted outside once the weather permits. Although the farm has explored several strategies to extend the growing season, it has not used hoop houses on a larger scale during the winter months, largely because it is difficult to secure these lightweight structures against stormy winter winds. In 2013, Brooklyn Grange began to cultivate microgreens in their Navy Yard greenhouse and mushrooms in an indoor space during the winter months.

In addition to its two green-roof farms, Brooklyn Grange operates New York City's largest commercial apiary. With over 30 beehives, the apiary in the Brooklyn Navy Yard produces a large amount of honey per year, as well as comb honey, wax, propolis, and pollen.

Distribution Strategy, Labor Division, and Volunteerism

As in its production, Brooklyn Grange relies on diversification for its distribution system. The company sells its produce at a local farmers' market and at their farm stand once a week, works with over 18 restaurant and catering partners, delivers to several small grocery stores, and runs a small CSA.

Brooklyn Grange is currently managed by three of the five original founding partners and several farm and project managers. In addition to this core team, the farm has a dedicated network of interns, apprentices, investors, landlords, community partners, and fellow farmers. Each 1-acre (4,000 m^2) rooftop farm demands one full-time farm manager and two to three additional farmers. Interns and volunteers provide much of this additional labor. The farm also features several educational programs: an internship program, a refugee and immigrant program, and a special youth curriculum offered through its nonprofit partner, City Growers.

Financing

Although installation costs are much less expensive than those for controlled-environment agriculture (CEA), productive green roofs still require substantial start-up capital. Brooklyn Grange used two different funding models for its two

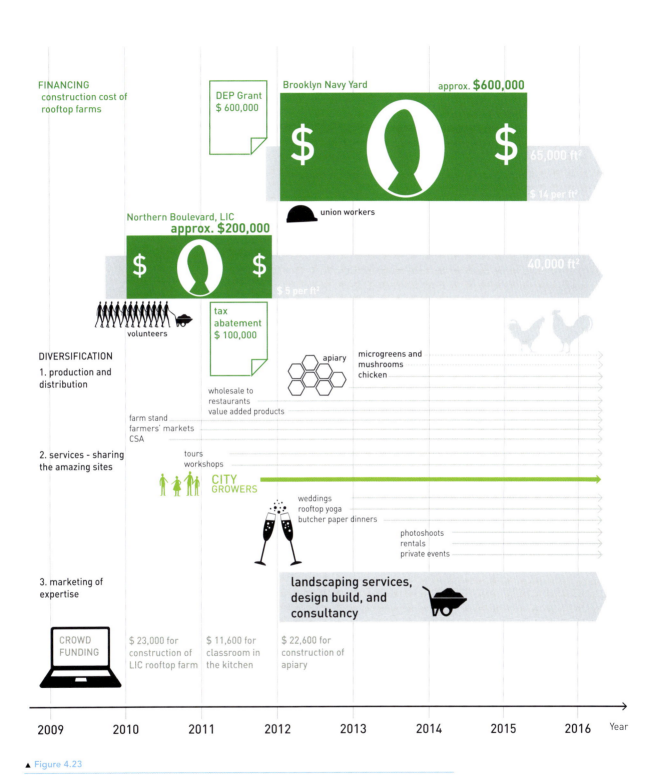

▲ Figure 4.23

Financing and diversification strategies, Brooklyn Grange

rooftop farms, demonstrating that with much creativity and enthusiasm, private funding of urban agricultural projects is possible, though additional grant money allows for an easier start.

Northern Boulevard
The start-up funding for the first farm at Northern Boulevard was achieved through a combination of private equity, small loans, grassroots fundraising events, and crowdfunding platforms. Brooklyn Grange's first Kickstarter campaign generated over $23,000 alone.[40] In total, the farm was able to raise about $200,000 for the substrate and other material expenses. This translates into a remarkably low construction cost of $5 per square foot ($54 per m²), which was only possible thanks to a tremendous amount of volunteer labor during the installation process.

Bromley Caldari Architects helped to secure tax abatements for the green-roof construction. Because this incentive is normally only granted to extensive green roofs, they applied for special consideration. The farm also found an advocate in Christine Quinn, the former speaker of the New York City Council, who saw Brooklyn Grange as an important source of local food. Quinn's advocacy helped the farm qualify for the maximum award of $100,000.

Brooklyn Navy Yard
Two years after the construction of its first rooftop farm, Brooklyn Grange received a $600,000 grant from the DEP's Green Infrastructure Stormwater Management Initiative. This grant primarily financed the installation of the second rooftop farm.[41] Such generous financial support made it possible to install the farm in the Brooklyn Navy Yard, where only union workers can perform construction. The cost of approximately $14/ft² ($150/m²) is still low in comparison to the $20–25/ft² ($220–270/m²) cost usually estimated for construction of intensive green roofs.

Design and Building Integration

The first step in Brooklyn Grange's development was finding the appropriate rooftop, which needed to accommodate an operation of at least 1 acre (4,000 m²) and to produce substantial amounts of produce without the need for any structural retrofits. In addition, the landlord had to be willing to take on a rooftop farm as a tenant. After several failed negotiations, Brooklyn Grange's team settled on the Standard Motor Products Building in Long Island City, Queens, a six-story warehouse built in 1919.

At that point, the Standard Motor Products Building was being converted from a single-tenant to a multi-tenant commercial space under the guidance of Bromley Caldari Architects. Structural considerations were the first step in the process of creating the rooftop farm. The building was originally designed to carry additional stories (a standard practice in that era), therefore the reinforced concrete slab of the top deck offered the same load allowance (130 pounds/ft², 640kg/m²) as all the other floors below. Allied Engineering surveyed the deck through x-ray imaging and confirmed that the roof could hold the required load of 70 pounds/ft² (340 kg/m²) without additional retrofit. Bromley Caldari

▲ Figure 4.24
United Nations food gardens, design-build project assisted by Brooklyn Grange, Manhattan, New York, 2015

▼ Figure 4.25
United Nations food gardens next to the East River, design-build project assisted by Brooklyn Grange, Manhattan, New York, 2015

worked with Brooklyn Grange to accommodate their needs in the renovation and ensured that the farm complied with building codes in terms of access, aisles, cross aisles, and stair bulkheads. (Egress became an important issue when the roof turned into an accessible work and event space.) They also stepped in as a professional consultant to help with the installation of the green roof.

Installation

To install Brooklyn Grange's first rooftop farm, 600 tons of substrate were lifted up six stories with a crane. The crane could not be erected above the subway along the north side of the building without additional permitting. With a rail yard on the south and an arterial connection bridging the rail yard on the east, the crane could only stand on the west side. This position required significant manual labor to distribute the substrate over the entire 500-foot- (150-meter-) long roof. With the help of two dozen volunteers, it took 10 days to install the full substrate layer. The farm operation and crop cultivation began immediately after the completion of the green roof.

Strengths and Innovations

Brooklyn Grange's primary innovation is its transformation of well-established green-roof principles into a productive system on a commercial scale. This not only offers environmental benefits for urban stormwater management, but also activates an underutilized urban resource: rooftops. The farm and business draw financial advantages from these environmental benefits through tax abatements and DEP grants for green-roof construction, which supported the construction of the two farms.

The farm's second great strength is its smart business model and strong, diverse team that capitalizes on the growing interest in urban agriculture and acknowledges that urban farmers and entrepreneurs need to embrace multi-disciplinary approaches. With the relatively low productivity of a nine-month soil-based growing system, the farm would not be able to generate enough revenue to support long-term operations, even with start-up costs covered by grants. The farm therefore relies on diversified business activities that fall into three main categories: (1) a varied and expanding farm operation; (2) marketing the unique rooftop farms for event spaces; and (3) selling their expertise by consulting and building successful rooftop farms for clients. By combining these three different business segments, Brooklyn Grange has become one of the best-known and most successful urban agricultural operations in the United States.

Design professionals have also been important to Brooklyn Grange's success. The expertise of designer-collaborators like Bromley Caldari Architects was essential to successfully install the green roofs and to apply for grant support. The farm's business success, combined with its environmental benefits, should encourage designers to incorporate productive green roofs in their work.

▶ Figure 4.26

Aquaponic raft culture, Plant Chicago

CASE STUDY 9: THE PLANT

Organization:	The Plant (for-profit)
	Plant Chicago, NFP (nonprofit)
Founder:	John Edel
Architects:	SHED Studio, Ryan Wilson, Marcus de la Fleur
Engineers:	dbHMS engineering
Location:	Chicago, IL, United States
Operation:	under construction since July 2010
Tenants:	first tenants since winter 2010
Growing Systems:	aquaponic indoor growing, soil-based outdoor farming
Growing Area:	aquaponic farming area of 30,000 ft^2 (2,800 m^2) once completed
	outdoor growing area of 90,000 ft^2 (8,700m^2) once completed
Growing Season:	year-round for indoor; April–October for outdoor (42° N latitude)
Main Distribution:	weekly farmers' market, store on site, direct to restaurants

Operation: Farm Management, Business Planning

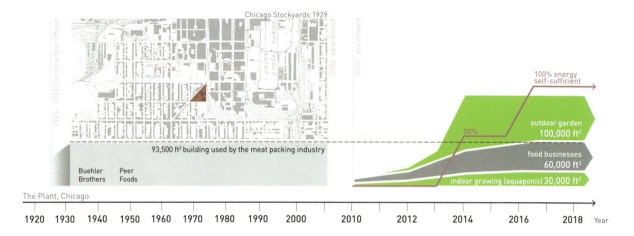

▲ Figure 4.27

Timeline and site plan (1929), The Plant, Chicago

The Plant, located in Chicago's Back of the Yards neighborhood, transformed a former meatpacking facility into a net-zero vertical farm and food business incubator.[42] The building, constructed between 1925 and 1931, served over 80 years in the meat-processing industry before closing in 2006. The Plant's founder, John Edel, spearheaded the facility's return to food production in 2010 when he bought the 93,500-ft^2 (8,700-m^2) building and its 3-acre (12,000-m^2) lot and began to convert it to a closed-loop production operation with the support of a small team of employees and numerous volunteers (Figures 4.27 and 4.28). Meanwhile, The Plant has established a larger, more robust leadership team.

Vision and Development

The Plant's mission is "to develop circular economies of food production and promote building reuse through research, education, and development." To achieve these goals, The Plant has created a closed-loop system in which one

◀ Figure 4.28

Building exterior with new windows, The Plant, Chicago

tenant's waste is another's resource and the building uses the energy it produces. One-third of the structure will house closed-loop aquaponic farming systems, and two-thirds will provide space for sustainable food businesses such as commercial kitchens, bakeries, breweries, and mushroom farms. Tenants will be attracted by low rent, low energy costs, and a licensed shared kitchen. Although established as individual businesses, each with their own closed-loop cycle, the different tenants create an integrated, complex "ecological" network of "producers, consumers, and decomposers." These engineered ecologies work on multiple scales, from molecular processes to the overall energy and resource exchange system within the building and the urban environment.

Nutrient Cycles

The Plant's closed-loop system is primarily based on a nutrient cycle that mimics nature, with "producers" that create organic matter, "consumers" that digest this matter, and "decomposers" that break down organic waste into mineral nutrients and accessible energy.

Producers

The Plant's main productive systems are aquaponic farms, which operate partly for research purposes and partly for commercial enterprises. Plant Chicago, the nonprofit companion to The Plant, runs the research aquaponic systems in the basement. Cultivation begins with seedlings grown in special hydroponic growing beds. After two weeks, the starts are transplanted into a raft system with trays floating on nutrient-rich water in growing pools (Figures 4.29a, 4.29b and 4.29c). The growing cycle lasts between 20 and 30 days depending on the crop, during which time the trays advance from one side of the growing pool to the other for harvesting. The water continually circulates through the growing pools, sedimentation filters, and fish tanks.

In nature, photosynthesis is driven by sunlight; in The Plant, it is powered by electrical light. Grow lights enable year-round cultivation at any location within the building. Currently, Plant Chicago's aquaponic lab is experimenting with different lighting options—LED and fluorescent—and is carefully monitoring which type of light and lighting fixture is most advantageous for which crop. The lab's findings help optimize operation and support the development of vertical growing systems. The Plant is planning to grow crops from floor to ceiling in the upper stories of the building with hopes of increasing the yield per square foot of growing area. In the future, Plant Chicago also plans to supplement the carbon dioxide (CO_2) concentration in the growing spaces with exhaust from other tenant operations.

In addition to accommodating closed-loop aquaponic growing systems throughout the building, The Plant is also in the process of establishing a greenhouse, a rooftop farm, and conventional gardens throughout most of the site (Figure 4.30). In these growing facilities sunlight will produce crops, sequester CO_2, and produce oxygen (O_2). Compost and in-house fertilizer will close the nutrient cycle.

◀ Figure 4.29a, b, & c

Aquaponic growing system: germination station, raft culture, and fish tanks, The Plant, Chicago

▲ Figure 4.30

Outdoor farm and mural on west façade, The Plant, Chicago

Consumers

Produce from the various growing operations of The Plant is consumed by the larger Chicago community. Consumers can access produce at a small store and the food businesses within the building, at the weekly on-site farmers' market, or at local restaurants. All of these distribution routes are beneficial for the local community because the area where the operation is located is considered a food desert. The Plant aims to actively build a relationship with the surrounding neighborhood by offering frequent events that complement the weekly farmers' market. The volunteer and internship programs allow interested residents to get actively involved in The Plant.

Decomposers

Several mushroom farms are located in the basement of The Plant. Mushrooms are fungi in the category of decomposers and can be grown on a wide range of media. In The Plant, they grow on in-house compost, fertilizer, and solid fish waste. While producing mushrooms for human consumption, the fungi make further use of spent materials. As powerful decomposers, they transform organic matter into mineral nutrients available for producers in the nutrient cycle. This process is essential for recycling the finite nutrients within an ecosystem. Eventually, the mushrooms will be harvested and the growing substrate used to amend the soil-based growing operations in the gardens. The decomposition of

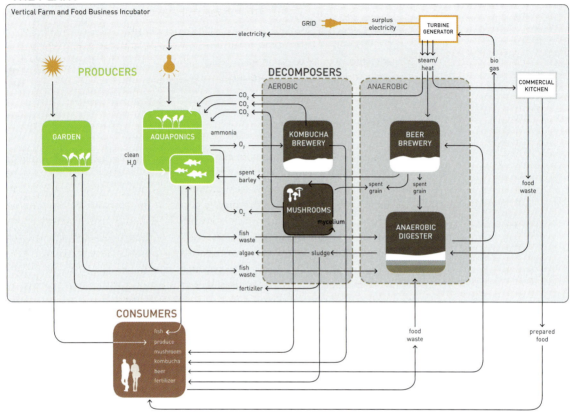

▲ Figure 4.31

Vertical farm and food business incubator—resource flows, The Plant, Chicago

organic material in the presence of oxygen is the ecological counterpart to photosynthesis. It requires O_2 and produces CO_2 and can work in resource exchange with the crop-growing operations at The Plant (Figure 4.31).

Fermentation

The Plant integrates both aerobic and anaerobic fermentation processes into its closed-loop systems. Typically, decomposition without oxygen results in fermentation, a process in which living anaerobic organisms, such as yeast, break down organic compounds. There are also fermentation processes in which organisms, such as kombucha cultures, work under aerobic conditions. The Arize Kombucha Brewery, one of the first tenants of The Plant, produces several flavors of kombucha tea. The brewing process inoculates tea with kombucha cultures or "mushrooms." The tea ferments over 5–10 days in the presence of oxygen, producing CO_2. This CO_2 will then be delivered to the growing rooms as CO_2 fertilization to improve photosynthetic plant growth by up to 20%. To contribute additional CO_2 and other byproducts, The Plant recruited a professional beer brewery as a tenant. The beer-brewing process involves alcoholic fermentation, in which yeast converts sugars from grain into cellular energy; ethanol and CO_2 are produced as metabolic waste. The brewing process requires larger amounts of heat, which is generated in The Plant's cogeneration plant, which also produces electrical power. At the same time, the brewery contributes spent barley and grains to the internal waste stream, which can be used for fish food, mushroom-growing media, and energy production.

Anaerobic Digester

The anaerobic digester is the core component of The Plant's alternative energy system, and it will primarily power the grow lights of the indoor farms. The digester is essentially a mechanical stomach that accepts organic waste and converts it into biogas, therefore greatly reducing the need for non-renewable fossil fuels. The Plant's anaerobic digester is currently under construction (Figure 4.32). Once completed, the enclosed, odorless, anaerobic digester will consume approximately 30 tons of food waste per day (around 10,000 tons annually), including all of the waste produced in the facility and by neighboring food manufacturers. The captured biogas will be converted to electricity by a combined heat and power (CHP) biogas engine. Additional products of the digestion process include biosludge that will be used as nutrient-rich fertilizer and solids that will be used as compost. These latter are especially useful in green-roof applications because of their light weight.

▶ Figure 4.32

Anaerobic digester installation, The Plant, Chicago

Energy Cycle

In The Plant's energy system, the CHP system will burn methane to produce electricity and heat. An absorption chiller will use excess heat to regulate the building's temperature. Most industrial buildings need to be cooled year-round because they generate too much heat. This is particularly true of The Plant, which is very well insulated and will produce heat from food manufacturing and grow lights. To even out the electric load of the building between day and night, the indoor growing operations will use the growing lights predominantly at night when electricity is available for a quarter of the daytime price. During the day, The Plant will be able to sell surplus electricity back into the grid at a higher rate.

Water Cycle

The aquaponic growing systems in The Plant are very water-efficient through their recirculating, closed-loop water systems. Beyond these aquaponic systems, The Plant has not yet installed or conceived of any water collection or recycling systems, although doing so could significantly improve their water-use footprint. Rainwater harvesting is a viable option in Chicago, where the annual precipitation is 33 inches (840 mm). The evapotranspiration rate during the summer is much higher than the rainfall during those months, so irrigation is necessary for any summer growing operation. Rainwater harvested on the roof of the building could irrigate the outdoor gardens and refill the aquaponic systems. Another possible water source is the condensate from the absorption chiller, available mostly during the summer months when additional irrigation water is needed. The food production businesses within The Plant offer another significant opportunity for water recycling. The Plant has the potential to close the loop of its water system just as it has with the nutrient cycle, which would greatly enhance the building's environmental performance.

Business Ecology and Operation

The Plant operates as a social enterprise model. This means it has both a non-profit and a for-profit side. Plant Chicago, NFP is the nonprofit side and focuses on social and environmental responsibility. It promotes sustainable food production, entrepreneurship, and adaptive reuse through education, outreach to the community, research, and development. Eventually, it will operate 22,000 ft^2 (2,000 m^2) of The Plant's 30,000 ft^2 (2,800 m^2) of aquaponic growing space, where research will take place. To serve as a business incubator and facilitate job creation, Plant Chicago will also operate the shared, licensed kitchen and obtain approval for processing goods produced on-site, especially the fish grown in the aquaponic farms. The nonprofit arm of the business will also educate the public about sustainable food production, job creation, renewable energy use, and green building renovation.

▶ Figure 4.33

Tenant "Peerless Bread and Jam" with custom-build oven, The Plant, Chicago

The Plant—the building itself—represents the for-profit side and is owned by its founder John Edel. The Plant is still in an adaptive reuse process. This construction process has been mainly financed by grants, online fundraising, volunteer work, and rent payments from the first tenants. Upon completion, The Plant will continue to function as the landlord for Plant Chicago and the other food-business tenants. As a food-business incubator, The Plant offers affordable rents, low energy costs, and other amenities. The hope is to attract new companies to the sustainable food industry and help them establish their businesses, creating up to 125 new jobs (Figure 4.33). The Plant also provides shared office space that is adaptable for different business sizes and needs and encourages communication among the different tenants. The communal atmosphere is fostered with a large tenants' lounge that offers event space and other opportunities for exchange. The hope is that these shared amenities will inspire consulting and collaboration among related businesses.

Design and Building Integration

The existing building provides ideal conditions for food-industry operations and growing systems. Because of its heritage as a meat-processing facility, all spaces have floor drains and many have food-grade surfaces. Since 70% of the original building was refrigerated, all existing walls are hyper-insulated. The decommissioned ammoniac cooling system provides piping that can be reused for the new cooling system or other infrastructure. What's more, the building's size is ideal for reuse as a vertical farm and food-business incubator. The many different food businesses and growing operations in The Plant will be ideal for establishing interconnected recycling networks, and the exchange of byproducts and resources will only grow with the diversity of tenants.

Adaptive reuse adds another level of sustainability. John Edel estimates that 80% of the building will be recycled; only minimal construction material will be trucked off-site during the remodel of the building. The Plant has also established several large material storage spaces for reusable material, allowing it to re-construct itself using its own resources. This is another hallmark of resource efficiency.

Strengths and Innovations

The Plant is an excellent model for integrating improved ecological performance and growing systems in an existing building. The building allows for complex interrelationships and exchanges among the products and byproducts of different users. It showcases how to incorporate ecological recycling and use organic substances, redefining conventional assumptions about building systems. Organic matter drives the energy production and all resource cycles of The Plant. The building provides a conceptual and infrastructural system that supports exchange among resources specific to biological processes.

Through its radical approach, The Plant challenges the established notion of best practices in environmental performance. The almost 100,000 ft^2 (9,000 m^2) building will eventually run its operations without fossil fuel and will house over a dozen food businesses. In the process of meeting its own heat and power needs, this operation will eventually divert over 10,000 tons of food waste from landfills each year.

Architecturally, The Plant develops a new relationship between abiotic and biotic materials and systems. Biotic systems are embedded into the existing building shell and will develop their own biodiversity over time. Just as natural ecosystems are inherently in flux, so too will the constructed ecologies of The Plant evolve as the building adapts to its new purposes. Eventually, both the building and the engineered ecological systems will perform on a variety of scales, from biological processes to large resource exchange systems to social connections between the project and its host neighborhood.

▶ Figure 4.34

Bok choy grown with Nutrient Film Technique (NFT), Lufa Farms, Ahuntsic, Montréal, 2011

CASE STUDY 10: LUFA FARMS

    Organization: Lufa Farms
      Founder: Mohamed Hage
     Cofounders: Kurt Lynn, Lauren Rathmell, Yahya Badran
      Architects: GKC Gross Kaplin Coviensky Architects
      Engineers: FDA Construction
      Location: Montréal, Ahuntsic-Cartierville, Quebec, Canada
     Operation: founded in 2009, first harvest in April 2011, expanding
 Growing System: hydroponic rooftop farm, polyculture
   Growing Area: prototype (Ahuntsic-Cartierville): 32,000 ft² (3,000 m²)
           second greenhouse (Laval): 43,000 ft² (4,000 m²)
Growing Season: year-round (45° N latitude)
    Annual Yield: 122 tons per acre
Main Distribution: CSA model

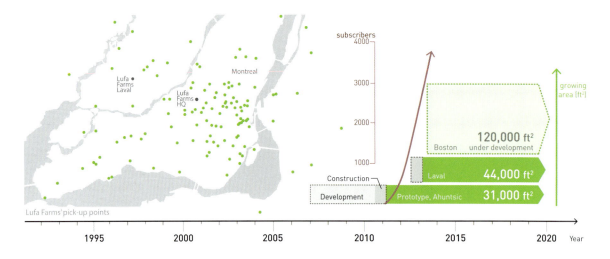

▲ Figure 4.35

Timeline, development and pick-up-points, Lufa Farms

Lufa Farms began operating its first commercial hydroponic rooftop farm in early 2011 on top of a two-story office building in Montréal and currently produces 210 tons of vegetables annually. Each week, it provides a growing number of customers with vegetables harvested the same day, never refrigerated, and directly distributed via community-supported agriculture (CSA) boxes at nearly 200 pick-up points throughout the greater Montréal area (Figure 4.35).[43]

Lufa Farms' Vision

The idea for Lufa Farms was born when cofounders Mohamed Hage and Kurt Lynn asked themselves how they could grow food more responsibly. Driven by concerns about food security, food justice, food safety, food nutrients, and food miles, they conceived of Lufa Farms as a very local urban farm that would create a direct link to consumers by bypassing the industrial food distribution network. According to Lynn, Lufa Farms' business model is based on six main premises:

1. *For profit.* Lufa Farms is a for-profit enterprise and strives to develop an economically sustainable operation to demonstrate the positive effect of rooftop farms on the urban food system.
2. *Market efficiency.* Instead of mimicking the existing unsustainable food system, Lufa Farms builds on a CSA distribution system. It removes the middleman to improve the freshness and quality of food and to maximize the profit margin for the farm itself.
3. *Production efficiency.* The farm grows in a controlled greenhouse environment for year-round production and higher yields. The first two greenhouses are situated in the extreme continental climate of Montréal, with its cold, snowy winters and hot summers, to test the worst-case scenario.
4. *Variety.* To guarantee customer satisfaction and diversity in the CSA boxes, the farm employs polyculture greenhouse management to allow for the concurrent cultivation of multiple crops.

5. *Closed cycles.* Production operates sustainably by harvesting water; abstaining from pesticides, herbicides, and fungicides; and recycling CO_2 and biomass.
6. *Proximity.* The two greenhouses are located fewer than 12 miles (20 kilometers) from the city center to increase proximity between the food's origins and its consumers.

Milestones

The founders began crafting a vision for a new form of responsible agriculture in 2006 alongside a group of engineers, architects, plant scientists, and farming experts. After four years of technical development, construction of the first greenhouse began on top of an office building (Figure 4.36). The first seeds were planted and the first crops harvested in early 2011. Conceived as a prototype for space-strapped urban farms, the first greenhouse is only 32,000 ft² (3000 m²) in size, relatively small in comparison to ground-based commercial hydroponic farms whose total greenhouse area typically ranges from 4–5 acres (16,000–20,000 m²). In 2013, Lufa Farms started operation in their second 43,000 ft² (4000 m²) greenhouse in the Montréal suburb of Laval.

Lufa Farms is planning to expand production soon to additional roofs in the larger metropolitan areas of Montréal, Toronto, and other North American cities. To increase operational efficiency, these new greenhouses will be up to

▼ Figure 4.36

Lufa Farms' first greenhouse, aerial view, Ahuntsic-Cartierville, Montréal, 2011

four times larger than the original prototype and will increase the company's total production area tenfold. A 120,000-ft² (11,100-m²) greenhouse on top of a new warehouse complex in Boston is under development. In addition, Lufa Farms is engaged in several research projects in collaboration with McGill University to further optimize their growing methods.

Nutrient Cycle and Growing Systems

Lufa Farms developed its own polyculture growing systems based on hydroponic growing methods. Conventional hydroponic greenhouses typically plant monocultures for the ease of operation and to maximize profits. Lufa Farms' system, though, supports the cultivation of multiple crops in the same greenhouse while achieving the same high yields as a monoculture operation. Software manages different microclimate zones in the greenhouse, which are created through an evaporative cooler and five heating circuits with separate controls for soil, plant height, roof, perimeter, and snowmelt. The colder zones accommodate various leafy greens, such as lettuce, chard, and mustard greens. Hot zones host fruit-bearing vine crops like tomatoes, peppers, cucumbers, and eggplants. In total, over 40 different vegetable cultivars are grown. These are selected for their taste and nutrient content to distinguish them from vegetables commonly available in supermarkets.

In addition to creating different microclimates, Lufa Farms also uses several different hydroponic growing methods to optimize growing conditions for each plant type. The plant-growing medium, type of irrigation, nutrients, and amount of light plants receive are all carefully customized and monitored for each crop. The farm uses two primary hydroponic growing methods: nutrient film technique (NFT) for leafy greens and a drip-irrigation system for vine crops, cultivated in an inert growing medium (Figures 4.37–4.39). The nutrient inputs

◀ Figure 4.37

Setting up high wire cultivation of tomatoes with drip irrigation, Lufa Farms, Laval, Montréal

▶ Figure 4.38

High wire cultivation of tomatoes with drip irrigation, Lufa Farms, Laval, Montréal

▼ Figure 4.39

High wire cultivation of tomatoes ready to be harvested, Lufa Farms, Laval, Montréal

into the system are inorganic minerals. These are stored in tanks in the basement to create customized hydroponic solutions for each crop. Instead of using synthetic pesticides, herbicides, and fungicides to control pests, Lufa Farms uses biological pest controls in the greenhouse environment. For example, ladybugs are introduced to control aphids.

With its rigorously managed greenhouses, Lufa Farms produces a large amount of organic waste. Training and de-leafing alone produce more than 1,100 lbs (500 kg) of organic material per week in each greenhouse. While Lufa Farms is not closing the nutrient cycle in its own hydroponic production, it does compost all its disposable plant material, organic waste, and cardboard boxes in an industrially-sized, low-energy composter in the basement. Lufa Farms uses this high-quality compost to grow potted herbs, sells it to its customers, and donates some to community gardens throughout Montréal. The farm also intends to establish a closed-loop, waste-into-energy system for their larger facilities currently under development.

Water Cycle

Lufa Farms aims to save and responsibly use water by collecting rainwater and recirculating nutrient solution within the greenhouse. The farm harvests rainwater from the roof of its first greenhouse and stores it in a 37,000-gallon (140-m^3) reservoir in the basement. The site receives 760,000 gallons (2,900 m^3) of rainwater per year, or an average of 61,000 gallons (230 m^3) a month. Of this, 60% can be stored in the rainwater reservoir. Lufa Farms is therefore able to cover a large percentage of its water needs with harvested water. It recirculates all of its irrigation water in its own patent-pending water circulation systems. The hydroponic operation generally reduces water needs to approximately 10% of that required by conventional field agriculture. The closed-loop water system also prevents harmful agricultural runoff and saves money in farm operations.

Solar Energy

Rooftops are underused urban spaces that often receive unobstructed solar radiation. This makes them an excellent location for food cultivation. Lufa Farms' roof, for example, receives 3.8 million kWh of annual insolation, or $400,000 in free solar energy every year. In Montréal's extreme continental climate, passive strategies to conserve energy are essential. Lufa Farms uses several of these strategies to reduce its energy consumption. This is essential because the energy needs of high-tech greenhouses are quite high, up to 12 times higher than for field-grown produce in northern climates (Figure 4.40).

The Lufa Farms greenhouse is thus designed to maximize passive solar gains and to absorb heat from the host building before tapping additional heat from high-efficiency natural gas boilers. Its urban location is an advantage; due to the urban heat island effect, nighttime temperatures in cities tend to

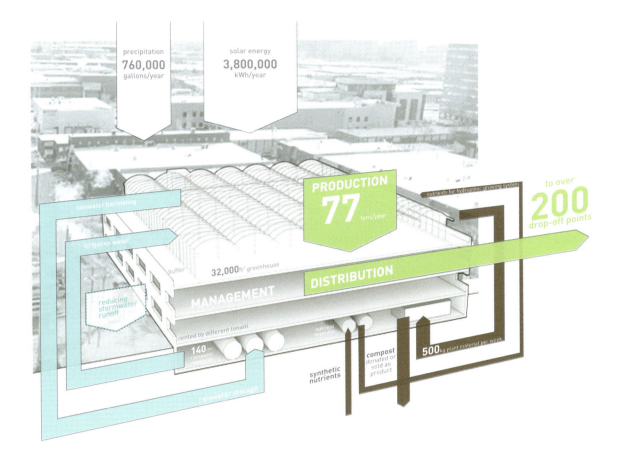

▲ Figure 4.40

Energy and resource flows, Lufa Farms, Ahuntsic, Montréal, 2011

be much higher than in the countryside. Heating demands for the greenhouse occur almost exclusively during cold winter nights. To prevent nighttime heat losses in winter, Lufa Farms deploys an automated, movable thermal screen. This semi-transparent energy curtain, a state-of-the-art greenhouse technology developed in the Netherlands, retains heat, resulting in a significant reduction in the energy needed to heat the greenhouse. The temperature above the energy curtain can be 14°F (-10°C) while the temperature below remains at 71–73°F (22–23°C). Montréal also has high average snow loads of 87 inches (220 centimeters) per winter. A large snow pack would exceed the live load on the roof and block out daylight, so Lufa Farms has two backup heaters to prevent snow buildup. In the summer, the fully operable glass structure vents excess heat.

Through effective passive temperature management, Lufa Farms uses only 50% of the natural gas that conventional greenhouse facilities use for winter heating. Lufa Farms' greenhouse also acts as an insulator for the host building below, making it more energy-efficient. In the winter, the greenhouse helps to save up to 20% of the energy needs for heating the building. In the summer, the combined respiration of all plants in the greenhouse reduces the heat island effect in comparison to a regular roof and reduces the cooling load of the host building by 5–10%.

Operation

Lufa Farms operates in four functional teams: research, greenhouse, consumer, and community. The founders and original research team members have backgrounds in business, engineering, and horticulture, and they contribute their expertise to various areas and oversee the four teams (Figure 4.41).

Research Team
The research team developed the prototype greenhouse, optimizes its operation, selects cultivars, and expands the operation by developing additional rooftop farms. This interdisciplinary operation includes advisors and consultants in construction, real estate development, architecture, greenhouse engineering, plant science, horticulture, and business consulting.

Greenhouse Team: Growing and Harvesting
The greenhouse team consists of members specializing in either growing or harvesting. The harvest team picks the ripe produce weekday mornings between 5 and 10 a.m. They follow a rigorous protocol, proceeding from the cold to the hot zone and from the "cleanest" crop in terms of pest pressure to the less-sensitive cultivars within each temperature zone. Afterwards, the harvest team cleans the growing infrastructure and vacuums any plant debris. In addition to taking care of the plants and harvesting produce, the chief greenhouse aid is also responsible for running the on-site compost operation.

Consumer Team: Distribution
The consumer team administers orders, packs, distributes, and delivers produce. Lufa Farms began operation based on a model similar to community-supported agriculture (CSA), in which consumers bought 12-week subscriptions for a market basket. Customers were able to select from two different content options: baskets composed exclusively of Lufa Farms-grown produce or baskets supplemented with locally grown, seasonal produce from a network of nearby organic farms. The farm has since switched to a pay-as-you-go plan. Lufa Farms curates baskets for customers, who are able to make substitutions and purchase additional products from Lufa Farms, partner farms, and other local food businesses. All ordering and business transactions are conducted on the company's website.

The distribution team packs the baskets for early-afternoon delivery the same day. The extremely short turnaround time of the Pick-and-Pack operation is possible through the use of a tablet application developed by Lufa Farms' IT team. The direct delivery guarantees best quality and is very energy-efficient, as Lufa Farms reduces food miles and energy costs for packaging, refrigeration, and long-distance transportation.

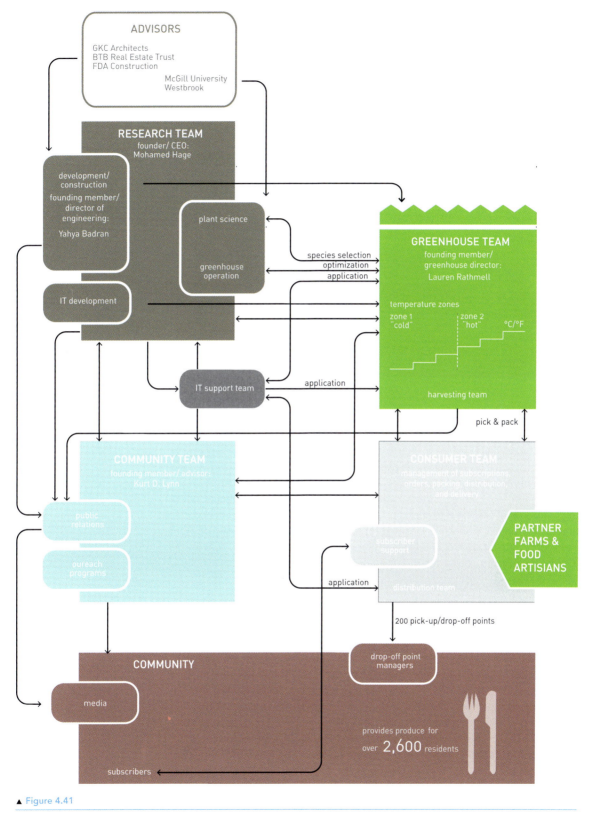

▲ Figure 4.41

Operation and team interaction, Lufa Farms, Montréal

▲ Figure 4.42

Packing of CSA boxes, pick-and-pack, Lufa Farms, Montréal

Community Team: Public Relations and Outreach
The community team is responsible for marketing, outreach, social media presence, consumer education, and public relations (Figure 4.42). Currently, Lufa Farms is not actively advertising its produce and market baskets, relying instead on word-of-mouth recommendations. Farm basket pick-up points at bakeries, cafés, health food stores, fitness centers, yoga studios, and university buildings throughout Montréal foster community by allowing for informal exchanges among customers. And while most hydroponic greenhouses are closed off from the public for pest control and the security of proprietary expertise, Lufa Farms also holds frequent, well-attended open houses.

Financing and Business Planning

Lufa Farms is a privately owned and financed company. Their start-up required courageous business planning and a $2 million up-front investment, primarily for the greenhouse construction. Lufa Farms was able to recruit open-minded partners not only to develop farming expertise but also to support its innovative business idea. The company signed a long-term lease with its building owner, a real estate investment trust that owns and manages several commercial buildings in the Montréal area. Cofounder Kurt Lynn underscores the importance of negotiating this secure long-term lease to ensure the stability of the operation. Clear agreements in the rental contract will also prevent their greenhouse structure from becoming the property of the building owner once the lease expires.

Lufa Farms' business operation has been very successful to date, breaking even after only one year of operation, with $1.2 million in revenue. The company announced in October 2012 that it had secured $4.5 million in equity investments, led by a venture capital fund, to support additional rooftop farming operations in Montréal, Toronto, and the United States.

Design and Building Integration

For its first prototype greenhouse, Lufa Farms selected a renovated two-story building designed to hold an additional floor that was never built. Therefore, it could support the weight of the greenhouse. The building owner also made some minor structural reinforcements and integrated additional stairs, a freight elevator, and a rainwater reservoir to facilitate the farm operation. The greenhouse covers almost the entire roof with its north-south-oriented bays, and the floor below is used for offices and operations. The farm also uses the basement of the building for water and nutrient tanks and for an on-site composter. It has no need, though, for the ground floor, which is rented by a different tenant. Lufa Farms' second greenhouse was developed on top of a new warehouse during construction (Figure 4.43).

While the City of Montréal was receptive to the Lufa project, Lynn admits that getting a rooftop greenhouse designated as an agricultural property in a commercially zoned area was complicated, especially since the agricultural area sits on top of an office building. For the building code, the city defaulted

▼ Figure 4.43

Lufa Farms' second greenhouse, aerial view, Laval, Montréal, 2013

to the most conservative assumptions. Due to concern about flammability, for example, it required Lufa Farms to use glass instead of lighter, less expensive rigid plastic panels as glazing material. The city also followed conservative fire and exit requirements, which conform to the standards for office buildings rather than those for agricultural structures; thus, Lufa Farms is a sprinkler-equipped greenhouse.

The engineering of the greenhouse took into consideration the structure of the building as well as wind velocity issues and the load of the plants. Because of the many complex technical issues, the planning and development phase of Lufa Farms took over four years. Water recycling (through water circulation and harvesting) and energy savings (through the use of passive solar and microclimate management software) were prime considerations for both economic and ecological reasons. The complex system design of the greenhouse highlights both the challenges the designers faced and the innovations they pioneered. It also illustrates the potential for resource recycling and system integrations for urban greenhouses. In comparison to the planning phase, the actual construction process was quite fast, taking less than three weeks.

Strengths and Innovations

Lufa Farms is succeeding in its goals to support the development of cities that feed their own inhabitants, to grow urban communities that are connected by farms, and to create opportunities for city dwellers to know their farmers and their food. Its greenhouse operation, environmental performance, and distribution system adapt existing hydroponic models effectively. Its most significant achievement, however, which made the operation possible in the first place, is the development of a successful enterprise. The founders were able to raise enough private capital to build the farm without relying on grant money. One and a half years after they started the operation, they were able not only to recoup their expenses but also to secure enough funding for expansion to additional rooftop sites in several North American cities.

▲ Figure 4.44

Interior of Gotham Greens' Greenpoint flagship rooftop greenhouse, Greenpoint, Brooklyn, New York, 2011

CASE STUDY 11: COMMERCIAL HYDROPONIC ROOFTOP FARMS: A COMPARISON

Hydroponic rooftop farms are extremely capital-intensive but are also usually economically viable in the long run, and this urban agricultural approach has recently been applied to commercial farms in several North American cities, such as Gotham Greens, New York; BrightFarms, New York; Local Gardens, Vancouver; and Lufa Farms, Montréal.[44]

     Hydroponic greenhouse systems fall into the category of controlled-environment agriculture (CEA). CEA systems allow for efficient year-round production. Moreover, hydroponic farms are resource-efficient because they recirculate water and nutrients, and they offer environmental benefits because they eliminate agricultural runoff. The light weight of some of the hydroponic growing infrastructure—like the nutrient film technique (NFT) and drip irrigation—is ideal for rooftop applications. Additionally, rooftops are an underused spatial resource in cities and offer excellent sunlight exposure. The installation of greenhouses on urban roofs may symbiotically improve both the performance of the commercial greenhouses and their host buildings. While these four hydroponic rooftop farms share most of these general benefits, they vary considerably in their operational approaches.

GOTHAM GREENS

Organization: Gotham Greens
Cofounders: Viraj Puri and Eric Hayley
Horticulturist: Jennifer Nelkin
Location: New York, United States
Operation: founded in 2008, first harvest 2011, expanding
Growing System: hydroponic rooftop greenhouses
Growing Area: Greenpoint, Brooklyn, New York City: 15,000 ft^2 (1,400 m^2)
Gowanus, Brooklyn, New York City: 20,000 ft^2 (1,900 m^2)
Jamaica, Queens, New York City: 60, 000 ft^2 (5,600 m^2)
Pullman, Chicago, IL: 75,000 ft^2 (7,000 m^2)
Growing Season: year-round greenhouse operation (40° N latitude)
Annual Yield: 400 tons per acre
Main Distribution: direct to supermarket

Founded in 2008 by Viraj Puri and Eric Haley, Gotham Greens designs, builds, and operates commercial-scale hydroponic greenhouse facilities. The team running Gotham Greens has experience in a variety of fields. Puri is well versed in technical research from his tenure with Ted Caplow at New York Sun Works (NYSW). Haley brings financial expertise and developed the long-term purchasing agreements with Whole Foods that financed the construction of the greenhouses. Jennifer Nelkin, head of greenhouse operations and partner since 2009, brings a knowledge of plant physiology and greenhouse systems from her work at the Controlled Environment Agriculture Center (CEAC) at the University of Arizona and at the NYSW Science Barge. Gotham Greens has built several commercial-scale rooftop greenhouses, including one in Greenpoint, Brooklyn (Figure 4.45), from 2011, a facility atop the Gowanus Whole Foods from 2013, a facility in Jamaica, Queens, and a greenhouse atop the Method factory in Pullman, on the far south side of Chicago. The latter two were completed in 2015.[45]

◀ Figure 4.45

Gotham Greens' flagship rooftop greenhouse with photovoltaic array in front of Manhattan skyline, Greenpoint, Brooklyn, New York, 2011

BRIGHTFARMS

Organization: BrightFarms
Founder: Dr. Ted Caplow, now chairman
CEO: Paul Lightfoot
Location: Headquarters: New York, United States
First farming operation: Yardley, Bucks County, PA, United States
Operation: in development since late 2006, first harvest in January 2013, expanding
Growing System: ground-based hydroponic greenhouses
Growing Area: 56,000 ft^2 (5,200 m^2)
Growing Season: year-round greenhouse operation (40° N latitude)
Annual Yield: 194 tons per acre
Main Distribution: direct to supermarket

In 2006, Dr. Ted Caplow founded the nonprofit organization New York Sun Works (NYSW) to research and develop educational models for hydroponic farming. NYSW's Science Barge proved to be a significant prototype for urban hydroponic farming (see Case Study 16). In 2007, Caplow founded BrightFarm Systems, a for-profit greenhouse consultancy that builds on the research of NYSW. BrightFarm Systems was involved in the development of several New York hydroponic farms, including rooftop greenhouses at the Manhattan School for Children (P.S. 333) and at Forest Houses in the Bronx. At the end of 2010, BrightFarms acquired BrightFarm Systems. Under the guidance of new CEO, Paul Lightfoot, the company shifted focus to being a builder, financer, and operator of greenhouse systems. In 2012, Gould and Caplow estimated that BrightFarms greenhouses could produce 250 tons of produce per acre and generate $1–1.5 million in annual revenue. BrightFarms currently operates one ground-based hydroponic greenhouse in Bucks County, Pennsylvania (Figure 4.46), and broke ground on another ground-based greenhouse project in Rochelle, IL.[46]

▶ Figure 4.46

Interior of BrightFarm's greenhouse, Bucks County, PA, 2012

LOCAL GARDEN

Organization:	Alterrus
CEO:	Christopher Ng
Location:	Vancouver, BC, Canada
Operation:	in development since 2008, production started 2012, bankrupt in 2014
First harvest:	2012
Growing System:	proprietary hydroponic rooftop greenhouses by VertiCrop
Growing Area:	6,000 ft² (560 m²) of greenhouse space
Growing Season:	year-round greenhouse operation (49° N latitude)
Annual Yield:	predicted 150,000 lbs (75 tons)
Main Distribution:	produce direct to supermarket; VertiCrop system to greenhouse management companies

Local Garden provided Vancouver with 150,000 pounds (68,000 kg) of microgreens annually from a 6,000-ft² (560 m²) rooftop greenhouse facility atop a parking garage. Local Garden was owned by Alterrus, designer and manufacturer of the VertiCrop hydroponic system. The Vancouver greenhouse primarily served as a demonstration ground for the VertiCrop system, which Alterrus hoped to sell to greenhouse owners.

The company began in 1996 as Valcent. Its early research focused on algae biomass technologies and other eco-friendly services. Company president and plant physiologist Glen Kertz also developed a vertical growing system known as VertiCrop. In 2008, the company shifted its focus to developing the VertiCrop system. The economic recession forced Valcent to move their operation from the United Kingdom to Canada, where the company changed its name to Alterrus. The company negotiated a low lease for a parking garage roof from the City of Vancouver, where they installed the Local Garden greenhouse in 2012 (Figure 4.47). Based on their previous mismanagement, and despite the promise of Local Garden, Alterrus was forced to declare bankruptcy in January 2014. In August 2015, a new owner started an online funding campaign to relocate the growing infrastructure and restart the operation.[47]

Timelines

Beginning in 2006, two independent teams developed models for hydroponic rooftop farms: Lufa Farms, led by Mohamed Hage in Montréal, and Ted Caplow's Science Barge group that developed into Gotham Greens and BrightFarms, both in New York. Gotham Greens was the first to develop a viable long-term purchasing agreement business model. All successful teams included partners with technical, financial, and hydroponic expertise to successfully develop and run these farms (Figure 4.48).

▲ Figure 4.47

Local Garden's rooftop greenhouse in operation, Vancouver, BC, 2013

Growing Systems and Greenhouse Operations

While all four farms in this comparison rely or relied on hydroponic growing systems and high-tech greenhouses, each operates or operated differently. Gotham Greens and BrightFarms began by focusing exclusively on leafy greens, one of the most profitable crops in hydroponic farming. Because only one growing system (NFT in this case) and one climate zone are needed, growing one crop type simplifies hydroponic operations. Gotham Greens' second greenhouse added another lucrative crop, tomatoes, grown in high-wire drip production systems. Lufa Farms, however, runs polyculture greenhouses that offer consumers 40 varieties of vegetables. Besides providing specialized nutrient compositions for each species, Lufa Farms' greenhouses integrate two different irrigation systems (NFT systems for leafy greens and high-wire drip systems for

Operation: Farm Management, Business Planning

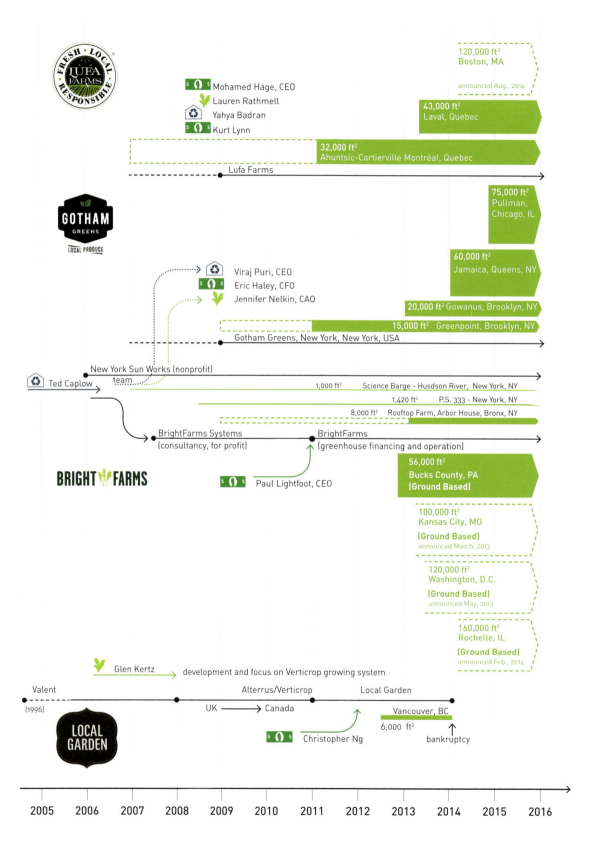

vine crops) and different microclimate zones to optimize the production of each crop. Local Garden, meanwhile, used the proprietary vertical growing system VertiCrop. Stacked 12 trays tall, this system uses space efficiently and purportedly yields leafy green and herb production 20 times higher than field crop production. Local Garden, however, had problems producing leafy green and switched to microgreens, which yield higher profits but require a more specialized customer base of local restaurants.

None of these four hydroponic farms is or was certified organic because, like most hydroponic farms, they dissolve or dissolved minerals as a nutrient source. Only Gotham Greens claims to use Organic Materials Review Institute (OMRI)-certified organic nutrients. At the same time, all four farms operate or operated without synthetic pesticides and herbicides and use or used biological pest management instead.

Water Systems

All four greenhouses integrate or integrated rainwater catchment systems into the design. Though environmentally conscious and economically efficient, integrating water storage into a rooftop greenhouse system can be difficult. The host building must have adequate structural integrity to transfer the concentrated loads of rooftop storage tanks from roof to ground. Lufa Farms solved this problem in its first greenhouse by locating the storage tanks in the basement, a common tactic in retrofitted buildings. Gotham Greens' Gowanus greenhouse was an entirely new construction; thus, proper structural considerations for rainwater storage were integrated from the beginning. In all four farms, collected rainwater irrigates or irrigated hydroponic crops so that these operations use or used ten times less water than conventional farming and produce or produced no agricultural runoff.

Solar Energy

All four greenhouses are or were situated in cities between 40–49° northern latitude and therefore work or worked within comparable climatic constraints while trying to use as much daylight as possible. Gotham Greens and Lufa Farms selected unobstructed roofs and a horizontal growing system to optimize their solar energy exposure, though their year-round operations require supplemental lighting during the winter. In addition to using passive solar and daylight for photosynthesis, Gotham Greens installed photovoltaic (PV) panels on its rooftops to generate electricity. Gotham Greens' Greenpoint greenhouse, for example, features a 60-kilowatt PV system, which offsets 50% of the farm's electricity demands. Its Gowanus greenhouse, meanwhile, features a 157-kilowatt combined heat and power plant (CHP) and a 325-kilowatt PV system, which provides electrical power for the greenhouse and Whole Foods below it. Because of its vertical, stacked growing systems and the limited daylight available in Vancouver, Local Garden required even more supplemental lighting than Gotham Greens and Lufa Farms.

◂ Figure 4.48

Commercial hydroponic rooftop farms: timeline and comparison of farms

Distribution Systems and Financing Models

All hydroponic farms produce close to their customer base to reduce food miles and deliver fresh, high-quality produce. Distribution and financing models vary considerably, though. BrightFarms, Gotham Greens, and Local Garden all rely or relied on high-end food retailers to sell their produce, competing against goods produced by traditional agricultural methods. Marketing is essential to convince buyers to choose produce from these farms rather than similarly priced or cheaper produce from elsewhere.

Gotham Greens and BrightFarms each engineered a close connection between the distribution and the financing model. Signing long-term purchase agreements with supermarket chains not only guarantees distribution of a large percentage of the produce but also helps to secure loans and raise funds to construct expensive greenhouses and hydroponic infrastructure. Gotham Greens started this approach in 2009 when they developed their first long-term contract with Whole Foods. BrightFarms was successful in partnering with several supermarket chains in 2012 but has only realized one ground-based greenhouse to date.

Gotham Greens and BrightFarms also receive significant funding through grants. For the construction of its Bucks County, PA, greenhouse, BrightFarms received $1.26 million from the Reinvestment Fund, a nonprofit community development institution that finances projects unable to obtain bank loans. Gotham Greens, meanwhile, has benefited from grants that include $900,000 from the state Regional Economic Development Council for its greenhouse in Jamaica, Queens.

Lufa Farms has taken a different route and bases its distribution approach on the community-supported agriculture (CSA) model. This model required the founders to raise private capital for the greenhouse construction but allowed them to create a strong community behind their operation (see Case Study 10).

Design and Building Integrations

Both Lufa Farms and Gotham Greens developed their first prototype greenhouses atop existing warehouses, a model that requires a search for an appropriate host building and a landlord willing to agree to this new tenant type and potential structural retrofits. The second greenhouses of both companies were integrated into new construction, allowing for more effective integration of greenhouse and host building and improved performances.

In order to meet the US Department of Energy's Better Building Challenge (reducing energy consumption by 20% by 2020), Whole Foods collaborated with Gotham Greens on their showcase supermarket in Gowanus, Brooklyn (Figure 4.49). This energy-efficient operation includes a 20,000-ft^2 (1,900-m^2) greenhouse on top of the supermarket building. Whole Foods acts as landlord, while Gotham Greens owns the greenhouse and hydroponic infrastructure. With the greenhouse, the supermarket operates 60% more efficiently, with annual energy savings of almost $400,000. The greenhouse works similarly to a green

▲ Figure 4.49

Gowanus rooftop greenhouse, Gotham Greens on Whole Foods supermarket, Gowanus, Brooklyn, 2013

roof by mitigating the urban heat island effect and adding insulation to the building during the winter. In return, the greenhouse absorbs heat from the market below so that the building requires less energy for heating.

Local Garden selected a city-owned parking garage as its host building based, in part, on a low rent negotiated with the City of Vancouver. A garage building, however, does not generate any performance benefits (either for the greenhouse or the host building) since it has does not have a climate-controlled interior.

Strengths and Innovations

These four case studies represent unique development and business approaches for the still-evolving enterprise of hydroponic rooftop farming. As shown from this comparison, no one farming model or business approach guarantees success or predicts failure.

Gotham Greens' solid performance may be attributed to its healthy investor and distribution connections with Whole Foods and the generous grant funding it received for its greenhouses. Furthermore, while New York is an expensive city for real estate and construction, it is also an ideal place to support rooftop farming and has a steady supply of customers willing to buy local produce at premium prices. Based on their success in New York City, Gotham Greens expanded to Chicago and completed the so far largest greenhouse

▲ Figure 4.50

Method factory and Gotham Greens' greenhouse, design by William McDonough + Partners, Pullman, South Side of Chicago, 2015

▲ Figure 4.51

Pullman rooftop greenhouse, Gotham Greens' greenhouse on Method factory, Pullman, South Side of Chicago, 2015

rooftop farm (75,000 ft² /7,000 m²) ever built with their new business partner, Method, a producer of cleaning products, in 2015 (Figures 4.50 and 4.51).

BrightFarms follows a similar business approach but is attempting to develop long-term purchase agreements with a more diverse set of supermarket chains outside of New York City. After building one ground-based greenhouse in the vicinity of Philadelphia, the company is trying to secure additional ground-based projects in other metropolitan areas. BrightFarms seems to have traded the rooftop challenge for a more conventional peri-urban approach. Although Gotham Greens and BrightFarms started with very similar bases of technical expertise, followed the same business model, and assembled strong management teams with diverse backgrounds, they are now, in 2015, at different points in realizing their business goals and farming philosophies.

Local Garden suffered from weak leadership and poor management; it was not the urban farm concept per se that failed. The idea to set up a prototype farm that sells local produce and demonstrates the VertiCrop growing system was a viable approach, but unfortunately, its promising start was not enough to save Local Garden from bankruptcy. Under new management and with the support of an online funding campaign, Local Garden attempted a new start in August 2015.

Finally, with an entirely different business model, Lufa Farms relies on building extensive community support for its expanding hydroponic rooftop operation through a CSA model that feeds more than 5,000 people each week in the Montréal area. The strong financial and entrepreneurial background of its founders allowed the team to build on private start-up funding. Within two years of operation, the group had raised $4.5 million to build a third rooftop greenhouse in Montréal and expand into other North American cities. Currently, the company is developing a 120,000-ft² (11,100-m²) greenhouse on a warehouse in Boston.

NOTES

1. Worldwatch Institute, "Globetrotting Food Will Travel Farther Than Ever This Thanksgiving," www.worldwatch.org/globetrotting-food-will-travel-farther-ever-thanksgiving.
2. Katherine H. Brown et al., "Urban Agriculture and Community Food Security in the United States: Farming from the City Center to the Urban Fringe" (Portland, OR: Community Food Security Coalition, 2003), 4. See also Kathrin Specht et al., "Urban Agriculture of the Future: An Overview of Sustainability Aspects of Food Production in and on Buildings," *Agriculture and Human Values* 31 (2014): 41.
3. Brown et al., "Urban Agriculture and Community Food Security," 5. See also Erin M. Tegtmeier and Michael D. Duffy, "External Costs of Agricultural Production in the United States," *International Journal of Agricultural Sustainability* 2 (2004): 1–20.
4. Brown et al., "Urban Agriculture and Community Food Security," 4.
5. Fifth AESOP Conference on Sustainable Food Planning, *Innovations in Urban Food Systems: Book of Abstracts* (Montpellier: Fifth AESOP Conference, October 2013), 6.

6. Food and Agriculture Organization of the United Nations (FAO), "Profitability and Sustainability of Urban and Peri-urban Agriculture," *Agricultural Management, Marketing and Finance Occasional Paper* 19 (Rome: FAO, 2007): 40.
7. Michael H. Shuman, "The Competitiveness of Local Living Economies," *The Post Carbon Reader Series: Economy* (Santa Rosa, CA: Post Carbon Institute, 2010), 287.
8. R. Vuattoux, "Intensive Vertical Urban Agriculture," Master's thesis, Malmö University, 2012.
9. USDA, *Adding Value to our Food Systems: An Economic Analysis of Sustainable Community Food Systems,* Sustainable Agriculture Research and Education Program (Logan, UT: Utah State University, 1997).
10. Brooklyn Grange, http://brooklyngrangefarm.com/produce/wholesale/.
11. Janine de la Salle and Mark Holland, *Agricultural Urbanism: Handbook for Building Sustainable Food & Agriculture Systems in 21st Century Cities* (Winnipeg: Green Frigate Books, 2010): 78.
12. Brooklyn Grange, http://brooklyngrangefarm.com/produce/wholesale/.
13. Eagle Street Rooftop Farm, "2012 Rooftop Farm Fact Sheet," http://rooftopfarms.org/.
14. Growing Power, www.growingpower.org/produce/rainbow/.
15. Silvio Caputo, "The Purpose of Urban Food Production in Developed Countries," in *Sustainable Food Planning: Evolving Theory and Practice*, ed. Andre Viljoen and Johannes S. C. Wiskerke (Wageningen, the Netherlands: Wageningen Academic Publishers, 2012): 265.
16. De La Salle and Holland, *Agricultural Urbanism*, 69.
17. Jerry Kaufman and Martin Bailkey, "Farming Inside Cities: Entrepreneurial Urban Agriculture in the United States," *Lincoln Institute of Land Policy Working Paper* (2000), 13–15.

Case Study 7: Growing Power

18. This case study is based on several presentations and interviews with Will Allen, founder and CEO of Growing Power, and partly supported by preliminary research conducted by Jessica Michalak in the author's graduate seminar.
19. "Certified Naturally Grown: Growing Power, Inc.,",www.naturallygrown.org/farms/3581.
20. Will Allen and Charles Wilson, *The Good Food Revolution: Growing Healthy Food, People, and Communities* (New York, N.Y: Gotham Books, 2012), 13–14.
21. Christine Grillo, "The Will Allen Index: Growing Power to the People" (Center for a Livable Future), www.livablefutureblog.com/2012/03/the-will-allen-index.
22. Elizabeth Royte, "Street Farmer," *The New York Times Magazine* (July 1, 2009), www.nytimes.com/2009/07/05/magazine/05allen-t.html?pagewanted=all.
23. "Growing Power Vision and Operation Outline," Growing Power Conference (2012).
24. Grillo, "The Will Allen Index."
25. W.K. Kellog Foundation, "Growing Power Awarded $5 Million Grant to Grow Community Food Projects across U.S.," www.wkkf.org/news-and-media/article/2012/09/growing-power-awarded-$5-million-grant.
26. "Growing Power Vision and Operation Outline," Growing Power Conference (2012).

27. Natalie Wickman, "Growing Power Provides a Record 40,000 Pounds of Carrots to Schools," *Milwaukee Neighborhood News Service* (January 24, 2014), www.milwaukeenns.org/2014/01/24/growing-power-provides-a-record-40000-pounds-of-carrots-to-schools/.
28. Joel McNally, "How Is This Man Changing The Way The World Grows Food?," *Milwaukee Magazine* (April 2010).
29. "GlobalGiving: Growing Power," www.globalgiving.org/donate/5278/growing-power/reports/.
30. Tom Philpott, "Walmart Drops $1 Million on Urban-Ag Pioneer Growing Power," *Mother Jones* (September 20, 2011), www.motherjones.com/tom-philpott/2011/09/walmart-drops-1-million-urban-ag-pioneer and https://foodfreedom.wordpress.com/2011/09/18/will-allen-walmart-greenwash/.
31. W.K. Kellog Foundation, "Growing Power Awarded $5 Million Grant to Grow Community Food Projects across U.S."
32. "Global Giving: Growing Power," www.globalgiving.org/donate/5278/growing-power/reports/.
33. Growing Power, www.growingpower.org/
34. Growing Power, "Vision and Operation Outline," Growing Power Conference (2012).
35. The Kubala Washatko Architects, Inc., "Growing Power Vertical Farm," www.tkwa.com/
36. Growing Power, "The Vertical Farm," www.growingpower.org/education/vertical-farm/; Allen and Wilson, *The Good Food Revolution*, Michael Broadway, "Growing Urban Agriculture in North American Cities: The Example of Milwaukee," *Focus on Geography* 52.3–4 (2009): 23–30.

Case Study 8: Brooklyn Grange

37. This case study is based on interviews with Brooklyn Grange's head farmer and president Ben Flanner; Michael Meier, a former farm manager; and founding partner Jerry Caldari of Bromley Caldari Architects.
38. Peter Hobbs, "Soil and Spreadsheets: A Look at the Past and Future of Rooftop Farming with Brooklyn Grange's Ben Flanner," Nona Brooklyn (March 20, 2013), http://nonabrooklyn.com/soil-and-spreadsheets-a-look-at-the-past-and-future-of-rooftop-farming-with-brooklyn-grange%E2%80%99s-ben-flanner/#.VYIVMVxVhBc.
39. "Rooftop Farming with Ben Flanner," Heritage Radio Network, www.heritageradionetwork.com/programs/96-Rooftop-Farming-with-Ben-Flanner.
40. "Kickstarter.com profile for Brooklyn Grange Rooftop Farm," www.kickstarter.com/projects/1909670623/brooklyn-grange-rooftop-farm?ref=nav_search.
41. Rachel Pincus, "First Look at Brooklyn Grange's Massive New Roof Farm at Brooklyn Navy Yard," *Gothamist* (August 2, 2012), http://gothamist.com/2012/08/02/brooklyn_grange_celebrates_first_ha.php#photo-1.

Case Study 9: The Plant

42. This case study is based on a tour and interview with The Plant's founder and owner John Edel and Melanie Hoekstra, a former director of operations. Additional sources: The Plant, www.plantchicago.com/.

Case Study 10: Lufa Farms

43. This case study is based on a presentation and interview with cofounder Kurt Lynn. Additional sources: Lufa Farms, https://lufa.com/en."Lufa Farm Launches Second Rooftop Greenhouse," *Market Wired* (September 23, 3013), www.marketwired.com/press-release/lufa-farms-launches-second-rooftop-greenhouse-1833546.htm. "Lufa Farms/Fermes Lufa," *Carrot City: Designing for Urban Agriculture*, www.ryerson.ca/carrotcity/board_pages/rooftops/lufa_farms.html. Michael Garry, "Montreal Greenhouse Operator Eyes U.S. Cities," *Supermarket News* (October 1, 2012), http://supermarketnews.com/produce/montreal-greenhouse-operator-eyes-us-cities. "TED talk by ted Mohamed Hage," (May 14, 2012), http://tedxtalks.ted.com/video/TEDxUdeM-Mohamed-Hage-How-rooft; Gerry Weaver, "Lufa Farms Expands with Second Rooftop Greenhouse," *The Produce News* (March 27, 2014), www.producenews.com/more-what-s-new/12559-lufa-farms-expands-with-second-rooftop-greenhouse. Richard Heinberg and Daniel Lerch. *The Post Carbon Reader: Managing the 21st Century's Sustainability Crises* (Healdsburg, CA: Watershed Media, 2010). "Lufa Farms Brings Large-Scale Rooftop Farming to Montreal," *Inhabit: Design with Save the World*, http://inhabitat.com/lufa-farms-brings-large-scale-rooftop-farming-to-montreal/bees/. Glenn Rifkin, "Cash Crops Under Glass and Up on the Roof," *The New York Times* (May 18, 2011), www.nytimes.com/2011/05/19/business/smallbusiness/19sbiz.html?pagewanted=all&_r=1. Michael Levenston, "Lufa Farms is Building a Third Greenhouse in Montreal Starting This Spring," *City Farmer News*, www.cityfarmer.info/2014/04/04/lufa-farm-is-building-a-third-greenhouse-in-montreal-starting-this-year/.

Case Study 11: Commercial Hydroponic Rooftop Farms: A Comparison

44. This case study profile is partly based on preliminary research conducted by Austin Kyle Boyd in the author's graduate seminar.

Gotham Greens

45. Gotham Greens, http://gothamgreens.com/. Laura Drotleff, "Gotham Takes Locally Grown Produce to a Whole New Level," *Greenhouse Grower* (June 27, 2014), www.greenhousegrower.com/news/gotham-greens-takes-locally-grown-produce-to-a-whole-new-level/#/BlackoutGallery/60760/9/. Ewa Kern-Jedrychowska, "Gotham Greens Begins Construction of Massive Rooftop Greenhouse in Jamaica," *DNAinfo* (April 3, 2015), www.dnainfo.com/new-york/20150403/jamaica/gotham-greens-begins-construction-of-massive-rooftop-greenhouse-jamaica. "The Greenhouse in Brooklyn," Whole Foods Market, www.wholefoodsmarket.com/service/greenhouse-brooklyn. Clare Trapasso, "Gotham Greens to Build One of the Country's Largest Commercial, Rooftop Greenhouses in Jamaica, Queens." *NY Daily News* (April 7, 2013), www.nydailynews.com/new-york/queens/gotham-greens-build-country-largest-commercial-rooftop-greenhouses-queens-article-1.1308662.

BrightFarms

46. BrightFarms, http://brightfarms.com/s/; "BrightFarms – A produce supply chain revolution: Paul Lightfoot at TEDxManhattan," YouTube, www.youtube.com/watch?v=3ZDLo8yNxgY.

Local Garden

47. Michael Levenston, "Vancouver's Rooftop Farm 'Local Garden' Bankrupt," *City Farmer News* (January 22, 2014), www.cityfarmer.info/2014/01/25/vancouvers-rooftop-farm-local-garden-bankrupt/. "Time Magazine Names Valcent's Vertical Farming Technology as one of the Top 50 Best Innovations of 2009," Bloomberg.com, www.bloomberg.com/apps/news?pid=newsarchive&sid=aHGDZlzUQlbk.

Chapter 5

Community
Education and Social Integration

ABSTRACT

Urban agriculture has the potential to reestablish lost connections between food production and consumption and to restore the social, economic, and cultural ties once embedded therein. By decreasing the physical distance food needs to travel and by sharing out knowledge and experience, community-initiated urban agricultural programs reduce the divide between producers and consumers in the current food system. Indeed, community support systems are as vital as growing systems to the success of an urban agricultural initiative, and it is helpful for designers to gain some familiarity with methods to facilitate community interaction. This chapter investigates different approaches to community involvement, from bottom-up movements to collaborative consumption and cogovernance models, demonstrating how communities and interest groups can be instrumental in creating and operating urban agricultural projects.

CURRENT COMMUNITY CHALLENGES

Urban residents worldwide are increasingly disconnected from the sources of their food. Our current food system is no longer transparent. Indeed, food production has been separated from its consumption,[1] resulting in decreased knowledge of food's nutritional value and how it is grown and prepared. The consumption of highly processed foods is on the rise because people lack access—physically, economically, and conceptually—to fresh, whole foods.

This disconnection from food affects community structure, cohesion, and resilience. A lost connection to food weakens the social, environmental, and economic networks in a society, because these systems traditionally evolved to support the local cultivation and sharing of food.[2] Community ties in cities are ever diminishing; urbanists and community planners, in fact, cite a growing condition of anomie, or social breakdown, in urban environments that has been traced to a lack of daily dependence both on ecological systems and on other people. Putting food on the table once required collaboration with nature and with our neighbors; today it can be achieved without either.[3]

The urban agricultural movement has grown in strength in recent decades as the result of an increasing awareness that globalization has disrupted such valuable local networks, with harmful social and environmental consequences.[4] This heightened interest in urban agriculture is closely associated with other

◀ Figure 5.1

Family shopping at a farmers' market in Detroit with Michigan's Double Up Food Bucks program

movements of community empowerment, revealing an overall dissatisfaction with the separation of two systems that should operate as one. The relationship between urban agriculture and its community support networks is reciprocal and mutually dependent; agriculture both requires and fosters community, and the community systems that maintain urban agricultural initiatives demand as much cultivation as the food that is grown. In an increasingly fragmented, unstable environment, urban agriculture offers a means to reconnect the social, spatial, ecological, and economic aspects of the city, and it requires that all of these systems be engaged to function optimally.

POTENTIAL EFFECTS OF URBAN AGRICULTURE ON COMMUNITIES

Today's urban agriculture movement is heir to a tradition that reaches back to the late nineteenth century, when an influx of immigrants to American cities, combined with an economic recession, inspired civic leaders to make surplus land available as a supplement during food shortages. Urban agriculture continued as an economically, socially, and politically important feature of urban life with Victory Gardens during World Wars I and II and the Great Depression (Figure 5.2). Though food production in cities declined after World War II, a resurgence of interest in community gardening occurred in the 1960s and 1970s as a response to urban decay, environmental degradation, and social disintegration.[5]

◄ Figure 5.2

Children's school Victory Gardens on First Avenue between 35th and 36th Streets, New York, 1944

These historical movements in urban agriculture were largely grassroots in nature and were initiated in the face of scarce resources—whether land, food, money, or all of the above. By the second half of the twentieth century, the movement was also motivated by a decline in environmental health and social connectivity. The early twenty-first century has seen a marked rise in the popularity of urban agriculture, as evidenced by the explosive growth of farmers' markets, a growing demand for organic and local produce, the rise of the community-supported agriculture (CSA) model, the continued success of community garden programs, and iconic crusades such as the Slow Food movement.

Civic Agriculture

The current popular interest in local, hands-on food production has the capacity to effect significant social, political, environmental, and economic change. Thomas Lyson, an influential sociologist at Cornell University, coined the term "civic agriculture," which conveys the interconnection between the act of growing our own food and our social, economic, and political systems. Citizen empowerment is a cornerstone of Lyson's concept of civic agriculture, which views participants as active agents in the production and consumption of their food rather than passive recipients at the end of a supply chain. Community agriculture thereby engenders a cooperative approach to problem-solving and economics, one that is collective rather than focused on individual competition.[6] This fosters a human support network that extends beyond the agricultural system itself and encourages larger-scale community empowerment.[7] The social capital, or the value of these social networks, has been identified as a powerful resource that supports community vitality, democracy, and sustainable development.[8]

Community Building and Education

According to historian Thomas Bassett, community gardens offer a lifeline for cultural systems in times of crisis.[9] Urban agriculture has been found to be an important mechanism for community building, offering opportunities for cross-cultural and cross-generational connections, and for creating ties between people of different socioeconomic backgrounds (Figure 5.3). This social mutualism, or the coming together of groups that are traditionally separated, has been identified as a critical design goal for increased social connectivity in cities.[10]

Collective food production is also a valuable means of preserving cultural heritage through the sharing of food and agricultural expertise (Figure 5.4).[11] Urban agricultural systems require stewardship from participants, nurturing the development of key social and workplace skills, including volunteerism, leadership, neighborhood engagement, and recruitment.[12] Red Hook Community Farm in Brooklyn offers volunteer events for organizations or companies to create meaningful, productive volunteer experiences. Through internships and job training programs, individuals are able to translate their experiences growing food to other professional and social pursuits.[13]

◀ Figure 5.3

Community building while establishing a community garden, R-Urban with Collectif Etc., Colombes, France

◀ Figure 5.4

Sharing cultural heritage in the Global Roots Garden, The Stop, Toronto, Canada

With a focus on reestablishing agricultural, ecological, and food literacy, educational programs in urban agriculture help ensure that the movement is strengthened and continues into the future. Educational efforts take many forms and are supported by schools as well as other organizations. Most emphasize integrating food production with traditional academic subjects, along with communication, cooperation, and leadership skills (see Case Study 16).

Access and Public Health

Despite the increased production availability of fresh food, food security is still a problem in cities, where many inhabitants lack access to fresh, nutritious food. These regions, known as "food deserts," are a result of larger-scale social and economic problems, including housing and income inequality, as well as our prevailing model of food production, which hides the true cost of "cheap," highly processed foods at the expense of human and environmental well-being.[14]

Urban agriculture influences public health at the scale of the individual as well as the community. Urban agricultural initiatives lead to increased fruit and vegetable consumption by participants and provide valuable opportunities for physical activity while promoting mental health and reducing health care costs.[15] At the community scale, urban agriculture promotes civic empowerment and builds social capital, both of which improve public health.[16]

The public health implications of decisions made in the built environment are receiving ever closer scrutiny, creating opportunities for designers to engage more meaningfully in larger urban systems issues. Urban agriculture as a means of improving public health will likely become increasingly important to urban design, both for the direct health benefits it confers and for the community networks it builds. Additionally, the social capital developed through urban agriculture will become even more crucial in the face of future challenges like global warming, which will demand quick, local responses to unpredictable change.

INTEGRATING URBAN AGRICULTURE INTO COMMUNITIES AND THE BUILT ENVIRONMENT

Potential Synergies

The spatial and social characteristics of the urban environment encourage agricultural techniques that have more in common with traditional cultivation methods than with today's large-scale agribusiness. In contrast to vast tracts of land producing a single crop with a heavy reliance on chemicals and mechanized equipment, agriculture in the city is typically achieved on a much smaller scale, with a greater intensity of land use and human effort, resulting in a greater diversity of produce. Urban environments are therefore uniquely poised to offer the environmental and sociocultural conditions necessary to encourage a return to a more socially integrated, decentralized form of food cultivation.

Designers and planners can identify synergies between the social, environmental, and spatial requirements of agriculture and of those provided by the city, allowing them to consider the full cycle of food production, distribution, and consumption at an integrated, systems-based level.[17] This holistic approach is beneficial at multiple scales, as illustrated by the growing realization that the socioeconomic and ecological resilience of cities go hand in hand, based on biodiversity, self-sufficiency, and integrated production and consumption.[18]

Integration Methods

Methods for initiating community-supported urban agricultural systems fall into broad categories, although each example is a site-specific response to the unique community and environmental context of the project. These models are alike, however, in the challenge they pose to prevailing relationships between food production and consumption.

Bottom-Up Movement

The first community gardening efforts in American cities were influenced by top-down management, often initiated by civic organizations and other reformers intent on "improving" disadvantaged groups of people. The revitalization of the movement in the 1960s and 1970s, however, took an increasingly grassroots approach associated with growing neighborhood activism and environmental awareness, supported by local and governmental programs and how-to literature.[19] This bottom-up approach has evolved today to include diverse initiatives that expand the traditional concept of a community garden to more actively engage social, spatial, and economic opportunities. Such efforts encourage increased civic involvement and empowerment by giving a voice to those who may feel excluded from local decision-making.[20]

Community-based urban agricultural programs also provide an important forum for cultural exchange, fostering cultural vibrancy and resiliency for groups faced with geographical and social upheaval. A model for grassroots cultural cultivation can be found in the Puerto Rican *casita* gardens in New York City, which serve as sites of community empowerment and enrichment. These gardens, each organized around a small wooden house, or *casita*, serve as the cultural, social, religious, and political nucleus of the community. Indeed, the garden's role in nurturing community may be even more important for these gardeners than its agricultural output or provision of green space.[21] New York Restauration Project (NYRP), in collaboration with TEN Arquitectos, developed pavilion-like structures that serve as *casitas* in restored community gardens and parks (Figure 5.5).[22]

Recent initiatives in urban agriculture emphasize the significance of community participation in food production, revealing that a human support system

▼ Figure 5.5

Casita in Willis Avenue Community Garden, New York Restoration Project (NYRP) in collaboration with TEN Arquitectos, Buro Happold and Urban Air Foundation, Bronx, New York, 2014

is just as necessary to agriculture as sunlight, water, and soil. The Paris-based program R-Urban strives to return autonomy to community cycles of production and consumption by empowering individuals to grow their own food, produce their own energy, and repurpose their own materials (see Case Study 14).[23] A three-part pilot project—including a self-sustaining urban agricultural unit, an educational facility devoted to recycled building materials, and an experimental housing complex—expands the local, responsive character of traditional agricultural systems to encompass present-day communities and the built environment.

The Prinzessinnengarten in Berlin is likewise based on a philosophy of open exchange (see Case Study 12).[24] Permeable to the surrounding city and open to all, the garden is an aggregation of moveable planting containers that can be constantly relocated according to cultivation and spatial needs. This mobility provides greater self-reliance for gardeners whose access to a community garden plot may be temporary and threatened by the sale of land to developers. The dynamism of the Prinzessinnengarten system allows participants an active hand in shaping both the spatial and social configuration of the garden. The garden itself becomes the raw material for cultural and social exchange, and this is expressed in an especially tangible manner as community members gather to build planting containers, harvest food, and assemble and reassemble their own public space.

Youth Involvement

School and youth-oriented programs offer another important source of spatial and social capital for community-based urban agriculture. The organizational frameworks and facilities associated with today's educational system can be readily appropriated to support food production in the city. School initiatives such as Alice Waters' Edible Schoolyard Project in Berkeley, California, and the Greenhouse Project in New York leverage underused urban spaces, including abandoned city lots, rooftops, and vacant building facilities to meaningfully integrate hands-on food production with curriculum requirements.

Since its founding in 1995, the Edible Schoolyard Project has grown into an international movement based on Waters' guiding principle that "food is an academic subject" (see Case Study 16).[25] More a method than a typology, Edible Schoolyard incorporates the cultivation and preparation of food into every school day. This comprehensive approach to education highlights the connection between food and environmental health while illustrating the practical application of academic disciplines and encouraging the development of real-world skills such as cooperation, communication, gardening, and cooking.

The Greenhouse Project similarly unites food production with academic programming, though it does so through a distinctive modular system that has been replicated on rooftops across New York City (see Case Study 16).[26] The program was founded by a group of parents and teachers who recognized that public school facilities in New York provided a wealth of underutilized opportunities for urban farming and environmental education. Each school is provided with a rooftop greenhouse and a suite of components to support a hydroponic farm. These rooftop science laboratories were directly inspired by the Science Barge, a floating prototype that has demonstrated an entirely closed-loop urban agricultural operation on the New York City and Yonkers waterfronts since 2007 (see Case Study 11).

Outside of the classroom, youth-focused organizations such as the Gary Comer Youth Center in Chicago and the Food Project in Boston offer opportunities for students to connect with their larger communities by building and sharing agricultural skills and by providing fresh produce to families in need and consumers seeking a local, seasonal food source.[27] Rather than a traditional after-school or summer program, these curriculum-integrated initiatives transform children from diverse backgrounds into advocates for urban agriculture by linking hands-on experience in the garden with business and training ventures that cultivate public speaking and leadership skills. In time, students take on increased responsibility within the program, selling specialty produce to Chicago-area chefs at the Gary Comer Youth Center, for example (Figure 5.6), or leading community workshops on gardening, nutrition, and food justice at the Food Project. The opportunity to teach as well as learn imparts an important sense of ownership to students, challenging traditional teacher-child-school dynamics and facilitating an atmosphere of colearning and self-reliance. The Added-value Youth Empowerment Program at the Red Hook Community Farm in Brooklyn and the Windy City Harvest Apprenticeship program at the Chicago Botanical Garden (Figure 5.7) prepare disadvantaged youth to qualify for the job market.[28]

▼ Figure 5.6

Rooftop vegetable and herb garden, Gary Comer Youth Center, Chicago, 2006

▶ Figure 5.7

Students harvesting at the training and production headquarters, Windy City Harvest, Chicago

Collaborative Consumption

A growing interest in collaborative consumption—or the sharing of resources across a group of people—offers another valuable framework to integrate urban agriculture with communities. The philosophy of collaborative consumption holds that community food resources are collective infrastructure, aligning spatial opportunities in the city with a willing community support network to maximize food production on both public and private land. This approach is not a new one, reaching at least as far back as the medieval English commons; however, it challenges current notions of property ownership that tend to impede city planning on a systems level.

Collaborative consumption initiatives occur at the city scale as well as on the scale of individual gardens. Projects such as Urban Gardenshare, Garden Swap, and Sharing Backyards (Figure 5.8) in several North American cities match avid gardeners who have no growing space with homeowners who may have too much backyard to manage on their own.[29] "Yes in My Backyard" (YIMBY), a similar initiative in Toronto and part of The Stop Community Food Centre (see Case Study 15), seeks to share land with low-income participants, strengthening connections between different socioeconomic groups while increasing urban agricultural production and providing a fresh source of produce for the gardeners.[30] In Eureka, California, Deborah Giraud of the University of California Cooperative Extension created a similar partnership program for Hmong refugee gardeners. The Hmong are able to preserve many of their cultural traditions through the practice of growing food, which they often share with the landowner.[31] Resource sharing in such programs extends beyond food and land, however, to include the exchange of expertise, cultural resources, equipment, and organizational capital. Programs including the Green Guerillas in New York City, Denver Urban Gardens, Chicago's GreenNet, Seattle's P-Patch, and the Natural Areas Network of Boston support community gardens by sharing information and other resources citywide.

Urban gleaning and foraging initiatives are also taking hold in cities worldwide and are organized around a comprehensive assessment of a city's long-term edible infrastructure, typically composed of its fruit and nut trees.

Community: Education and Social Integration

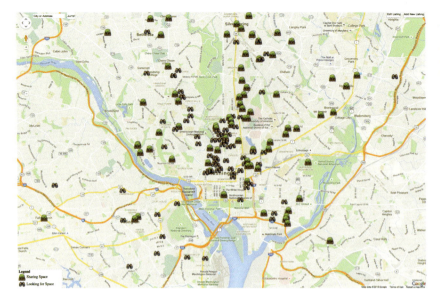

◀ Figure 5.8

SharingBackyardDC, online database connecting gardeners with homeowners who offer their backyard for gardening

Fruit- and nut-bearing trees are registered by nonprofit or governmental organizations that then facilitate the collection and distribution of produce to groups in need. Public utilities and local governments are increasingly involved in such projects, illustrating that collective food production is beginning to be accepted as a vital component of civic infrastructure. In Seattle, the Beacon Food Forest—the largest forest in the United States composed entirely of edible plants[32]—was established in 2009 on 7 acres formerly owned by Seattle Public Utilities, transforming one type of utility into another (Figure 5.9). Figure 5.10 shows Food Forests' Living Web, educational material showcasing permaculture principles.

In Tokyo, designers are relying on traditional and digital research techniques to map "fruit paths" through the city.[33] Each fruit path records a startling diversity of species grown in a wide range of spatial conditions while revealing the intricate network of human connections that ensure food distribution

▼ Figure 5.9

Beacon Food Forest site plan, Harrison Design Landscape Architecture, Beacon Hill, Seattle, WA, 2014

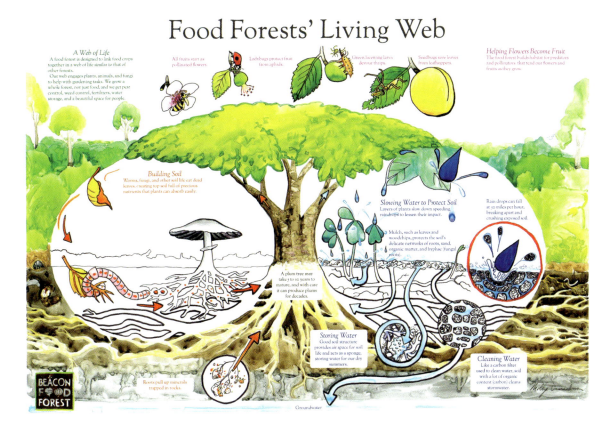

▲ Figure 5.10

Food Forests' Living Web, educational material showcasing permaculture principles, Molly Danielsson, 2013 (original size 36 x 24 inches/0.9 x 0.6m)

and consumption. The Tokyo Local Fruit program reinvigorates Tokyo's heritage as a fruit-growing city and inspires planners, designers, and residents to see abundant opportunities to cultivate food and social connections in their urban environment.

Commercial Community-based Projects

The city offers not only spatial and social potential for urban agriculture, but also economic opportunity. Economic benefits often go hand in hand with community integration. Most commercial ventures need community support of some kind to grow food efficiently and lucratively in urban environments. This support can range from political backing for setting up an urban farm to active volunteerism to build and operate the farm, youth, internship, and training programs to sustained patronage. Any of these forms of support generates a win-win situation between a community and an urban farm.

Growing Power, a nonprofit advocate for urban agriculture, is one of the most successful operations in connecting community support with the commercial aspect of their farm. It has leveraged existing distribution networks—among other tactics—to assist communities in growing and selling food in the city (see Case Study 7). Its youth and internship programs give important work experience to disadvantaged youth on their road to the labor market. Most urban agricultural operations also work with volunteers, whom they organize more or less stringently for volunteer hours, days, or events to strike a balance between instruction and need for assistance on the farm.

Conceived as a low-capital, local business venture accessible to everyone, small ground-based farming shows how a commercial enterprise can be integrated in a community. These small outlets depend on loyal customers to buy produce at farm stands and to sometimes even offer backyards as growing space. These small operations once again localize the economic exchange surrounding food and suggest an alternative model for commercial agriculture that reunites social, agricultural, and economic systems at a community scale.[34] The variety of economic models that may support urban agricultural systems promises nimble and responsive design possibilities for planners and city residents eager to facilitate such programs in their neighborhoods.

Cogovernance/Coproducers

Urban agricultural systems rely on complex synergies among governmental regulations, land-use policies, property ownership, community support, funding options, and the availability of growing space. Because they cannot exist without significant contribution from participants, successful initiatives in urban agriculture are largely the result of substantial grassroots efforts. Yet the long-term sustainability of these programs often requires some manner of top-down support, whether in the form of favorable laws and policies, administrative assistance from partner organizations, or government involvement. Though urban agriculture is, by nature, a grassroots practice, overarching legal and programmatic frameworks may be crucial for community-based efforts to thrive.

As illustrated by numerous case studies, urban food production has a strong interconnection with its community support network: each system relies on and, in turn, strengthens the other. The reciprocal relationship between urban agriculture and political leadership, a dynamic interaction between top-down and bottom-up efforts, has been described as "adaptive cogovernance," and it characterizes some of the most successful urban agricultural initiatives. Community garden programs in New York, Portland, and Seattle, for example, have reinforced both their community base and local government, fostering resilience in the face of changing political, economic, and land-use horizons. Adaptive cogovernance also encourages greater involvement and responsiveness on the part of government, which shares leadership responsibilities with community members. The resulting social capital benefits citizens and governments alike and ideally establishes an evolving, long-term rapport. As scholars Henry Barmeier and Xenia K. Morin state, "The government's presence in the garden is better understood as a process rather than a product."[35]

Collaboration between government and community gardening entities promises increasingly agile and substantive changes to spatial and economic policies. Municipal initiatives such as Baltimore's Adopt-A-Lot support the expansion of community gardening plots through short-term leases for gardeners on publicly owned lands.[36] At the state level, Michigan's Double Up Food Bucks program recalibrates the economic system to incentivize local food production and make fresh produce available to those with lower incomes; food assistance recipients receive tokens that can be used to purchase fruits and vegetables at Michigan farmers' markets (Figure 5.11). What started in 2009 at five farmers' markets in Detroit has since expanded to 150 sites in Michigan (Figure 5.12).[37] Often a top-down effort will catalyze long-term grassroots support, such as in the case of the Toronto FoodShare Program's Good Food Market. FoodShare was initially formed to fulfill a government mandate to coordinate food bank efforts in the city. In time, organizers transformed this overarching directive into a flourishing community-based, self-sufficient initiative, with projects such as the Good Food Market relying on community members to organize markets and distribute food to residents.[38]

One of the most compelling examples of government-assisted urban food production is in Cuba. In the days following the fall of the Soviet Union in 1991, the Cuban government maximized the cultivation of all available land in an effort

▶ Figure 5.11

Billboard of Double Up Food Bucks program in Michigan, Fair Food Network

▶ Figure 5.12

Results of the Double Up Food Bucks program in Michigan, Fair Food Network to feed its citizens. Organic urban farms and gardens known as *organopónicos* were established across cities such as Havana. Land-use regulations shifted to encourage food production on vacant lots, and produce grown in *organopónicos* was made directly accessible to consumers. This national movement has proved profoundly successful, providing farmers with a source of livelihood and making organic food available for consumers. By the year 2000, over 22,000 farmers in Havana were cultivating over 30 square miles of land within the city limits, producing 90% of all vegetables consumed by residents (see Case Study 13).

Design Considerations

Spatial, economic, and social analyses of cities reveal that they are well suited to support agriculture at a scale that allows for direct participation and community integration. Small-scale, non-mechanized operations require collaboration and create diversity and community empowerment. Indeed, they offers designers, planners, and residents unique opportunities to revive the intricate networks that have historically sustained civic agriculture.

Both individuals and urban communities benefit from urban agriculture. Access to fresh local food and environmental benefits from urban agriculture improve neighborhoods' public health. Expanded education programs and job opportunities support disadvantaged youth. These educational gardens are no longer only at ground-based grassroots operations, but can be found at sites like the green roofs in the Garry Comer Youth Center and the 20,000-ft^2 (1,900-m^2) green roof of the McCormick Place Convention Center used by the Windy City Harvest Apprenticeship Program in Chicago (Figure 5.13).

Urban agriculture fosters community, and community maintains urban agricultural operations. Often farms start operations in cities to make direct connections with their costumers and support base. The goal is to bring people into closer contact with their food again, and support and volunteerism benefit the realization and operation of a farm. For example, Brooklyn Grange's first green roof and large parts of The Plant were built through volunteer help (see Case Studies 8 and 9). The most important community support, though, is still patronage through a sustained customer base and strong identification with the local urban farm.

▼ Figure 5.13

Productive green roof farmed by the Windy City Harvest apprenticeship program, McCormick Place Convention Center, Chicago, 2013

▶ Figure 5.14

"Ernterundgang," Daily Harvest for the on-site café and restaurant, Prinzessinnengarten, Kreuzberg, Berlin, Germany

CASE STUDY 12: PRINZESSINNENGARTEN

Organization:	Nomadisch Grün
Founders:	Robert Shaw and Marco Clausen
Location:	Berlin, Germany
Operation:	since 2009
Growing System:	soil-based farming in containers
Growing Area:	64,000 ft^2/ 6,000 m^2
Growing Season:	April to October (52° N latitude)
Annual Yield:	500 varieties of organic crops
Main Distribution:	direct harvest, on-site purchase, café, and restaurant

Described as a "wasteland," the debris-choked lot that became the Prinzessinnengarten had stood empty in West Berlin since World War II. Filmmaker Robert Shaw and Marco Clausen, a historian and photographer, proudly proclaim that they knew nothing about gardening before they began to transform the soccer field-sized stretch of land—220 yards (200 m) from the former Berlin Wall—in 2009. Since then, a community garden has flourished, providing an alternate model for civic participation in urban space and connecting diverse groups of people through the production and sharing of food and knowledge. On land owned by the city, the Prinzessinnengarten cultivates 500 varieties of crops in entirely mobile containers, demonstrating the staying power of urban agriculture in an environment where land tenure is insecure.[39]

Background and Milestones

Prinzessinnengarten, which translates as the "Garden of the Princesses," has been a wildly successful gathering space since over 100 volunteers first cleared the land. Located at Moritzplatz in Berlin Kreuzberg, near a massive roundabout and a busy subway station, the garden is situated among diverse cultural groups, including first- and second-generation immigrants from almost every continent.

Inspired by urban agricultural operations in Cuba, cofounder Robert Shaw imagined the plot not only as a place for people to grow their own food but also to learn from one another and take an active hand in shaping city space, increasing biodiversity, and fostering community. Moveable planters crafted from repurposed food containers ensure that the garden could be relocated in the event that the property is sold (Figure 5.15). Raised beds are also an ideal solution given the site's compacted, contaminated soils. Other structures are equally mobile and built from recycled shipping containers; these include a café and bar along with storage and workshop spaces. These facilities support the garden's mission to create an informal venue to share food and information and to encourage spontaneous collaboration and exchanges.

Prinzessinnengarten attracts an average of 60,000 visitors per year, along with approximately 1,000 volunteers. The garden has transformed itself from an esoteric experiment to an internationally recognized model. In 2012, the city threatened to sell the Kreuzberg parcel, drawing criticism and inciting a very public debate about the management of municipally owned lands. In December of that year, the Berlin Property Fund returned the property into the charge of the borough, thus preventing the closure of the garden. The organization aims to agree to a lease of at least five years with the city so that it can have planning security with its educational programs and with its funding options, including grant applications. Berlin ought to consider the added social and ecological value gained through the project, especially since the city is already using the internationally recognized project in its PR campaigns.

Socio-Spatial System

Shaw and Clausen emphasize that the amateur nature of the garden has been crucial to its success; everyone learns by doing—even if the process is slow—resulting in a space that is shaped from the bottom up, empowering people to take risks, share acquired knowledge, negotiate territory, and accept collective responsibility. Clausen notes that the Prinzessinnengarten differs from traditional allotment gardens in which gardeners tend their own individual plots and strive

▲ Figure 5.15

Container-based Prinzessinnengarten at Moritzplatz, Kreuzberg, Berlin, Germany

for a sense of escape from the city: here no one owns a particular bed, and the energy and dynamism of the urban environment are welcomed with open arms into the garden. This laboratory for alternative urban development and civic participation is held together by a common human interest in growing and eating food and in enjoying leisure time in a vibrant, beautiful place. In addition to enticing regular and occasional gardeners, Prinzessinnengarten has become a prime social destination for Berliners who live well outside the neighborhood (Figure 5.16).

Built with minimal resources and no expert knowledge, the garden imaginatively illustrates what Clausen calls "Pioneer Use." This term draws a parallel

▶ Figure 5.16

On-site café, Prinzessinnengarten, Kreuzberg, Berlin, Germany

◀ Figure 5.17

Constructing container growing beds at "Ablegergarten" (branch container garden) at Sophien Kita (daycare), Berlin, Germany

between ecological succession and the potential evolution of land use in urban settings, suggesting an alternate pattern for public space development. The execution of tangible, discrete projects in collaboration with others (Figure 5.17) helps build conceptual bridges to larger concerns, including global warming, food insecurity, decreasing biodiversity, and reduced community connectivity in urban settings. Prinzessinnengarten's founders underscore that the networks and flexible support systems nurtured in the garden are those that will prove most useful in the face of these future urban challenges.

Growing Systems

The organic growing system in the Prinzessinnengarten is composed entirely of materials recycled from the traditional food production industry. These include bakery crates, milk and juice cartons, and jute sacks for staples such as rice and potatoes. Imaginative reuse of containers is highly encouraged, as Shaw observes when he notes that a teapot may serve as an ideal place to cultivate a radish. The portable buildings can likewise be rearranged, offering an additional benefit in that their temporary status does not trigger permit requirements.

Prinzessinnengarten's productivity is high. More than 500 varieties of organic vegetables and herbs are cultivated in the garden, which is also home to more than 10,000 bees. Produce includes root crops such as carrots, parsnips, potatoes, and turnips; greens like kale, chard, sorrel, and mustard greens; a vibrant selection of edible flowers and herbs; and statuesque tomatoes trained on tall trellises.

Operation

Reliant on a team of 12 employees, a core group of regular gardeners, plus hundreds of drop-in volunteers, who donate as many as 30,000 hours per year,

▶ Figure 5.18

Garden dinner at Prinzessinnengarten, Kreuzberg, Berlin, Germany

the garden is partly financially sustained by the sale of vegetables and revenue from a highly successful café and restaurant, which also host garden dinners, events, and concerts (Figure 5.18). Shaw and Clausen took a pragmatic view of the project's finances from the outset, realizing that the initiative could not be supported by produce sales alone. A nonprofit organization called Nomadisch Grün (Nomadic Green) was founded in tandem with the garden and provides the financial structure needed to maintain the project. The partners stress the importance of balancing money-generating activities with non-money-making programs. They have supplemented the garden's income with programs that further its primary goal to connect people and food cultivation; these include educational programs, workshops, tours, outside consulting, landscaping commissions, presentations, donations, opportunities for sponsorship, installations, and mobile garden units that catalyze urban agriculture in other parts of the city (Figure 5.19). Meanwhile, the organization used its established container systems to build 40 satellite vegetable gardens for social institutions like daycares and schools.

Community: Education and Social Integration

◀ Figure 5.19

Prinzessinnengarten volunteers demonstrate mobility of community garden by moving growing beds through Kreuzberg, Berlin, Germany

Strengths and Innovations

Prinzessinnengarten is a highly successful community garden that fosters a culture of food production, preparation, and communal consumption. Its existence in the center of Berlin generates a unique connection between garden and city that encourages the rethinking and cultivation of a different type of city. The mobility celebrated by the Prinzessinnengarten suggests that the social connections formed by urban agriculture may be more crucial to a project's success than its spatial resources and location. The collaborative, productive momentum generated by the project has the potential to grow and change over time, regardless of location. Paradoxically, the garden has galvanized much community support in its recent effort to stay put. The successful campaign to extend its lease at the Moritzplatz has provoked a critical debate in Berlin that may significantly influence city-planning decisions. Identifying spaces that are prime candidates for "Pioneer Use" could profoundly shape the way we imagine urban land use opportunities in the future, offering a special place for urban agriculture in this municipal succession.

▲ Figure 5.20

Farmer with rake at Organopónico Vivero Alamar, Havana, Cuba

CASE STUDY 13: ORGANOPÓNICOS

Organization:	Organopónicos
Founder:	community with Cuban government
Location:	Havana, Cuba
Operation:	beginning in 1991
Growing System:	soil-based farming in raised beds
Growing Area:	30 miles^2 (80 km^2) within city limits
Growing Season:	year-round (23° N latitude)
Annual Yield:	11 tons per acre (at Organopónico Vivero Alamar)
Main Distribution:	direct sale from farm at produce stands

With the fall of the Soviet Union in 1991, Cuba lost its primary source of imported food. In response, the Cuban government amended land use and food distribution policies. Havana, the capital, innovatively addressed the resulting food shortage by developing *organopónicos*—urban gardens and farms—throughout the city, with government and local citizens banding together. The city now grows 90% of its produce in these *organopónicos*.[40]

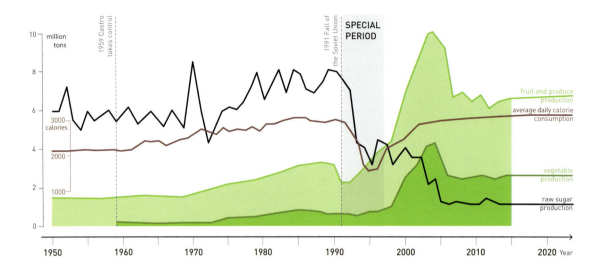

▲ Figure 5.21

Timeline of agricultural production in Cuba

Data adapted from Cuba's Food and Agriculture Situation Report, Office of Global Analysis, FAS, USDA, March 2008.

Background and Milestones

Before 1991, Cuba's agricultural industry was heavily export-oriented, relying primarily on sugar cane exported to the Soviet Union in return for discounted oil, fertilizer, and food. Up to 63% of all food and 90% of all oil imported to Cuba in this period arrived through its Soviet trade relationship. Fuel and fertilizer were required to support Cuba's domestic agricultural production, which relied on large-scale farming techniques and the capacity to transport food from rural to urban areas.

With the disintegration of the trade agreement between Cuba and the USSR, a food and fuel shortage besieged the country, affecting urban communities in particular. Average caloric intake among Cuban citizens dropped from approximately 2,600 calories per day to about 1,500 calories by 1993. During this time of food scarcity, known as the "Special Period," starving local citizens took over vacant city land in order to grow crops (Figure 5.21).

The need for food was so great that the Cuban government made food security its most pressing issue—even higher than reevaluating its foreign policy—and set the goal of making individual cities, including Havana, home to 20% of Cuba's population, self-sufficient for their food supply. Urban agriculture became vital to the city's survival, and policies were established to support urban farmers. These included forming a new Department of Urban Agriculture, providing higher education and wages to farmers, and creating seed banks and tool- and compost-sharing networks. By 2000, with urban agriculture promoted by the government, 58% of the country's vegetable stock came from within cities. In Havana, by the same year, over 22,000 food producers were cultivating over 30 square miles (80 km^2) of land within city limits.

▶ Figure 5.22

Price list at gate for on-site produce sales, Organopónico Paseo, Havana, Cuba

Government Policies

Innovative government-sponsored initiatives have supported the development of *organopónicos*. Land-use and food-distribution laws have been adapted to facilitate in-city cultivation. Citizens may appropriate unused urban land if they use it for farming. While the Soviet-era food distribution system required the government to serve as an intermediary between farmers and consumers, today's food distribution policies encourage farmers to use farmers' markets and produce stands to sell fruit and vegetables directly to customers. Crops in excess of a farm's government food quota are sold for profit, providing growers with financial incentive to increase their food output. Produce stands on the same land as the farm eliminate the need for scarce and costly food transport while reducing the lag between harvest and consumption (Figure 5.22). The government has also supported research centers on biological pest control. Eleven of these centers are located in the city of Havana alone and provide education and resources for chemical-free treatment of plant pests and diseases since Cuba was not able to import industrial pesticides.

Growing Systems

Different types of *organopónicos* have been established, reflecting varied agricultural techniques that range from personal rooftop gardens to extensive urban farms—*organopónicos populares*—that are run by commercial operators and illustrate organic gardening methods on a large scale. The *organopónicos* system is based on raised beds (Figure 5.23) and is ideal for growing food in a city where soil quality is generally poor. These raised beds separate plants from contaminated or infertile soil in a modular approach suitable for vacant lots or rooftops.

Compost provides vital organic matter and nutrients to the operation and is created from farm and domestic waste generated in the city. Over 1,000 tons of organic waste are discarded every day in Havana, translating to around 220 tons of compost per day, or 80,000 tons a year. Rather than relying on fossil

◂ Figure 5.23

Growing beds constructed from recycled building materials, Organopónico Paseo, Havana, Cuba

fuels to transport waste out of the city, compostable materials are collected by 12 cooperative organizations that process the compost and redistribute it to farms, agriculture shops, and educational centers.

Producing compost, vermicompost, and natural pesticides on an industrial scale is especially crucial because the country has no access to synthetic fertilizer and pesticides. Soil conservation once again became important to farmers; instead of adding fertilizer for quick gains, farmers carefully cultivated and maintained healthy soil over the years. In the *organopónico* system, compost is regularly applied to the beds, which are rarely left unplanted for more than 48 hours. Growing is a year-round endeavor in Cuba's consistently warm climate.

Operation: Organopónico Vivero Alamar

Though the operation of each *organopónico* varies, the management of the Organopónico Vivero Alamar is reflective of the organization of many urban farms in Havana (Figure 5.24 and 5.25). Located on the outskirts east of the city, Vivero Alamar was established in 1997 by five partners and runs as a cooperative. By 2013, the operation had expanded to employ more than 170 people, approximately 90% of them as members of the cooperative, and it produces 300,000 tons of food in four to six crop rotations per year.

The Organopónico Vivero Alamar is one of Havana's most successful urban farms. It mainly grows lettuce, vegetables, and fruit on its 27 acres (11 hectares) of land. In addition, it produces added-value products such as dried herbs, condiments, sauces, and pickles as well as compost, vermicompost, and substrates.

The *organopónico* sells 90% of its produce to the public at its farm stands. The remaining harvest is sold at a discounted price to social institutions like

▶ Figure 5.24

Main office, Organopónico Vivero Alamar, Havana, Cuba

▶ Figure 5.25

Growing beds with shading cloth, Organopónico Vivero Alamar, Havana, Cuba

schools and hospitals or through the Ministry of Agriculture to local hotels. In addition to providing a large quantity of quality produce, the *organopónico* is a valuable employer in the city, hiring highly educated workers and furthering their education with additional training and experimentation facilities.

Community: Education and Social Integration

Strengths and Innovations

Organopónicos were created in the face of dire need and illustrate the crucial role that government can play in promoting and achieving food security. Flourishing *organopónicos* have reshaped the urban fabric of Havana, as formerly empty land and unused rooftops now host thriving and vibrant gardens that provide the city with fresh, local food as well as job opportunities for the city's residents. In addition, the reuse of food waste into compost recycles unused produce into crop production and nurtures local soils. That the *organopónicos* have affected the city at so many levels is a testament to the collaboration between government and citizens and between urban land and innovative farming techniques.

▲ Figure 5.26

"Espace Technique" (technical and service area), participatory community design project, atelier d'architecture autogérée/R-Urban with Collectif etc., Colombes, France, 2012

CASE STUDY 14: R-URBAN

Organization:	R-Urban
Founders:	Constantine Petcou and Doina Petrescu
Architects:	aaa (atelier d'architecture autogérée)
Location:	Colombes, France
Operation:	construction of model units begun in 2012, expanding
Growing System	soil-based, outdoors and in hoop houses
Growing Area:	not specified
Growing Season:	April to November outdoors (49° N latitude)
Annual Yield:	3.3 tons
Main Distribution:	on-site market, public weekly lunches, and direct harvest from garden on demand

Developed by architects Constantine Petcou and Doina Petrescu of the Parisian firm aaa (atelier d'architecture autogérée), R-Urban proposes an alternative model of production and consumption based on community networks and collectively produced space. Urban agricultural practices are part of a larger system that also addresses flows of water, energy, waste, and local skills, culture, and economics. Petcou and Petrescu engage architecture to express these systems and facilitate their connection between the key activities of food production, habitation, and economic development. Their architectural interventions catalyze the socio-spatial and ecological processes that will encourage these self-sustaining community networks to spread and thrive.[41]

Background and Milestones

Since its founding in 2001, aaa has fought to make collective urban spaces that are managed by residents and support everyday activities. This group of architects, landscape architects, artists, planners, sociologists, and neighbors identifies and leverages underutilized urban spaces to support the autonomous social and ecological networks formed by practices such as gardening, socializing, cooking, and DIY fabrication. Earlier projects such as ECObox and Passage 56 in Paris illustrated the generative role of design in the development of community connections and sustainable urban lifestyle practices. Tactics emphasize "mobility, temporality, and informality," empowering participants to shape their own spaces and systems by building, moving, taking apart, and reassembling gardens in new locations.

Initiated in 2011, R-Urban is a larger-scale experiment based on collective facilities, or hubs, and the networks that expand between them. A three-part system has been deployed in Colombes, a town and suburb of Paris with a population of 84,000, that includes an urban agricultural unit, a platform to support recycled building materials, and a cooperative housing unit. AgroCité, the unit for urban agriculture, was launched in 2012, the same year that the collective began construction of the RecycLab, a facility devoted to repurposing urban waste for construction. EcoHab, a self-built cooperative housing unit, is still in the planning phase (Figure 5.27).

Socio-Spatial System

Architecture is used to disseminate knowledge and facilitate community interaction. The AgroCité and RecycLab facilities illustrate sustainable building techniques and provide venues for gathering, for hands-on education and experimentation, and for distributing resources (Figure 5.28). The structures themselves model the viability of the R-Urban system as a whole and have inspired interest in other European municipalities, including in Spain, Germany, Belgium, and Romania. Because the architectural hubs are mobile and adaptable, the system can be transferred to other locations worldwide. But because each facility is collectively produced, using repurposed materials and engaging local skill, each permutation of the system will necessarily be unique and responsive to site-specific conditions.

In their attempt to recalibrate social, agricultural, and economic relationships in the city, the designers of R-Urban have enabled micro-scale

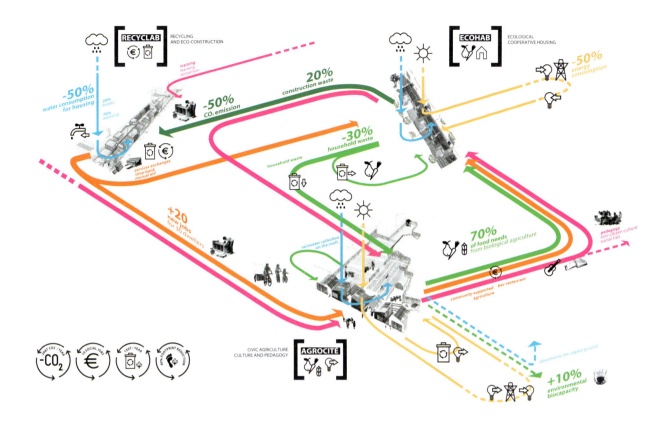

▲ Figure 5.27

R-Urban pilot facilities and cycles: AgroCité, RecycLab, and EcoHab, atelier d'architecture autogérée/R-Urban, proposal for Colombes, France, 2010

changes—beginning with individual lifestyle choices—to effect transformation at the neighborhood, regional, and even national and international levels. Each unit is crafted as an urban retrofit, making use of existing spatial, social, and material resources to empower local production and consumption. This allows

▶ Figure 5.28

AgroCité street façade, atelier d'architecture autogérée/R-Urban, Colombes, France, constructed 2012

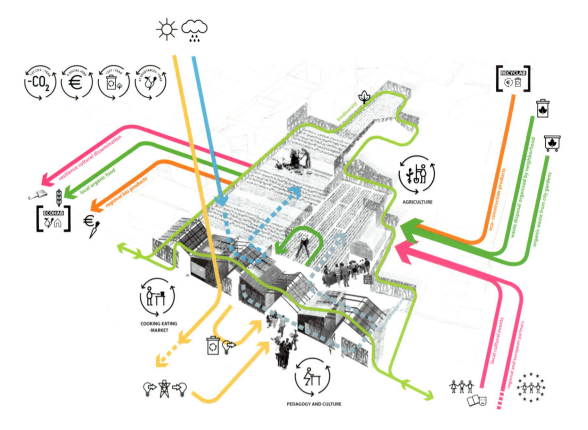

▲ Figure 5.29

AgroCité, civic-agricultural, cultural, and pedagogical unit, atelier d'architecture autogérée/ R-Urban, Colombes, France, 2012

participants to take a leading role in creating their own food, water, energy, and materials, and to alter prevailing economic and lifestyle frameworks to support such locally based cycles. This participative strategy creates autonomous networks and sustains their expansion both within the parent community and beyond.

Growing and Operation Systems

The AgroCité model attempts to sustain a full community system of agriculture from the seed to the table, and programs range from youth education to advanced experimentation and testing. The unit comprises an experimental urban farm (the AgroLab, which experiments with new methods of intensive production), a shared community garden for neighborhood residents, an educational garden, beehives, a chicken coop, a compost production facility, and a shared greenhouse equipped with solar panels and rainwater catchment technologies. The building itself is used to display various urban agricultural techniques and environmental systems (Figure 5.30). Thus multiple scales, functions, and levels of intensity and technology are embedded in the unit.

The RecycLab platform for recycled and eco-building technology also strives to enable locally based, closed-loop cycles of materials, energy, and skills. This facility showcases the construction potential of repurposed materials and the importance of reducing energy consumption by extending the lifecycle of construction materials while providing a repository for material donation and a venue for training opportunities.

▲ Figure 5.30

AgroCité, community garden and garden façade, atelier d'architecture autogérée/R-Urban, Colombes, France, 2012

AgroCité produce is distributed at a weekly vegetable stall, in a shop selling the urban farm's products, and at regular Thursday lunches that are open to the public for a small fee. Team members will also harvest vegetables for customers on demand. The unit additionally contains a seed library, bread oven, and traveling kitchen and connects community members to local farmers by serving as a distribution site for CSA boxes. RecycLab hosts material exchanges and even a barter-based flea market for trading products.

Project goals include a 40% reduction of the ecological footprint of each unit (AgroCité, RecycLab, and EcoHab), the recycling or reuse of more than 75% of all waste associated with the program, and the involvement of at least 15% of the host community of Colombes. R-Urban also welcomes collaboration with other organizations. For example, the garden infrastructure for the AgroCité site was designed and constructed in 2012 with the assistance of Collectif etc., an association of 11 architects and collaborators that supports participatory urban experiments (Figure 5.31). In addition, organizers seek to demonstrate the feasibility of the R-Urban model as a grassroots environmental governance strategy that could be employed in other municipalities.

The day-to-day operation of AgroCité and RecycLab is volunteer-driven and sustained by the European Union's LIFE program for environmental governance. Partners in the initiative include aaa and the City of Colombes. Collective land ownership is made possible by a specially formed cooperative bank that finances the acquisition of available land in urban and suburban neighborhoods.

In addition to on-site educational opportunities such as workshops and demonstrations, R-Urban also supports a robust online platform for participants to share experiences and other resources; this platform is used to disseminate information on a worldwide scale.

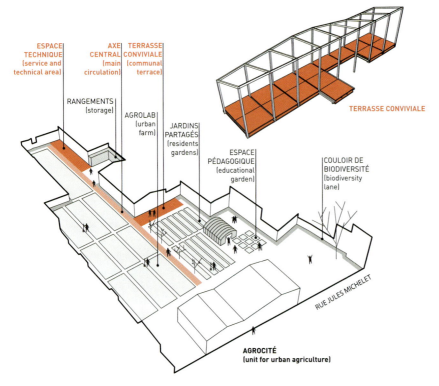

◀ Figure 5.31

Layout of participatory community design project, atelier d'architecture autogérée/R-Urban in collaboration with Collectif etc., 2012

Strengths and Innovations

Perhaps the most innovative aspect of R-Urban is its integration into existing urban systems—whether spatial, material, social, economic, or political. R-Urban demonstrates how private individuals and community groups can come together with governmental organizations to collectively shape a shared space and establish healthy, local cycles of supply and consumption. Until recently, the significance of this collaboration was reflected in the municipal policy of the City of Colombes, which supported the initiative as a win-win situation for all entities involved. Unfortunately, the city's newly elected mayor terminated this promising partnership and has threatened to move the RecycLab and evict AgroCité to make space for a temporary parking lot. In the face of this unexpected challenge, R-Urban is drawing more strongly than ever on its robust social capital and hopes to successfully petition the mayoral decision.

For designers, R-Urban illustrates how small interventions in the spatial realm can engender participative networks and facilitate lifestyle changes that may gradually effect much larger transformations. Urban agriculture is one element in a comprehensive system that strives to alter the prevailing patterns of resource use, economic exchange, and social connectivity in the city. These micropolitical gestures affect the social and environmental ecologies of the individual, of the community, and of production and consumption cycles at large.

▶ Figure 5.32

The Stop's greenhouse in the Green Barn, DTAH Architects, Artscape Wychwood Barns, Toronto, Canada, 2009

CASE STUDY 15: THE STOP COMMUNITY FOOD CENTRE

Organization: The Stop Community Food Centre
Founder: Nick Saul (urban agriculture and expanded operations)
Architects: Joe Lubko, du Toit Architects Limited (DTAH)
Engineers: Stantec Consulting (mechanical/electrical/LEED) and Blackwell Bowick Partnership (structural)
Location: Toronto, Ontario, Canada
Operation: food bank (1982), expanded operations (1999), Green Barn (2009)
Growing System: soil-based farming and greenhouse operation
Growing Area: 10,000-ft^2 (950-m^2) gardens located in public parks
3,000-ft^2 (280-m^2) greenhouse
Growing Season: year-round indoors, May to October outdoors (44° N latitude)
Annual Yield: 5 tons per acre
Main Distribution: food bank, community kitchen, farmers' market

The Stop Community Food Centre (CFC) has grown from humble beginnings as a food bank organized from a church basement in the 1970s to a much larger, community-based nonprofit organization committed to providing healthy food choices to marginalized populations in Toronto. As the organization has grown, it has expanded its services to include urban agricultural initiatives and various community outreach programs, all focused on empowering local citizens.[42]

Background and Milestones

From its beginnings, The Stop combined its primary goal of delivering food aid during emergencies with a community-building approach. The organization always fostered bigger, more long-term political, social, and educational solutions to the many issues affecting impoverished citizens. In 1995, The Stop expanded its programs and facilities by moving its main offices to West Davenport, northwest of downtown Toronto. Residents come here to use various community services. A satellite office, known as the Green Barn at Wychwood Barns, northeast of The Stop's primary facility, was established in 2009 to offer most of the organization's urban agricultural services, such as education in sustainable food production, a greenhouse and compost center, a farmers' market, and the Global Roots Garden.

Social Programs

Ensuring that marginalized people have access to fresh, local food remains the chief goal of The Stop, but it also provides those same populations with learning opportunities about urban agriculture, healthy food, and life skills. The Stop also operates many food and social services as part of its urban agricultural program. One of the longest standing and most successful is the Healthy Beginnings initiative, which provides nutritional education and support for pregnant women and new mothers with their babies.

Another key program is the Community Action Program, which includes peer advocacy services and civic engagement work. The program assists low-income participants to obtain additional social services to help sustain healthy lives and enables community members to engage on issues and become change-makers. Overall, The Stop operates on a "place-based" model, in which many programs are conducted at the same location, encouraging environmental, social, and economic sustainability. Approximately 15–20 outreach services and programs operate simultaneously.

Several initiatives cultivate community connectedness through gardening. The Global Roots Garden, for example, brings different cultures together to celebrate their heritage through an arrangement of eight small garden plots. The Global Roots Oral History Project recorded the memories and experiences that the gardeners with international backgrounds brought to the site. Another, Yes In My Backyard, or YIMBY program, connects Toronto residents who have garden space to share with low-income gardeners in need of a plot of land. The

▶ Figure 5.33

The Stop's community kitchen, DTAH Architects, Artscape Wychwood Barns, Toronto, Canada, 2009

▶ Figure 5.34

The Stop's dining space in the Green Barn, DTAH Architects, Artscape Wychwood Barns, Toronto, Canada, 2009

Stop supports the YIMBY program by organizing a tool-share platform, hosting skill workshops, and offering free seedlings.

Growing Systems and Urban Agriculture Infrastructure

The urban agricultural system at The Stop is composed of four main programmatic pieces, all of which employ typical soil-based growing methods: the two

8,000-ft² (750-m²) Earlscourt and Hillcrest Community Gardens, a 3,000-ft² (280-m²) greenhouse (Figure 5.35), eight Global Roots plots at the Green Barn, and nearly 60 small, residential garden plots throughout the community. Wychwood Barns, where the Green Barn is located, is a recently renovated tram depot containing various shops, offices, artist studios, and residential units. The previous tram garage—in the form of a covered street—has become a large event space which hosts farmers' markets during the winter months.

The Stop's growing facilities intentionally moved into this location to strengthen urban agriculture's ties to these more typical urban programs. The Wychwood Barns strive for environmentally sustainable performance. Their roofs collect rainwater for irrigation; the buildings use geothermal heat to offset traditional heating requirements; and the compost demonstration center receives food scraps from residents, The Stop's kitchen, and other community participants. This nutrient-rich compost is then used in the community gardens and greenhouse or sold back to the community.

Operation

The Stop's community gardens, located in neighborhood parks, as well as the greenhouse and plots at the Green Barn are almost entirely volunteer-operated. The program places an emphasis on child and youth involvement through after school programs, class visits of elementary schools, and summer camps (Figure 5.37). Food produced in the greenhouse and community gardens is distributed among The Stop's food hampers (food banks), the Drop-In kitchen, and the volunteers.

◀ Figure 5.35

Exterior view of the greenhouse in the Green Barn, DTAH Architects, Artscape Wychwood Barns, Toronto, Canada, 2009

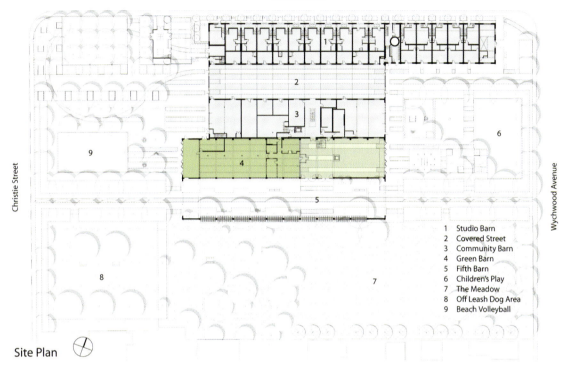

▲ Figure 5.36

Site plan, DTAH Architects, Artscape Wychwood Barns, Toronto, Canada, 2009

The Stop yields 5,000 lbs (2,270 kg) of organic produce annually through urban agricultural production, which takes place year-round in the greenhouse and seasonally in the outdoor plots. In 2013, the organization served approximately 19,000 individuals in need through its food bank program, hosted 1,000 visitors at its weekly farmers' market (Figure 5.38), and provided 60,000 meals through its Drop-In community kitchen. The Drop-In serves breakfast and lunch four days a week (up to 150 meals at breakfast and up to 200 at lunch). Unlike a

▶ Figure 5.37

Young community gardeners, The Stop, Toronto, Canada

◀ Figure 5.38

Farmers' market organized by The Stop, Artscape Wychwood Barns, Toronto, Canada, 2009

typical soup kitchen, the Drop-In is organized as a restaurant (patrons are seated and served instead of lining up cafeteria-style) to lessen the stigma of food need. Donated produce, meat, and dairy items supplement the vegetables and fruit grown in-house.

Funding is raised through events, galas, and facility rentals. Despite these income-generating practices, 90% of the funds required to operate The Stop's programs are received as private donations. Though the organization employs full- and part-time staff to oversee day-to-day operations and achieve long-term milestones, The Stop also relies on community volunteers to make high-quality programs and produce. In 2013, 70 individuals volunteered in the food bank, while over 6,900 volunteer hours were logged in the Drop-In. Volunteers additionally participate in the maintenance of the gardens and with harvests. Approximately 60% of volunteers are themselves benefactors of The Stop's food and social services, collecting vouchers that can be redeemed for organic produce at a discounted price.

Strengths and Innovations

The Stop uses urban agriculture to benefit otherwise marginalized populations through education, solving hunger issues, promoting healthy lifestyle choices, and creating stronger relationships in communities. The organization has evolved from a food bank to a much larger institution serving and served by the community. It folds urban agriculture into a broader goal of educating and providing better health options. The food center recognizes that simply handing out food to those in need will not make a lasting impact. Instead, its innovation lies in its understanding that healthy food production and consumption are intimately linked to civic empowerment and communal change. The coupling of food access and community-building programs is core to all of The Stop's work.

▲ Figure 5.39

Edible Schoolyard at P.S. 216 in Gravesend, Brooklyn, New York

CASE STUDY 16: SCHOOL GARDENS: MICROCOSMS OF URBAN AGRICULTURE

The growing popularity of urban agriculture has revitalized an interest in school gardens. Children are enthusiastic and receptive audiences for the practices and values of urban agriculture. Parents and educators, particularly of urban children, cite a desire to connect youth with nature and the outdoors and describe the importance of demonstrating green building technologies, sustainable food production, healthy eating habits, and the connection between garden and table. This interest is reinforced by prominent examples such as Michelle Obama's vegetable garden at the White House. New York City is a good example of the large number of newly implemented school gardens in cities. Between 2010 and 2012, the number of school gardens there increased from 45 to 230.

School gardens are not a new phenomenon and have played a vital role in every urban garden movement since the 1890s. Gardening was seen then as a way to instill values, such as hard work, collaboration, and good character, as well as support practical pursuits and academic subjects.[43] These applications can still be made from urban agricultural practices in schools, where they are now complemented by environmental and general health education. Today, however, it is more difficult in increasingly dense cities to find space for school gardens. In view of limited spatial resources, garden projects are relying more and more on imaginative and sometimes complex building retrofits to exploit previously untapped growing spaces—notably rooftops. Today's school gardens are more diverse than ever, reflecting the ever-growing repertoire of urban agricultural practices, responding to the distinct conditions of every site and group of gardeners, and ranging widely in complexity and cost of installation. Web-based forums share resources and ideas and connect projects worldwide, demonstrating that the school garden remains a compelling cornerstone of the urban agricultural movement. This case study will investigate the Edible Schoolyard Project, the Greenhouse Project and three unique green roof school gardens projects.

THE EDIBLE SCHOOLYARD PROJECT

The recent resurgence of the school garden movement can arguably be traced to Alice Waters and her development of a garden at Martin Luther King Jr. Middle School in Berkeley, California (Figure 5.40). Waters is a renowned chef and owner of the famed restaurant, Chez Panisse, and her focus from the outset was to illustrate the connection between the garden and kitchen. From the beginning, the garden was conceived as a place to increase food literacy among urban children and to cultivate the idea that wholesome, sit-down lunches are a nonnegotiable component of every school day.[44]

In 1996, motivated by the poor condition of the King Middle School campus, Waters launched a pilot garden project on a stretch of untended land adjacent to the school. Three years after the garden's construction, the school's long-abandoned kitchen was renovated to support food preparation and interactive teaching (Figure 5.41). The Edible Schoolyard soon blossomed, becoming an integral part of the school curriculum in every subject; students learn principles of ecology, biology, and chemistry while working in the garden, making

◀ Figure 5.40

Composting, Edible Schoolyard at the Martin Luther King Jr. Middle School, Berkeley, California

▲ Figure 5.41

Preparing red bean stew in the kitchen classroom, Edible Schoolyard, Berkeley, California

compost, preparing food, eating a salad, or cultivating and grinding heirloom grains to make bread as part of a history lesson. Transforming a scrubby 1-acre parcel into a student-designed and -constructed teaching garden has inspired educators, politicians, activists, and students worldwide. A global network of Edible Schoolyards is forming to provide resources and training for schools that want to establish gardens and kitchens as hands-on classrooms.

Affiliated Programs

Since 2006, the founding of six affiliated Edible Schoolyard Projects throughout the United States has illustrated that the concept is applicable everywhere, with approaches tailored to each program's unique climate, participants, and spatial resources. The Edible Schoolyard Project (ESYP) illustrates how the existing spatial resources and organizational capacity of the present-day educational system can be leveraged to reintroduce traditional cycles of food production and consumption into urban environments. Available school facilities, willing educators, and engaged parents and community members are vital ingredients to the success of such endeavors.

The Edible Schoolyard Project will always result in gardens and kitchens that are as unique as their settings. Whereas the growing system in the Berkeley

Edible Schoolyard consists of mud-and-wattle raised beds built by students, future prototypes planned for New York City, for example, will need to contend with more limited ground space. Edible Schoolyard NYC currently plans to establish five "Showcase Schools," one in each borough. The first was completed in 2014 at P.S. 216 in Gravesend, Brooklyn, and the second is under development at P.S. 7 in East Harlem and will incorporate a rooftop teaching garden. The architecture firm WORKac in New York designed both "showcase" edible schoolyards (see Architect's Profile 5). To disseminate resources and case studies as widely as possible, an online network established by the ESYP makes it easy to find and list affiliated projects all over the world, share knowledge, and provide participants with a sense of belonging to a much larger movement.

THE GREENHOUSE PROJECT

In 2010, a pilot greenhouse laboratory was completed at P.S. 333 on Manhattan's Upper West Side. Designed and installed in collaboration between the architecture firm Kiss + Cathcart (see Architect's Profile 2) and nonprofit New York Sun Works (NYSW), the greenhouse was developed as a rooftop science lab to illustrate sustainable agricultural techniques for a dense urban setting (Figure 5.42). The Greenhouse Project was originally founded in 2008 by a

▼ Figure 5.42

Rooftop greenhouse, Kiss + Cathcart with New York Sun Works, P.S. 333, Upper West Side, New York, 2010

group of parents and educators seeking to connect urban children to agriculture through the lens of science. Inspired by the self-sustaining Science Barge, developed by NYSW in 2007, these parents and teachers saw an unexploited resource in the rooftops of New York City's public schools and proposed that the closed-loop production and consumption lessons of the barge be brought to every child. Each greenhouse laboratory is outfitted with hydroponic and aquaponic systems, rainwater catchment cisterns, solar panels, a vermicompost facility, an evaporative cooling system, and prototypes illustrating space-saving agricultural techniques. With a goal of establishing 100 greenhouse labs by the year 2020, the Greenhouse Project seeks to demonstrate that New York's rooftops can be harnessed to supply produce not only to public school students but to the rest of the city as well.[45]

NYSW was founded in 2004 and three years later launched the Science Barge, a floating educational prototype for organic food production with a net zero carbon footprint. Based on a recirculating hydroponics system, the Science Barge produces lettuce, tomatoes, peppers, and cucumbers in a greenhouse powered by solar and wind energy and biofuels (Figure 5.43). Water is supplied by rainfall and the Hudson River. The technology demonstrated by NYSW in the Science Barge greenhouse catalyzed two new ventures: (1) the nonprofit Greenhouse Project; and (2) BrightFarm Systems, a for-profit consultancy to support commercial urban greenhouse production (see Case Study 11). NYSW's technical expertise—equally suitable for high-yield commercial projects—sets the Greenhouse Project apart from other school garden initiatives.

▼ Figure 5.43

Science Barge in Yonkers, New York Sun Works, built in 2007

GREEN ROOF SCHOOL GARDENS

Greenroof Environmental Literacy Laboratory: P.S. 41

The growing interest in testing different kinds of rooftop farming at school gardens is most notable in New York City.[46] The Greenroof Environmental Literacy Laboratory, or GELL, was founded at P.S. 41 in the West Village in 2006. The brainchild of parent Vicki Sando, the project developed as an offshoot of an already existing garden program at street level. From the outset, Sando sought to create an environmental literacy focus and conceived of the roof as a hands-on classroom to integrate subjects such as ecology, agriculture, nutrition, technology, biology, chemistry, and mathematics. At 15,000 ft^2 (1,400 m^2), the green roof is the largest on any public school in New York City (Figure 5.44), though the building could only support a shallow soil growing system due to structural limitations. Rather than intensive vegetable beds, the garden is based on a modular tray system for growing shallow-rooted species such as herbs, which are sold to local restaurants. Despite its limited depth, the green roof is

▼ Figure 5.44

Green roof, P.S. 41, Green Roof Environmental Literacy Laboratory GELL, Greenwich Village, New York, 2012

highly effective at absorbing stormwater and reduces energy costs by regulating the temperature of the building in summer and winter. One-third of the roof is devoted to urban wildlife habitat. The estimated $1.7 million required for construction has been funded by a variety of nonprofit organizations, local businesses, and the New York School Construction Authority.

Fifth Street Farm Project: Robert Simon School Complex

Serving three East Village Schools—the Earth School, P.S. 64, and Tompkins Square Middle School—the Fifth Street Farm Project is a successful example of a green roof retrofit that could serve as a model for other schools in older buildings (Figure 5.45). Like the GELL in the West Village, this rooftop project was initiated by a group of parents and teachers, notably parent and award-winning architect, Michael Arad. In 2007, the Fifth Street Farm Project was formed to

▼ Figure 5.45

Rooftop garden, Fifth Street Farm, Robert Simon School Complex, East Village, New York, 2012

Community: Education and Social Integration

expand a small garden program already underway at ground level; the team envisioned a 2,400-ft² (220-m²) rooftop farm with raised beds for cultivating vegetables and ornamentals. To solve the structural limitations of the existing building, Arad leveraged a technique known as rooftop dunnage, which is used to support heavy mechanical equipment on roofs. The platform he devised hovers 4 feet above the roof slab and rests on two new steel beams tied into the existing building structure. The rooftop garden was planted in fall 2012 after a $1.1 million installation funded by grants from state and city politicians.

P.S. 84: Lillian Weber School of the Arts

A rooftop garden project at P.S. 84, on the Upper West Side, reveals another potential source for collaboration: university professionals and students. Since 2011, parents and teachers have partnered with landscape design students in Columbia University's School for Continuing Education to develop a rooftop garden to augment the school's burgeoning urban agricultural program. A design proposed by the students was selected; it includes a greenhouse, eight raised planters, sheltered gathering spaces, and a rainwater catchment system. The cost to implement the plan will be estimated by other students in Columbia's School for Continuing Education, whose programs in construction and fundraising will similarly support the endeavor.

Strengths and Innovations

Recent school garden initiatives demonstrate a range of growing practices, from ground- and community-based farming to productive green roofs and hydroponic rooftop operations. This diversity of operations is similarly reflected in the different values and skills acquired by the children who learn in these gardens.

Edible Schoolyards focus on soil-based, organic plant cultivation and the culture of food preparation. The garden and kitchen are equally important locations where students learn to grow, prepare, and consume food communally. The movement primarily intends to reach children in underprivileged neighborhoods or food deserts where access to healthy food and food culture is limited, similar to the original Edible Schoolyard in North Berkeley.

The Greenhouse Project addresses the science of urban agriculture through the installation of "laboratories" on school rooftops. Technology is the primary focus of these learning spaces. Rooftops are retrofitted with greenhouses that house hydroponic and aquaponic growing systems, where pupils learn how to monitor and control the inputs and outputs of nutrient cycles. Here, scientific understanding takes priority over hands-on plant cultivation.

The green roof projects emphasize the environmental benefits of urban agriculture. In addition, they bring vegetation to barren roofscapes in environments where few ground-based growing areas are available. Depending on the specific local conditions and structural capacity of the host building, these projects may require compromise as to the soil depth, selection of plant species, or improvement of the building performance. Despite these constraints, these projects serve as powerful models of sustainability for children and the community while creating unique outdoor classrooms in the city.

Each school garden case study also describes the work of a visionary individual able to inspire a group of supporters to create an urban school garden. A committed team typically includes some combination of parents, teachers, school and political leaders, designers, and nonprofit organizations to work through several phases of design, development, permitting, and fundraising. In this way, these projects demonstrate the extensive community capital that has historically been required for school gardens to succeed in the long term.

The popularity of the Edible Schoolyard, Greenhouse Project, and these green roof projects—each beginning as a discrete prototype and inspiring a movement—demonstrates the immense interest in school gardens. A tangible, compelling example, along with an existing framework and network for development, seems particularly helpful in motivating other parents, teachers, and schools to establish similar programs. Some schools or parent groups are able to raise millions of dollars for expensive rooftop infrastructures, while others struggle to finance a few hundred dollars to buy gardening supplies. This is where nonprofits can help. The enrichment of the learning environment will differ according to the urban agricultural strategy selected, but, as these case studies suggest, students and teachers will benefit no matter what the growing system.

NOTES

1. Thomas Lyson, *Civic Agriculture: Reconnecting Farm, Food, and Community* (Medford, MA: Tufts University Press, 2004), 5.
2. Ibid., 8.
3. Randolph T. Hester, *Design for Ecological Democracy* (Cambridge, MA: MIT Press, 2006), 3.
4. A. Gilchrist, "Design for Living: The Challenges of Sustainable Communities," in *Sustainable Communities: The Potential for Eco-Neighbourhoods*, ed. E. Barton (London: Earthscan Publications, 2000), 147–59.
5. Laura Saldivar-Tanaka and Marianne E. Krasny, "Culturing Community Development, Neighborhood Open Space, and Civic Agriculture: The Case of Latino Community Gardens in New York City," *Agriculture and Human Values* 21 (2004): 399.
6. Lyson, *Civic Agriculture*, 77.
7. Kate H. Brown and Andrew L. Jameton, "Public Health Implications of Urban Agriculture," *Journal of Public Health Policy* 21.1: 20–39. See also Ellen Teig et al., "Collective Efficacy in Denver, Colorado: Strengthening Neighborhoods and Health through Community Gardens," *Health & Place* 15 (2009): 1115–22.
8. Jim Diers, *Neighbor Power: Building Community the Seattle Way* (Seattle: University of Washington Press, 2004), 14.
9. Thomas Bassett, "Reaping the Margins: A Century of Community Gardening in America," *Landscape Journal* 25.2: 1–8, cited in Jeffrey Hou, Julie M. Johnson, and Laura J. Lawson, *Greening Cities, Growing Communities: Learning from Seattle's Urban Community Gardens* (Seattle: University of Washington Press, 2009), 13–14.
10. Hester, *Design for Ecological Democracy*, 60.

11. Donna Armstrong, "A Survey of Community Gardens in Upstate New York: Implications for Health Promotion and Community Development," *Health & Place* 6 (2000): 319–27.
12. Teig et al., "Collective Efficacy in Denver," 1119.
13. Hou, Johnson, and Lawson, *Greening Cities, Growing Communities*, 27.
14. Carolyn Steel, "Sitopia—Harnessing the Power of Food," in *Sustainable Food Planning: Evolving Theory and Practice*, ed. Andre Viljoen and Johannes S. C. Wiskerke (Wageningen, the Netherlands: Wageningen Academic Publishers, 2012), 40.
15. Katherine Alaimo et al., "Fruit and Vegetable Intake among Urban Community Gardeners," *Journal of Nutrition Education and Behavior* 40 (2008): 94–101. See also Lacey Arneson McCormack et al., "Review of the Nutritional Implications of Farmers' Markets and Community Gardens: A Call for Evaluation and Research Efforts," *Journal of the American Dietetic Association* 110 (2010): 399–408.
16. Teig et al., "Collective Efficacy in Denver," 1120.
17. Paul A. de Graaf, "Room for Urban Agriculture in Rotterdam," 533–45.
18. Paul Hawken, *The Ecology of Commerce: A Declaration of Sustainability* (New York: HarperBusiness, 1993), 146.
19. Hou, Johnson, and Lawson, *Greening Cities, Growing Communities*, 15.
20. Teig et al., "Collective Efficacy in Denver," 1115–22.
21. Saldivar-Tanaka and Krasny, "Culturing Community Development, Neighborhood Open Space, and Civic Agriculture," 399–411.
22. NYRP, www.nyrp.org/green-spaces/garden-details/willis-avenue-community-garden/. See also TEN-arquitectos, www.ten-arquitectos.com/projects/160.
23. R-Urban, http://r-urban.net/en/.
24. Prinzessinnengarten, http://prinzessinnengarten.net/about/.
25. Alice Waters, *Edible Schoolyard: A Universal Idea* (San Francisco: Chronicle Books, 2008), 43.
26. NY Sun Works, "The Greenhouse Project: 100 Labs by 2020," http://nysunworks.org/thegreenhouseproject.
27. Gary Comer Youth Center, www.gcychome.org/?project=green-initiatives. See also Food Project, http://thefoodproject.org/.
28. Added-value Youth Empowerment program, www.added-value.org/what-we-do/. See also Windy City Harvest Apprenticeship program, www.chicagobotanic.org/urbanagriculture/apprenticeship.
29. Urban Gardenshare, www.urbangardenshare.org/. Sharing Backyards, www.sharingbackyards.com/. Garden Swap, http://gardenswap.org/gardenswap/Welcome_to_garden_swap.html.
30. YIMBY, The Stop, http://thestop.org/yes-in-my-back-yard.
31. Deborah D. Giraud, "Shared Backyard Gardening," in *The Meaning of Gardens: Idea, Place, and Action*, ed. Mark Francis and Randolph T. Hester Jr. (Cambridge, MA: MIT Press, 1980), 166–71.
32. Robert Mellinger, "Nation's Largest Public Food Forest Takes Root on Beacon Hill," *Crosscut.com: News of the Great Nearby* (February 16, 2012), http://crosscut.com/2012/02/16/agriculture/21892/Nations-largest-public-Food-Forest-takes-root-on-B/.
33. Chris Berthelsen, Jared Braiterman, and Jess Mantell, "Tokyo, a Fruitful City," in *Farming the City: Food as a Tool for Today's Urbanization*, ed. Francesca Miazzo and Mark Minkjan (Amsterdam: Valiz/Trancity, 2013), 94–101.
34. Sami Grover, "$50,000 from a Backyard Farm? The Enticing Promise of Spin Farming," Treehugger (September 7, 2011), www.treehugger.com/green-food/50000-from-a-backyard-farm-the-enticing-promise-of-spin-farming.html.

35. Henry Barmeier and Xenia K. Morin, "Resilient Urban Community Gardening Programmes in the United States and Municipal Third-sector 'Adaptive Co-governance,'" in *Sustainable Food Planning: Evolving Theory and Practice*, ed. Andre Viljoen and Johannes S. C. Wiskerke (Wageningen, the Netherlands: Wageningen Academic Publishers, 2012): 159–72.
36. Jane Schukoske, "Community Development through Gardening: State and Local Policies Transforming Urban Open Space," *Agriculture and Human Values* 21 (2004): 371.
37. Fair Food Network, www.fairfoodnetwork.org/what-we-do/projects/double-up-food-bucks.
38. Jennifer Sumner, J. J. McMurty, and Michael Classens, "Possibilities and Pitfalls: Urban Food Security," in *Farming the City: Food as a Tool for Today's Urbanization*, ed. Francesca Miazzo and Mark Minkjan (Amsterdam: Valiz/Trancity, 2013), 74–75.

Case Study 12: Prinzessinnengarten

39. Prinzessinnengarten, http://prinzessinnengarten.net/. Nomadisch Grün, ed., *Prinzessinnengarten: Anders Gartnern in der Stadt* (Köln: DuMont Verlag, 2012). Pim Bendt, Stephan Barthel, and Johan Colding, "Civic Greening and Environmental Learning in Public-access Community Gardens in Berlin," *Landscape and Urban Planning*, 109 (2013): 18–30. Marco Clausen, "Cultivating a Different City," http://prinzessinnengarten.net/about/. George Eich, *Prinzessinnengärten Berlin: Urban Farming*, video, www.architekturclips.de/prinzessinnengarten/, 2010. Adalbert Evers, Benjamin Ewert, and Taco Brandsen, eds., "Princesses Gardens," in *Social Innovations for Social Cohesion* (Liege, Belgium: WILCO, 2014), www.wilcoproject.eu/downloads/WILCO-project-eReader.pdf, 116. Ellen Mey, "Interview with Robert Shaw," trans. Naomi Hanada, http://prinzessinnengarten.net/about/. Joseph Redwood-Martinez, *Prinzessinnengärten—Berlin, Germany*, video, http://prinzessinnengarten.net/about/. Jacobo Zanella, *Prinzessinnengärten, Berlin*, Monocle video, http://prinzessinnengarten.net/about/, 2010.

Case Study 13: Organopónicos

40. This case study profile is partly based on preliminary research conducted by Gabrielle Glass in the author's graduate seminar. Additional sources: Martin Bourque and Kristina Canizares, "Urban Agriculture in Havana, Cuba," *Urban Agriculture Magazine* 1 (2005): 2. Andrew Buncombe, "The Good Life in Havana: Cuba's Green Revolution," *The Independent* (August 8, 2006), www.independent.co.uk/news/world/americas/the-good-life-in-havana-cubas-green-revolution-410930.html. Scott Grahm Chaplowe, "Havana's Popular Gardens and the Cuban Food Crisis," (Master's Thesis, University of California, Los Angeles, 1996), 47. Sinan Koont, *Sustainable Urban Agriculture in Cuba*. (Gainesville, FL: University Press of Florida, 2011): 133. See also Bourque and Canizares, "Urban Agriculture in Havana," 2. Mario Gonzalez Novo and Gunther Merzthal, "A Real Effort in the City of Havana: Organic Urban Agriculture," *Urban Agriculture Magazine* 6 (2002): 26. André Viljoen, Katrin Bohn, and J. Howe, *Continuous Productive Urban Landscapes: Designing Urban Agriculture for Sustainable Cities* (Amsterdam; San Diego: Elsevier/Architectural Press, 2005), 136–91.

Case Study 14: R-Urban

41. R-Urban, http://r-urban.net/en/. Atelier d'Architecture Autogérée (AAA), "R-Urban: Resilient Agencies, Short Circuits, and Civic Practices in Metropolitan Suburbs," *Harvard Design Magazine* 37: 1–6. European Union, LIFE Programme, "R-URBAN: Participative Strategy of Development, Practices and Networks of Local Resilience for European Cities," http://ec.europa.eu/environment/life/project/Projects/index.cfm?fuseaction=search.dspPage&n_proj_id=3965. Constantin Petcou and Doina Petrescu, "R-Urban Resilience," in *Atlas: Geography, Architecture, and Change in an Interdependent World*, ed. Melissa Butcher (London: Black Dog Architecture, 2012), 64–71. Doina Petrescu, "*Relationscapes:* Mapping Agencies of Relational Practice in Architecture," *City, Culture and Society* 3 (2012): 135–40. Doina Petrescu and Constantin Petcou, "Tactics for a Transgressive Practice," *Architectural Design* 83.6: 58–65. Elvia Wilk, "R-Urban Prototypes for an Urban Ecology," *Uncube Magazine: Urban Commons* 20: 19–22, www.uncubemagazine.com/magazine-20-12467995.html#!/page19.

Case Study 15: The Stop Community Food Centre

42. This case study profile is based on a visit to The Stop in Toronto, communication with The Stop's Communications Manager, Kathe Rogers, and preliminary research conducted by Claire Shigekawa Rennhack in the author's graduate seminar. Additional sources: The Stop Community Food Centre, www.thestop.org. Community Knowledge Centre, Toronto Community Foundation, "The Stop Community Food Centre," http://ckc.torontofoundation.ca/org/stop-community-food-centre. N. Saul, "The Name Gain," *The Stop News*, Fall 2002: 1. C.X. Levkoe and S. Wakefield, "The Community Food Centre: Creating Space for a Just, Sustainable, and Healthy Food System," *Journal of Agriculture, Food Systems, and Community Development* 2011, advance online publication available at http://dx.doi.org/10.5304/jafscd.2011.021.012. Elizabeth Fraser, "CFCC Urban Agriculture Summit 2012," *The Stop CFC Vimeo*, http://vimeo.com/48041800. Kathryn Scharf, Charles Levkoe, and Nick Saul, *In Every Community a Place for Food: The Role of the Community Food Centre in Building a Local, Sustainable, and Just Food System* (Toronto: Metcalf Foundation, 2010). Cheryl Roddick, "Stronger Together," *The Stop Community Food Centre 2013 Annual Report* 2. Carole Counihan and Penny Van Esterik, *Food and Culture: A Reader* (New York: Routledge, 2013), 591–94. Nick Saul and Andrea Curtis, *The Stop: How the Fight for Good Food Transformed a Community and Inspired a Movement*, 1st ed (Brooklyn, NY: Melville House Pub., 2013).

Case Study 16: School Gardens: Microcosms of Urban Agriculture

43. Laura J. Lawson, *City Bountiful: A Century of Community Gardening in America* (Berkeley: University of California Press), 51–92.

The Edible Schoolyard Project

44. Alice Waters, *Edible Schoolyard: A Universal Idea* (San Francisco: Chronicle Books, 2008). The Edible Schoolyard Project, "Explore the Network," http://edibleschoolyard.org/network. WORKac, http://work.ac/tag/agri-culture/.

The Greenhouse Project

45. Kiss + Cathcart, http://www.kisscathcart.com/productive_architecture.html. NY Sun Works, "The Greenhouse Project: 100 Labs by 2020," http://nysunworks.org/thegreenhouseproject. BrightFarms, "Our History," http://brightfarms.com/s/#!/about_us/our_history.

Green Roof School Gardens

46. Mark Gorgolewski, June Komisar, and Joe Nasr, *Carrot City: Creating Places for Urban Agriculture*, 1st ed. (New York: Monacelli Press, 2011), 174–79. Jill Stern, "Funding Growing for P.S. 41 Roof," *The Villager* 78.46 (April 2009), http://thevillager.com/villager_312/fundinggrowing.html. See also Greenwich Village School, "Greenroof Environmental Literacy Laboratory," www.ps41.org/groups/gell. Fifth Street Farm Project, www.5thstreetfarm.org/. Alex Davies, "A NYC School Teams Up with Columbia to Build a Rooftop Garden and Classroom," Treehugger, www.treehugger.com/urban-design/columbia-students-build-green-roof-elementary-school.html

Chapter 6

Design

From Urban Visions to Building Integration

ABSTRACT

Designing for urban agriculture requires multidisciplinary knowledge. Designers, as discussed in the previous chapters, must synthesize a full spectrum of environmental factors and human inputs—including growing systems, the nutrient cycle, sustainable water supplies, access to sunlight, farm operation, finances, marketing, and community integration. Juggling so many disciplines is a challenge, but it also opens opportunities for integrative collaboration. This chapter will discuss how design professionals in multidisciplinary teams can shape urban agricultural projects. It will also describe typical roadblocks to establishing farming operations in cities, in particular, issues relating to code and policy, as well as recent changes in municipal regulations that improve feasibility. Despite the challenges, design professionals have developed many approaches, illustrated here by a diverse array of innovative projects. The exemplary work of several outstanding firms will be highlighted in a series of concluding profiles.

ARCHITECTS' FASCINATION WITH URBAN AGRICULTURE

Design professionals are increasingly fascinated by urban agriculture. Nowhere is this more apparent than at the Universal Expo in Milan 2015. To fulfill the exposition's theme—"Feed the Planet, Energy for Life"—the USA Pavilion extends as an open green plane, a vertical farm stretching the length of a football field. Architect James Biber's striking display of edible crops raises provocative questions about the future of food and farming worldwide (Figure 6.2). Designers have been grappling with these ethical, practical, and aesthetic questions for decades, however, and many have begun to rigorously incorporate urban agriculture into their work. More and more buildings integrate plant material and other living systems: examples include green roofs, eco-machines, and building-integrated agriculture (BIA), which is the most complex application. In addition, urban agriculture is now widely considered to be a key component of large urban design projects, an encouraged element of many urban building codes, and a requirement of sustainability rating systems. Urban agriculture is uniquely poised to integrate ecological, cultural, social, and educational systems within the built environment and has thus become a favorite studio and thesis topic in architecture schools around the world.

◀ Figure 6.1

Vertical farm façade, Biber Architects, USA Pavilion at the Universal Expo in Milan, Italy, 2015

▲ Figure 6.2

Entrance and southwest-facing façade, Biber Architects, USA Expo Pavilion in Milan, Italy, 2015

The idea of cultivating food in cities sparks new urban visions and utopian ideas of urban self-sufficiency. As sustainability becomes a crucial component of all design projects, urban agriculture offers a new set of tools for increasing resilience. It offers an array of benefits, expanding environmental and sustainability improvements, increasing social and health gains, and creating new businesses and economic profits. Design professionals are increasingly captivated by the notion of food production as a cultural component of our urban lives and are more and more motivated to search for design expressions that make this culture a part of the city. The broad field of urban agriculture enriches the repertoire of designers, with manifestations ranging from community gardens to building-integrated vertical greenhouses.[1] The multifaceted requirements of urban agriculture also present opportunities for interdisciplinary collaboration that parallels design professions' current work to develop holistic, integrated approaches to shape the built environment.

Because of their fascination with urban agriculture, designers are a driving force in advancing and promoting the field. Design professionals continue to publicize urban agriculture by producing innovative ideas for the built environment. Many design professionals have integrated urban agriculture into their research, speculative work, competitions, design proposals, and realized projects. This work contributes to the development of new conceptual ideas, the public support for urban agriculture, the feasibility of building integration, and the development of concrete projects or new initiatives, often actively supported by the architects themselves.

New Urban Visions

Urban food production has long inspired visions for self-sustaining communities and utopian city plans, as illustrated by the research initiative *49 Cities* by WORKac[2] (see Architect's Profile 5). This project compares a collection of visionary city plans from ancient Rome to the present day. As these examples demonstrate, today's designers are part of long historical tradition of imagining agriculture in the city. And contemporary architects are leveraging urban agriculture and its practices to transform the city on a larger scale than ever before.

A recent example of this type of vision is the concept of Continuous Productive Urban Landscapes (CPULs), developed by architects Katrin Bohn and André Viljoen and first published in 2005 (Figure 6.3).[3] Bohn and Viljoen imagine a network of agricultural operations integrated with multifunctional urban spaces. Collectively, these connected interventions have a much larger

▶ Figure 6.3

The Continuous Productive Urban Landscapes CPUL concept, Bohn & Viljoen Architects

Design: Urban Visions to Building Integration

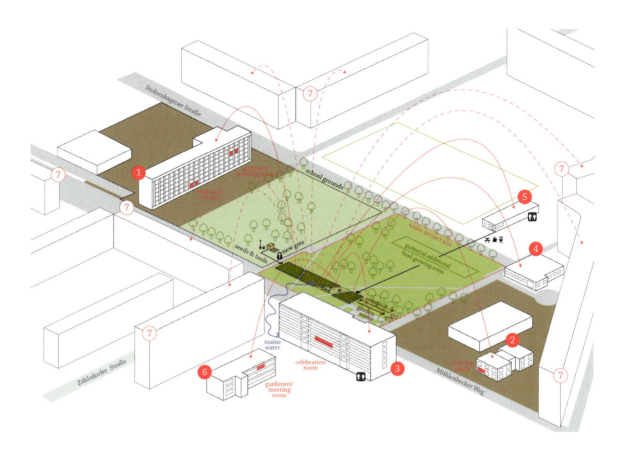

Figure 6.4

Growing Food Together, Spiel/Feld Marzahn, Berlin, Germany, 2011– ongoing

positive effect than individual projects. In their 2014 book, *Second Nature Urban Agriculture: Designing Productive Cities*, Bohn and Viljoen investigate how CPULs are changing the way designers address current urban food systems, urban agriculture, urban landscapes, and participatory design.[4] They illustrate "the emergence of urban agriculture as design subject" and introduce numerous international hands-on, community-based projects (Figures 6.4–6.6).

Architect and scholar, C.J. Lim takes the integration of agriculture and urban infrastructure a step further. In his proposals for "Smartcities," Lim develops new cities around agriculture, rather than vice versa. He further synthesizes his design ideas into policy frameworks that support the implementation of urban agriculture in Smartcities like Guangming, China, and Nordhavnen, Denmark (see Architect's Profile 1).

Technical Viability and Incorporation

Questions of technical viability present fascinating challenges for design professionals seeking to integrate agriculture into buildings to improve both building performance and the operation efficiency of an urban farm. Recently, architects have begun to aspire to higher degrees of building integration by establishing

▲ Figure 6.5

Starting a productive urban landscape, Spiel/Feld Marzahn, Berlin, Germany, 2011–ongoing

symbiotic relationships between growing and building systems. Crops become part of active and passive systems, making productive use of building byproducts such as exhaust heat and air and greywater.

The Vertical Integrated Greenhouse (VIG) by Kiss + Cathcart (see Architect's Profile 2) and the vertical greenhouse by Plantagon (see Case Study 5) not only harvest solar radiation on south-facing façades but also utilize the environmental performance benefits of double façades while contributing to their buildings' passive air-conditioning systems. A team of

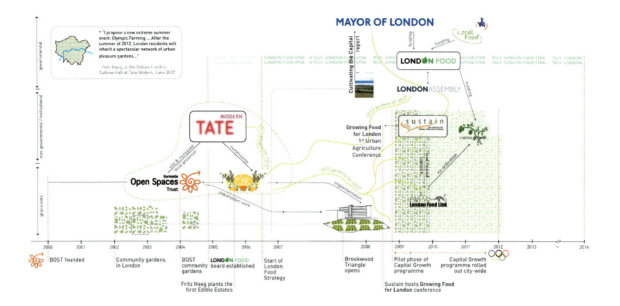

▲ Figure 6.6

A process diagram for *Capital Growth*, design research, Bohn & Viljoen Architects with Department of City and Nutrition, TU Berlin

architects and engineers has applied a similar system to grow algae within the façade of a five-story residential building. The BIQ in Hamburg, Germany, is the first building with a façade-integrated algae bioreactor, which grows algae in the cavity of double-glazed window panels. Currently, the system produces and harvests algae as biomass for energy production for its fifteen residential units, though it could alternatively grow algae for food or as a dietary supplement.[5]

Operational and economic viability are also key factors in realizing BIA projects. Design professionals are often the driving force behind developing financial models for BIA projects, and many compete to solve the technical and economic challenges associated with urban agricultural operations in order to realize their first building-integrated farm (see Case Study 4). Other architecture firms focus on grant writing and alternative funding for their urban agricultural projects. The Seattle-based architecture firm Weber Thompson (see Architect's Profile 3) has been developing models for BIA operations as part of mixed-use projects since 2009. In addition to considering how farm operations can be economically viable, the firm searches for new financing models for developers and building owners who invest in infrastructure for urban agriculture.

Design and Building Integration

Integrating growing systems—juxtaposing plant cultivation and architectural structures—both inspires and challenges design professionals working in the field. Combined with the widespread interest in designing sustainable, or "living," buildings, integrating productive living systems, such as plants and crops, becomes even more compelling. Designing green roofs, green walls, hydroponic systems, greenhouses, and vertical greenhouses has become an inspiring and popular challenge.

Vegetation boosts the well-being of occupants and urban dwellers, and many architects see urban agriculture as an educational, public health, and cultural resource that enriches life in cities. The Gary Comer Youth Center is a realized educational project that features urban agriculture in the form of a productive green roof that introduces children and young adults in the south side of Chicago to food cultivation (Figure 6.7). At the same time, the green roof is a central architectural element that makes a strong statement about the project's identity. The protected roof garden (Figure 6.8) has become a symbol for learning about ecological resilience while fostering the resilience of disadvantaged youth.[6]

Elmslie Osler Architect embraces urban agriculture as an important cultural resource by combining food production, retail services, and health care in one community center. This proposal for a food and health center in Syracuse, New York, connects two programs via a rooftop farm: an existing neighborhood supermarket and a new health-care facility (Figure 6.9). An aquaponic greenhouse, meanwhile, bridges a new shared community plaza. The center intends to improve the public health of the community by providing resources and educational opportunities, such as access to nutritional counseling, cooking classes, healthy food, and preventive health services.[7]

The two firms that most frequently address the design and cultural integration of urban agriculture are SOA in Paris (see Architect's Profile 4) and

▼ Figure 6.7

Productive green roof, Hoerr Schaudt Landscape Architects, Gary Comer Youth Center, Chicago, IL, 2009

◀ Figure 6.8

Productive green roof creating a hidden, protected garden, Hoerr Schaudt Landscape Architects, Gary Comer Youth Center, Chicago, IL, 2009

WORKac in New York (see Architect's Profile 5). SOA situates BIA projects in prominent urban sites and juxtaposes highly visible growing operations with everyday programs like supermarkets and residential buildings. Their work demonstrates that urban agriculture is an important cultural component of today's cities and that people are meant to be at the center of this movement and these projects.

WORKac similarly promotes a visionary and visible approach to urban food production while also emphasizing the cultural importance of soil-based growing in each project. This combination of innovation and soil-based agriculture often generates new urban typologies. Thanks to this unique approach, the firm is one of the few to both successfully implement realized projects and put forward imaginative proposals. Their work also demonstrates that advancing the

▲ Figure 6.9

Food and health center, proposal, Elmslie Osler Architect, EOA Syracuse, NY, 2012

design integration of urban agriculture relies on a creative design process that builds conceptually strong projects.

CHALLENGES MOVING TOWARDS REALIZATION

While many design professionals are captivated by the architectural possibilities of urban agriculture, realizing the integration of plant cultivation and food production in built projects remains a challenge. Designers need to navigate interdisciplinary knowledge, building codes, and other regulations. Many regulatory policies are changing, albeit slowly, in support of productive agricultural systems and programs. Finding the right niche in this complex landscape of regulatory frameworks and operational and marketing opportunities is often the key to success. Many design professionals state that the greatest challenges are bringing clients, developers, and landlords on board and establishing new forms of operation and business models. Therefore, creativity and innovation in areas far beyond the usual parameters of design are often required to introduce agricultural production to the urban built environment.

Multidisciplinary Knowledge and Teams

Integrating urban agriculture may be challenging for architects, landscape architects, and planners because it requires them to engage systems and fields of expertise that are outside their training and comfort zone. Just as urban farmers need to "wear multiple hats," as Ben Flanner from Brooklyn Grange (Case Study 8) observes, designers working in urban agriculture need to acquire multidisciplinary knowledge—including input from the fields of agriculture, horticulture, ecology, agronomics, and economics. At the same time, these challenges afford exciting opportunities to engage with other practices and fields of knowledge. Working with consultants and experienced farmers, developing research labs, or collaborating with students on competitions or pilot projects allow designers to gather information from different parties and to address problems with more versatility and creativity.

Zoning and Regulations

Over the past decade, city zoning and code regulations have begun to change rapidly to allow for food production in various forms. Although food production was an integral part of cities for centuries, agriculture was systematically moved out of cities in the years after World War II. While urban farming had been greatly encouraged and legitimized during wartime to support food security, it was not considered compatible with the post-war lifestyle. It was banned due to perceived health and safety concerns and its lack of compatibility with segregated land-use regulations. Recent cultural shifts, including the popularity of local food movement and growing ecological awareness, have made cities more receptive to alternative land-use practices.

Due to the broad set of concerns that urban agriculture projects try to address—such as food security, community support, climate change, and economic development—food policy advisory councils (FPCs) and private advocacy groups have become important activists for new land-use planning and policy-making.[8] Together with these stakeholders, cities have started to develop new planning tools for urban agriculture. Design professionals have also been active in this process, helping to identify and spatially contextualize opportunities so that synergies can be recognized.[9]

Building Codes

In many municipalities, the integration of crop cultivation in building design directly conflicts with the prevailing building code. For example, adding an agricultural use on top of commercial or residential uses conflicts with the land-use code of many cities. As a result, some cities have begun to adapt their codes not only to allow but also to incentivize building-integrated agriculture. One strategy is to exempt rooftop greenhouses from floor area and height limits as long as they do not include residences. In New York City, these greenhouses are limited to 25 ft (8 m) in height, require a 6-ft (2-m) setback, and must use water-efficient technology.[10]

Yet because this practice is still fairly uncommon, many cities classify these greenhouses as office buildings (and not agricultural structures) in terms of fire protection code, requirements for material choices, sprinkler inclusion, and egress. These heightened building and safety standards are one reason why building-integrated greenhouses are disproportionately more expensive than conventional ground-based construction.

Environmental Policies and Regulations

In addition to establishing the legal frameworks for access to adequate growing space, city governments also regulate the essential inputs for growing operations, such as soil, nutrients, and water. For example, health concerns caused by soil contamination or water pollution often trigger restrictions. Historically, these regulations have also been strict and unfavorable to reclaiming nutrient and water sources, due largely to concerns about hygiene based on outdated recycling practices. Urban farmers and designers have started to campaign for the repeal of these restrictions in order to increase resource conservation and the sustainable benefits of their urban agricultural projects.

Land Tenure

Due to the high demand for land in densely populated cities, urban agricultural operators compete with developers for available growing sites and are often displaced when the land becomes valuable enough to sell. Therefore, urban agriculture has long been seen as a temporary instead of a permanent land use. Thanks to public advocacy, however, new zoning regulations in some cities protect urban agriculture for the benefit of the community, especially to prevent the destruction of vibrant community gardens.

City Farm, an entrepreneurial farm in Chicago, has turned old zoning regulations to its advantage. In operation since the early 1990s, City Farm leases sites awaiting future development. The farm prefers sites one acre (4000 m^2) or larger and available for at least three to five years. Arrangements like this create win-win conditions: they improve the situation for soil-based farmers by offering affordable leases and provisions for a new site in the event that the land is developed while improving the value of the land and the neighborhood while the site remains undeveloped.[11]

Site Selection

It can be a challenge to find available and affordable sites for urban agricultural operations. Design professionals are trained to evaluate site conditions and constraints that will potentially restrict farm operations, such as zoning and code regulation, accessibility, operational frameworks, cost, land tenure, lease conditions, and other economic challenges. Environmental conditions and the specific microclimate of an urban site must also be evaluated. Soil quality determines the opportunities for a ground-based operation on a specific site. Similarly, finding an ideal host building for a BIA project is equally critical.

Host Building Selection

A host building has to be conducive to the intended mode of operation—rooftop farming, indoor farming, or façade farming—and the landlord has to be willing to take an urban farm as a tenant and to negotiate acceptable leasing conditions. The list of criteria for the host building includes structural integrity and allowable load capacity (especially on rooftops), access, egress, transportation infrastructure for vertical circulation and freight transport, access to resources, and appropriate size.

Historic industrial and warehouse buildings are particularly desirable, as they were originally constructed to accommodate heavy loads and often designed to accommodate additional floors if needed. The Brooklyn Grange flagship farm, for example, sits atop the muscular Standard Motor Products Building, built in 1919 and able to withstand up to three times the load that its 43,000-square-ft (4000 m²) rooftop is currently carrying (see Case Study 8) (Figure 6.10).[12]

Interior warehouse spaces and large basements can serve as suitable sites for indoor growing, aquaculture, mushroom, and vermiculture operations. In Chicago, The Plant urban farm operates in a former meatpacking plant (see Case Study 9); Buffalo's Village Farms has created an extensive hydroponic tomato-growing operation on the site of a former Republic Steel mill; and the Biospheric Project in Manchester, United Kingdom, combines a multisystem urban farm and research center in a three-story former mill adjacent to a low-income housing estate.[13]

Much like secure land tenure, reliable, long-term leases are essential for building-integrated operations. They have to be long enough for the farm operation to be viable. The higher the up-front investment, the longer the lease should be to allow for enough time to turn a profit. When they lose their farm sites, building-integrated projects must also grapple with losing some of the infrastructure installed on the site, such as greenhouse structures and other growing systems not easily transferred to a new host building. Recently,

▼ Figure 6.10

Standard Motor Products Building, host building of Brooklyn Grange flagship rooftop farm, Long Island City, Queens, built 1919, renovated 2010

established rooftop farms have negotiated leases of 10 years or more and have secured the ownership of the installed infrastructure.

Building-Integrated Agriculture: New Construction Versus Retrofit

When beginning a BIA project, designers must first determine whether to build a new structure or retrofit an existing building. Both approaches are feasible, though each is associated with different drawbacks. Most rooftop farms currently in operation have selected warehouses—existing or new constructions—to support their operational needs. The first hydroponic rooftop farms at both Lufa Farms (Case Study 10) and Gotham Greens (Case Study 11) were retrofits, whereas the second greenhouses for each operation were integrated into the construction of a new warehouse or supermarket. The companies, as this trend shows, have been increasingly successful at convincing investors to support custom-built infrastructure.

Architecture & food, a London-based design consultancy for BIA, makes the possible synergies between host buildings and hydroponic farms the focus of its design investigations for both retrofits and "new-builds."[14] The development process starts with feasibility studies in multiple steps that lead to design development, planning, and construction, if viable. The retrofit process begins with lease negotiations with the building owner and a viability analysis of the existing host building, while "new-builds" are initiated in dialog with developers and an architectural design team. In the case of new construction, core concerns like structural viability, egress, and supply infrastructure for hydroponic rooftop farms can be solved during the design phase, making a positive outcome more likely. Architecture & food has consulted about integrating urban agricultural operation primarily in terraced housing in London (Figure 6.11).[15] Similar to its work is a realized project called Arbor House in the South Bronx, New York. The affordable housing complex has had an 8,000-ft² (740-m²) commercial hydroponic rooftop greenhouse in operation since 2013.

▼ Figure 6.11

Rooftop greenhouse retrofit proposal, Architecture & food with Hyde Group, Adas UK, Arup, and the May Barn Consultancy, Ringcross Estate in Islington, London

DESIGN CONSIDERATIONS

This is a unique time for designing with urban agriculture. Public support of the movement is now strong and growing; many growing systems have been tested; and architects and designers are just shy of establishing compelling strategies to finance and realize urban farming operations. Strong advances in urban agricultural technology, operation, and design have been documented in this book.

In the last few years, designers and entrepreneurs have developed and implemented pioneering growing systems. Some of these include innovative greenhouse design and building-integration technologies that maximize the benefits of urban growing conditions (see Case Studies 1–6). These technological advances have led to a number of successful commercial operations, many of which are—at least in part—community-supported. The success of these large-scale realized projects usually hinges on a strong operating and business administration framework. Due to the density of urban growing conditions, most initiatives are building-integrated, at least to a certain degree: this includes both low-tech, do-it-yourself growing infrastructure as well as commercially manufactured, high-tech systems and greenhouses (see Case Studies 7–11). With the popularity of the urban agricultural movement, new forms of community gardens have emerged, either through community-driven construction and operations or through existing social organizations or parent groups that shepherd projects through development, fundraising, and construction (see Case Studies 12–16).

Architects and design professionals play an important role in these advances, whether serving as technical advisors or the visionary masterminds behind projects. Integrating urban agriculture can enrich architecture and its allied design professions. The wide spectrum of approaches and applicable scales underscores this potential: designers have the opportunity to engage in explorations ranging from large urban design projects to the detailing of a "productive" façade, and from community-supported initiatives to high-tech commercial ventures (see Architects' Profiles 1–5).

Realization Challenges

While designers have visionary ideas for integrating urban agriculture and while tested technologies are numerous and growing, design professionals still struggle to realize their urban agriculture projects. To date, few of the many inspiring proposals have been constructed, chief among them WORKac's two showcase projects for the Edible Schoolyard NYC initiative (see Architect's Profile 5), as well as the first constructed vertical farm of Vertical Harvest (see Case Study 4). Realized large-scale BIA projects in new construction are especially rare, although examples include the Gowanus Whole Foods supermarket (see Case Study 11), Lufa Farms' Laval greenhouse (see Case Study 10), and the Arbor Houses in the South Bronx.

Why does realization remain the biggest hurdle? The challenges vary depending on the scale, location, budget, and primary goals. While small-scale projects may be challenged by land tenure and zoning issues, by recruiting adequate political and community support, and by fund-raising, large-scale, high-tech, and capital-intensive BIA projects may struggle with code restrictions, with financing, and with client and investor involvement and support. Many investors and financiers do not yet view an urban agricultural operation as a trusted business model and are waiting to see successful, built precedents before they invest their money in a new field.

Next Steps

To make urban agriculture a widespread, viable operation and to realize more building-integrated projects, design professionals need to intensify their collaborations with all stakeholders. Municipalities, design professionals, and public advocates must continue to transform the regulatory landscape of urban zoning, building codes, and health regulations to foster urban agriculture. Changes in urban regulations will promote environmental improvements, increased resilience and food security, economic and business development benefits, and community building. To take better advantage of these benefits, municipalities need to more strongly incentivize urban agriculture by facilitating the permitting process as well as establishing alternative financing options. Cities, neighborhoods, and local businesses often use outstanding urban agricultural operations as marketing tools. This is an additional enticement for them to support new farms in their communities with start-up capital or long-term purchasing agreements.

People should be at the heart of every urban agricultural intervention, regardless of whether they grow the food, benefit from newly created jobs, or support the urban farm as consumers. Integrating growing systems and environmental support systems into buildings and public spaces will make sustainable systems more visible and recognizable for building users and urbanites. Most urban agricultural projects have the potential to involve the entire community in the process of design and food production. Stronger community involvement means that more and more residents will have a voice in shaping their food system and urban futures.

The future of urban agriculture depends, to a large degree, on the current student generation, and support for it is formed in design education programs. Students' research, inquisitive design work, and willingness to approach problems and urban infrastructure from a fundamentally different perspective will solve many of the hurdles that the urban agriculture movement currently faces. Food systems and urban agriculture have only recently, though, become the subject of university research and teaching. Including urban agriculture and food production in design education will help advance the field and will also address various topics important for design in the built environment, including interdisciplinary collaboration, innovative design research, community collaboration, action research, integration of environmental systems, and sustainable design.

To develop successful urban agricultural operations, designers need to work from the beginning in strong interdisciplinary teams that include agriculturists, horticulturists, suppliers, entrepreneurs, and marketing experts. By collaborating, designers can connect their visionary ideas with the environmental and operational strategies of operating farms. Establishing the right growing infrastructure, identifying a farm operator, setting up a distribution system, and connecting to the local food system are all crucial.

As with the operational requirements, designers also need to better understand the entrepreneurial side of urban agriculture so that larger-scale commercial projects can be realized. More successfully built projects will show the long-term viability of growing food in cities. If the rapid development of technically feasible building-integrated projects over the past 10 years is any indication, the field is on the verge of a major breakthrough.

Most importantly, urban agriculture is an opportunity for architects, landscape architects, and planners to creatively integrate sustainable design while simultaneously addressing critical aspects of environmental, social, and economic resilience. In addition, they need to make use of the synergies in the built environment, getting beyond metrics, rating systems, and technologies. With this perspective, urban agriculture helps to redefine the role of the architect in sustainable, holistic design.

▲ Figure 6.12

Farmers (as the New Eco-Warriors), CJ Lim/Studio 8 Architects, Guangming Smartcity, China, 2007

ARCHITECT'S PROFILE 1: CJ LIM/STUDIO 8 ARCHITECTS

Partner/Principal: CJ Lim
Location: London, United Kingdom
Year founded: 1994
Web address: www.cjlim-studio8.com

C.J. Lim founded the London-based Studio 8 Architects in 1994 as a multidisciplinary practice in architecture, landscape architecture, and urban design.[16] Focusing on cultural, social, and sustainability issues, his design research has led to a transformative new urban design paradigm, which Lim calls the "Smartcity." Urban agriculture is a central component of this innovative approach. Lim explores Smartcities in numerous urban proposals and in two of his most recent books, *Smartcities and Eco-Warriors* (2010) and *Food City* (2014). Lim is also the Professor of Architecture and Urbanism at the Bartlett School of Architecture, UCL, in London. In his teaching, he uses the Smartcity concept to explore urban environmental and social sustainability from a designer's perspective. He has won numerous awards for his designs, research, and contributions to education.

Design: Urban Visions to Building Integration

Background

The Smartcity paradigm imagines future urban environments in which nature and built form create an ecological symbiosis. It posits that sustainable urban development can be achieved through embedding mutually supporting closed systems into each other within cities. The Smartcity reintegrates cultivated land within an urban economic and ecological context via architectural and urban design solutions. The hybridization of urban agriculture and the city as well as the establishment of city-dwelling farmers can lead to a production-consumption relationship that is symbiotic rather than parasitic, reducing carbon emissions and food shortages and adding other equally significant environmental and social benefits (Figure 6.13).

C.J. Lim's framework for the Smartcity and the integration of urban agriculture as an "urban transformation tool" began in 2007 with the master plan for the Guangming Smartcity in the Guangdong Province in southeast China. In the following years, Lim worked on several projects based on this new urban framework. The 15 examples included in the book *Smartcities and Eco-Warriors* respond to or were commissioned by international initiatives, including those of the Chinese and Korean governments and regeneration agencies in Denmark, the United Kingdom, and the United States.

Guangming and Nordhavnen Smartcities

The Guangming Smartcity proposal exerted the biggest influence on Lim's research and established many of the manifestos and policies of his Smartcity,

▼ Figure 6.13

Symbiotic resource flows in the Smartcity, CJ Lim/Studio 8 Architects

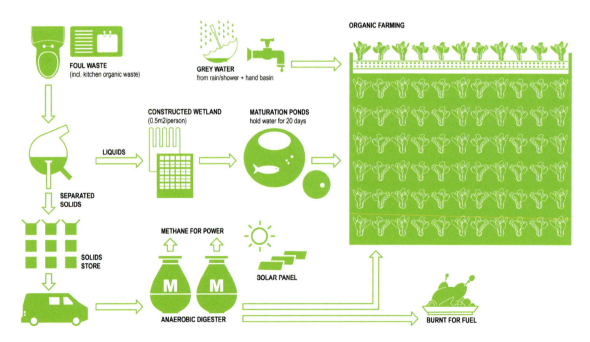

Human Expertise

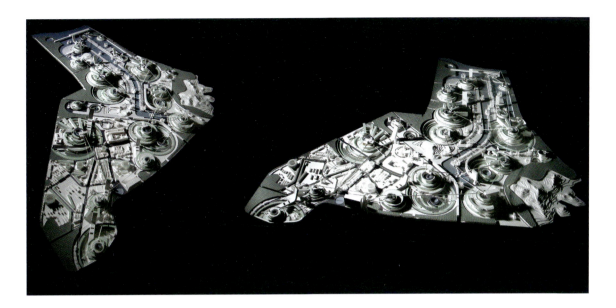

▲ Figure 6.14

Site model, Guangming Smartcity, China, 2007 CJ Lim/Studio 8 Architects

including the integration of urban agriculture into city planning. Commissioned by the Shenzhen Municipal Planning Bureau, Guangming is an urban development proposal covering three square miles (eight square km, more than twice the area of Central Park), housing 300,000 inhabitants, and combining agricultural tradition with twenty-first-century lifestyles. The housing is composed of self-sufficient towers and "craters," which augment the natural landscape and combine dwelling and agricultural fields in a series of circular, terraced forms (Figure 6.14). At the forefront of the Guangming Smartcity manifesto stands urban agriculture, which is based on building-integrated rooftop farming methods and livestock grazing fields and orchards between buildings (Figure 6.15). Lim's design also draws on the agrarian background of many of China's new urban dwellers.

A new part of Shenzhen, the Guangming Smartcity will be an ecological subcenter independent from the high-tech industrial sprawl of the region, and it will balance socio-cultural issues with economic growth. Additionally, the proposal has the opportunity to influence both China's environmental and socio-economic policies. The country currently houses 22% of the world's population but possesses only 10% of the world's cultivated land and has eclipsed the United States in the consumption of basic agricultural and industrial goods, becoming the world's largest consumer of grain, meat, coal, and steel. It is anticipated that half of China's population will move from the countryside to cities for economic reasons. Migration from these rural areas has resulted in the decline of a rural Chinese culture built upon ties to place of origin. The Chinese government has been supportive of Smartcity design policies, which hopefully will be widely implemented within the next few years. The government intends to make Smartcity implementations into political showcases, presenting China's ecological policy to international communities.

Nordhavnen Smartcity takes Guangming's philosophies and infrastructural elements and situates them within water-dominated Copenhagen (Figure 6.16).

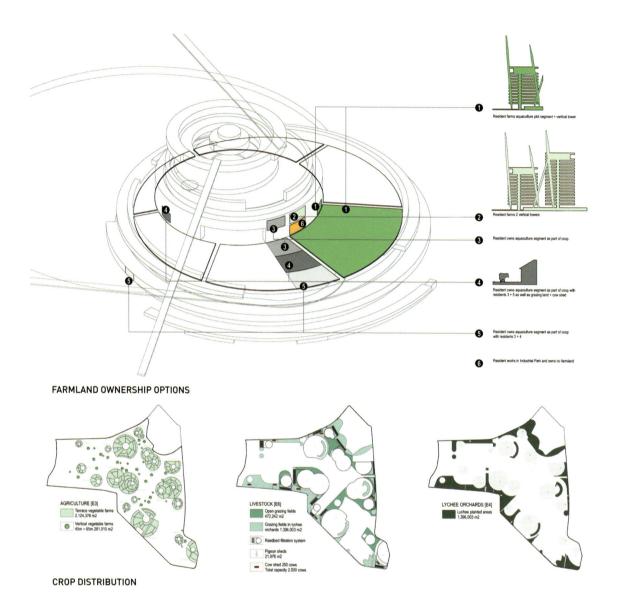

Already a world leader in sustainable living, Copenhagen aims to be the world's leading environmental capital, and the transformation of Nordhavnen into a sustainable new waterfront city is seen as key to that ambition. Lim's proposal for a 420-acre (1.7 km^2) "arable kitchen-garden park" on a former industrial and shipdocking yard in Nordhavnen was commissioned by the Copenhagen Port Authority to demonstrate sustainable farming principles (Figure 6.17). Over 80% of the ground would be dedicated to farmland, interspersed with grazing fields (Figure 6.18). Compact car-free suburb clusters are then stitched together by an elevated ribbon of vegetable farming draped with hydroponic curtains (Figure 6.19). The Nordhavnen Smartcity will be able to absorb most of Copenhagen's expected population increase while integrating state-of-the-art environmental approaches.

▲ Figure 6.15

Farmland ownership options and crop distribution, Guangming Smartcity, China, 2007 CJ Lim/ Studio 8 Architects

▶ Figure 6.17

Aerial view, Nordhavnen Smartcity, Denmark, 2008, CJ Lim/Studio 8 Architects

▲ Figure 6.16

Master plan, Nordhavnen Smartcity, Denmark, 2008, CJ Lim/Studio 8 Architects

◂ Figure 6.18

Housing units elevated over farmland, Nordhavnen Smartcity, Denmark, 2008, CJ Lim/Studio 8 Architects

◂ Figure 6.19

Housing clusters stitched together by elevated ribbon of farming, Nordhavnen Smartcity, Denmark, 2008, CJ Lim/Studio 8 Architects

Design Philosophy and Approach

Lim sees Smartcities as opportunities to realign with a grounded value system that rejects rampant consumerism and exploitation. For him, design should offer intelligent solutions that demonstrate added value, regain public and political confidence, and reaffirm the value of the profession. In times that demand sustainable design, this assessment requires a shift in values away from beauty based on aesthetics toward elegance created by efficient arrangements and systems.

The work of Lim and his firm demonstrates how to develop a new urban vision and how to design with urban agriculture on a large scale. This approach requires multidisciplinary sustainable design that combines architecture, planning, geography, hydrology, and environmental engineering to develop a holistic model of an alternative urban form. Lim and Studio 8 Architects demonstrate alternative ways to realize this vision by disseminating the new urban paradigm and maximizing its impact on multiple levels. In so doing, Lim applies strategies that other architects often do not consider in integrating urban agriculture. These include:

Policy development
The aim of his research is to influence government policies. Through his collaboration with government agencies and other scientific disciplines, he works toward a policy-level implementation of his speculative visions and research.

Publications
As a prolific author, Lim has published his work on the design integration of urban agriculture and urban food systems in two recent books. Both are written from a designer's perspective to disseminate the new paradigm of the Smartcity and to inspire other designers.

Awards
The recognition of the Smartcity approach through a series of international awards and exhibitions further increases its reach and influence. Collectively, the work on Smartcities has won seven international urban design and environmental prizes. The Smartcity projects have also been exhibited in the United Kingdom, China, the United States, and Japan, including exhibitions funded by the European Union and Japan's Ministry of Environment and an international traveling exhibition curated by Toyo Ito. *Smartcities and Eco-Warriors* was honored with the 2010 RIBA International Research Award and nominated for the Urban Design Group UK "best urban design book 2008–10."

Public Outreach

Lim attests that growing advocacy about climate change and the food crisis over the last decade has increased public awareness of the issues he promotes. Though scientific, statistical proof about both crises is well documented, it is

Figure 6.20

Food Parliament, CJ Lim, *Food City*, 2014

mass media presentations of that proof—like Davis Guggenheim's documentary *An Inconvenient Truth* about global warming or Robert Kenner's *Food Inc.* about the food industry—that are providing the compelling and engaging wake-up calls the public at large needs. Lim champions these storytellers, observing that they are essential to laying the groundwork for government officials and designers to solve these pressing issues.

He also calls on farmers to achieve the same level of advocacy. The Smartcity prototype identifies farmers as essential to instructing and advising communities on food cultivation. Lim thus asks them to become leaders in managing energy and ecosystems. He sees future farmers as managers of the environment, actively balancing competing needs for carbon sequestration and wildlife habitat with food, biomass, and timber production.

By using urban relationships to reframe the spaces of food consumption and production, Lim's newest book, *Food City*, raises serious questions about the priorities of the world's governing bodies. The book continues his explorations into ways previous cultures have dealt with food creation, storage, and distribution and what contemporary designers and policy-makers may learn from historical precedents (Figure 6.20).

Strengths and Innovations

Lim's work as an architect, urban designer, policy advocate, and author reveals his enormous versatility and offers a model for how architects and landscape architects should think broadly about their work to design urban agriculture. For example, Lim's architectural voice adds the perspective of the designer to the current debate surrounding sustainability issues and more specifically creates awareness of the need to integrate urban agriculture. He expands this thinking about the urban scale to policy development, thus revealing alternative ways to approach urban agricultural integration and realization. Instead of attempting to build a single building-integrated project, he attempts to clear the way for other architects by advocating for the implementation of thoughtful policies.

Lim influences the political consciousness by converting dry data into speculative design with aesthetics that capture the public imagination. While his proposals incorporate very real sustainable urban agricultural practices and have been commissioned by high-profile clients, his work, which equally involves his writing as much as design, remains intent upon promoting a cultural shift in the way the public, governments, and designers think about cities. His ideas for the Smartcity coalesced from long-standing sustainable principles, which he combines with striking aesthetics and persuasive rhetoric that tap into an increased desire for healthier, more sustainable lifestyles.

▲ Figure 6.21

Rooftop greenhouse, Kiss + Cathcart with New York Sun Works, P.S. 333, Upper West Side, New York, 2010

ARCHITECT'S PROFILE 2: KISS + CATHCART, ARCHITECTS

Partners/Principals: Gregory Kiss and Colin Cathcart
Location: Brooklyn, New York, United States
Year founded: 1983
Web address: www.kisscathcart.com

Kiss + Cathcart, Architects is an innovative architecture firm that has worked since its inception in 1983 to integrate cutting-edge sustainable and environmental systems into its projects.[17] The firm calls its work "productive architecture," or architecture that generates positive human, environmental, and economic benefits through good design. Integrated systems, including integrated agriculture, are the primary focus of the practice. Kiss + Cathcart's work related to urban agriculture ranges from hydroponic educational greenhouses to prototypes for vertical greenhouses, including a proposal for a 150-story building featuring building-integrated agriculture (BIA).

Background

Much of the firm's early work incorporated photovoltaic technology, which converts solar energy into electricity, well before the term building-integrated photovoltaics (BIPV) was coined. The technical and aesthetic challenges of photovoltaic work sensitized Kiss + Cathcart to related issues involving the sun—such as daylighting, shading, and passive solar heating—as well as other environmental factors including natural ventilation and rainwater collection. Multifunctional solutions to these issues improved the quality and raised the value of the firm's designs. Explorations around sunlight also led the firm to embrace vegetation as another productive element, not only in terms of landscape design but also as an integral component of building systems. Plants themselves are effective solar devices, capturing and storing the energy of the sun. In addition, vegetation mitigates stormwater through evapotranspiration, creates a cooling effect, improves the microclimate, sequesters CO_2, and produces oxygen. Building-integrated vegetation also offers an aesthetic value, which improves people's well-being. These tangible benefits create values that can be much greater than just that of the electricity produced by PV panels. In this sense, growing food in buildings can be seen as the most complex form of integrated solar production.

A 2007 visit to the Science Barge—New York Sun Works' off-grid farm-on-a-raft (see Case Study 16)—initially inspired Kiss + Cathcart to integrate urban agriculture into their projects. The demonstration of hydroponic technologies, and the nutrient film technique (NFT) system in particular, sparked ideas for building integration. In collaboration with New York Sun Works and Arup, Kiss + Cathcart proposed a vertical NFT system in a double-skin façade for the Buckminster Fuller Institute competition in 2009. This was the first example of what has become known as a Vertical-Integrated Greenhouse, or VIG (Figure 6.22). This growing system suspends NFT troughs on a cable-stay system between two vertically oriented pulleys in the cavity of a double-skin façade. This plant cable lift (PCL) moves the plants like a conveyer belt through the vertical space to guarantee homogeneous light exposure for all plants and to bring the crops to the harvesting station at the bottom of the loop. Kiss + Cathcart has since developed the VIG idea in a number of other projects, none yet built, though with New York Sun Works they have prototyped a VIG, and other architects have subsequently pursued similar ideas.

Building-Integrated Agricultural Projects

Kiss + Cathcart's collaboration with New York Sun Works has led to successful, highly visible, and highly publicized projects. One of these projects is the Greenhouse Project, which builds greenhouses as science classrooms on the rooftops of New York City public schools such as P.S. 333 and P.S. 84 (see Case Study 16) (Figure 6.23). These science labs are adaptations of standard greenhouses, customized for their dual growing and learning missions as well as their installation on a rooftop. These greenhouses illustrate the enormous potential

◄ Figure 6.22

Vertical growing system prototype, Kiss + Cathcart with New York Sun Works and Arup, Vertical-Integrated Greenhouse (VIG), 2009

▼ Figure 6.23

Interior space of greenhouse, Kiss + Cathcart with New York Sun Works, P.S. 333, Upper West Side, New York, 2010

for hydroponic rooftop greenhouses by demonstrating the technological viability of BIA as well as by introducing children and the public to the idea that food can be grown on urban rooftops. Kiss + Cathcart continues to refine its knowledge of the practical aspects of integrating greenhouses into existing buildings, developing requirements for environmental science classrooms, and advancing hydroponic growing systems.

VIGs will create more opportunities for hydroponic installations in a range of building types and spaces, and Kiss + Cathcart has started to deploy more advanced VIG systems in forthcoming projects. The Bronx High School of Science, the 2020 Tower, and the Masdar Green Market (Figure 6.24) are examples of BIA systems based primarily on VIG principles. In three very different building types, these projects demonstrate how VIGs can produce a substantial quantity of crops. At Bronx High School of Science and in the 2020 Tower, the greenhouse elements are scaled to produce the total amount of fresh produce consumed on site by the buildings' populations: 3,000 students and faculty for the former and 30,000 inhabitants and workers for the latter. The Bronx Science design integrates both vertical and horizontal greenhouses into the lobby, while the 2020 Tower's façade houses vertically integrated hydroponic systems (Figure 6.25). The Masdar Green Market uses the same system as a double-skin façade to provide spatial definition, shading, and cooling while producing crops that are primarily sold in the market itself. These projects also demonstrate the aesthetically and thermally beneficial aspects of building-integrated systems.

Another project, the Bronx River House, employs a different approach that could easily be adapted to produce edibles. As a building in a park, it appropriately has a dynamic, green façade—a metal mesh covered in vines and plants (Figure 6.26). The vegetated enclosure is an active system that affects building performance, creating a favorable microclimate that moderates temperature by

▼ Figure 6.24

Masdar Green Market, Kiss + Cathcart, Abu Dhabi, United Arab Emirates

◀ Figure 6.25

2020 Tower commissioned by the National Building Museum, Kiss + Cathcart with Arup, New York

▼ Figure 6.26

Vegetated green façade, Kiss + Cathcart, The Bronx River Greenway River House, Bronx, New York, 2007

cooling the surrounding area up to 15°F (8°C), controlling sun exposure, and improving air quality through evapotranspiration. It is also a stormwater management system, harvesting rainwater and putting it to productive use while keeping it out of the sewer system. The project won the 2007 New York City Public Design Commission award.

Design Approach

Kiss + Cathcart begins each project by evaluating its greatest productive potential in an effort to maximize the environmental building performance. This includes quantifying the direct input of environmental resources—insolation, rainfall, and wind—as well as alternative urban resources and by-products. The second step is to analyze which building system could make best use of these resources. This approach parallels best practices in design with urban agriculture. Identifying the best use of urban resources and supporting urban synergies is a key strategy to create sustainable urban agricultural operations.

Available solar radiation sets an aggregate limit for photovoltaic electricity generation, solar thermal production, passive space heating, and naturally powered photosynthesis. If any or all of these strategies seem to make sense for the program and budget, the firm moves forward by weighing the costs and benefits of each, always seeking to realize the maximum value in terms of the project's performance. The evaluation of which strategies, inputs, and technologies are most beneficial depends greatly on the specific situation, location, budget, and program of the project. While PV panels are an established technology—they are even subsidized through incentives in some places—VIGs still have to prove their technical and economic viability. Regardless, the firm continues to solicit opportunities to realize its first VIG.

Kiss + Cathcart completed their second rooftop greenhouse for the Greenhouse Project at P.S. 84 in Brooklyn in 2015 (Figures 6.27a and 6.27b). With the exception of the school greenhouses, Kiss + Cathcart has never been hired specifically for an urban agricultural project. The same may be said for the firm's other sustainable integrations, such as employing advanced environmental principles like BIPV, green roofs, and rainwater harvesting. But thanks to its reputation for working with environmental systems, Kiss + Cathcart has been very successful in proposing these practices to their clients and in integrating them into their projects.

Strengths and Innovations

Kiss + Cathcart primarily embraces VIGs as an alternative strategy to capture solar radiation on building envelopes. This endeavor started based on the firm's long experience with PV technology and environmental building systems. This interest in integrating productive building technologies led quite naturally to the development of the VIG as a new façade system, which offers additional benefits though the living plants. The firm believes that BIA is potentially the

most productive use of a building's envelope, contributing to energy efficiency, resilience, building performance, and quality interior spaces.

Though the firm heavily invests in research into building-integrated growing practices, additional investigations into technical and economic feasibility are needed to make such integration a widespread reality, particularly at larger scales and in real-world settings. As with many innovative systems, there is often resistance to integrating something new. BIA is often dismissed because of clients' and users' lack of familiarity, code issues, and questions of cost and payback. Nonetheless, Kiss + Cathcart remains committed to realizing better-quality, higher-performance projects by integrating productive, multifunctional program elements such as urban agricultural systems.

▲ Figure 6.27a and b

P.S. 84 Rooftop greenhouse, (a) View from street level, (b) Roofscape with Williamsburg Bridge, Kiss + Cathcart with New York Sun Works, P.S. 84, Brooklyn, New York, 2015

▲ Figure 6.28

Close-up of façade, Weber Thompson, Eco-Laboratory, Seattle, WA, 2008

ARCHITECT'S PROFILE 3: WEBER THOMPSON

Partners/Principals: Blaine Weber, Scott Thompson, Kristen Scott
Location: Seattle, Washington, United States
Year founded: 1988
Web address: www.weberthompson.com

Weber Thompson is an award-winning, interdisciplinary architecture and design practice advancing environmental and sustainable approaches. The firm has 25 years of experience in residential, mixed-use, and commercial projects and, since 2008, has worked with sustainable building-integrated agriculture (BIA). Beyond mastering the challenging technical integration involved in these projects, the firm's goal is to integrate agriculture as an economically viable component of commercial building projects while realizing the environmental and health benefits it confers to the community.[18]

Background

The firm first embraced urban agriculture in 2008, with an entry in the Living Future Design Competition for Emerging Green Builders of the Cascadia Green Building Council. Employees Myer Harrell, Brian Geller, Chris Dukehart, and Dan Albert designed a mixed-use building called Eco-Laboratory to meet the Living Building Challenge (a holistic building standard and certification tool), designing energy, water, waste, and ventilation systems in tandem with building-integrated growing systems (Figure 6.29). Urban agriculture united these systems, allowing the building to produce (not just consume) resources by harvesting alternative energy (solar, wind, and methane) and cultivating produce. The project won the regional competition and later competed nationally against Emerging Green Builders throughout USGBC chapters at Greenbuild 2008. It won first place overall and received online coverage from Treehugger and other green-building blogs.

Dr. Dickson Despommier, professor emeritus at Columbia University and author of the 2010 book *The Vertical Farm*, touted the project in online magazines, on television, in print, and in exhibits, including "Why Design Now?" at the Cooper Hewitt National Museum of Design in 2010. Through outreach to advocates, including politicians, urban farmers, and university researchers, the firm leveraged the success of Eco-Laboratory to galvanize support for sustainable, high-yield urban food production. Following this publicity, Weber Thompson received many inquiries regarding urban agricultural integration. Though most

◀ Figure 6.29

Building in site context, Weber Thompson, Eco-Laboratory, Seattle, WA (Living Future Design Competition for emerging green builders, 1st place), 2008

of these requests for design investigations were too grand or far-fetched for cost-effective realization, a few led to fruitful explorations.

Design Approach and Urban Agricultural Projects

The Newark Vertical Farm was Weber Thompson's first commissioned design study, and it allowed the firm to continue its design studies with urban agriculture (Figure 6.30). The project proposed a research and demonstration lab to develop controlled-environment agriculture (CEA) while utilizing sustainable site strategies for the building's orientation and outdoor growing facilities. Initiated by the Mayor's Office of Newark, New Jersey, to revitalize the city's downtown, it was intended to be operated in a partnership between the city and a private developer (Figures 6.31 and 6.32). The firm's resulting systematic design approach in subsequent projects integrated commercial growing operations in mixed-use buildings. It documented its workflow in a diagram that tracks the design decision-making process needed to establish economically viable urban farms (Figure 6.33).

The first step is to establish the vision or priority for the urban agricultural project. Does the client favor the potential social, environmental, or economic benefits? The next three questions can be answered in any order, but must be answered before the next steps can be taken to determine financial viability: What should be grown? Which growing system should be used? And what is the ideal interface between the growing system and the building? Based on the answers to these questions, the architects have enough background information to begin to calculate potential yields and outputs. After establishing a framework for resource flows, the operation and management methods now need to be selected. Taken together with the business model, these planning factors can

▼ Figure 6.30

Vertical farm with site context, Weber Thompson, Newark Vertical Farm, Newark, NJ, 2010

Design: Urban Visions to Building Integration

Figure 6.31

Atrium space, Weber Thompson, Newark Vertical Farm, Newark, NJ, 2010

predict the farm's income and whether it will exceed its expenses, which in turn indicates whether the operation will be profitable and economically viable. With this holistic approach, Weber Thompson's design team is pioneering a comprehensive design integration of urban agriculture. Their work highlights that while design concept and environmental integration of physical systems are key aspects of the design process, the operational and economic systems of urban agricultural projects are equally important design questions to solve.

Figure 6.32

Exterior façade, Weber Thompson, Newark Vertical Farm, Newark, NJ, 2010

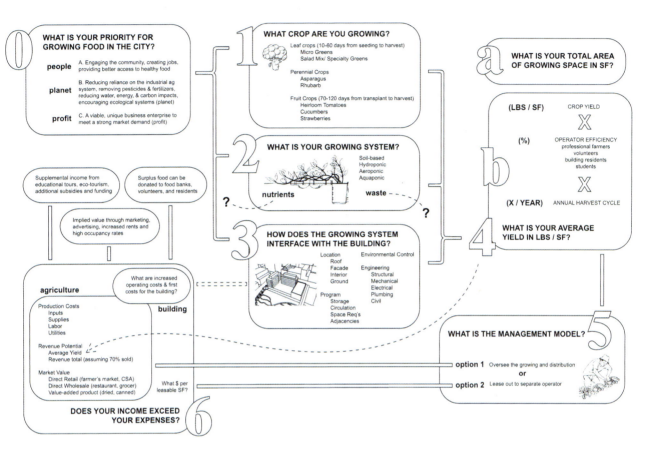

▲ Figure 6.33

Workflow diagram for establishing economically viable urban farms, Weber Thompson

Beyond this overarching approach, some of Weber Thompson's projects have focused on the development of specific farming methods and their technical integration. The firm has tested and detailed numerous growing systems for new construction and retrofits. In 2012, for example, a conceptual rooftop installation was a model for retrofitting a rooftop with a limited-capacity mild concrete slab, demonstrating that the firm could focus the additional weight of soil-based farming where concrete columns support the roof (Figure 6.34). Weber Thompson thus integrated a steel frame touching down exactly over these existing concrete columns. This frame carries lightweight panels and planters.

Understanding where and how projects will be provided with soil, water, nutrients, and light are other crucial questions. Rooftop farming provides the most reliable daylight access in cities. Since agricultural production is only one way to make use of rooftop solar access, different farming methods need to be evaluated in comparison to each other and in comparison to the installation of other systems, such as photovoltaic arrays. In 2013, Weber Thompson used a large, urban, mixed-use residential project to systematically study how to integrate different farming options and rooftop uses while considering architectural expression, productivity, and economic viability (Figure 6.35). The client did not commission this study; it was initiated by the firm's commitment to adapting

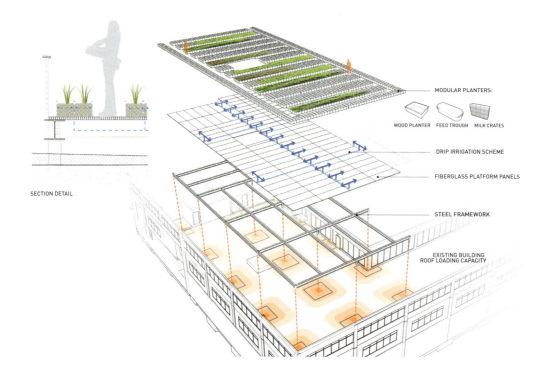

▲ Figure 6.34

Structural analysis and prototype for commercial urban agriculture rooftop retrofits, Weber Thompson, 2012

underused rooftop spaces. By comparing soil-based and hydroponic approaches, the firm decided that hydroponic greenhouses are currently the most viable economic use of the rooftop. Data suggested that the hydroponic greenhouses would produce approximately 75–100 tons of leafy greens annually, compared to 4–5 tons using conventional soil-based methods (Figure 6.36). Hydroponic greenhouses are thus the only growing model to produce a high enough product yield to cover the costs of the necessary infrastructure and production.

◀ Figure 6.35

Study for soil-based rooftop farm on top of a large mixed-use building, Weber Thompson, 2013

▶ Figure 6.36

Study for hydroponic greenhouse rooftop farm on top of a large mixed-use building, Weber Thompson, 2013

Another important step in the design process for Weber Thompson is an evaluation of code requirements and the existing land-use framework. An affordable housing development begun in 2011 was their first project intended to take full advantage of revised land-use code provisions implemented by the City of Seattle Department of Planning and Development in August 2010. Despite these revisions, which allow for a 15-ft (4.5-m) exemption to height limits for food-producing rooftop greenhouses, the project found itself in conflict with local building code. The maximum height and number of occupied stories could not be waived for building code requirements even though the land-use code used additional allowable height. In order to addresses this obstacle, city staff would need to work across departments.

Farm Operation and Distribution Models

Many urban agricultural projects fail to sufficiently design the operational and distribution systems. Weber Thompson acknowledges that a functional growing system without a proper distribution system will likely fail. Engineering the entire production chain at the initial design stage—including securing purchasing agreements—reduces the risk involved in commercial urban agriculture and will also drive the project's design.

Weber Thompson suggests an alternate business model for commercial urban agriculture that separates the role of the building owner from the role of the farm operator. In this model, a separate company manages the farm operation. It will install the growing system and oversee operation, maintenance, training, and the distribution of produce. The building owner will provide either usable rooftop space and utility hook-ups or install the static farm infrastructure, such as greenhouses. With this model, the operator leases space like other commercial and industrial tenants, providing a familiar business model and reducing risk for the owner. The first few projects would help determine the market rate for urban agricultural space. If a zoning incentive like height increases can be captured, this is simply additional leasable area that would not otherwise be available.

Strengths and Innovations

Weber Thompson uniquely tackles the economic integration of BIA in commercial building projects, and its experiences expose the main challenges—lack of built examples and the necessity of demonstrating economic viability—that prevent commercial urban agricultural projects from being realized. For clients, commercial viability is key. The firm acknowledges that, currently, little data exist on successful commercial urban agricultural projects, especially those incorporated into new construction. Therefore investors remain timid about integrating costly growing infrastructure into large-scale commercial projects. Finding ways to reduce risk for the building owner will encourage more investors to back urban agricultural projects, which can result in many additional benefits such as higher profits and media exposure. Most clients support high-yield urban food production in the conceptual and schematic design phases, but at the first sign of additional cost or code issues, they abandon the idea, sometimes for more familiar programs such as amenity space and rooftop photovoltaic arrays.

Besides its advocacy for a tenant model for urban rooftops, Weber Thompson also promotes the environmental benefits that urban agricultural infrastructure provides. By integrating productive systems to improve building performance, the firm also supports its strong sustainability agenda. To prove economic viability, feasibility studies and design proposals also tend to include farm operation methods and distribution models.

Though Weber Thompson has developed many urban agricultural prototypes, the firm has not yet realized a commercial urban agricultural project. Regardless, the practice remains confident that once a pilot project has been built and produces data about cost, crop yield, and revenue, more and more commercial urban agricultural projects will follow. The firm is optimistic that commercial urban agriculture will become a significant urban movement. In its work, Weber Thompson never loses sight of the fact that commercial urban agriculture presents an opportunity to fundamentally change the industrial food system, dramatically reducing the miles food travels and allowing produce to be selected not for its shelf life and hardiness, but for its taste and texture.

▲ Figure 6.37

Superfarm, research study for hydroponic rooftop farm visually connected with "host" supermarket, SOA Architectes

ARCHITECT'S PROFILE 4: SOA ARCHITECTES

Partners/Principals:	Pierre Sartoux and Augustin Rosenstiehl
Location:	Paris, France
Year founded:	2001
Web address:	www.soa-architectes.fr/

SOA is an architecture firm in Paris, France, that has embraced integrated urban agricultural proposals in their design work for over a decade. The firm's primary scope of work includes multifamily housing; educational, cultural, and commercial projects; and urban design schemes. SOA acquires its projects both through prestigious competitions and public and private commissions. Since 2005, the firm has also increasingly focused its research on urban agriculture, culminating in a series of widely publicized projects and the cofounding of the Agricultural Urban Lab (Le Laboratoire d'Urbanisme Agricole, LUA).[19]

Background

Pierre Sartoux and Augustin Rosenstiehl started SOA Architectes in 2001. The two founding partners enrich the firm's collaborative design approach through their multidisciplinary backgrounds in architecture, design, ethnology, urbanism, and conceptual art. Early projects included small remodels, additions, and competition entries. The firm's first project of note came with the Tour Vivante building, when they comprehensively incorporated urban agriculture by imagining a vertical farm integrated with residential and office space in an energy-efficient tower. The project brought recognition to the firm and attention to building-integrated agriculture (BIA).

SOA realized its first built urban agricultural project in 2009 with an educational farm and eco-museum in a Paris suburb. After several initial studies in urban agriculture with Dickson Despommier and the Paris School of Engineering, SOA launched the Agricultural Urban Lab (LUA) in 2012 in collaboration with Le Sommer Environnement, an environmental engineering consultancy, and Le Bureau d'Etudes de Gally, which specializes in landscape design and agricultural innovations. LUA has published articles about urban agriculture and presented various speculative urban agricultural schemes to the public in collaboration with multidisciplinary teams.

Design Approach

SOA's and LUA's primary research and design intent are to develop case studies that "question the limits of compatibility between the technical requirements of intensive agriculture and the cultural heritage" of European cities. They see agriculture as an untapped cultural component of urban dwelling and want to reintegrate humans at the heart of agricultural systems without relying on traditional farming methods. To test the compatibility between food production and cities, their projects develop different scenarios for vertical farms in specific urban conditions, such as prominent downtown locations, brownfields, vacant lots, leftover spaces, and underutilized rooftops. These proposals also illustrate different modes of farm management and diverse types of social integration. In their projects, farming is usually juxtaposed with everyday activities like dwelling, grocery shopping, and commuting. Seeing food production every day builds connections between urban dwellers and the sources of their food. Highly visible urban farms thus allow people to come into direct contact with farming and food production.

SOA tested these design premises in a series of speculative projects intended to capture the public imagination by placing vertical urban farms in prominent locations in the heart of Paris:

- The Tridi farm, supported by a massive, modular steel structure, functions as a large-scale intensive production farm whose green monolith rises prominently within the Place de la Concorde (Figure 6.38).
- Urbanana similarly sites an intensive banana farm in a seven-story greenhouse on the Champs Elysées (Figure 6.39).

▲ Figure 6.38

Tridi Farm, research study on urban farming, SOA Architectes

▲ Figure 6.39

Urbanana, research study on urban farming, SOA Architectes

- Mini-Farm, a group of small local farms in three- to five-story towers, occupies the public open space between housing slabs and operates as a cooperative network (Figure 6.40).
- The vertical farming system Cactus multiplies the small footprints of vacant lots and leftover spaces by maximizing the vertical growing space in structures up to 460 ft (140 m) high.
- Superfarm utilizes not only underused urban rooftop space but also highlights the concept of cross-programming by stacking and visually connecting a hydroponic farm on top of a large supermarket.

These remarkable proposals suggest that various forms of urban farming and food production should be incorporated into the city.

Building-Integrated Agriculture

While exploring such conceptual ideas, SOA has also thought about the practicalities of some of their BIA projects by tackling questions of constructability, economy, and operation. These latter projects address pertinent architectural issues for designers working in the existing urban context, including innovations in urban housing, the improvement of existing public housing estates, and issues of adaptive reuse.

SOA's 2005 Tour Vivante project provided BIA and vertical farming with architectural legitimacy (Figure 6.41). This project was the first to propose a detailed system integrating mutually beneficial water collection, hydroponic

◀ Figure 6.40

Mini-Farm, research study on urban farming, SOA Architectes

◀ Figure 6.41

Integration of vertical, BIA greenhouse in mix-use tower, SOA Architectes, Tour Vivante, Rennes, France, 2005

growing, and alternative energy systems. The project introduces 75,000 ft² (7,000 m²) of hydroponic greenhouse space for growing tomatoes, strawberries, and leafy greens into a 30-story, 540,000-ft² (50,000-m²) commercial and residential building in Rennes, France (Figure 6.42). SOA developed a new architectural experience by juxtaposing growing spaces with the other building programs. The integrated greenhouse not only provides fresh food in the center of the city, it also plays an essential role in regulating the indoor climate of tenant spaces (Figure 6.43). This regulation is achieved by controlling solar gain, thermal and humidity fluctuations, and cooling via evapotranspiration. The greenhouse forms one continuously connected spiral, rising from the bottom of the building to the top. Heat captured in the greenhouses in the winter is stored in the thermal mass of the building's concrete structure. After winning the 2005 Cimbéton positive-energy building competition, the Tour Vivante was featured in many respected publications, including *Le Monde*, the *New York Times*, and *National Geographic*.

SOA has also integrated urban agricultural scenarios into existing buildings. A rooftop farm in Romainville, a Paris suburb, proposes a building retrofit that makes full use of urban rooftop space while reactivating and upgrading an existing housing project (Figure 6.44). It integrates a series of two-story rooftop greenhouses on three existing apartment blocks joined by sky bridges. The existing buildings do not have the structural integrity to support the greenhouses, so SOA has added a concrete structural system to the exterior of the existing housing blocks, creating, at the same time, additional balconies for the apartments. This unbuilt project is awaiting funding from the French government.

The firm is also fostering a new culture of urban agriculture at the Ferme Musicale (or Ferme Darwin) in Bordeaux, France (Figure 6.45). The Ferme, designed in collaboration with the Paris-based design firm Holdup, unites urban

▶ Figure 6.42

Greenhouse with tomatoes, SOA Architectes, Tour Vivante, Rennes, France, 2005

◀ Figure 6.43

View from office space into the greenhouse, SOA Architectes, Tour Vivante, Rennes, France, 2005

◀ Figure 6.44

Rooftop greenhouse and balcony additions, SOA Architectes, Rooftop Farm, Romainville, France, 2012

▲ Figure 6.45

Rooftop farm on music venue, SOA Architectes, Ferme Musicale (Musical Farm) in Bordeaux, France, 2012

farming and cultural activities. The ground floor houses a musical stage for outdoor concerts, gallery space, service facilities for the farm, and educational spaces devoted to agriculture. Above, a lightweight steel structure supports four levels of growing infrastructure. The building is housed within the one-story shell of an old barrack. The contrast between the heavy masonry walls below and the transparent steel structure above gives the impression that the crop cultivation rises out of the existing urban fragment. The project, which brings together natural and cultural elements, reinforces SOA's commitment to highlighting urban agriculture's cultural importance for cities.

SOA's most recent urban agricultural project is a competition entry for the French Pavilion at the Universal Expo in Milan 2015 (Figure 6.46). The theme for the expo was "Feeding the planet, energy for life." SOA's competition entry draws from the iconic form of the greenhouse and market hall, both long-standing cultural symbols of agricultural production. The structure is elevated one story and appears to float in a large, lush market garden and orchard. The pavilion and grounds, meanwhile, exhibit France's ancient and contemporary crops and culinary sciences. On the top floor of the pavilion is a restaurant and bar that showcase the country's culinary culture. The pavilion poetically expresses the technical pragmatics of greenhouses by employing typical greenhouse technology with operable apertures to regulate internal temperature.

◂ Figure 6.46

Front façade, SOA Architectes, Competition Entry, French Pavilion at the Universal Expo in Milan, 2015

Strengths, Innovations, and Influence

SOA's main contribution to the field of urban agriculture is its strong interest in design integration with the city, work underscored by a belief that urban agriculture is an important cultural component of cities in the twenty-first century. The firm's projects increase the visibility of food production in the city and integrate people into the center of the urban food system, all the while proposing innovative farming models. SOA advances its efforts through research and multidisciplinary collaborations in the LUA. With its understanding of urban agriculture as an interdisciplinary field, the firm aspires to work with farmers, engineers, and designers; with experts in agronomy, biology, sociology, art, and philosophy; and with faculty at architecture schools. And in order to reach a broad audience, SOA seizes opportunities to publish its projects widely and place them in respected competitions.

SOA's conceptually and visually striking projects have generated significant public and professional interest. In addition, the firm is making important steps towards realizing its projects through detailed development of architectural integration strategies. Its multifaceted research, continued commitment to these issues, and refined design sensibility ensure that SOA remains not only an influential voice in the realm of urban agricultural design but also an important advocate in advancing its real-life integration.

▲ Figure 6.47

Aerial view, P.S. 216 in Brooklyn Gravesend, WORKac, showcase project for Edible Schoolyards NYC, Brooklyn, New York, 2014

ARCHITECT'S PROFILE 5: WORKac

Partners/Principals: Amale Andraos and Dan Wood
Location: New York, United States
Year founded: 2003
Web address: http://work.ac

WORKac (WORK Architecture Company) is an award-winning, New York-based, globally operating architectural firm that positions its work at the intersection of urban and natural environments. Urban agriculture is an important component of its quest for urban innovation and alternate scenarios for the future of cities. The firm's work focuses on cultural civic projects, museums, commercial offices, retail spaces, educational projects, and large-scale master planning. Principals Amale Andraos and Dan Wood are long-time teachers at architecture schools in the United States and beyond, which allows them to engage in a vivid exchange about their research interests between academia and practice. In September 2014, Andraos was appointed Dean of Columbia University's Graduate School of Architecture, Planning and Preservation.[20]

Background

WORKac was founded in 2003 by Amale Andraos and Dan Wood. The firm's interest in the connections among design, ecology, urbanism, and food production began with its research project "49 Cities," initiated while both Andraos and Wood were teaching at Princeton University (Figure 6.48). The project compares historically important, visionary city plans designed worldwide between 500 B.C.E. and 2006 and explores each plan's integration of urban, rural, and natural systems, including agriculture. Many of the 49 utopian proposals include farming—a detail that has often been overlooked in previous studies. For example, Le Corbusier's Radiant City incorporates both kitchen gardens for each resident that together form communal gardens as well as an innovative operation strategy with automated irrigation and overseen by an expert farmer.

The research on "49 Cities" inspired the idea for Public Farm1 (PF1), WORKac's winning entry for MoMA's Young Architects Program in 2008. In this invited competition contribution, the firm envisioned the environment for the "Warm Up" summer parties at MoMA PS1 (contemporary art center) as a working urban farm. PF1 was constructed as a temporary installation on the grounds of MoMA PS1 in Long Island City. The popularity of this highly visible project introduced the topic of urban agriculture to a large audience. In the

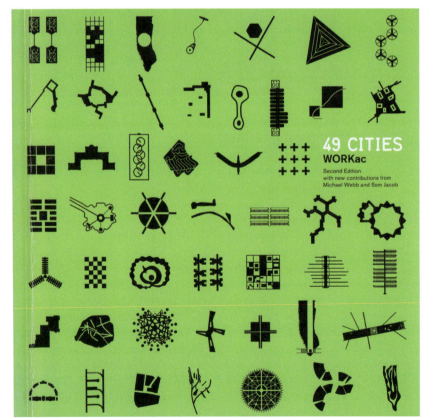

◀ Figure 6.48

Book cover, WORKac, *49 Cities*, 2nd Edition, 2006

following years, the firm has further explored this realm of inquiry through a series of evolving, large-scale projects.

Design Approach

WORKac has substantially advanced the design integration of food production in cities by expanding its research on food systems and urban agriculture while always assessing the potential for intersection with urban systems. Its research and design work on this subject range from incorporating experimental growing systems to integrating with building typologies and neighborhoods. The firm's inquiries and conversations with farmers and consultants led them to the conclusion that vertical farming in high-rise buildings (as publicized in the 2010 book *Vertical Farm* by Dickson Despommier) does not align with their vision. Controlled-environment agriculture (CEA) at the building scale is too resource- and energy-intensive without offering the important cultural component or reconnecting urban dwellers to their source of food. Soil-based growing strategies reestablish this lost connection more easily. WORKac developed its alternative position and approach as a combination of soil-based and building-integrated farming. The soil-based approach also allows the firm to establish a stronger cultural link to the history of rural farming in the United States and to develop urban food production as more of a cultural component than a technical add-on.

WORKac collaborated with the Dutch firm MVRDV on a study for the Governors Island "Pioneers of Change" celebration in 2009 that imagined the steps needed to locally produce all food for the greater New York area. Following their ground- and soil-based premise, WORKac proposed the project "New Ark," which rethought the foodshed within a 100-mile radius of the city, while MVRDV visualized the enormous building volume that would be needed to produce Manhattan's food supply in multistory greenhouse extensions on top of existing buildings. In general, collaboration—within the WORKac team, with consultants, and with artists—is an important part of the firm's design process. Andraos and Wood see exchange and creative input from outsiders as important contributions to the success of their design projects.

WORKac seeks to expand urban agriculture by implementing culturally and environmentally integrated projects that are not primarily evaluated according to productivity. To further this goal, the firm works on two scales. It develops large-scale conceptual projects as well as smaller realized projects. The construction of these small projects is a vital link between conceptual thoughts and the realities of the built environment, which will allow the firm to integrate food production into larger projects in the future. In all cases, the firm has been able to leverage strong public outreach to publish and promote its projects.

Conceptual Projects

The provocative proposals for Locavore Fantasia (commissioned by *New York Magazine*) (Figure 6.49) and Plug-Out (commissioned by New York's Downtown

◀ Figure 6.49

Conceptual project: Locavore Fantasia, WORKac, New York, 2008

Alliance) imagine vertically stacked growing spaces in combination with multi-story housing on sites in downtown Manhattan. Other speculative projects integrate architecture, landscape, sustainable technologies, and food planning at large urban scales. For example, the Wild West Side—the firm's proposal for New York's Hudson Yards—imagines ecological infrastructure (including food production) that transforms a proposed high-density neighborhood into a natural living system. The firm's Infoodstructure project develops a vision for a new food infrastructure in underserved neighborhoods in Brooklyn that face health issues linked to poor diet. A network of community farms, local food stores, greenmarkets, distribution hubs, and an aquaponics network increase access to healthy local food.

Built Projects

The popularity of the firm's PF1 installation inspired another high-profile urban agricultural opportunity. After PF1's completion, Alice Waters' Chez Panisse Foundation approached WORKac about designing the showcase Edible Schoolyards, with one in each New York borough (see Case Study 16). In collaboration with the nonprofit Edible Schoolyards NYC (ESNYC), WORKac completed the first showcase project at P.S. 216 in Brooklyn Gravesend in 2014. Over several years, the project transformed a half-acre parking lot into a thriving organic garden. An adjacent greenhouse/kitchen classroom ensures the year-round usability of the Edible Schoolyard (Figure 6.50). WORKac's structure consists of three major parts: an aluminum greenhouse clad in polycarbonate; the kitchen classroom covered with colorful shingles creating a pixelated flower pattern; and a light blue, rubber-coated "system wall" (Figures 6.51 and 6.52). The "system wall" consists of a series of one-story volumes that contain a cistern, composting facility, toilet, toolshed, and chicken coop.

The second Edible Schoolyard at P.S. 7 in East Harlem is in the design phase. Due to space constraints, the project will occupy an existing courtyard, classroom, and rooftop. The program elements will be similar to the first showcase

▲ Figure 6.50

Greenhouse/kitchen classroom at P.S. 216 in Gravesend, WORKac, showcase project for Edible Schoolyards NYC, Brooklyn, New York, 2014

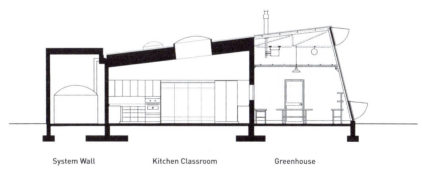

System Wall   Kitchen Classroom   Greenhouse

▶ Figure 6.51

Section and plan of greenhouse/kitchen classroom at P.S. 216, WORKac, showcase project for Edible Schoolyards NYC, Brooklyn, New York, 2014

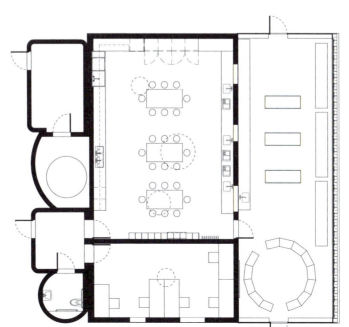

▲ Figure 6.52

Greenhouse interior, P.S. 216 in Gravesend, WORKac, showcase project for Edible Schoolyards NYC, Brooklyn, New York, 2014

project. In the first, completed phase, colorful planters provide outdoor growing opportunities for immediate use (Figure 6.53). In the second phase, the greenhouse, kitchen classroom, and rooftop garden will be installed on an adjacent one-story building (Figure 6.54). To formally connect and brand the different showcase projects, WORKac incorporates the same design elements and customizes them for the school's specific needs. The "system wall" of the first ESNYC project translates into playful infrastructure displays at P.S. 7, including a blue water tank centrally located in the greenhouse and visible as a flower-shaped waterwheel from the entire schoolyard.

◀ Figure 6.53

Planters as growing beds at P.S. 7 in Harlem, WORKac, Phase 1, showcase project for Edible Schoolyards NYC, New York, 2014

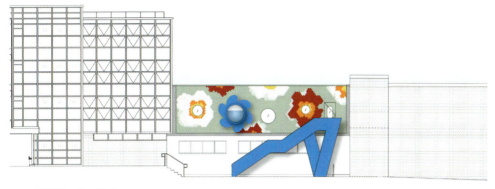
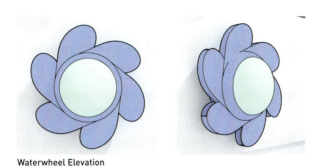

▲ Figure 6.54

Elevation studies and cistern mechanism for P.S. 7 in Harlem, WORKac, Phase 2, showcase project for Edible Schoolyards NYC, New York, 2014

The Edible Schoolyard projects underscore WORKac's design philosophy to emphasize the cultural importance of food production. The Edible Schoolyards projects foster cultural change by offering children first-hand experience with food production. They educate students in a novel way and introduce them to the culture of food through growing, harvesting, cooking, eating, and composting.

Strengths and Innovations

WORKac sees its globally operating practice following a paradigm in architecture that embraces an integrated design approach and addresses social issues. In particular, its designs focus on the relationships among nature, the city, and urban food production. Their innovative balance of considered research, imaginative risk taking, and engaging presentation adds a new important perspective to the design integration of urban agriculture.

WORKac's urban-scale investigations culminate in the Nature-City proposal for MoMA's exhibit "Foreclosed: Rehousing the American Dream" (Figure 6.55). Nature-City reimagines the suburban plan of Keizer Station, Oregon, by envisioning a variety of new housing typologies (and their supporting economic frameworks) that work as ecological infrastructure, generate their own power, clean water, compost organic waste, and grow their own food. Nature-City is five times denser than nearby suburbs and offers three times as much open space, consisting of forests, wetlands, and farms (Figures 6.56–6.58).

While working on high-caliber projects that are very often in urban sites, the firm develops new forms of building-integrated food production that are not reliant on CEA like most BIA projects. Instead, its urban agricultural projects depend predominantly on soil-based operations, clearly illustrating the firm's emphasis on the cultural component of soil-based agriculture. In its projects, WORKac folds together innovative urban typologies and the cultural importance of food. The firm sees itself as part of a new generation of architects aware of their moral responsibility to create work that benefits the public while developing sensitive and pioneering environmental infrastructure for food production in cities.

WORKac is one of the few firms working in urban agriculture to successfully make the challenging leap between conceptual, imaginative proposals and completed projects. Its success is due, in part, to its collaborations with highly visible organizations, its energetic outreach efforts, and its work in architectural education. Through its academic work, the firm has another platform to encourage visionary thinking, speculative design ideas, and innovative research. Andraos, Wood, and their team provide a highly influential and very public voice for the design integration of urban agriculture.

▶ Figure 6.55

Nature-City model, WORKac, MoMA exhibit "Foreclosed: Rehousing the American Dream," Keizer Station, Oregon, 2012

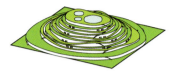

COMPOST HILL
TERRACED HOUSING
+
METHANE DOME
+
SPIRAL PARK

THRU-DE-SAC
CUL-DE-SAC COURTYARDS
+
GEOTHERMAL
+
FORAGING GARDENS

FIELD HOUSES
BROWNSTONES
+
GEOTHERMAL
+
COMMUNITY GARDENS

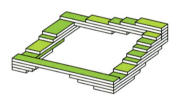

ANGLE
STEPPED SLABS
+
WILDLIFE PASS-THROUGH
+
ROOFTOP LANDSCAPES

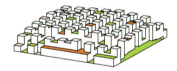

PIXEL
STAGGERED TOWNHOUSES
+
MUSHROOM & CANNING FACTORIES
+
CHECKERBOARD GARDENS

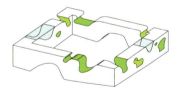

CAVERNS
SLABS
+
WILDLIFE PASS-THROUGH
+
LANDSCAPED CAVERNS

HOUSING TYPOLOGIES

▲ Figure 6.56

Nature-City, housing typologies, WORKac, MoMA exhibit "Foreclosed: Rehousing the American Dream," Keizer Station, Oregon, 2012

HUTONGS
PATIO HOUSING
+
FUEL CELL / POWER PLANT
+
PRIVATE COURTYARDS

TOWER OF HOUSES
STACKED LIVE-WORK "HOUSES"
+
WATER PRESSURE WATERFALL
+
FARMER'S MARKET

SOLAR COURTYARDS
INNER COURTS
+
PUBLIC SCHOOL
+
FLOWER GARDENS

HOUSING BRIDGE
PARTY-WALL, MULTI-FAMILY HOUSES
+
LANDSCAPE BRIDGE
+
CARVED COURTYARDS

WATER GARDENS
HILL HOUSES
+
NATURAL WATER TREATMENT
+
PONDS AND AQUAPONICS

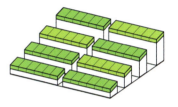

POTATO ROWS
ROW HOUSES
+
ROOFTOP GREENHOUSES
+
WINTER GARDEN

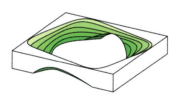

STADIUM
ARENA HOUSING
+
WILDLIFE PASS-THROUGH
+
JOGGING PATHS

LOWRISE OF HOMES
PARTY-WALL, MULTI-FAMILY HOUSES
+
LANDSCAPE EDGE
+
CARVED COURTYARDS

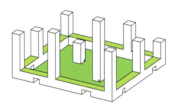

TOWER CLUSTER
STACKED INDIVIDUAL APTS
+
GEOTHERMAL
+
SPORTS FIELDS

▲ Figure 6.57

Nature-City, Town-Country and Doug Fir Forest, WORKac, MoMA exhibit "Foreclosed: Rehousing the American Dream," Keizer Station, Oregon, 2012

▶ Figure 6.58

Nature-City site model, WORKac, MoMA exhibit "Foreclosed: Rehousing the American Dream," Keizer Station, Oregon, 2012

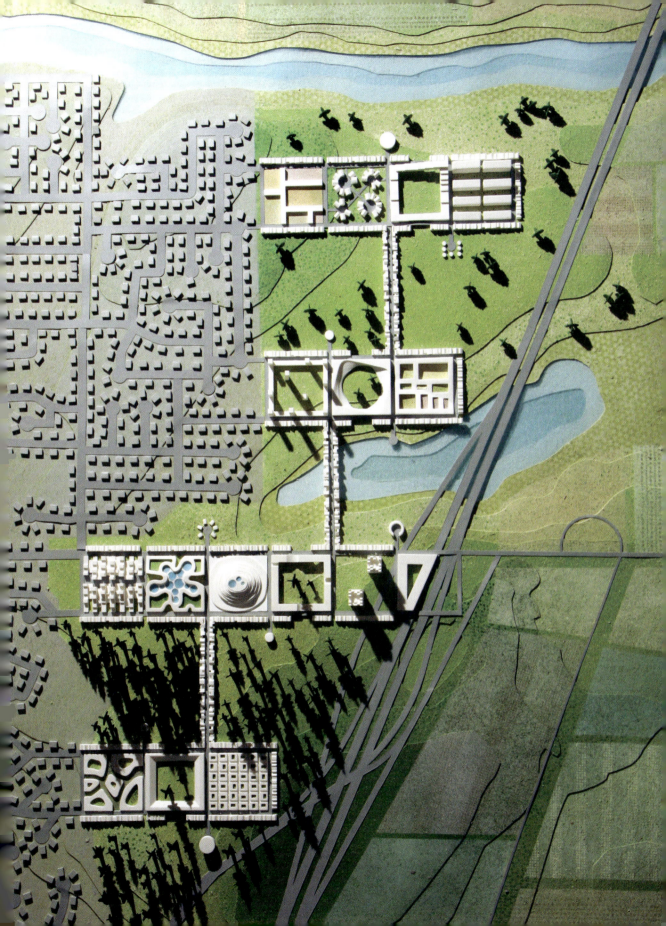

NOTES

1. Nina Mukherji and Alfonso Morales, "Zoning for Urban Agriculture," *Zoning Practice* 3.10: 2.
2. WORKac, *49 Cities*. 2nd ed. (New York: Storefront for Art and Architecture, 2010).
3. André,Viljoen, Katrin Bohn, and J. Howe. *Continuous Productive Urban Landscapes: Designing Urban Agriculture for Sustainable Cities* (Oxford: Architectural Press, 2005).
4. Katrin Bohn and André Viljoen, *Second Nature Urban Agriculture: Designing Productive Cities* (London: Routledge, 2014).
5. IBA Hamburg, "Smart Material Houses BIQ," *International Building Exhibition IBA Hamburg*, www.iba-hamburg.de/en/themes-projects/the-building-exhibition-within-the-building-exhibition/smart-material-houses/biq/projekt/biq.html.
6. Gary Comer Youth Center, http://www.hoerrschaudt.com/
7. Elmslie Osler Architect, www.eoarch.com/
8. Nevin Cohen, "Planning for Urban Agriculture: Problem Recognition, Policy Formation and Politics," in *Sustainable Food Planning: Evolving Theory and Practice*, ed. Andre Viljoen and Johannes S. C. Wiskerke (Wageningen, the Netherlands: Wageningen Academic Publishers, 2012),103.
9. Paul A. De Graaf, "Room for Urban Agriculture in Rotterdam: Defining the Spatial Opportunities for Urban Agriculture within the Industrialized City," in *Sustainable Food Planning: Evolving Theory and Practice*, ed. André Viljoen and Johannes S.C. Wiskerke (Wageningen: Wageningen Academic Publishers, 2012), 533.
10. NYC Planning, "Zone Green Text Amendment—Approved!," www.nyc.gov/html/dcp/html/greenbuildings/index.shtml.
11. City Farm, www.cityfarmchicago.org/.
12. Brooklyn Grange, "Flagship Farm," http://brooklyngrangefarm.com/about/farms/flagship-farm/.
13. Specht, Kathrin, Rosemarie Siebert, Ina Hartmann, Ulf Freisinger, B. Sawicka, Magdalena Werner, Armin Thomaier, Susanne Henckel, Dietrich Walk, and Heike Dierich. (2014) "Urban Agriculture of the Future: An Overview of Sustainability Aspects of Food Production in and on Buildings," *Agriculture and Human Values* 31.1: 36, 38. See also: Helen Pidd and Sarah Dawood, "Manchester International Festival: An Urban Farm Feeding a Deprived Area," *The Guardian*, www.theguardian.com/culture/2013/jul/08/manchester-international-festival-urban-farm.
14. Architecture & food, www.architectureandfood.com/.
15. Rachel Dring, "The Rooftop Revolution," Sustainable Food Trust, http://sustainablefoodtrust.org/articles/can-urban-growing-feed-cities/.

Architect's Profile 1: CJ Lim/Studio 8 Architects

16. This profile is based on an interview with C.J. Lim and was completed with his permission. Additional sources: C.J. Lim and Ed Liu, *Smartcities + Eco-Warriors* (London: Routledge, 2010). C.J. Lim, *Food City* (New York: Routledge, 2014).

Architect's Profile 2: Kiss + Cathcart, Architects

17. This profile is based on interviews with Gregory Kiss and Colin Cathcart, completed with their permission. Additional source: Gregory Kiss, "Solar Energy in the Built Environment," in *Metropolitan Sustainability: Understanding and Improving the Urban Environment*, ed. F. Zeman (Sawston, Cambridge, UK: Woodhead Publishing, 2012), 431–56.

Architect's Profile 3: Weber Thompson

18. This profile is based on interviews with Scott Thompson and Myer Harrell, completed with their permission. Additional sources: Todd Woody, "A Crop Sprouts Without Soil or Sunshine," *The New York Times*, http://green.blogs.nytimes.com/2010/09/20/a-crop-sprouts-without-soil-or-sunshine/?_r=0. Lloyd Alter. "Two Visionaries in Vertical Farming Plan Project In New Jersey," *Treehugger*, www.treehugger.com/sustainable-product-design/two-visionaries-in-vertical-farming-plan-project-in-new-jersey.html.

Architect's Profile 4: SOA Architectes

19. This profile was written with the permission of SOA Architectes. Additional sources: Agricultural Urban Lab (LUA), www.lua-paris.com/. Emmanuelle Borne, "Les Fermes Urbaines de SOA (Interview)," *Le Courrier de l'Architecte*, www.lecourrierdelarchitecte.com/article_1662. Peter Fairley, "Urban Agriculture Grows Up," *Architectural Record*, http://archrecord.construction.com/tech/techfeatures/2013/1307-urban-agriculture-grows-up.asp.

Architect's Profile 5: WORKac

20. This profile is based on an interview with Amale Andraos and was completed with WORKac's permission. Additional sources: "Interview with Architects Dan Wood and Amale Andraos of WORKac," *Designboom*, www.designboom.com/architecture/workac-interview-dan-wood-amale-andraos-10-17-2014/. Alexandra Lange, "Dan Wood," *The Design Observer Group*, http://designobserver.com/feature/dan-wood/22728/. Alexandra Lange, "Edible Schoolyard for P.S. 216, Designed by WORKac," *Architect*, www.architectmagazine.com/design/edible-schoolyard-for-brooklyn-ps216-by-workac_o. Laura Mirviss, "WORKac Unveils Edible Schoolyard in Brooklyn," *Architectural Record*, http://archrecord.construction.com/news/2013/11/131112-WORKac-Unveils-Edible-Schoolyard-at-PS-216-in-Brooklyn.asp. James Petty, "Architectural Startup: Dan Wood," *Petty Design*, www.pettydesign.com/2014/11/05/architectural-startup-dan-wood/.

Glossary

Aeroponics—hydroponic (soil-less) growing methods that creates a mist environment of growing solution around the plant's root zone

Anaerobic digestion—a biological process by which anaerobic bacteria convert organic matter into two main products: biogas and digestate in the absence of oxygen

Aquaponics—a combination of aquaculture (raising fish or aquatic animals) and hydroponics (cultivating plants in water) that generates self-fertilizing, recirculating ecosystems

Biogas—a mixture of gases produced during the anaerobic breakdown of organic matter

Biogeochemical cycles—fluxes of chemical element (such as carbon, water, oxygen, nitrogen, and phosphorus) between biotic and abiotic spheres (biosphere, atmosphere, hydrosphere, and lithosphere)

Biomimicry—the designing of structures and systems that emulate biological forms and processes to help solve human problems

Biosolids—organic matter generated as the byproduct of the wastewater treatment process

Building-integrated agriculture (BIA)—greenhouses, vertical façade systems, and stacked indoor growing facilities—usually with hydroponic growing systems (cultivating plants in water)—that are actively integrated with building systems to capture byproducts (waste heat, exhaust air, rainwater, AC condensate, foundation drain water, etc.) and utilize synergies between the built environment and growing systems

Carbon fixation—the transformation of inorganic, atmospheric carbon dioxide into organic compounds by living organisms (primarily during photosynthesis)

Carbon sequestration—the process by which atmospheric carbon dioxide is removed from the atmosphere and put in long-term storage or carbon pools

Cash crop—a crop grown for its high commercial value and easy marketability

Chlorophyll—the green pigment in plants and in photosynthetic algae and bacteria, responsible for the absorption of energy from light that fuels photosynthesis

Cogeneration—see Combined heat and power (CHP)

Combined heat and power (CHP)—simultaneous production of heat and electricity from a single fuel source

Compost tea—vermicompost dissolved in water and used as liquid fertilizer

Composting—the process of creating soil amendments or fertilizer from decomposing organic matter, particularly food waste, plant clippings, and cardboard

Controlled-environment agriculture (CEA)—the cultivation of plants in an indoor growing environment (such as a greenhouse or warehouse-like structure) engineered to provide optimal growing conditions year round

Crop water requirement—the amount of water needed for a particular crop to grow optimally

Cultivar—a crop variety that has been cultivated by selective breeding or (rarely) by special selection from the wild

Denitrification—transformation of nitrates by bacteria in the soil into nitrogen gas (and the greenhouse gas nitrous oxide), which escapes into the atmosphere

Digestate—liquid residue generated during anaerobic digestion

Double-skin façade—a glass façade with two layers; the outer layer protects from environmental impacts (sun, wind, and rain); the inner layer controls the interior climate; and the naturally ventilated cavity between the façade layers works as a buffer to help heat and cool the building

Eco-Machine, also Living Machine—a man-made wastewater treatment system that breaks down and cleans wastewater via natural processes

Energy curtain—horizontal, movable screens in greenhouses that prevent heat loss during the night (and often function as adjustable shading systems). Energy curtains are also known as thermal screens, movable curtains, or heat blankets.

Environmental remediation—the removal of contamination from soil, surface water, and groundwater

Eutrophication—a process in which aquatic ecosystems accumulate overly high amounts of nutrients, often tied to excess algae growth

Evapotranspiration—the transfer of water into the atmosphere by a combination of evaporation from the soil and transpiration from plants

Feedstock—raw material that fuels a chemical or industrial process

Food desert—an urban area lacking access to healthy food in grocery stores, farmers' markets, or farm stands. Readily available food comes only from convenience stores and fast-food chains

Food miles—the geographical distance food travels from farm to customer

Food security—physical and economic availability and access to a variety of healthy foods and knowledge about nutrition and healthy diet

Foodshed—"the flows of people, goods, materials and knowledge that create urban food systems and reshape rural/urban linkages," as defined by the fifth AESOP Conference in October 2013

Green Stormwater Infrastructure (GSI)—the set of best management practices for reducing stormwater runoff by simulating the natural ecosystem processes of retention, evapotranspiration, and infiltration

Greenhouse gas (GHG)—gas in the atmosphere that absorbs infrared radiation (IR) and reradiates it in all directions, for example, carbon dioxide, methane, and nitrous oxide. This GHG-induced warming is the major cause for global warming

Groundwater recharge—the movement of water from surface to groundwater and the process that replenishes aquifers

Gutter-connected greenhouses—an array of greenhouses connected by their gutters at the low points of their pitched roofs

Heat island effect—the phenomenon by which urban areas have a higher temperature than adjacent rural areas, caused by the large amount of heat-absorbing surfaces in cities as well as generated by heat escaping buildings and vehicles

High-wire production systems—growing systems for vine crops, according to which the plant is trained into a single stem, usually combined with a hydroponic drip irrigation system

Hoop house—a low-tech greenhouse made up of a tubular, semicircular structure sheathed in polyethylene; also known as a polytunnel, polyhouse, or high tunnel

Humus—organic material in the soil from decaying plants and animals

Hydroponics—soil-less growing systems, which provide plants with nutrients through a nutrient solution. Recirculating hydroponic systems reduce resource inputs, raise water and nutrient efficiency, and increase productivity

Infrared (IR)—electromagnetic radiation with a wavelength greater than the visible (red) spectrum and shorter than microwaves (800nm–1mm)

Intercropping—a polyculture with two or more crops grown in proximity and usually in alternating order

Light-Emitting Diode (LED)—lamps producing light by passing an electric current through a semiconductor material. The electrons moving through the material release photons, particles carrying energy in the form of light

Lithosphere—the solid outer part of the Earth consisting of the crust and a portion of the mantle

Microclimate—a localized area featuring different climatic characteristics than its surrounding climate zone

Monoculture—a large stand or greenhouse of a single crop

Multi-cropping—a polyculture in which two or more crops are grown simultaneously in one growing bed

Nitrification—the biological process in which ammonia is transformed into nitrite and then into nitrate, thus replenishing nitrate (an important nutrient for plants) in the soil

Nitrogen fixation—the fixation of atmospheric nitrogen into compounds, either naturally by bacteria in the root balls of legumes or by industrial chemical processes

Nutrient film technique (NFT)—the hydroponic method (cultivating plants in water) that suspends plant roots in a long narrow trough through which the nutrient solution trickles; the most productive and frequently employed hydroponic growing method for leafy greens

Pathogen—a biological agent that causes disease

Peri-urban—the zone at the outskirts of the city, between urban and rural

Permaculture, also Food forest—originally permanent agriculture; generates self-sustaining agriculture systems by mimicking natural ecosystems

Photosynthesis—a plant process that uses energy from (sun) light to synthesize carbon dioxide and water into chemical energy

Photosynthetically active radiation (PAR)—the light spectrum which powers photosynthesis (with a wavelength between 400 and 700 nm)

Photovoltaics (PVs)—a technology using semiconducting material to convert solar energy into direct current electricity

Polyculture—multiple crop species in one growing bed or greenhouse, including intercropping and multi-cropping

Resilience—toughness; ability to recover easily from adverse conditions or adjust to change

Respiration—the process in which a living organism produces energy by taking in oxygen (and carbohydrates) and releasing carbon dioxide and water

Root ball—the network of roots at the base of a plant

Soil water availability—the water capacity of the soil—or amount of water available—for plants

SPIN farming—small, plot-intensive farming that combines the cultivation of several small plots in an urban neighborhood to aggregate a larger growing area

Stormwater—a liquid volume generated when precipitation comes into contact with ground-level impervious surfaces. In developed urban areas, about 75% of city rainfall turns into stormwater runoff

Sub-irrigation—an irrigation method in which water is delivered to the root zone of the plants from below and absorbed upwards, as in the ebb and flow irrigation method

Surface irrigation—an irrigation process in which plants receive water from the top surface of the soil

Symbiosis—a relationship or interaction between two organisms that is to the mutual benefit of both

Terrestrial biosphere—the area encompassing vegetation and soil and holding the largest biological carbon reservoir

Transpiration—the natural process by which plants evaporate water into the atmosphere through the pores (stomata) in their leaves after absorbing it through their roots

Ultraviolet (UV)—electromagnetic radiation with a wavelength shorter than the visible (violet) spectrum and longer than x-rays (380nm–250nm)

Vermiculture, also vermicomposting—a composting process augmented by the presence of worms (usually red wigglers or red earthworms) that break the compost down even further and refine it through worm castings

Selected Bibliography

The books and journal articles listed here have been the most influential in the development of this book. Additional sources I consulted are documented in the notes. This bibliography is intended to serve readers by introducing them to other sources that look at the environmental benefits and design integration of urban agriculture.

Ackerman, Kubi. (2011) *The Potential for Urban Agriculture in New York City: Growing Capacity, Food Security, and Green Infrastructure*. Urban Design Lab at the Earth Institute, New York: Columbia University.
Allen, Will, and Charles Wilson. (2012) *The Good Food Revolution: Growing Healthy Food, People, and Communities*. New York: Gotham Books.
Andraos, Amale, Dan Wood, and P.S.1 Contemporary Art Center. (2010) *Above the Pavement—the Farm! Architecture & Agriculture at PF1*. 1st ed. New York: Princeton Architectural Press.
Benyus, Janine M. (2002) *Biomimicry: Innovation Inspired by Nature*. New York: Perennial.
Bernstein, Sylvia. (2011) *Aquaponic Gardening: A Step-by-step Guide to Raising Vegetables and Fish Together*. Gabriola, BC: New Society Publishers.
Bohn, Katrin, and André Viljoen, eds. (2014) *Second Nature, Urban Agriculture: Designing Productive Cities*. London: Routledge.
Carpenter, Novella, and Willow Rosenthal. (2011) *The Essential Urban Farmer*. New York: Penguin Books.
Cockrall-King, Jennifer. (2012) *Food and the City: Urban Agriculture and the New Food Revolution*. Amherst, NY: Prometheus Books.
Cordell, Dana, Jan-Olof Drangert, and Stuart White. (2009) "The Story of Phosphorus: Global Food Security and Food for Thought," *Global Environmental Change* 19.2: 292–305.
Coyne, Kelly, and Erik Knutzen. (2010) *The Urban Homestead: Your Guide to Self-sufficient Living in the Heart of the City*. Port Townsend, WA: Process Media.
De La Salle, Janine M., Mark Holland, and H.B. Lanarc. (2010) *Agricultural Urbanism: Handbook for Building Sustainable Food & Agriculture Systems in 21st Century Cities*. 1st ed. Winnipeg, Manitoba: Green Frigate Books.
Despommier, Dickson. (2010) *The Vertical Farm*. New York: Thomas Dunne Books.
Frey, Darrell. (2011) *Bioshelter Market Garden: A Permaculture Farm*. Gabriola Island, BC: New Society Publishers.
Gao, Li-Hong, Mei Qu, Hua-Zhong Ren, Xiao-Lei Sui, Qing-Yun Chenand, and Zhen-Xian Zhang. (2011) "Ecological Benefit of a Single-slope, Energy-efficient Solar Greenhouse in China," Beijing: College of Agronomy and Biotechnology, China Agricultural University.
Giacomelli, Gene. (2004) "Engineering Design of Plant Nutrient Delivery Systems," *Acta Horticulturae* 648: 71–81.
Giacomelli, Gene. (2009) "New Products and Innovations in Greenhouse Engineering," presented at International Symposium on High Technology for Greenhouse Systems (GreenSys).

Gorgolewski, Mark, June Komisar, and Joe Nasr. (2011) *Carrot City: Creating Places for Urban Agriculture*. 1st ed. New York: Monacelli Press.

Haeg, Fritz, and Diana Balmori. (2008) *Edible Estates: Attack on the Front Lawn*. New York: Metropolis Books.

Heinberg, Richard, and Daniel Lerch. (2010) *The Post Carbon Reader: Managing the 21st Century's Sustainability Crises*. Berkeley, CA: Watershed Media (Contemporary Issues Series); Post Carbon Institute; Distributed by the University of California Press.

Heinrich Böll Stiftung, ed. (2009) *Urban Futures: Visionen künftigen Städtebaus und Urbaner Lebensweise*. Schriften zur Ökologie, Band 5, Berlin: Heinrich Böll Stiftung.

Hemenway, Toby. (2009) *Gaia's Garden: A Guide to Home-scale Permaculture*. White River Junction, VT: Chelsea Green Publishing.

Hester, Randolph T. (2006) *Design for Ecological Democracy*. Cambridge, MA: MIT Press.

Hislop, Hannah, ed. (2007) *The Nutrient Cycle: Closing the Loop*. London: Green Alliance.

Hoekstra, Arjen Y. (2012) "The Hidden Water Resource Use Behind Meat and Dairy," *Animal Frontiers* 2.2 (April).

Hoekstra, Arjen Y., and A.K. Chapagain. (2007) "Water Footprints of Nations: Water Use by People as a Function of Their Consumption Pattern," *Water Resources Management* 21.1: 35–48.

Hou, Jeffrey, Julie Johnson, and Laura J. Lawson. (2009) *Greening Cities, Growing Communities: Learning from Seattle's Urban Community Gardens*. Case Study in Land and Community Design, Washington, D.C.: Landscape Architecture Foundation in Association with University of Washington Press.

Jeavons, John. (2002) *How to Grow More Vegetables: (and Fruits, Nuts, Berries, Grains, and Other Crops) than You Ever Thought Possible on Less Land than You Can Imagine: A Primer on the Life-giving Sustainable Grow Biointensive Method of Organic Horticulture*. 6th ed. Rev. ed. Berkeley, CA: Ten Speed Press.

Jones, J.B. Jr. (1997) *Hydroponics: A Practical Guide for the Soilless Grower*. Boca Raton, FL: St. Lucie.

Kirby, Ellen, and Elizabeth Peters. (2008) *Community Gardening*. Brooklyn Botanic Garden All-region Guides; Handbook #190. Brooklyn, NY: Brooklyn Botanic Garden.

Ladner, Peter. (2010) *Agricultural Urbanism: Handbook for Building Sustainable Food Systems in 21st Century Cities*. Winnipeg: Green Frigate Books.

Lawson, Laura J. (2005) *City Bountiful: A Century of Community Gardening in America*. Berkeley, CA: University of California Press.

Lim, C.J. (2014) *Food City*. New York: Routledge.

Lim, C.J., and Ed Liu. (2010) *Smartcities + Eco-Warriors*. London: Routledge.

Lyson, Thomas. (2004) *Civic Agriculture: Reconnecting Farm, Food, and Community*. Medford, MA: Tufts University Press.

Mandel, Lauren. (2013) *Eat Up: The Inside Scoop on Rooftop Agriculture*. Gabriola, BC: New Society Publishers.

Mars, Ross, and Martin Ducker. (2005) *The Basics of Permaculture Design*. White River Junction, VT: Chelsea Green Publishing Company.

Mason, John. (2003) *Sustainable Agriculture*. 2nd ed. Collingwood, Vic.: Landlinks Press.

Mentens, J., D. Raes, and M. Hermy. (2006) "Green Roofs as a Tool for Solving the Rainwater Runoff Problem in the Urbanized 21st Century?" *Landscape and Urban Planning* 77.3: 217–26.

Muckherji, Nina, and Alfonso Morales. (2010) "Zoning for Urban Agriculture," *Zoning Practice*, American Planning Association, Issue Number 3, Practice Urban Agriculture.

Müller, Christa, ed. (2011) *Urban Gardening: Über die Rückkehr der Gärten in die Stadt*. München: Oekom Verlag.

Nomadisch Grün, ed. (2012) *Prinzessinnengarten: Anders Gärtnern in der Stadt*. Köln: DuMont Verlag.

Nordahl, Darrin. (2009) *Public Produce: The New Urban Agriculture*. Washington, D.C.: Island Press.

Pinderhughes, Raquel. (2004) *Alternative Urban Futures: Planning for Sustainable Development in Cities Throughout the World*. Lanham, MD: Rowman & Littlefield.

Pollan, Michael. (2008) *In Defense of Food: An Eater's Manifesto*. New York: Penguin Press.

Postel, Sandra. (1999) *Pillar of Sand: Can the Irrigation Miracle Last?* New York: W.W. Norton & Co.

Resh, Howard M. (2013) *Hydroponic Food Production: A Definitive Guidebook for the Advanced Home Gardener and the Commercial Hydroponic Grower*. Boca Raton, FL: CRC Press.

Ruddle, Kenneth, and Gongfu Zhong. (1988) *Integrated Agriculture-aquaculture in South China: The Dike-pond System of the Zhujiang Delta*. Cambridge: Cambridge University Press.

Saul, Nick, and Andrea Curtis. (2013) *The Stop: How the Fight for Good Food Transformed a Community and Inspired a Movement*. 1st ed. Brooklyn, NY: Melville House Pub.

Shiva, Vandana. (2002) *Water Wars: Privatization, Pollution and Profit*. Cambridge, MA: South End Press.

Solomon, Steve. (2007) *Growing Vegetables West of the Cascades: The Complete Guide to Organic Gardening*. 6th ed. Seattle, WA: Sasquatch Books.

Specht, Kathrin, Rosemarie Siebert, Ina Hartmann, Ulf Freisinger, B. Sawicka, Magdalena Werner, Armin Thomaier, Susanne Henckel, Dietrich Walk, and Heike Dierich. (2014) "Urban Agriculture of the Future: An Overview of Sustainability Aspects of Food Production in and on Buildings," *Agriculture and Human Values* 31.1: 33–51.

Steel, Carolyn. (2008) *Hungry City: How Food Shapes Our Lives*. London: Chatto & Windus.

Steen, Ingrid. (1998) "Phosphorus Availability in the 21st Century: Management of a Nonrenewable Resource," *Phosphorus and Potassium* 217: 25–31.

Ting, K.C., and Gene A. Giacomelli. (1987) "Solar Photosynthetically Active Radiation Transmission through Greenhouse Glazings," *Energy in Agriculture* 6.2: 121–32.

Todd, Nancy Jack, and John Todd. (1994) *From Eco-cities to Living Machines: Principles of Ecological Design*. Berkeley, CA: North Atlantic Books.

Viljoen, André, Katrin Bohn, and J. Howe. (2005) *Continuous Productive Urban Landscapes: Designing Urban Agriculture for Sustainable Cities*. Oxford: Architectural Press.

Waldheim, Charles, ed. (2006) *The Landscape Urbanism Reader*. New York: Princeton Architectural Press.

Waters, Alice, Daniel Duane, and David Liittschwager. (2008) *Edible Schoolyard: A Universal Idea*. San Francisco: Chronicle Books.

White, Mason, Maya Przybylski, and InfraNet Lab. (2010) *On Farming*, Bracket; Almanac 1. New York: Actar.

WORKac. (2010) *49 Cities*. 2nd ed. New York: Storefront for Art and Architecture.

Wortman, Sam E. and Sarah Taylor Lovell. (2013) "Environmental Challenges Threatening the Growth of Urban Agriculture in the United States," *Journal of Environmental Quality* 42.5: 1283–94.

Zeman, Frank, ed. (2012) *Metropolitan Sustainability: Understanding and Improving the Urban Environment*. Sawston, Cambridge, UK: Woodhead Publishing.

Image Credits

1.1	Kokhanchikov/Shutterstock.com
1.6	based on drawing by Paul de Graaf, with permission
1.8	Jennifer Baynes
1.11	based on drawing by Hayley Buckbee, with permission
1.12	Martin Crawford
1.15a	anekoho/Shutterstock.com
1.15b	Lufa Farms
1.16a	Chicago Botanic Garden
1.16b	Lufa Farms
1.16c	Mavadee/Shutterstock.com
1.18	based on drawing by Kevin Xiaochen Zhang and Andrea Gousen, with permission
2.1	Nomad_Soul/shutterstock.com
2.3	Timm Kekeritz/www.virtualwater.eu
2.9	John Stamets
2.10	2020 Engineering
2.11	Weber Thompson
3.1	Lufa Farms
3.7	Beccy Lane/positive image photography
3.9	Kräss GlasCon GmbH
3.10b	T.W. van Urk/Shutterstock.com
3.10c	zhengzaishuru/Shutterstock.com
3.12	chinahbzyg/Shutterstock.com
3.15	Lutz Igiel/Lugfoto.de
3.16a	Franz Schreier/EBF GmbH
3.16b	Franz Schreier/EBF GmbH
3.18	Lutz Igiel/Lugfoto.de
3.20	Lutz Igiel/Lugfoto.de
3.21	Lutz Igiel/Lugfoto.de
3.22	Tadashi Aizawa/*The Japan Journal*
3.23	Tadashi Aizawa/*The Japan Journal*
3.26	Granpa Co.Ltd
3.27	Granpa Co.Ltd
3.28	Sky Greens Pte Ltd.
3.30	Sky Greens Pte Ltd.
3.32	Sky Greens Pte Ltd.
3.34	Sky Greens Pte Ltd.
3.35	E/Ye Design/Vertical Harvest
3.36a	E/Ye Design/Vertical Harvest
3.36b	E/Ye Design/Vertical Harvest
3.37	E/Ye Design/Vertical Harvest
3.38	E/Ye Design/Vertical Harvest
3.39	Alexander Herring
3.40	Alexander Herring
3.41	Plantagon. Illustration: Sweco

3.42	based on drawing by Plantagon/Sweco, with permission
3.43	based on drawing by Plantagon/Sweco, with permission
3.44	based on drawing by Plantagon/Sweco, with permission
3.45	Plantagon. Illustration: Sweco
3.46	Caliber Biotherapeutics
3.47	FarmedHere
3.48	AeroFarms
3.49	Caliber Biotherapeutics
3.50	AeroFarms
4.1	Lufa Farms
4.4	Jennifer Baynes
4.6	Plant Chicago NFP
4.7	Plant Chicago NFP
4.9	Lufa Farms
4.10	Jennifer Baynes
4.11	Douglas Gayeton for Lexicon of Sustainability
4.14	Jennifer Baynes
4.15	Jennifer Baynes
4.17	Jennifer Baynes
4.18	The Kubala Washatko Architects, Inc.
4.19	Steven Bornholtz/Creative Commons Attribution-Share Alike 4.0 International
4.21	Map Data: Google
4.22	Map Data: Google
4.24	United Nations/John Gillespie/Flickr Creative Commons License
4.25	United Nations/John Gillespie/Flickr Creative Commons License
4.26	Plant Chicago NFP
4.29a	Plant Chicago NFP
4.29b	Plant Chicago NFP
4.29c	Plant Chicago NFP
4.30	Plant Chicago NFP
4.32	Plant Chicago, NFP
4.33	Plant Chicago, NFP
4.34	Lufa Farms
4.36	Lufa Farms
4.37	Lufa Farms
4.38	Lufa Farms
4.39	Lufa Farms
4.41	Lufa Farms
4.43	Lufa Farms
4.44	Gotham Greens
4.45	Gotham Greens
4.46	BrightFarms
4.47	Andrew Larigakis
4.49	Gotham Greens and Ari Burling
4.50	William McDonough + Partners, Architects
4.51	Gotham Greens
5.1	Chuk Nowak for Fair Food Network
5.2	Edward Meyer/Library of Congress
5.3	Collectif, Etc
5.4	The Stop Community Food Center/Zoe Alexopoulos
5.5	photo by 'Emily Kinsolving' courtesy of New York Restoration Project

5.6	courtesy of Hoerr Schaudt Landscape Architects, photographer: Scott Shigley
5.7	Chicago Botanic Garden
5.8	Sharing Backyards/www.sharingbackyards.com
5.9	Harrison Design	Landscape Architecture
5.10	Molly Danielsson, 2013
5.11	Fair Food Network, Jordi C/Shutterstock.com
5.12	Fair Food Network
5.13	Chicago Botanic Garden
5.14	Marco Clausen/Prinzessinnengarten
5.15	Marco Clausen/Prinzessinnengarten
5.16	Marco Clausen/Prinzessinnengarten
5.17	Marco Clausen/Prinzessinnengarten
5.18	Marco Clausen/Prinzessinnengarten
5.19	Marco Clausen/Prinzessinnengarten
5.20	Alexandra Dare Porter
5.22	Nancy Rottle
5.23	Nancy Rottle
5.24	Alexandra Dare Porter
5.25	Nancy Rottle
5.26	Zumtobel Group AG
5.27	Atelier d'Architecture Autogérée (aaa)
5.28	Atelier d'Architecture Autogérée (aaa)
5.29	Atelier d'Architecture Autogérée (aaa)
5.30	Atelier d'Architecture Autogérée (aaa)
5.31	Collectif, etc
5.32	The Stop Community Food Center/Matt O'Sullivan
5.33	The Stop Community Food Center/Zoe Alexopoulos
5.34	Tom Arban/DTAH Architects
5.35	Tom Arban/DTAH Architects
5.36	DTAH Architects
5.37	The Stop Community Food Center/Zoe Alexopoulos
5.38	The Stop Community Food Center/Zoe Alexopoulos
5.39	Iwan Baan/WORKac
5.40	Katie Standke/Edible Schoolyard
5.41	Erin Scott/Edible Schoolyard
5.42	Kiss + Cathcart
5.43	Hughes Marine Firms
5.44	Barbara Norman/GELL
5.45	Douglas Fountain
6.1	Saverio Lombardi Vallauri
6.2	Saverio Lombardi Vallauri
6.3	Bohn & Viljoen Architects (assisted by Eva Benito), 2002
6.4	Bohn & Viljoen Architects (assisted by Nishat Awan (FG Stadt & Ernährung TU Berlin)), 2012
6.5	Bohn & Viljoen Architects, 2012
6.6	Katrin Bohn and Nishat Awan (FG Stadt & Ernährung TU Berlin) (assisted by Kristian Ritzmann and Susanne Hausstein (FG Stadt & Ernährung TU Berlin)), 2012
6.7	photo by Scott Shigley, courtesy of Hoerr Schaudt Landscape Architects
6.8	photo by Scott Shigley, courtesy of Hoerr Schaudt Landscape Architects
6.9	Elmslie Osler Architect, EOA
6.10	T. Carrigan/Flickr Creative Commons License

6.11	Oscar Rodriguez/Architecture and Food
6.12	CJ Lim/Studio 8 Architects
6.13	CJ Lim/Studio 8 Architects
6.14	CJ Lim/Studio 8 Architects
6.15	CJ Lim/Studio 8 Architects
6.16	CJ Lim/Studio 8 Architects
6.17	CJ Lim/Studio 8 Architects
6.18	CJ Lim/Studio 8 Architects
6.19	CJ Lim/Studio 8 Architects
6.20	CJ Lim/Studio 8 Architects
6.21	Ari Burling/Kiss + Cathcart, Architects
6.22	Kiss + Cathcart, Architects
6.23	Kiss + Cathcart, Architects
6.24	Kiss + Cathcart, Architects
6.25	Kiss + Cathcart, Architects
6.26	Starr Whitehouse/Kiss + Cathcart, Architects
6.27	Kiss + Cathcart, Architects
6.28	Weber Thompson
6.29	Weber Thompson
6.30	Weber Thompson
6.31	Weber Thompson
6.32	Weber Thompson
6.33	Weber Thompson
6.34	Weber Thompson
6.35	Weber Thompson
6.36	Weber Thompson
6.37	SOA Architectes
6.38	SOA Architectes
6.39	SOA Architectes
6.40	SOA Architectes
6.41	SOA Architectes
6.42	SOA Architectes
6.43	SOA Architectes
6.44	SOA Architectes
6.45	SOA Architectes
6.46	SOA Architectes
6.47	Iwan Baan/WORKac
6.48	WORKac
6.49	WORKac
6.50	Iwan Baan/WORKac
6.51	Iwan Baan/WORKac
6.52	WORKac
6.53	WORKac
6.54	WORKac
6.55	James Ewing/WORKac
6.56	WORKac
6.57	WORKac
6.58	WORKac

All other images are by the author.

Index

Page numbers in *italics* refer to figures.

added-value products 154
Adopt-A-Lot initiative 242
aerobic composting 18, 21–2, *22*
AeroFarms in Newark, New Jersey 139, *139*, *143*, 146
aeroponics 34–6, *35*, 346
aggregate cultures 31–2
"A-Go-Gro" vertical farming system 116, 119
agricultural runoff 7, 9
Agricultural Urban Lab (LUA) 324, 330
Agri-Food and Veterinary Authority (AVA) in Singapore 116
AgroCité 258, *261*, 261–2
air-conditioner condensate 65
alcoholic fermentation 198–9
Allen, Will 173–4, 178; *see also* Growing Power
Allied Engineering 190
alternative nutrient and energy sources 13, 14
alternative water sources 54, 63–5
ambient temperature 76–8
ammonia (NH_3) 10
anaerobic digestion: definition 346; feces 24; organisms 198; overview 21–2, *22*; The Plant in Chicago 199, *199*; sewage sludge 23
Andraos, Amale 332
anthropogenic activities 71
aquaponic growing systems 24, 36–7, *37*, 346
Aquaponic Solar Greenhouse in Neuenburg am Rhein, Germany: excess solar energy into electrical energy 104–5, *104*–*5*; growing system 101; introduction *100*, 101; light transmission 103–4, *104*; overview 16, 83, 92; passive solar energy 101–3, *102*; solar energy 101; strengths and innovations *106*, 106–7
Arbor House 296

Arize Kombucha Brewery 198
Arthur and Friends 128
Atlanta's Botanical Garden 30
atmosphere 71

Barmeier, Henry 242
Bastille (kitchen garden) 167
Beacon Food Forest 240, *240*
Bedford Park, Illinois: FarmedHere in Bedford Park, Illinois 138, *138*
beer-brewing processes 198–9
Berkeley, California: Edible Schoolyard Project (ESYP) 237
Berlin *see* Prinzessinnengarten in Berlin
Better Building Challenge 222
Biber, James 283
biogas 18, 21, 25, 346
biogeochemical 2, 7, 69, 346
biointensive farming methods 27–8, *28*
biological pest controls 208
biomass production 86
biosolids 23, 346
Biospheric Project in Manchester 294
blackwater 64
Bohn, Katrin 285–6
Bosch, Carl 10
Boston: Food Project in Boston 238
bottom-up movement *236*, 236–7
branding operations in urban agriculture 168–9
BrightFarms in New York 217, *217*, 222, 225
Bromley Caldari Architects 190, 192
Bronx River House project 311
Brooklyn Grange in New York: Brooklyn Navy Yard funding 190; design and building integration 190–2, *191*; distribution strategy 188; diversified operation and business strategies 186, *187*; financing 188–90, *189*; growing and harvesting 188; installation 192; introduction *183*, 184; irrigation 185–6; milestones 184, *185*; Northern Boulevard funding 190; nutrient cycle

Brooklyn Grange in New York (*cont.*) and growing systems 184–5; operations concerns 167, 169–70; rooftop gardening 56, 107, 163, *187*, 244; stormwater management 62; strength and innovations 192; water cycle and water retention 185
brown water 64–5
Bryan, Texas: Caliber Biotherapeutics in Bryan, Texas, United States 141, *141*
Buffalo, New York: Village Farms in Buffalo, New York 294
building code challenges 292–3
building-integrated agriculture (BIA): definition 346; design considerations 283, 296–8; designing for urban agriculture 288–91, *289–91*; environmental systems for indoor growing 80, 81–6, *82*; Kiss + Cathcart, Architects 309–13, *310, 311–12*; Net-Zero water system 58; new construction vs. rooftop 295, *295*; SOA Architectes *325*, 325–9, *326–30*; Weber Thompson 315
building-integrated photovoltaics (BIPV) 309
Bullitt Center in Seattle 58, *59*
burning of crop residues 73
business considerations: Brooklyn Grange 186, *187*; ecology 200–1, *201*; Growing Power farm *179*, 179–80; Lufa Farms 212–13; Plantagon International 135–6; urban agriculture 321–2; Weber Thompson 321–2

Caliber Biotherapeutics in Bryan, Texas 141, *141*
Caplow, Ted 216, 217
carbon cycle: human impact on 7; industrial agriculture, impact on 73–4; introduction 69–70, *70*; natural pools and sinks 70–1; urban agricultural impact on 78–9
carbon dioxide (CO_2): fertilization with 85, 198; global warming 71–3, *72, 73*; increasing levels of 69; introduction 18; solar energy and 74–6, *75, 77*; supplementation in nutrient cycle 195
carbon pools and sinks 70–1
Cascadia Green Building Council 316
casita gardens 236, *236*

Chicago: McCormick Place Convention Center in Chicago 244, *244*; *see also* The Plant in Chicago
Chicago's GreenNet 239
Chinese greenhouses 91–2, *92*
chlorophyll 69, *75*, 76, 346
cisterns for rainwater harvesting 63
cities *vs.* urban agriculture 3–4
City Farm Fish 107
City Growers, nonprofit 170
civic agriculture 233
Clausen, Marco 245–7, 249
closed-loop production: aquaponic growing systems 195, *196*; building integrated agricultural systems 58, 60; cyclical systems 1–2; Lufa Farms 205; waste-into-energy system 208
cogovernance/coproducers in urban agriculture 242–4, *243*
cogeneration 85, 346
Cohen, Alison 175
collaborative consumption 239–41, *240–1*
Colombes, France *see* R-Urban in Colombes, France
combined heat and power (CHP) biogas engine 199, 346
combined sewer overflows (CSOs) 50, 185
Commercial Urban Agriculture Program (Growing Power) 174
Community Action Program (The Stop) 264
community building 233–4, *234*
community gardens 56, 181, 232–7, *236*, 242–3, 245, 260, *261*, 266–7, *267*
community-initiated urban agricultural programs: access and public health 234–5; bottom-up movement *236*, 236–7; civic agriculture 233; cogovernance/coproducers 242–4, *243*; collaborative consumption 239–41, *240–1*; commercial projects 241–2; community building 233–4, *234*; current challenges 231–2; design considerations 244, *244*; effects of urban agriculture on 232, 232–5, *234*; integration methods 235–6; introduction *230*, 231; potential synergies 235; youth involvement 237–8, *238–9*; *see also* urban agriculture
community-supported agriculture (CSA) 167, *168*, 178, 210, 222, 233
compact fluorescent lights (CFL) 96

composting: aerobic composting 18, 21–2, *22*; anaerobic digestion 21–2, *22*; definition 346; heat recovery systems 19–20, *20*; industrial scale 254; introduction 18–19, *19*; processing 175, *175*; vermicomposting 18–19, 176, *177*; windrow composting 19
consumers in nutrient cycle 196, *196*
container gardens 15, 28–30, *29*; *see also* Prinzessinnengarten
Continuous Productive Urban Landscapes (CPULs) 285
controlled-environment agriculture (CEA): definition 346; growing mediums and 14, 16; installation costs 188–90, *189*; Newark Vertical Farm 317–18, *317–18*; operations 89; overview 60, 96; PlantLab 142; rooftop farm operations 160; WORKac 333
Controlled Environment Agriculture Center (CEAC) at the University of Arizona 216
cooling systems for greenhouses 84
cooperatives 168
Cooper Hewitt National Museum of Design 316
cover materials for greenhouses 93–5, *94*
crop water requirement 48–9, *49*, 347

daily light integral (DLI) 96
decomposers in nutrient cycle 196–7, *197*
decomposition 9, 11, 18
deforestation 74
Denver Urban Gardens 239
denitrification 74, 347
Department of Crop Sciences, University of Illinois 2
Department of Environmental Protection (DEP) 62, 185
Department of Urban Agriculture in Cuba 252
design and building integration: Brooklyn Grange 190–2, *191*; for greenhouses 85–6; Local Garden greenhouses 222–3, *223*; The Plant in Chicago 201–2; urban agriculture 170–1
designing for urban agriculture: building codes 292–3; challenges 296–7; challenges to realization 291–5, *294*, *295*; design and building integration 288–91, *289–91*; design considerations 296–8; environmental policies 293; introduction *282*, 283; land tenure 293; new urban visions 285–6, *285–6*; professional fascination with 283–4, *284*; site selection 293; technical viability 286–8, *287–8*; zoning and regulation 292
Despommier, Dickson 316, 324, 333
direct-to-buyer distribution model 165–7, *166*
digestate 21, *22*
distribution models: Brooklyn Grange 188; direct-to-buyer distribution model 165–7, *166*; Local Garden greenhouses 222; in urban agriculture 155, 165–8, *166*, *168*; Vertical Harvest system 128
domestic wastewater 64–5
double-skin façade *130*, 131, *134*, 309, 311, 347
Double Up Food Bucks program 243
drip-irrigation 32–3, *33*, 52, 206
Drop-In kitchen 266

Eagle Street Farm 167, 184
Earlscourt and Hillcrest Community Gardens 266
East Anglia Food Link 168
ebb-and-flow system 31–2, 131, *132*
EcoHab project 258
ecological succession 248
Eco-Machines 24–6, *25*, 347
Edel, John 201
Edible Schoolyard Project (ESYP) in Berkeley, California 237
Edible Schoolyard Project (ESYP), New York: overview *270*, 270–2, *271*; WORKac 296, 334–8, *335–8*
electrical lighting for greenhouses 84, 143–4, *144*
Elmslie Osler Architect 289
Energy Biosphere Food (EBF) 92
energy curtain 83, 347
energy cycle: balance of growing systems 86; building integration 80, *81*; Growing Power farm 178; introduction *68*, 69; The Plant in Chicago 200; urban agriculture and 86; urban growing conditions 78; *see also* carbon cycle; solar energy
energy needs of fertilizer production 10–11

energy recovery strategies 16–18, *17*, 23–4
environmental challenges: response to 2
environmental policy challenges 293
Environmental Protection Agency (EPA) 23, 74
environmental systems for indoor growing 81–5, *82*
ethylene tetrafluoroethylene (ETFE) greenhouse film 95, 101–2, *102*, 106, 110–11
European Union's LIFE program 261
eutrophication 2, 9, *10*, 347
evapotranspiration 48–9, 78–9, 347

façade-integrated algae bioreactor 288
FarmedHere in Bedford Park, Illinois 138, *138*
farmers' markets 165, 243, *268*
Farm-to-City Market Basket Program 170
fermentation in nutrient cycle 197–8
fertilizer production 10–11
feedstock 19, 21, 347
financing concerns: Brooklyn Grange 188–90, *189*; Growing Power farm *179*, 179–80; Local Garden greenhouses 222; Lufa Farms 212–13; Plantagon International 135–6; Vertical Harvest system 128, *129*
fish fertilizer systems 24, 36–7, *37*; see also aquaponic systems
fish tanks in Aquaponic Solar Greenhouse 101–3
flood-and-drain system 31–2
fluorescent lighting 96
food banks 264, 267
food business incubator (The Plant) 194
Food City (Lim) 307
food desert 234, 276, 347
food forests 239–41, *240–1*
Food From the 'Hood (FFTH) initiative 169
Food Inc. (film) 307
food miles 79, 146, 347
Food Project in Boston 238
food security 170, 234, 297, 347
foodshed 154, 347
Forbes magazine 174
49 Cities (WORKac) 285
fossil fuel consumption 69
foundation drain water 65

From Eco-Cities to Living Machine (Todd, Todd) 25

Gary Comer Youth Center 238, *238*, 244, 289, *289*
geological carbon pool 71
geothermal heat 266
Giraud, Deborah 239
glass for greenhouses 93
Global Roots Garden 264
Global Roots Oral History Project 264
global warming 2, 71–3, *72*, *73*
Good Food Market (FoodShare in Toronto) 243
Good Food Revolution 173, 180
Gotham Greens in New York: overview 58, 295; rooftop gardens *215*, 216, *216*, 221–5, *223–4*
Gowanus greenhouse 221
Gowanus Whole Foods 216, 296
Graaf, Paul de 3
Granpa Co., Ltd. 109
Granpa domes in Yokohama, Japan: construction and milestones 109; growing system 109–10, *110*; introduction *108*, 109; operation of 111–13, *112*, *113*; strengths and innovations 113–14, *114*; structure of 110–11, *111*
Green Guerillas 239
greenhouse effect 72
greenhouse gas emissions 2, 9, 71–2
The Greenhouse Project in New York *272*, 272–3, *273*
greenhouses: biological pest controls in 208; carbon dioxide (CO_2) fertilization 85; Chinese greenhouses 91–2, *92*; cooling systems 84; cover materials 93–5, *94*; design considerations 85–6; electrical lighting for 84, 143–4, *144*; environment of 31; ethylene tetrafluoroethylene (ETFE) greenhouse film 95, 101–2, *102*, 106, 110–11; glass for 93; gutter-connected greenhouse 91; heating 84–5; high-tech greenhouses 79, 89–91; lighting technologies 96–9, *97*; low-tech greenhouses *88*, 89; microwave use in 106; open-roofed greenhouses 83; overview 80; passive solar 87, *88*, 89, 91–2; rigid plastic for 95; Science Barge greenhouse 273, 309;

shading systems and energy curtains 83; typologies 87–92, *88, 90, 92*; ventilation systems 81–3, *82*; Vertically Integrated Greenhouse 36, 287; *see also* Aquaponic Solar Greenhouse; Local Garden greenhouses
green infrastructure 43
Green Infrastructure Stormwater Management Initiative 62
Greenroof Environmental Literacy Laboratory (GELL) *274,* 274–7, *275*
green roofs 15, 192, 244; *see also* productive green roofs; rooftop agriculture/farms
green stormwater infrastructure (GSI) 50, 62, 347
greywater 64
ground-based farming 242
growing mediums/systems: aquaponic growing systems 24, 36–7, *37*; Aquaponic Solar Greenhouse 101; Brooklyn Grange 188; controlled-environment agriculture 14, 16; distance concerns 153; environmental systems for 80, 81–6, *82*; evaluation and design integration 15–16; Granpa domes 109–10, *110*; impact on urban agriculture 14–16, *15*; integrated, recirculating growing systems 57–8; nutrient cycle and 184–5; Plantagon International 131, *132*; potential yields 16; Prinzessinnengarten 248; Sky Greens 116–17, *117*; urban farms 13, 14; vertical growing structures 30, 36; water-efficient growing methods 86; *see also* hydroponic (soil-less) systems; soil-based growing systems; Vertical Harvest system
Growing Power in Milwaukee: background and development 173–4, *174*; community support with 241–2; design and building integration 181; education 180; financing and business planning *179,* 179–80; introduction 19; operations concerns 168, 170, 178; overview 89, 157, 165, *171,* 172–3; social effects *180,* 180–1; strengths and innovations 182; systems and nutrient cycle 175–8, *177–8*; vertical farming 181–2, *182*; water and energy cycles 178

Growing Underground in London 140, 146
grow lights 195, *196*
Guangming Smartcity 300–1, *301, 302*
Guggenheim, Davis 307
gutter-connected greenhouse 91, 347

Haber, Fritz 10
Hage, Mohamed 218
Haley, Eric 216
hardiness zone maps 77–8
Havana, Cuba *see* organopónicos in Havana, Cuba
heating for greenhouses 84–5
heat island effect 49, 50, 78, 85, 347
high-intensity discharge (HID) 98
high-pressure sodium (HPS) 98
high-tech greenhouses 89–91
high-wire production system 32, 348
High Tunnel Initiative (USDA) 89
hoop-house farms 89, 157–9, *158–9*, 348
hydroponic (soil-less) systems: aeroponics 34–6, *35*; aggregate cultures 31–2; aquaponic growing systems 24, 36–7, *37*; costs *164*; definition 348; drip-irrigation hydroponic system 32–3, *33*; ebb-and-flow hydroponic system 131, *132*; introduction 31; Mulberry dike-pond system 37–8, *38*; nutrient film technique *32,* 32–3, 34; overview 14, 16; packaging needs 168; PlantLab 142; raft culture 34; rooftop farm operations 160, *214,* 215, *215*; vertical growing structures 30, 36; Village Farms 294; water cultures 34–8; *see also* Vertical Harvest system

An Inconvenient Truth (film) 307
indoor growing facilities 80
industrial agriculture: food system concerns 154; impact on carbon cycle 73–4; phosphorus and 12, *13*; supply chains 165; water use in 44–5; *see also* urban agriculture
infrared radiation (IR) 93, 95
in-house market selling 165
integrated, recirculating growing systems 57–8
Integrated Food and Energy Systems (IFES) 101
intercropping 14, 348

irrigation systems: Brooklyn Grange 185–6; drip-irrigation 32–3, *33*, 52, 206; manual irrigation systems 52; micro-irrigation systems 52; net irrigation water requirement 48–9; rainwater irrigation 185–6; sprinkler irrigation systems 52; sub-irrigation systems 52; water cycle and 52–3

Jackson, Wyoming *see* Vertical Harvest in Jackson, Wyoming
Japan *see* Granpa domes in Yokohama, Japan; Mirai, Co. in Miyagi Prefecture, Japan
Japanese Ministry of Economy, Trade, and Industry 109

Kellogg Foundation 175
Kenner, Robert 307
Kertz, Glen 218
Kiss + Cathcart, Architects: background 309; building-integrated agriculture 309–13, *310*, *311*–*12*; design approach 313; introduction 308, *308*; strengths and innovations 313–14, *314*
kombucha cultures 198
Kubala Washatko Architects 181

land tenure challenges 293
land-use conversions 74
Larssen, Thomas 125
"Let's Move!" campaign 174
Liebig's Law of the Minimum 8
life-cycle assessments concept 86
light-emitting diodes (LEDs): definition 348; overview 98–9; PlantLab 143–4, *144*; vertical indoor farming 137; vertical indoor farms 160
Lightfoot, Paul 162, 217
light/lighting: Aquaponic Solar Greenhouse 103–4, *104*; compact fluorescent lights 96; daily light integral 96; fluorescent lighting 96; greenhouses 84, 143–4, *144*; grow lights 195, *196*; high-pressure sodium (HPS) lighting 98; plasma lights 99; quality/intensity for plant growth 74–6, *75*, *77*; sole-source lighting 96; supplemental lighting 96; technologies for greenhouses 96–9, *97*
Lillian Weber School of the Arts 276–7

Linköping, Sweden *see* Plantagon International in Linköping, Sweden
Lim, CJ 286: background 300; design philosophy 305; introduction 299; public outreach 305–7, *306*; smartcity projects 300–2, *301*, *302*, *303*–*4*; strengths and innovations 307
lithosphere 27, 71, 348
livestock manure management 73
Living Future Design Competition for Emerging Green Builders 316
local adaptation and value 154
Local Garden in Vancouver: design and building integrations 222–3, *223*; distribution systems and financing 222; introduction 218; operations *219*, 219–21, *220*; solar energy 221; strength and innovations 223–4, 223–5; timelines 218; water systems 221
locavorism 167
London: Growing Underground in London 140, 146
long-term purchasing agreements 168
Lovell, Sarah Taylor 2, 16
low-profit, limited liability company (L3C) model 129, 136
low-tech greenhouses *88*, 89
Lufa Farms in Montréal: design and building integration *213*, 213–14; financing and business planning 212–13; introduction *203*, 204, *204*; milestones *205*, 205–6; nutrient cycle and growing system *206*–*7*, 206–8; operation 210–12, *211*–*12*, 219, 221; overview 295; solar energy 208–10, *209*; strength and innovations 214; vision 204–5; water cycle 208
Lynn, Kurt 212
Lyson, Thomas 233

MacArthur Fellowship 174
McCormick Place Convention Center in Chicago 244, *244*
Manchester: Biospeheric Project 294
Manhattan School for Children 217
manual irrigation systems 52
Martin Luther King Jr. Middle School 270, *271*
metal-halide (MH) lamps 98
methane gas 18, 23
microclimate 50, 78, 348

microgreens 144–5
micro-irrigation systems 52
microorganisms 18, 63
Milwaukee *see* Growing Power in Milwaukee
Mirai, Co. in Miyagi Prefecture, Japan 140
MoMA's Young Architects Program 332
mono-nitrogen oxides (NO) 10
monoculture 206, 348
Montréal *see* Lufa Farms in Montréal
Morin, Xenia K. 242
Mulberry dike-pond system 37–8, *38*
multi-cropping 14, 348

National Oceanic and Atmospheric Administration (NOAA) 71
natural pesticides 254
Nature-City (WORKac) 338, *339*–43
neighborhood activism 236
Nelkin, Jennifer 216
net irrigation water requirement 48–9
Net-Zero water system 58, *59*, 194
Neuenburg am Rhein, Germany *see* Aquaponic Solar Greenhouse in Neuenburg am Rhein, Germany
New Alchemy Institute 24
Newark, New Jersey: AeroFarms in Newark, New Jersey 139, *139, 143*, 146
Newark Vertical Farm (Weber Thompson) 317–18, *317–18*
New York: BrightFarms in New York 217, *217*, 222, 225; The Greenhouse Project in New York 272, *272*–3, *273*; *see also* Brooklyn Grange in New York; Edible Schoolyard Project in New York; Gotham Greens in New York
New York Restauration Project (NYRP) 236
New York Sun Works (NYSW) 272–3
Ng, Jack 116
niche products and markets 155
nitrogen cycles: energy needs of fertilizer production 10–11; introduction 7–8, 9–10, *10*; plant needs 8, *9*
nitrogen dioxide (NO_2) 10
nitrogen fixation 9, *9*, 348
nitrous oxide (N_2O) 9, 73
non-money-making programs 249
Nordhavnen Smartcity 300, *301*–2, *303*–4
NPK rating system 8, *9*
nutrient film technique (NFT) *32*, 32–3, 34, 206, 219, 309, 348

nutrient needs of plants 8, *9*
nutrient systems: anaerobic digestion 21–2, *22*; Brooklyn Grange 184–5; closing nutrient cycle 7–8; composting 18–20, *19, 20*; design considerations 25–6; growing mediums and 14–16, *15*; Growing Power farm 175–8, *177–8*; introduction 6, *7*; Lufa Farms 206–7, *206–8*; The Plant in Chicago 195–8, *196–8*; plant needs 8, *9*; strategies with 16–18, *17*; urban agriculture impact on 13–14; wastewater 21, *22*–5

Obama, Michelle 174, 269
oceans as carbon source 71
on-site cafés 169
on-site treatment of organic waste 26
open-roofed greenhouses 83
operations in urban agriculture: assembling a team 155–6, *156*; Brooklyn Grange 186, *187*; challenges 153–4; community support and integration 169–70; complementary farming 161; costs of 163–5, *164*; design considerations 155–77, 170–1; distribution models 155, 165–8, *166, 168*; economics of 157; Growing Power farm 178; hoop-house farms 157–9, *158–9*; introduction 2–3, 153; local adaptation and value 154; Local Garden greenhouses 219, 219–21, *220*; Lufa Farms 210–12, *211–12*, 219, 221; niche products and markets 155; organopónicos 254–5, *255*; The Plant in Chicago 200–1, *201*; positive effects of urban agriculture 154–5; prices and farm models 155, *162*; Prinzessinnengarten 248–9, *249, 250*; processing, packaging, and branding 168–9; productive green roofs 159–60; soil-based urban farms 157; start-up funding 161–3, *162*; The Stop Community Food Centre (CFC) 266–8, *266–8*
Organic Materials Review Institute (OMRI)-certified organic nutrients 221
organic matter 18, 175, *175*
organopónicos in Havana, Cuba: background and milestones 252, *252*; government policies 253; growing and operation systems 260–1, *261*; growing systems 253–4, *254*; introduction 251,

organopónicos in Havana, Cuba (*cont.*) *253*; operations 254–5, *255*; socio-spatial system 258–60, *259–60*; strength and innovations 262; strengths and innovations 256
Organopónico Vivero Alamar 254, *255A*
over-fertilization 7, 10
oxygen (O_2) 195

packaging operations in urban agriculture 168–9
Paris School of Engineering 324
passive solar energy 101–3, *102*
passive solar greenhouses 87, *88*, 89, 91–2
passive temperature management 209
peri-urban 167, 348
permaculture techniques 27
Petcou, Constantine 257
Petrescu, Doina 257
phosphorus cycle: industrial agriculture 12, *13*; introduction 7–8, *11*, 11–12; plant needs 8, *9*; waste management 12
photosynthesis 69–70, *70*, 74–6, *75*, *77*, 348
photosynthetic active radiation (PAR) 93, 95, 348
photovoltaic (PV) panels *104*, 104–5, 348
Pick-and-Pack operations 210
Plantagon International in Linköping, Sweden: building integration 134–5, *134–5*; business model and financing 135–6; energy systems 132–4, *133*; growing system 131, *132*; introduction *130*, 131; milestones 131; operation 135, 162; overview 287; strengths and innovations 136
PlantaSymbioSystem 132, *132*
plant cable lift (PCL) 309
The Plant in Chicago: anaerobic digestion 199, *199*; business ecology and operations 200–1, *201*; design and building integration 201–2; energy cycle 200; introduction *193*, 194; nutrient cycles 195–8, *196–8*; operations concerns 170; overview 21, *22*, 25; site selection 293; strengths and innovations 202, vision and development *194*, 194–5; water cycle 200
PlantLab in 's-Hertogenbosch, Netherlands 142–6, *144*, *145*
plant physiology 48

Plant Production Units (PPUs) 142, 146
plasma lamps 106
Pollan, Michael 174
pollution concerns 9, 44
polyculture 27, 206, 348
polyethylene (PE) film for hoop houses 89
potassium cycle 8, *9*
prices and farm models 155
Prinzessinnengarten in Berlin: background and milestones 246; growing systems 248; introduction 245–6; operations 248–9, *249*, *250*; overview 237; retail opportunities 169; socio-spatial system 246–8, *247*, *248*; strength and innovations 250
processing operations in urban agriculture 168–9
producers in nutrient cycle 195, *196*
productive green roofs: impact of 80; operations 159–60; overview 30; water management 56–7, *57*
public relations and outreach 212
Puri, Viraj 216
PVC pipes for hoop houses 89
PVC roofing systems 119

Quinn, Christine 190

raft-based hydroponic systems 34, 111, 113
rain gardens 56
rainwater harvesting *55*, 55–6, 63
rainwater irrigation 185–6
raised bed gardens 15, 30
reclaimed water 65
RecycLab 260, *261*, 262
Red Hook Community Farm 233, 238
resilience 20, 231, 235, 242, *260*, 348
resistance/insulation value (R-value) 93
resource conservation 51–4, *53*
resource-efficient growing methods 13, 14
respiration in carbon cycle 69–70, *70*, 349
rigid plastic as greenhouses cover material 95
rooftop agriculture/farms: Brightfarms 217, *217*; Brooklyn Grange 56, 107, 163, *187*, 244; Gary Comer Youth Center *289*, 289, *290*; Gotham Greens 58, 215, 216, *216*; Greenroof Environmental Literacy Laboratory *274*, 274–7, *275*; hydroponic (soil-less) systems 160, 214,

215; introduction 3; Kiss + Cathcart, Architects 311; new construction *vs.* 295, *295*; operations for hydroponic farms 160; rainwater irrigation 185–6; water-efficient growing methods in 86; Weber Thompson 319–21, *320–1*; *see also* green roofs; productive green roofs
Rosemary (kitchen garden) 167
Rosenstiehl, Augustin 324
runoff *see* water runoff
R-Urban in Colombes, France: background and milestones 258; introduction *257*, 257–8; overview 237

Sartoux, Pierre 324
school gardens: Edible Schoolyard Project *270*, 270–2, *271*; The Greenhouse Project *272*, 272–3, *273*; Greenroof Environmental Literacy Laboratory *274*, 274–7, *275*; introduction *269*, 269–70
Schreier, Franz 106
Science Barge 273, 309
Seattle's P-Patch program 239
Second Nature Urban Agriculture: Designing Productive Cities (Bohn, Viljoen) 286
semi-transparent energy curtain 209
sewage sludge 23
shading systems 83
Shaw, Robert 245–6, 249
's-Hertogenbosch, Netherlands: PlantLab in 's-Hertogenbosch, Netherlands 142–6, *144*, *145*
site selection challenges 293
Singapore *see* Sky Greens in Singapore
Sky Greens in Singapore: background and milestones 116; design of 118–19, *119*; growing system 116–17, *117*; introduction *115*, 116; operation 119–21, *120*, *121*; strengths and innovations 121–2; yield and efficiency 117–18
Slow Food movement 233
Smartcity paradigm 300–2, *301*, *302*, *303*–4
SOA Architectes: background 324; building-integrated agriculture *325*, 325–9, *326–30*; design approach 324–5, *325*; introduction *323*, 323; strengths and innovations 330
social capital from urban agriculture 235

social effects *180*, 180–1
social programs 264–5, *265*
socio-spatial gardening system 246–8, *247*, *248*
soil-based growing systems: biointensive farming methods 27–8, *28*; constructed soil-based grounds 28–30, *29*; container gardens 28–30, *29*; design of 25; natural soil-based systems 27–8, *28*; overview 14, 15; permaculture techniques 27; productive green roofs 30; urban farm operations 157; vertical growing structures 30; WORKac 333; *see also* Sky Greens
soil fertility factors 7, 185
soil water availability 48, 349
solar energy: Aquaponic Solar Greenhouse 101; carbon dioxide and 74–6, *75*, *77*; Local Garden greenhouses 221; Lufa Farms 208–10, *209*; passive solar energy 101–3, *102*; transforming into electrical energy 104–5, *104–5*; urban agriculture and 79
sole-source lighting 96
source separation 24
SPIN farming, small plot-intensive farming *158*, 349
sprinkler irrigation systems 52
start-up funding 161–3, *162*
The Stop Community Food Centre (CFC) in Toronto: background and milestones 264; collaborative consumption 239; growing systems and infrastructure 265–6; introduction 263–4; operations 266–8, *266–8*; social programs 264–5, *265*; strengths and innovations 268
stormwater management 54–7, 64
student-run gardens 169
Studio 8 Architects *see* Lim, CJ
sub-irrigation systems 52, 349
supplemental lighting 96
supplementation in nutrient cycle 195
surface irrigation 52, *53*, 349
Symbiocity initiative 136

Takaaki, Abe 109
terrestrial biosphere 70
TESS (Thermal Energy Systems Specialists) 181
T5 linear fluorescents 96
Thompson, Weber 60, 288

Todd, John 24–5
Tohoku earthquake and tsunami 109, 114
Tokyo Dome 109
Tokyo Local Fruit program 241
Tompkins Square Middle School *275*, 275–6
Toronto: Good Food Market (FoodShare in Toronto) 243; *see also* The Stop Community Food Centre (CFC) in Toronto
Toronto FoodShare Program 175, 243
Tower Garden system 36
transpiration 48, *49*, 349
Tridi farm 324, *325*

ultraviolet radiation (UV) 93, 95
Uncommon Ground 167
Universal Expo in Milan (2015) 329
urban agriculture: alternative nutrient and energy sources 13, 14; business model for 321–2; energy cycle and 86; environmental challenges 2; future steps 297–8; growing systems 14–16, *15*; hydroponic growing systems 31–8, *32–3*, *35*, *37–8*; impact on carbon cycle 78–9; impact on nutrient cycle 13–14; impact on water cycle 50–1, *51*; introduction 1–2; operational alternatives 2–3; resource-efficient growing methods 13, 14; soil-based growing systems 27–30, *28*, *29*; solar energy and 79; strategies 16–18, *17*; synergy between cities and 3–4; *see also* closed-loop production; community-initiated urban agricultural programs; industrial agriculture; operations in urban agriculture; rooftop agriculture/farms; vertical indoor farming
Urbanana farm 324, *325*
urban growing conditions 49–50, 78
urban rooftops *see* rooftop agriculture/farms
urban waste streams 16–18, *17*
urban water challenges 44
US Department of Agriculture 77
US Department of Energy 222
Utzinger, Michael 181

ventilation systems 81–3, *82*
vermicomposting (vermiculture) 18–19, 176, *177*, 254, 349

The Vertical Farm (Despommier) 316, 333
Vertical Harvest in Jackson, Wyoming: background and milestones 124; collaboration with organizations 128; distribution 128; energy requirements 125–7, *126*; financing 128, *129*; growing systems 124, *125*; introduction *123*, 124; operation *127*, 127–8; strengths and innovation 129, *129*; yield and efficiency 127
vertical indoor farming: AeroFarms 139, *139*, *143*, 146; Caliber Biotherapeutics 141, *141*; FarmedHere 138, *138*; Growing Power farm 181–2, *182*; growing structures 30, 36; Growing Underground 140, 146; introduction 137, *137*; Kiss + Cathcart, Architects *310*, 311; Mirai, Co. 140; Newark Vertical Farm 317–18, *317–18*; operations 160; PlantLab 142–6, *144*, *145*; *see also* hydroponic (soil-less) systems; Sky Greens Vertical Harvest
Vertically Integrated Greenhouse (VIG) 36, 287
VertiCrop system 218
Victory Gardens 232, *232*
Viljoen, André 285–6
Village Farms in Buffalo, New York 294

Washington State's King County Loop 23
WasteCap Wisconsin 175
waste-into-energy system 208
waste management 12, 26
wastewater: blackwater 64; building of 65; from composting 21; domestic wastewater 64–5; greywater 64; overview 21, 22–5; reclaimed water 65; urban agricultural impact on 50; yellow/brown water 64–5
water cultures 34–8
water cycle: alternative water sources 54, 63–5; Brooklyn Grange 185; building-integrated, Net-Zero water system 58, *59*; challenges 43–6; closed-loop, building integrated agricultural systems 58, 60; cost of water 45–6; design considerations 60–2, *63*; efficiency and resource conservation 51–4, *53*; evapotranspiration 48–9; Growing Power farm 178; industrial agriculture 44–5; integrated, recirculating growing

systems 57–8; introduction 43; irrigation strategies 52–3; Lufa Farms 208; The Plant in Chicago 200; plant needs 48–9, *49*; plant physiology 48; productive green roofs 56–7, *57*; rain gardens 56; rainwater harvesting *55*, 55–6, 63; reclaimed water 65; resource conservation 51–4, *53*; stormwater management 54–7, 64; urban agricultural impact on 50–1, *51*; urban growing conditions 49–50; virtual water footprint 46, *47*

water runoff 7, 9, 44, 185

Waters, Alice 237

water systems: drip-irrigation 32–3, *33*, 52, 206; ebb-and-flow system 31–2, 131, *132*; Local Garden greenhouses 221; *see also* irrigation systems

water use efficiency (WUE) 16

wavelength conversion 106

Weber Thompson: background *316*, 316–17; business model for commercial urban agriculture 321–2; design approach 317–21, *317–21*; introduction 315, *315*; strengths and innovations 322

windrow composting *19*

Windy City Harvest Apprenticeship program 238, *239*, 244

Wood, Dan 332

WORKac (WORK Architecture Company): background *332*, 332–3; built projects 334–8, *335–8*; conceptual projects 333–4, *334*; design approach 333; introduction 331, *331*; Nature-City proposal 338, *339*–43; overview 290; strengths and innovations 338

Wortman, Sam 2, 16

Wychwood Barns 266

yellow water 64–5

Yes in My Backyard (YIMBY) initiative 239, 264–5

Youth Corps program 174

youth involvement 174, 237–8, *238–9*

YWCA programs 174

zoning and regulation challenges 292